CHICANA PORTRAITS

EDITED BY

Norma E. Cantú

WITH PAINTINGS BY RAQUEL VALLE-SENTÍES

CHICANA PORTRAITS

Critical Biographies of Twelve Chicana Writers

THE UNIVERSITY OF
ARIZONA PRESS

TUCSON

The University of Arizona Press
www.uapress.arizona.edu

We respectfully acknowledge the University of Arizona is on the land and territories of Indigenous peoples. Today, Arizona is home to twenty-two federally recognized tribes, with Tucson being home to the O'odham and the Yaqui. Committed to diversity and inclusion, the University strives to build sustainable relationships with sovereign Native Nations and Indigenous communities through education offerings, partnerships, and community service.

ISBN-13: 978-0-8165-5182-8 (hardcover)
ISBN-13: 978-0-8165-5181-1 (paperback)
ISBN-13: 978-0-8165-5183-5 (ebook)

Cover design by Leigh McDonald
Cover art via Steve Johnson/Unsplash
Typeset by Leigh McDonald in Berling 10.5/14, Harlie WF and Aboriginal Sans (display)

Publication of this book is made possible in part by the proceeds of a permanent endowment created with the assistance of a Challenge Grant from the National Endowment for the Humanities, a federal agency.

Library of Congress Cataloging-in-Publication Data
Names: Cantú, Norma E., 1947– editor. | Valle-Sentíes, Raquel, illustrator.
Title: Chicana portraits : critical biographies of twelve Chicana writers / edited by Norma E. Cantú ; with paintings by Raquel Valle-Sentíes.
Description: Tucson : University of Arizona Press, 2023. | Includes bibliographical references and index.
Identifiers: LCCN 2022058183 (print) | LCCN 2022058184 (ebook) | ISBN 9780816551828 (hardcover) | ISBN 9780816551811 (paperback) | ISBN 9780816551835 (ebook)
Subjects: LCSH: Hispanic American women authors—Biography. | American literature—Hispanic American authors—History and criticism.
Classification: LCC PS153.H56 C45 2023 (print) | LCC PS153.H56 (ebook) | DDC 810.9/92870896872073—dc23/eng/20230405
LC record available at https://lccn.loc.gov/2022058183
LC ebook record available at https://lccn.loc.gov/2022058184

Printed in the United States of America
♾ This paper meets the requirements of ANSI/NISO Z39.48-1992 (Permanence of Paper).

CONTENTS

ACKNOWLEDGMENTS

First and foremost, I want to thank Raquel Valle-Sentíes for her generosity of spirit and her artistic talent, without which this book would not exist. ¡Gracias! Thank you to the brilliant literary critics, whose essays present the writers in words and enrich and expand our knowledge of their work, for responding to my invitation to write these critical biographies. ¡Gracias! To Elvia Niebla for her patience and understanding as I prepared the final draft of this manuscript. ¡Gracias! Finally, to la Virgen de Guadalupe and all spiritual guides and teachers who are with me every step of the way. ¡Gracias!

Norma E. Cantú

My most sincere thanks to Dr. Norma E. Cantú, whose friendship, patience, and belief in me have made possible the longtime dream of having my paintings of some of the Chicana writers who paved the way for the rest of us to be published. The paintings evolved slowly over the years. I'm thrilled to still be around to share my joy with these Chicana writers.

Raquel Valle-Sentíes

CHICANA PORTRAITS

LAREDO AND ITS DISCONTENTS

An Introduction

NORMA E. CANTÚ

I T IS a balmy May evening in Laredo, Texas, in 2001 when we gather in el Café del Barrio, a small café/bookstore that the artist and poet Raquel Valle-Sentíes owns and operates out of her Victorian-era home on Matamoros Street. At this particular gathering, we are celebrating the writers from Nuevo Laredo, Tamaulipas, and Laredo, Texas, who are attending the IV Letras en el Borde (Letters on the Border) conference. The brainchild of José Luis Velarde and Guillermo Lavín, a couple of writers from Ciudad Victoria, Tamaulipas, the annual transnational event has taken place for several years with support from Texas A&M International University (TAMIU), Laredo Community College(LCC), and the cultural affairs office of the city of Nuevo Laredo under the direction of Héctor Romero Lecanda. Like any other literary festival, Letras en el Borde features writers reading their work and academic papers by critics and scholars; because it is being held in the two Laredos and the organizers want to emphasize the transnational aspects of our region, the conference focuses on border writing. The meal and performances—readings and music—at Café del Barrio are a highlight of the conference.[1]

Our host, Raquel Valle-Sentíes herself, is active in the local literary scene. Her dream of owning a bookstore has come true, and it is all she had hoped it would be. In the 1980s Valle-Sentíes had begun writing poetry and taking art classes at Laredo Community College (now Laredo College) with Martha Fenstermaker. I was then a professor at Laredo State University (now Texas A&M International University), and we—the *literatontos*, as some jokingly referred to us—were a handful who were keeping Chicanismo alive as we engaged with community projects that addressed the raging problems of the day: immigration, illiteracy, erasure of our history, historic preservation, et cetera. By the 1990s, we had coalesced into a force engaged in important interventions, launching a chapter of Amnesty International to do our work in the migrant detention center run by the private carceral company Corrections Corporation of America and establishing the Refugee Assistance Council to provide legal services to migrants. It was the days of massive migration from Central America due to the United States incursions into that region of the Americas. Many of our members were also involved in the feminist group Las Mujeres, and we hosted an annual women's conference, Primavera, to promote and recognize the accomplishments of women in our community.[2] I discuss Las Mujeres below as I contextualize the work of Café del Barrio and Raquel Valle-Sentíes.

HISTORICAL CONTEXT

Cultural life along the U.S.-Mexico borderlands is anything but the wasteland some have described. Many who do not live on the border see it as a cultural desert, devoid of any literary or artistic activity. In fact, it is rife with cultural events and home to a rich and vibrant population of cultural creators that includes poets, fiction writers, dramatists, painters, muralists, sculptors, and many traditional artists whose ephemeral art (such as piñatas and elaborately decorated cakes) and more permanent art (like landscaping, quilting, and wood carving) attest to the varied and deeply rooted aesthetics of the community. Border art and literature are often political and expressive of the sociocultural reality of those who live along the border. Groups spring up and create spaces for art as well as for political undertakings. Such activity is not new; it has deep roots in the cultural life of the borderlands. The history of Laredo, indeed of South Texas, attests to the cultural activity amid the always contentious political dramas that have played out in our community. From its beginnings in the mid-eighteenth century, Laredo has grappled with class issues and the legacy of a colonialist mentality that exists in all sectors of its social strata, a point that Elaine Peña makes in her 2020 book *¡Viva George! Celebrating Washington's Birthday at the U.S.-Mexico Border.* Yes, George Washington's birthday is the reason for the city's main—and incongruous—annual celebration.

Various historians have pointed out that the original inhabitants of the region—mostly the Coahuiltecan groups that roamed the area around what became Laredo and the Spanish, as well as other Indigenous groups that came with them from the interior of Mexico, like the Tlaxcaltecs—shaped its history and forged a *mestizaje* of Indigenous and European cultural expressions. Indeed, the area was home to many Indigenous groups centuries before the European arrival. According to John A. Adams Jr., the "oldest indication of farming in the region was discovered in the Ocampo Caves in southwest Tamaulipas, Mexico; gourds, squash, and jerk beans have been dated from about 7000 to 5500 BCE. Corn, or maize, was found in the same caves and was radiocarbon dated from 2772 BCE" (208). W. W. Newcomb Jr. also cites the many nomadic groups that lived in what is now South Texas (56). The rich folklore of the area has roots in this Indigenous past as well as in the deeply Catholic Spanish culture that was first documented by folklorist John Bourke in the late nineteenth century. Among historians who explore the sociohistorical legacy of these groups, we find agreement that religion and political or military history blend. In seeking to understand the contemporary sociopolitical conditions that some would say plague Laredo, Gilberto Hinojosa and Carlos Castañeda explored the intersection of economic and social life from its founding in 1755. Hinojosa situates the ways the community has evolved since its founding within a matrix of religious and political factors. Castañeda's *Our Catholic Heritage in Texas, 1519–1936* explores the role of the church in the foundation of Texas and in its seven volumes offers a cultural and social history along with an examination of the military and evangelizing mission of the Catholic Church in early Texas history and along the border. More recently and in a different style, historian Jerry Thompson presents a pictorial history of Laredo in his 1986 publication highlighting key events of the twentieth century, like the 1954 flood, as well as key figures.

As this rich historical groundwork delving into the established hierarchy of colonialist structures suggests, the two sectors—the military and the church—played a pivotal role in the city's history. As evidence of this matrix, I present the fact that the streets of Laredo were named after prominent political and military heroes of both the United States and Mexico (Farragut, Matamoros, Houston, et cetera) and the intersecting avenues after saints (Santa Ursula, San Francisco, San Eduardo, et cetera) (Cantú). The entrenched political system that came to be known as el Partido Viejo (the Old Party), and which was formally registered as the Independent Club, emerged in the twentieth century and unsurprisingly perdures, some would say, in the social and cultural ties within the community's social systems today.

Allow me to place this in perspective by leaping from the early colonial period to the 1960s and '70s. Well, perhaps not the '60s, as Laredo remained in the periphery of any '60s social justice movements save for a few isolated events; any earlier political activity, such as labor strikes or demonstrations, remained in the past. A common joke was that the '60s took a decade to get to us, and it was not until the '70s, when the established patron system was upended, that we saw any real progress. We had been under what Fernando Piñon described in his book *Patron Democracy*. Having been under the thumb of a corrupt and powerful political party, the Independent Club, the community was slowly flexing its muscles and moving toward an inclusive and less abject condition.[3] In the midst of the heyday of political activism that the '70s brought to Laredo, a sense of commitment to the arts as well as to social justice issues flourished.

It was into this milieu that Laredo-born Raquel Valle-Sentíes returned from Veracruz, where she had gone after her marriage and where she gave birth to her sons and lived until 1978. In the 1980s and '90s, I joined colleagues like Stanley Green at Laredo State University and Carlos Flores, Lucy Cárdenas (RIP), and Vicente Molina at Laredo Junior College, as well as other fellow faculty members and students, to create an active and exciting ambience of political activity. I remember attending the statewide rallies of the Chicano political party Raza Unida, interspersed with rock music concerts, at various plazas in town. I was at the time working at a local utilities company, and a Saturday afternoon rally with folks from Austin talking about the need for a third political party attracted me and a few others, mostly those associated with the local community college. While it was exciting and we felt that the political voter registration drives were essential—we called ourselves the Action League of Laredo—I don't think any of us had hopes that we would actually change things much. We knew the history of the Reform Party that had unsuccessfully tried to change things in the 1950s. But we had hope, and we worked hard in door-to-door canvasing to register people to vote and later to get the vote out for elections like Frances "Sissy" Farenthold's run for governor and for Raza Unida candidates.

ARTIVISM AND LAS MUJERES

In the 1980s, along with students and faculty members from Laredo State University and Laredo Junior College and a group of community activists, we started the feminist group Las Mujeres with the aim of hosting an annual conference called Primavera to celebrate women's accomplishments, sponsoring events for Women's History Month and a few activists and artists who had started an Amnesty International chapter. Raquel's Café del Barrio served as a meeting place, as Carlos Flores points out in his essay on Valle-Sentíes in this volume; the community college had a writing program, and many of the writers congregated there. The café was an oasis as it provided a space for our cultural and political activities and our encounters with out-of-town writers who visited from both Mexico and the United States.

As mentioned earlier, it was not until almost twenty years after the heyday of 1960s activism that we were equipped to challenge the Laredo institutions that were still pretty much strangling any kind of political and social justice and to actually institute change in our community. How did we do this? Mostly through organizing and getting our own groups to do the work. Through Las Mujeres, we organized visits to the detention center that housed undocumented Central American migrants; we led literacy classes, forming the Literacy Volunteers of Laredo; and we started the Refugee Assistance Council to provide legal assistance to those in the local detention center with funding from various organizations. Las Mujeres had as its goal to do what Gloria Anzaldúa would call "work that matters."[4] In addition to producing the annual Primavera Conference in Laredo, we put on a yearly Brindis a la Mujer (Toast to Women), where we joined with women from our sister city across the river, Nuevo Laredo, for a transnational celebration of International Women's Day. For over fifteen years, Primavera hosted academic and cultural events celebrating women in our community.

Throughout the 1980s and '90s, we continued to immerse ourselves in the work of Las Mujeres and in the local literary activities, including gatherings of writers from Northern Mexico and South Texas in Nuevo Laredo hosted by the city's office of cultural affairs. In the '90s, Letras en el Borde brought writers together thanks to the efforts of cultural workers like Héctor Romero Lecanda and Antonio Sarabia in Nuevo Laredo and Las Mujeres members, principally Valle-Sentíes, Rosa Burgess, and Rose T. Treviño, in Laredo. Another significant experience was hosting the Mujeres Activas en Letras y Cambio Social (Women Active in Letters and Social Change) gathering in Laredo in 1992, for it brought writers from Mexico like Elena Poniatowska and Chicana literary critics and scholars like Norma Alarcón and Sonia Saldívar-Hull to a national gathering; it was an exciting and transformational event.

Many visual artists had been taking art classes and successfully exhibiting their work at the Laredo Center for the Arts after it opened in 1993. Laredo artists like sculptor Armando Hinojosa and painter Amado Peña had developed a reputation outside of Laredo, but the latter moved away, and only a handful of painters, including Valle-Sentíes, remained. In 1998, when she began painting the Chicana writers she was reading, Valle-Sentíes shifted away from the more traditional subjects of still life and family portraits she had been engaged with; the writers' portraits were a coming home, a celebration.

A BRIEF INTERVIEW WITH RAQUEL VALLE-SENTÍES

I was still living in Laredo when things were happening at the Café del Barrio. I have memories of going for lunch and enjoying the just-made agua fresca (watermelon was my favorite) and delicious Mexican cuisine that included dishes from Veracruz cooked with *hoja santa*, a plant that Valle-Sentíes grew in her own yard. I relished the fact that Laredo had a bookstore where I could buy Chicana and Chicano authors as well as work by Mexican writers. While I recalled our gatherings at the café, such as the one I described at the opening of this essay, I was unclear as to how it all came about. In my view, the café was a gift to Laredo, and I wondered why she closed it down. So, in preparation for writing this introduction and in a desire to contextualize her work, I contacted Valle-Sentíes and asked for her narrative around the opening of el Café del Barrio. She told me the café was born of a need for a space where poets and other writers could gather:

> I bought the Victorian house known as the Wormser House, built in 1883, on Matamoros Street in 1991, and I opened el Café del Barrio in the summer of 1998. At first it was just a coffee and gift shop; it was the first bookstore in Laredo devoted to Latinx and Chicanx literature. The menu was limited to coffee, soups, sandwiches, and desserts, all made by me. I was cook, waitress, dishwasher, and cashier. I was writing poetry by then and had just published my first book of poetry, *Soy como soy y qué*.
>
> As time went on, I felt there was a need for a place where people could gather to share their love of poetry by reading their poems or hearing poets read. I was encouraged by my teachers and friends at Laredo Community College (LCC), Carlos Flores and Randy Koch, who did the flyers for our monthly readings. The poetry nights became quite popular where local published and unpublished writers as well as those from San Antonio and the Valley had book presentations. . . . We also had music—Jazz, Hindu, and Chamber music by local musicians, and ceremonia by "danzantes concheros." In the gift shop, besides books in English and Spanish by Mexican and Latinx authors, I sold rebozos from Santa María del Río [in San Luis Potosí]; huipiles; silver jewelry, black pottery, and alebrijes from

Oaxaca; bilingual Christmas and all-occasion cards, paintings, post-ers, and retablos and nichos by Ene-Art, Enedina Vásquez, the artist from San Antonio whose famous pieces sold all over the country, including museums.

Valle-Sentíes held onto the dream as long as possible, but sadly, as time went by, she realized she couldn't keep on doing all the work at the café and continue attending classes at LCC while also writing and painting, so she closed the café and sold her house. She jokingly tells stories of another factor that drove her to close: the "neighbor from hell . . . who thought she owned the street" and was not pleased when the café held gatherings and the usually quiet Matamoros suddenly had traffic coming and going. Valle-Sentíes says that it "broke her heart to close el Cafe del Barrio and sell my lovely home." But she saw no other option if she was to continue creating art. The dream had come to an end.

The interlude is a critical period in Laredo's literary history, as were two earlier key events. In 1980–82, Carlos and Dora Flores published a literary magazine, *Revista Río Bravo*, which featured Chicana and Chicano authors from around the country; and in the 1990s, the Flo-reses and Lucinda Farrokh established the South Texas Writing Project (STWP). Valle-Sentíes's Café del Barrio would become the focus for the STWP participants.

When Valle-Sentíes and I began discussing the possibility of a vol-ume that would include the images from her *Chicana Writers* series and critical biographies by scholars, I asked why she began the series at all. Valle-Sentíes expressed her admiration for the authors, yes. But she also told me that artists in other lands and other times had painted the leading writers of their day; she felt that no one was doing that for Chicanas. Although she didn't initiate the project with this idea in mind, the series slowly grew as she became more and more interested in documenting the Chicana writers she was reading. While she had been painting for almost twenty years, the subjects had been mostly members of her family; her still life paintings had won awards in local contests. She and Fenstermaker, her teacher, had developed a rich friendship, and she just knew she was ready to venture into portraits outside of her family.

Later, in an email, she told me about painting the *Chicana Writers* series:

> I started the Chicana Writers Series in 1998. It was my way of showing my admiration and paying tribute to them. They had paved the way for the rest of us who had just started writing. I had never heard of these women before and was thrilled when Norma Cantú brought Sandra Cisneros to read at Laredo Community College (LCC), now Laredo College. . . . She was the first painting of the series, and I was thrilled when LCC used my painting of Sandra on the invitation to one of our Art Shows. The next one was of Norma, and [thus] I unknowingly started what became "the Chicana Writers Series." Norma's is the only one I ever sold, as I decided to keep the others as a collection. Some have been in art shows and have been awarded their ribbon. It is my wish that they remain together as a collection.

Indeed, many of the writers in the *Chicana Writers* series have come to Laredo to read, but not all. Some have a stronger connection to the region. Both Valle Senties and I are from Laredo: she was born in Laredo, and I was born in Nuevo Laredo and grew up in Laredo. Montserrat Fontes was born in Laredo as well. Others, such as Demetria Martínez and Denise Chávez, write about borders but are from New Mexico. Angela de Hoyos was born in Mexico but lived and wrote in San Antonio; she too wrote about borders. Sandra Cisneros and Ana Castillo were born in Chicago and also have connections to Laredo: Cisneros's family crossed into Mexico through Laredo, as she writes in her novel *Caramelo*, while Castillo's family resided there for a while.

THE AUTHORS AND THEIR PORTRAITS

This collection includes the portraits of twelve Chicana authors painted by Valle-Senties over a period of several years; the portraits are accompanied by critical biographies written by noted scholars and offer information on the life and work of the authors. It is my hope that these biographies will inspire readers to seek out the authors' writings. I have arranged the essays in chronological birth order.

A second major impetus for putting this book together is to offer recognition for work that may otherwise go unnoticed. Valle-Sentíes merits not only recognition but gratitude for her years as a cultural artivist in Laredo, one whose unwavering commitment has been to her art and her writing; her work has inspired young writers and artists and remains a testament to her *fronteriza* aesthetics. The first two essays in this book focus on Raquel Valle-Sentíes (1936–) and her work and are accompanied by her self-portrait; it is the most recent of the *Chicana Writers* portraits, and she painted it at my request—sort of. Since she herself is a writer, I felt it only fair to include her in the collection and to solicit essays on her work. The two complementary essays are written by contributors who know her work well: a friend, Carlos Flores, and a scholar, María Jesús Castro Dopacio.

Valle-Sentíes had a special connection to Angela de Hoyos (1924–2009); her first poetry collection, *Soy como soy y qué*, was published by de Hoyos through M&A Editions, the press that de Hoyos and her husband, Moisés Sandoval, founded and ran for many years. I first met de Hoyos in the 1980s when she graciously hosted me in her home on one of my trips to a conference in San Antonio. It was to be the first of many such visits as we deepened our friendship. She and her husband were instrumental in my reestablishing a connection to San Antonio, for they had an extended network of activists, artists, and literary movers and shakers in the community that included Chicana artist Terry Ybáñez and writer Max Martínez. Moisés and Angela played a critical role for writers in San Antonio, with M&A Editions publishing many young Chicanx poets' chapbooks. I remember one incident a colleague shared with me that exemplifies the reach of de Hoyos's work back in the 1980s. My friend's teenage son was picked up for possession of a joint and found Angela's poem—a broadside—on the wall of the juvenile detention center where he waited to be processed; her poem welcomed young people who were detained and offered words of affirmation and pride in being Chicano. I was deeply saddened when she passed in 2009. María Esther Quintana and María Magdalena Guerra de Charur collaborated in writing the critical biography; de Hoyos's work has rarely been written about with such care.

Montserrat Fontes (1940–), or Montsy, as she is affectionately known, was born in Laredo and lives in Glendale, California. Mary

Pat Brady's essay not only provides a critical biography focusing on her literary output but also explores the varied influences and contexts for Fontes's novels, which are set on the border. Moreover, she explicitly highlights that Montsy is a teacher and as such has influenced numerous writers and actors.

The passing of Chicana queer thinker and writer Gloria E. Anzaldúa (1942–2004) left an undeniable void in Chicana queer letters. In her honor, and to continue her legacy, I founded the Society for the Study of Gloria Anzaldúa two years after her death. The epitome of the border scholar whose work revolutionized both border studies and queer studies, Anzaldúa forged new ways of writing and thinking. The recently dedicated Dr. Gloria E. Anzaldúa Literary Landmark at her alma mater in Edinburg, Texas, reads:

> Gloria Evangelina Anzaldúa (1942–2004), queer Chicana poet, writer, and scholar, was born and raised in the Rio Grande Valley and graduated in 1968 from Pan American College, legacy institution of the University of Texas, Rio Grande Valley. Her internationally renowned writings reflect the varied experiences of the south Texas borderland region—la frontera. Nevertheless, her pathbreaking ideas, theories, and concepts written in Tex-Mex resonate with other border realities and have influenced many queer and feminist writers across the globe.

In her critical biography, Cordelia E. Barrera provides a brilliant overview of Anzaldúa's work and her impact all around. Barrera herself is a border dweller, a former student from my days at TAMIU, who has become a friend; through her work in and out of academia Barrera is doing "work that matters," as Anzaldúa urged us all to do.

My own portrait, Norma Elia Cantú (1947–), hangs on my living room wall. I am honored to have scholar Gabriella Gutiérrez y Muhs write the essay for this book. She provides a sensitive look at the creative output and the cultural context for my work. As editor of *Word Images: New Perspectives on* Canícula *and Other Works by Norma Elia Cantú*, in which thirteen contributors explore the themes and issues raised in my work, she is more than familiar with my literary output.

Denise Elia Chávez (1948–) is known mostly as a dramatist and performer, but as Myrriah Gómez demonstrates, her life and work weave together beautifully, like the fine handspun wool of a traditional Rio Grande blanket. Gómez, a scholar of New Mexico literature and culture, brings a unique perspective to the critical biography of such a luminary. Chávez remains a committed activist, most recently initiating Libros para el Viaje (Books for the Journey), a book drive that brings bilingual literature to the many migrants in detention along the border. Her celebration of young writers and her indomitable spirit of performance are ably captured by Gómez.

Jen Yáñez-Alaniz's essay on Carmen Tafolla (1951–) is an intimate portrait in words to go along with the painting. The critical biography by Yáñez Alaniz takes us, the readers, to Tafolla's varied and important literary work as well as the personal space where she writes and lives.

Lourdes Torres's critical biography of Chicana queer theorist, poet, and prose writer Cherríe Moraga (1952–) also complements Valle-Sentíes's painting; in her essay, we find a discerning and critical eye that explores the facets of Moraga's work.

Meagan Solomon's critical biography of Ana Castillo (1953–) draws from her dissertation work on women's friendships and queer love in Chicana feminist literature. Solomon, a recent PhD graduate from Texas Christian University, brings a fresh approach to the fiction of this extraordinary writer.

Eliza Rodríguez deftly explores themes and highlights significant aspects of Lorna Dee Cervantes's poetry. Rodríguez edited the anthology *Stunned into Being: Essays on the Poetry of Lorna Dee Cervantes*, so she was an obvious choice to write the critical biography.

Georgina Guzmán writes on Sandra Cisneros (1954–), adding to a vast repertoire of critical work on this pioneering Chicana author as she explores the intricate relationships Cisneros inhabits. The critical biography perforce has an element of literary critical analysis and takes on the intersections of her life and her work; Guzmán demonstrates that indeed the work, rooted as it is in Chicana cultural expressions and literary history, can be read also as history and as social justice work.

Cristina Herrera's critical biography of the journalist and writer Demetria Martínez (1960–) concludes the book. In her essay, Herrera explores the political and literary aspects of Martínez's work.

With a look to the past and with hopes for the future, these essays and paintings attest to a vibrant present. The last twenty years or so have been for me filled with joy and excitement as I see the younger writers come into their own, note how many more books by Chicanas are published each year, and witness the number of Chicanx literary scholars grow, as evidenced by their presence at the Modern Language Association annual meetings. My fellow pathbreakers in these academic spaces, Tey Diana Rebolledo and María Herrera-Sobek, and I celebrate them and are heartened by their work. Our hope is that those who came before them not be left in obscurity and that they recognize the writers who have shaped our literary history, such as those in this volume. Some of these authors' place in the literary canon is assured—such is the case for Moraga, Castillo, and Cisneros, for example—but so many others, such as Martínez, Fontes, and de Hoyos, merit attention and remain understudied.

My hope is that these portraits and the critical biographies will inspire readers—both those new to the writers and those seasoned scholars of Chicana literature who recognize and know their work well—to learn more about these twelve Chicana writers and to read or reread their work. I offer this introduction to *Portraits of Chicana Writers* with deep love for the writers, for the scholars, and for the artist who so lovingly painted the portraits. I feel a sense of gratitude to all of them for their work and for allowing me the gift of putting the collection together.

NOTES

1. As Arturo Zárate notes in his review of the conference on the Literatura Virtual website, the fact that we were on the border prevented at least two participants from attending the events: "Orlando Ortiz no pudo disfrutar las actividades en Laredo porque no traía papeles para pasar a Estados Unidos. José Cardona no pudo disfrutar las actividades en Nuevo Laredo porque no tenía papeles para regresar a los Estados Unidos." Curiously, Zárate does not mention ANY of the women who presented or who hosted the event. I was one of the first persons to host the event when I was teaching at TAMIU. In 2001, it was William Nichols who is credited. Two other women were certainly involved: Valle-Sentíes hosted at her establishment, and Rose T. Treviño also hosted. Rebecca Bowman and several other women writers and scholars presented papers and read their work but remain erased in his review.

2. The Laredo Commission for Women was established by the Laredo City Council in 1994 through the efforts of council member Cecilia Moreno, one of the women we recognized at a Brindis a la Mujer (Toast to Women) at a Primavera Conference. Las Mujeres member Lucy R. Cárdenas also worked diligently to make this happen; thus we ensured that the work of Las Mujeres in recognizing women continued in a more institutionalized fashion through the Laredo Women's Hall of Fame that the commission sponsors every year.

3. See Fernando Piñon's *Patrón Democracy* (1985) for a brief political history of the period that led to the shift in power away from the Old Party.

4. For more information on the group, see Norma E. Cantú, "Las Mujeres," *Texas State Historical Association Handbook of Texas*, https://www.tshaonline .org/handbook/entries/las-mujeres.

BIBLIOGRAPHY

Adams, John A., Jr. *Conflict and Commerce on the Rio Grande: Laredo, 1755–1955*. College Station: Texas A&M University, 2008.

Bolton, Herbert E. *The Spanish Borderlands*. Albuquerque: University of New Mexico, 1966, 35–41.

Bourke, John Gregory. "Folk-Foods of the Rio Grande Valley and of Northern Mexico." *Journal of American Folklore*, April–May 1895.

———. "Notes on the Language and Folk-Usage of the Rio Grande Valley (With Especial Regard to Survivals of Arabic Custom)." *Journal of American Folklore*, April–June 1896.

Cantú, Norma E. "Barrio and Street Names in Laredo, Texas." Unpublished paper, 1974.

Castañeda, Carlos. *Our Catholic Heritage in Texas, 1519–1936*. 7 vols. Edited by Paul J. Foik. Prepared under the auspices of the Knights of Columbus of Texas. Austin, Tex.: Von Boeckmann-Jones, 1936–1958.

Hinojosa, Gilberto Miguel. *A Borderlands Town in Transition: Laredo, 1755–1870*. College Station: Texas A&M University, 1983.

Newcomb, W. W., Jr. *The Indians of Texas from Prehistoric to Modern Times*. Austin: University of Texas Press, 1961.

Peña, Elaine. *¡Viva George! Celebrating Washington's Birthday at the U.S.-Mexico Border*. Austin: University of Texas Press, 2020.

Piñon, Fernando. *Patron Democracy*. Mexico City: Contraste, 1985.

Rodríguez y Gibson, Eliza. *Stunned into Being: Essays on the Poetry of Lorna Dee Cervantes*. San Antonio: Wings Press, 2012.

Thompson, Jerry. *Laredo: A Pictorial History*. Laredo, Tex.: Webb County Heritage Foundation, 1986.

Zárate, Arturo. "El IV Encuentro Letras en el Borde." Literatura Virtual (website). https://www.angelfire.com/va3/literatura/IV_Letras_en_el_Borde.htm.

RAQUEL VALLE-SENTÍES

RAQUEL VALLE-SENTÍES

Portrait of a Poet, Painter, and Playwright

CARLOS NICOLÁS FLORES

F IRST, THE Mexican colors struck me: bright red and orange and
yellow and green, especially vivid against the gray and blue institutional ambience. I was looking for the human resources office at
Texas A&M International University, and I was lost. Then, there they
were: the faces of women, only women. Since I seldom visited the
campus and had never wandered this far in Killam Library, this was
the first time I saw them displayed in all their splendor: Raquel Valle-
Sentíes's series of portraits of prominent Chicana writers Sandra Cisneros, Lorna Dee Cervantes, Ana Castillo, Denise Chávez, and others.

Having seen on Facebook one of her latest paintings, a Galveston
beach landscape, I had meant to talk to Raquel and tell her I loved it.
Now I needed to call her and tell her about my encounter with the
women's faces and that, in addition to being remembered for her poetry
and plays, she will also definitely be remembered for the portraits.

A GRAND STYLE

My first impression of Raquel when we met in a classroom at Laredo Community College in 1987 was of a well-dressed, dignified,

sumptuous, decorous woman—in other words, a woman of grand style—and that has continued to be my impression throughout the years. For instance, today she lives in an hacienda-style house in J. S. J. Estates, an exclusive neighborhood in north Laredo, surrounded by family memorabilia, her paintings, Mexican *artesanía*, books, and rustic furniture. An accomplished cook, she always regales her guests with an exquisite and varied Mexican cuisine.

The creative writing class in 1987 was divided into three parts and taught by three different instructors: Robert Sanford taught poetry, Carlos Morton, playwriting, and I, fiction. Even though the arrangement would provide only a cursory introduction to writing in each of the three genres, my colleagues and I were pleased to have the renowned Chicano playwright Carlos Morton on board and agreed everything would work out. As doubtful as the teaching arrangement might have been, it laid the foundation for subsequent developments in Laredo's incipient literary community. For instance, Luis Flores (*My Little Mexican* and other plays), who later was important in the establishment of Teatro Chicano de Laredo, was present the first night. So was Lisha Adela García (*Blood Rivers: Poems of Texture from the Border*), who later moved to San Antonio, where she figured among the poets flourishing in that city's storied literary culture. And Raquel—a superbly dressed middle-aged woman, elegant and poised—was there.

"She doesn't belong here," I thought, stereotyping her as a Mexican aristocrat. "She belongs in a beauty salon."

I soon learned she was fluent in both English and Spanish and was a successful businesswoman, owner and CEO of Taylor Rental Center, which rented everything from chairs, tables, and awnings for parties to heavy construction machinery such as backhoe tractors and dump trucks. She was not Mexican per se either. Born in Laredo, Texas, she was a Mexican American and a citizen of the United States. However, she had lived in Veracruz, Mexico, for many years and raised five boys. Then, in 1979, she returned to Laredo and in 1989 divorced her husband.

I forget how the class itself turned out, but the friendships formed led to get-togethers off campus, where we ate, drank, and discussed the history of Laredo, the problems besetting the border, and the promise of Chicano literature, which many of us were discovering for the first time. I remember sitting in the backyard of one of the seigniorial houses in the historic district, within walking distance of downtown and the Rio Grande, looking at the moon and marveling that this literary experience was occurring in a border town far from mainstream literary centers in both the United States and Mexico. Of course, the big question that always underlies such endeavors is whether anything will come of it—the writing and publication of an important book, a successful literary career, or a social or political movement that would lead to the transformation of Laredo, which many viewed as a backward, even feudal, community with little interest in literature or art. Elsewhere in the United States—San Antonio, Austin, El Paso, Albuquerque, New York, and Los Angeles—Chicanos and other marginalized groups were making history. Would we, who lived in a forgotten province between the so-called First and Third Worlds, ever participate in the shaping of that history?

"I had always wanted to take a creative writing course," Raquel said years later. "So when my cousin told me about this course, I signed up immediately. As a middle-aged woman, I felt self-conscious when I arrived. Then I was overwhelmed by taking a creative writing class in fiction, playwriting, and poetry. Eventually, I got used to it. Then I took other creative writing classes, one with the late Terry Wiggs and a workshop with Sandra Cisneros.[1] Now that I look back on those days, I marvel at all that came of it. Who would have thought?"

CAFÉ DEL BARRIO AND CHICANOS

In 1985, while enrolled in the graduate program at the University of Texas at El Paso during the summer, my wife, Dora, learned of the West Texas Writing Project's (WTWP) success in improving Mexican American students' writing skills. She thought establishing such a project in Laredo would help local teachers address our students' difficulties in writing English. So in the summer of 1995, Dora, Laredo Community College instructor Lucinda Farrokh, and I traveled to El Paso, where we enrolled in WTWP and trained as directors. Upon returning to Laredo, we established the South Texas Writing Project (STWP),[2] which we saw as an opportunity to introduce new and up-and-coming Chicano writers to the community, all in an effort to enrich our lives educationally and culturally.

The STWP became the impetus for our literary community, and at the heart of this enterprise was Raquel's El Café del Barrio.

Raquel had bought a two-story Victorian house in Laredo's historic district. Dating from the turn-of-the-century economic boom created by the arrival of the railroad, it could have been the set for a Tennessee Williams play. It was within walking distance of the old train depot and railroad tracks, which connected with the "Black Bridge" straddling the Rio Grande. West of those tracks was Laredo Community College, once the site of Ft. McIntosh. After refurbishing the old house, Raquel filled the glass-cases in her living and dining rooms with dolls of Marilyn Monroe, Rhett Butler, and Scarlet O'Hara. Here poet and journalist Randy Koch interviewed her for *LareDOS*:

On a January afternoon, Raquel and I sat on the couch in the front room of her large Victorian house with the tape recorder between us. Her paintings [were] set on the floor and leaned against furniture and the wall in a corner and beneath a window to my left. On the large wall hung several paintings from the series she's doing on Chicana writers—Cherrie Moraga, Sandra Cisneros, Norma Cantú, and a self-portrait. In the top half of the tall window to our right was the poster used to promote the Latina Letters Conference on Literature and Identity held last July at St. Mary's University in San Antonio. Raquel's portrait of Denise Chavez—burnt red in the background, a black cloud of hair, a dark green dress, and hands holding her elbows— filled the top three-fourths of the poster. Raquel complained that several people have pointed out that it's her, not Denise Chavez, in the painting, and there are some similarities. However, her self-portrait, while of a much younger Raquel ("People say that I gave myself a lot of plastic surgery," she says and laughs), is her—reddish hair, a full face, and sharp brown eyes; the absence of her large glasses contributes to the portrait's youthfulness. (42)

Finally, it was here, too, that she and I sat on antique chairs, drank coffee, nibbled on pan dulce, and worked on what would become her first collection of poems, *Soy como soy y qué*. However, across the hall separating the two sides of the house was the room that fascinated me the most: the bookstore. While the living room felt like part of an antebellum plantation home in the deep South, the room lined with bookshelves seemed like some market, museum, or art gallery—or a combination of all three—in southern Mexico. Strings of beads, wine colored and green, hung across the tall windows and filtered the late afternoon sunlight. A high ceiling crowned the fuschia and yellow walls. Books by or about Hispanics filled some shelves: Rudolfo Anaya, Sandra Cisneros, Carmen Tafolla, Angela de Hoyos, Victor Villaseñor, Carlos Morton, Helena María Viramontes, Lorna Dee Cervantes, and many others. Carlos Fuentes, Octavio Paz, and Sor Juana Inés de la Cruz, and other Latin American writers occupied their own shelf. Then, there was the Mexican artesanía—the Catrinas, retablos, black pottery, alebrijes from Oaxaca, ceramics, and jewelry. If the house overall impressed me with its aging grandeur, this room stunned me with its Mexican chic. Raquel, after living in Mexico twenty years, had returned to the Mexican American border with impeccable taste for all things Mexican, including not only artesanías but also Mexican cuisine. In the screened-in patio in the rear of the house, our fledgling literary community gathered for open-mic readings, which concluded with Raquel reading her latest poems and, always, "Soy como soy y qué."

Our efforts—STWP, el Café del Barrio, open-mic readings, and eventually el Teatro Chicano de Laredo—were rooted in the models and inspiration provided by the Chicano activists and writers José Flores Peregrino, the late Cecilio García-Camarillo, the late Angela de Hoyos, Linda Armas, and others. In effect, Raquel's artistic and literary career has been part not only of Laredo's cultural development but also of Mexican Americans' efforts to create a national literature that illuminates their struggle and triumph as strangers in their own land. Those were wonderful, heady days, and Raquel was a key player.

TEATRO CHICANO DE LAREDO

Laredo has a rich theater history, but the productions have been, by and large, mainstream American plays and musicals. If you want to see a play dealing with Mexico or Latin America and in Spanish, you must cross the border to one of a handful of theaters in Nuevo Laredo, Tamaulipas. To be fair, some Chicano plays, such as Luis Valdez's *Soldado razo*, Carlos Morton's *El jardín*, Raquel's plays, and others, had been produced locally. Teatro Chicano de Laredo (TCdeL), however, which Rene Montemayor and I, with the support of Laredo Community College, founded in 2009, sought to break ground by developing and producing new plays by local—though not exclusively Hispanic—playwrights about life on the Mexican American border.

That year, I spoke to Raquel about offering a playwriting workshop. After all, not only was she an actor, but she had already written and produced two plays. First, during the drama portion of the three-part creative writing class with Carlos Morton, she wrote *Alcanzando un sueño*, a play about an impoverished Mexican family seeking to cross the border into the United States. It won third place in the 1989–90 Chicano/Latino Literary Prize contest.[3] Later, she wrote and produced *La mala onda de Johnny Rivera*, which dealt with teens in school, their problems, and their lives. In 1995, she worked on *La mala onda* during a two-week Isadora Aguirre Workshop in San Francisco, after which the play had a stage reading by professional actors at that city's Teatro de la Esperanza. Finally, the late María Eugenia (Jeannie) López, a longtime icon of the local theater scene, was a good friend of hers. As a director, actor, and theater arts teacher, Jeannie was associated with the hundred-year-old Laredo Little Theatre. She could help us.

Raquel loved the idea.

The night of our first workshop , some forty people—students and members of the community alike—showed up at LCC's Arena Theater. Raquel had promoted the workshop extensively in the theater community, making sure Jeannie and others were there. Six weeks later, we extended the workshop another four weeks so we could accommodate all the one-act plays that had been written and submitted. By the end of the ten weeks, participants had composed some forty plays, and in the fall of 2009, we produced nine of them, including Kimberly Peña's *Spaghetti Is Straight . . . 'til It's Hot*, in TCdeL's first festival at the Laredo Little Theatre. We had standing-room-only audiences. Between 2009 and 2014, participants wrote and, with a minimum of resources, we produced twenty-seven original plays, some full-length and all by local playwrights.

Two of Raquel's plays were produced during TCdeL's five-year run: *Nothing to Declare* and *Fashionably Late*, both ten-minute one-acts that satirize the idiosyncrasies and challenges of life in Laredo.

Nothing to Declare, featured in a video on Jesús Treviño's *Latinopia* guest blog, dramatizes two women's experiences while crossing the border from Nuevo Laredo to Laredo one hot afternoon. Sizzling in a convertible, Regina and Mague, upper-middle-class and middle-aged Mexican American women, must not only deal with waiting in line to cross the bridge to Laredo but must fend off a young *ambulante*, or street vendor, as well as a gruff and imposing U.S. Customs inspector. Laurence Wensel, a third-year doctoral candidate at University of Texas at Dallas, in his dissertation on TCdeL, states that "we witness how [Raquel's play] reflects a culture affected by policies to control the uncontrollable aspects of the *frontera*" (413).

In *Fashionably Late*, Mague and Regina, the same characters from *Nothing to Declare*, quibble about punctuality as Mague takes her time getting ready to attend a party to which their friend Alicia has invited them. When she asks Regina for advice on which dress and shoes to wear, the latter, who hates being late, urges her to hurry. The title itself highlights a characteristic of Laredoans' behavior—namely, a casual attitude toward punctuality and a concept of time different from that of the Anglo-American world. Steve, Alicia's Yankee husband, despises this as well, calling it "the border attitude." In any case, the two women arrive late and are scolded by Alicia for their tardiness—until Steve himself shows up not only later but drunk, turning the stereotype of Yankee punctuality versus Laredoans' mañana attitude on its head.

A third play from that period, though not produced by Teatro Chicano, is, in fact, Raquel's favorite: *Path of Marigolds*. The action occurs on *la noche del Día de los Muertos*, when Ariana, an interior decorator, throws a party for her closest friend, Consuelo, and three special guests. After engaging in some entertaining banter about the afterlife, fulfilling the Mexican custom of setting up an altar to honor the dead, and Ariana inviting three special guests—Marilyn Monroe, Frida Kahlo, and Sor Juana Inés de la Cruz—they decide to play on a Ouija board. Before long, they hear knocking at the door. It turns out to be Marilyn Monroe, and eventually, Frida and Sor Juana arrive as well. All claim to have been summoned in order to help Ariana decide whether she should leave her alcoholic, unfaithful, and abusive husband, Roberto, a handsome baseball player from Mexico. In the unfolding drama, each of the women gives her view and recommendations based on her history and experience with men. In a surprise ending, Ariana's closest friend, the highly skeptical and sarcastic Consuelo, solves her problem in a most unexpected manner. The play went on the road to McAllen and San Antonio, where the Mexican American singer Vikki Carr, who was in the audience, loved it and congratulated Raquel; she also took pictures with her and the cast. Later, Raquel staged a special performance at the Laredo Country Club for the Women's City Club of Laredo. In McAllen a journalist liked it so much he attended all the performances and wrote a very favorable newspaper review titled "Broadway Bound." No doubt many will see the play as her most feminist piece of writing, since it resonates with the themes of identity and gender issues that appear throughout her poetry.

SOY COMO SOY Y QUÉ

In 1997, *Soy como soy y qué* won the Premio Nacional de Literatura José Fuentes Mares en Letras Chicanas awarded by the Universidad Autónoma de Ciudad Juárez in Mexico. Raquel reports that since the prize's inception ten years earlier, only men had won it. The fact that she and another woman won is also a milestone in border consciousness of gender inequities. In her introduction to the book, Norma Elia Cantú states, "Esta colección añade una voz más a la canción, a la vida de nuestra tierra fronteriza, cruza fronteras pero jamás ignora que existen, y nos ofrece nueva fe para salir adelante y hacer camino al andar en estos terrenos de fin de siglo" (10). In a blurb on the back cover, the ever-sassy Sandra Cisneros declares, "Feroz, fuerte, y sensual como la frontera. I love the voice Raquel Valle-Sentíes gives to Texas writing. Malcriada, hocicona, traviesa, sinvergüenza, in other words, an excellent woman."

The book is divided into three sections. In the first, titled "Laredo," Raquel introduces us to her world in "Los colores de mi mundo," "Laredo," "Eavesdropping," "Border Distortions," and "Hasta en la sopa los encuentro." In "La feria nupcial," she highlights the delusional aspects of expensive traditional weddings, which too often end in disastrous unions. In "¿Velada o velorio?" she skewers the hypocrisy of some wakes. In "Raquel," "Raquel a los seis años," "Growing Up en Laredo," "El rompevientos," "Mal de ojo," "Puntos de vista," and "Did Gringos Have *Piojos?*" she reminisces about growing up in Laredo. Then, in "Pa' Chano," about her love and admiration for her grandfather Chano, and "Padre ausente," about her father's absence, we get a hint of her looming troubles with men. Poems in the second section, "Veracruz," transport us to Mexico and provide glimpses of her encounter with a thoroughly *machista* culture, her subjugation and humiliation at the hands of a abusive and unfaithful husband, her struggle with spiritual and cultural isolation, and finally her decision to divorce her husband: "Pregunta sin respuesta," "Vislumbre," "Retrato de un hombre," "Egoísmo," "Aquella Navidad," "Culpas," "El varón domado," "El festín," "Soñando a orillas del Papaloapan," "En agradecimiento," and "Es mejor cortar por lo sano." In the final section, "Ahora," Raquel reflects on her lost youth, sympathizes with Marilyn Monroe's tragic life, and brings closure to the collection's narrative with defiant self-acceptance in the poems "Dos mujeres," "Where Did That Girl Go?," "M. M.," "Caminos," "Hacia el infinito," and "Soy como soy y qué."

The title poem, "Soy como soy y qué," like other poems in this collection, has always been a hit with Spanish-speaking and bilingual audiences. In her *LareDOS* interview with Koch, she states that her poems

appeal to the younger audience because even if they're not living the same experiences, maybe they heard their moms talking about such a time. And, of course, since I'm writing in Spanglish, they can relate to that. A lot of the poems are funny, and they laugh. One time when I [was going to] read to third graders, I thought, "I don't want to go read to third graders." And these little kids were one of the greatest audiences I ever had. They didn't want me to stop. And when I did the online discussion with the students from Ohio and Utah, it was so unbelievable that these people could enjoy these poems because some people think, "Oh well, they're local, they're regional, they're ethnic and just a certain group of people would be interested." That's not true. People from all over relate to them, especially "Soy como soy y qué." They're interested in how I handled the duality of citizenship, of being both and none. That poem brings out a lot of emotion. People cry when I've read it; they like it very much. (43)

Perhaps the line that most resonates with me is the opening of "Soy como soy y qué": "Soy flor injertada que no pegó" (91).[4] Here, Raquel declares she is a "grafted flower" that never "took." As a misfit, she undertakes the struggle to make sense of her world, especially life on the Mexican American border, and confesses she is a Mexican without being one and an American without feeling it. Though she lived many years in Mexico and loves its culture—the huapangos, Mexico's national anthem, the cuisine, et cetera—Mexicans always remind her, "No, you're not Mexican." On the other hand, she gets goosebumps when she hears the American national anthem, even though Americans look at her as if saying, "You're not American!" In much the same way that "two loves" cannot fit inside her, "two homelands" don't fit either.

No longer able to tolerate the unreality of this displacement, she embraces the reality of the Mexican American border: "I'll have to say, / I'm from the border, / from Laredo." Yet it is a "strange world":

neither Mexican nor American,
where at sunset the smell of
fajitas grilled over mesquite
makes my mouth water,
where on birthdays
we sing "Happy Birthday"
and "Las Mañanitas."
Where who knows why we celebrate
George Washington's birthday.
Where tourists get culture shock,
and people can live here for years
and still be considered outsiders,
where in many places
the green, white, and red flag
waves proudly beside
the red, white, and blue. (93)

Her return to the border does not relieve the tension. In fact, it mirrors and highlights her contradictions. A series of metaphors describe a conflicted self:

> I'm like the Rio Grande,
> once a part of Mexico,
> displaced.
> I'm a puppet
> jerked by the strings of two cultures
> that clash.
> I'm la mestiza
> la pocha,
> la Tex-Mex, *la Mexican-American,*
> la *hyphenated*
> who lacks identity
> and struggles to find it,
> who no longer wants to
> ignore a reality
> that strikes her,
> that wounds her,
> who no longer wants
> to bite her tongue
> who in Veracruz
> defended the United States
> tooth and nail,
> who defends Mexico
> tooth and nail. (93)

This strange world leaves her no choice but to live in ambivalence, flouting all expectations of who she should or could be and affirming the value of the Mexican American border and her life here:

> I'm a walking contradiction.
>
> In other words, like Laredo,
> I am who I am! So what. (93)

ON THE PATH TO REDEMPTION

Many of Raquel's poems touch briefly and indirectly on the subject of sex and infidelity. Once, a woman friend, after hearing Raquel talk about her marital issues in Veracruz, told her, "You have to write those stories . . . about things that people go through [because] they are not being told. You have to write about it." Raquel admits she has written about "abused women because in a certain way I am—verbally, of course; emotionally, definitely; physically, some" (Koch, "Raquel Valle-Sentíes," 69). Even though seemingly reluctant to see herself as an "abused woman," she was very much abused. So why did it take her twenty-five years to leave? The answer is simple: it is difficult. That is why many women—and some men—endure years of pain and misery in bad marriages. Yet she was able to do it. Today, she conveys a message of hope: "And women need to know that no matter how bad it is, how awful, or how long it takes, you can remake your life and get out of this horrible situation" (69).

In one especially powerful poem, "In Gratitude," she takes us to the heart of the matter. Here, she describes the emotional triangle involving herself, her husband, and the other woman. All three are walking contradictions. The other woman, Elizabeth, is plain and ungainly but professionally accomplished. The husband is handsome, "charismatic," and athletic but short and abusive. Raquel is "the betrayed wife," clueless and grieving. First, as we see in the following translation by Raquel, she introduces us to the other woman:

Goes by an English name
a queen's name,
the virgin queen of England,
a name too grand for her.
It clashes with her indigenous aspect
and her Spanish last name.
She stoops as she walks
trying to dissimulate her height,
dragging big feet impossible to ignore.

Young, without grace
whose large shifty eyes as dark
as her intentions save her
from being ugly. Tall and thin
like a candle's wisp with
a cloying voice so different
from mine. A gray woman
from humble origins,
a medical doctor. (68)

Next appears the husband. In "Him" we see a much older version of the "handsome" young professional baseball player Raquel "fell in love with" in Laredo:

Of medium height with all
the complexities of the short man,
silver sideburns rim a swollen face
where remnants of the handsome
man I fell in love with are still visible.
Traces of yesterday's athlete
in his agile, slender frame.

Charismatic man, outstanding baseball
player, loving son, respectful,
generous and loyal friend,
unfaithful and violent husband,
absent and incomprehensible father,
the Don with a resounding last name,
the fairytale prince
for an ordinary woman. (69)

In "Me," Raquel includes herself in the comparison:

The betrayed wife,
How did I fail?
What does she have that I lack?
Questions that I no longer ask myself. (69)

However, she shies away from taking a good, hard look at her own deficiencies, physical or otherwise. Perhaps it is enough of a failure to be a "betrayed wife." Perhaps that betrayal was so traumatic that it left her oblivious. After all, the dynamics of a broken heart are often too complex to understand, especially when one finds oneself in its grip. Nevertheless, she insists on coming to terms with the situation:

> I'm grateful to them,
> especially Her.
> I've been to Europe,
> I've had a sincere friendship with a man,
> the pleasure of being free,
> the pleasure of being
> alone without feeling loneliness.
> If it hadn't been for Her,
> I wouldn't be a writer,
> nor an artist, nor an actress.
> I would still be tied
> to that insignificant man
> with a narrow mind.
> I would still have obligations
> but no rights,
> living in a spiritual desert. (70)

While the poem sheds light on her life in Veracruz, it also raises some interesting questions. For example, who is the "ordinary woman"—Elizabeth or Raquel? How about both? Why doesn't Raquel, an attractive woman with European features, describe her own appearance? Was he, in fact, an "insignificant man"? After all, they lived together for twenty years, and she bore him five boys, all grown men today, and he would haunt her for many years after their divorce in 1989. If not for him, she may never have experienced and absorbed a side of Mexico many of us as Mexican Americans never see. But at the heart of Raquel's artistic achievements is her survival of a disastrous marriage. At one time she may have been an ordinary woman; she is no longer.

THE ONES SANTA ANNA SOLD

"Rich with the ancient dust that falls on the Río Grande and with the sweet airborne pollen of blooms from the Mexican tropics," writes Carmen Tafolla in her introduction to Raquel's second poetry collection. *"The Ones Santa Anna Sold* is a powerful slice of borderland experience." She continues:

> In it, Raquel Valle-Sentíes brings to life the bilingual, bicultural world of Laredo, Texas, with all of its binational contradictions, its Washington and Juárez icons, and its street lore of *coyotes* (people smugglers) and *come hombres* (man-eaters). With a bald-eyed honesty and the freshness of morning gossip, Valle-Sentíes blows the breath of life and the blood of reality into both world-famous celebrities and the unknown homeless, both the impassioned adolescents and the scarred *veteranos* peering warily over the edge of life. (9)

The book contains fifty-one poems. However, seventeen mostly untranslated Spanish poems also appeared in *Soy como soy y qué*, so the collection, like Raquel herself, is another "grafted flower." An interesting one, for all that. Read in conjunction with the first collection, it is, in fact, a footnote to the first book. But more than that, it is the final section of the first book, since it completes the narrative of the disastrous marriage. "Some of the best of Valle-Sentíes's work woven through this collection," observes Koch in an unpublished book review, "involves the man she married sixty years ago and whose memory still haunts her. When read together, ten of these—'First Kiss,' 'Repercussion,' 'A Lover's Nest,' 'M. M.,' 'Day of the Dead,' 'Anniversary Waltz,' 'Dance of Madness,' 'Earthbound,' 'Sifting through the Ashes, and 'Exorcism'— form a complicated and sometimes tragic narrative of young love, marriage, exile, betrayal, death, and, ultimately, forgiveness."

Of special interest to me is "Earthbound," where she addresses the ghost of her husband:

> Many years ago, when afraid
> to let go, we clung
> together like strands of a woven

palm. I said, "I'd rather
you were dead than living
with another woman." You laughed,
"You're mean, *mujer*." (62)

Even though she was finally able to leave him, she could not free herself from her past until she received news of his death, which turned out to be a comedy of sorts, reminiscent of the stories in Carlos Fuentes's *Where the Air Is Clear* or Gabriel García Márquez's *One Hundred Years of Solitude* and *Love in the Time of Cholera*:

I imagined
your rage when the coffin didn't fit
inside the tomb and you, who hated
to wait, waited and kept
everyone else waiting
while a smaller one was brought. (62)

The scene in the cemetery becomes macabre:

You raged when you were lowered
into the grave where the bones
of your ancestors and pieces
of their faded shrouds floated
in the muddy water like paper ships.
You raged so loud that your loved
ones' nightmares made them
exhume, cremate then scatter
your ashes over your beloved land. (63)

The final stanza is a farewell and a reconciliation made possible not only by time but by Raquel's art:

Time has healed our wounds,
freed us both. No longer
lurking in the purple shadows,
you have walked into the light. (63)

"THE ONES SANTA ANNA SOLD": TITLE POEM

The title poem demands attention. According to Tafolla, "'The Ones Santa Anna Sold' tells simply and unsentimentally our collective history as residents of one country and descendents [*sic*] of another. A matter-of-fact litany of our experiences as Mexican-Americans and Mexicans in the U.S., it exposes the *desprecio* with which human beings can be treated for political and monetary reasons and echoes an unspoken indictment of the injustices of those treated as spoils of war, 'collateral' damage and irrelevant 'natives' of the land" (10).

Raquel turns her attention from her fate as a native of the Mexican American border and an abused wife in Veracruz to the history of the border when she invokes the name of Antonio López de Santa Anna, the controversial president of Mexico during the Texas Revolution (1835–36), the Mexican-American War (1846–48), and the Gadsden Purchase (1854). But why would she choose such a title—clever and engaging yet enigmatic? Consider the poem:

We are
those who fled
the land of our birth,
those who built the great pyramids—
mute witnesses of Cortes's destruction,
those who invented the Aztec calendar,
those who left our mothers,
our wives,
our children,
because our country
rich in oil can't feed us.

We are
the wetbacks that cross
the Río Bravo,
the brave ones that cross
the desert,
that drown,
that die of thirst,

that are killed by vigilantes,
border guards or *coyotes*,
those who passively conquer
the most powerful nation in the world,
taking back what once belonged to Mexico.

We are
the traitors,
the starving Indians,
the *pochos*,
the *chicanos*.

We are the ones Santa Anna sold. (24–25)

First, as Tafolla states, the poem is a "litany" of the socioeconomic and political conditions that have beset Mexican Americans as a result of Santa Anna's questionable actions. Nothing new here, of course, since readers have encountered such litanies in numerous other poems by Chicanos. Also, the "litany" lacks the rich imagery and metaphors that characterize Raquel's best poems. However, what saves the poem is the last line—"We are the ones Santa Anna sold"—because only a Mexican, not a Chicano or Mexican American, would say this about Mexican Americans. Yet Raquel, a Mexican American herself and one familiar with Mexicans' customs and vernacular, says it, appropriating the phrase and satirizing it. When I asked her where she picked up the statement, she said, "From the Mexicans, of course. That's what I heard them call us who were from over here."

"*¿Con desprecio?*" I asked.

"Well, yes and no," she replied.

In tandem with what many other Chicano writers and activists have done—namely, flipped a pejorative on its head, including the once denigrating label "Chicano"—Raquel has flipped the Mexicans' snide reference to Santa Anna's betrayal on its head. In her hands, it becomes a Chicano affirmation.

THE EXCITING LIFE OF AN UNHAPPY WOMAN

"I've always thought, 'My goodness, I've never been happy,'" Raquel declares to Koch. "Some people can look back and say, 'Oh, I had such a wonderful childhood.' Well, my mother was a good mother, but I still have not felt that love and family thing that you'd want to have as a child." Koch probes, pointing out that throughout her poems and plays, men are seldom cast in a positive light, since they figure primarily as "victims," "boor[s]," or "abusive" men. Finally, he confronts her: "I'll ask the question that Carlos [Flores] asked: 'Are you a man hater?'" She laughs, then says: "I guess I'm envious of the few women that have good marriages or good relationships with men because I didn't have it, and I didn't see it. Most of the time I see the bad marriages, the bad relationships. It's very rare to see really good relationships anymore. I think it's such an important part of life to love but also to be loved. And I have never felt what it's like to be loved. It's not that I hate men. I don't know why that should come out as man hating" (42–43).

Raquel is always full of surprises, whether it be in her choice of a two-story Victorian house or her taste in Mexican decor or switching from one genre to another in expressing herself. Perhaps no one is more surprised than she in how her life has turned out as a result of her courage and love of art. Toward the end of the interview, she adds a lighter note: "Usually, you think of old age as winding down into oblivion [laughs], or the rocking chair gets you, and for me it's been very different. My life has been more exciting with more happening in the latter part of it. Usually, you don't think these things will happen after a certain age, and with me—well, most of my friends are retiring from their jobs, and I've got all these things in my mind, which really makes life very interesting" (70).

A FINAL NOTE: SPIRIT AND COURAGE

I am delighted that all that work we invested in during the heyday of the South Texas Writing Project, the Café del Barrio, and Teatro Chicano de Laredo has culminated in a contribution to Mexican

Americans' history: Raquel's body of work. It is a product of a chapter in the history of Chicanos and South Texas that remains unacknowledged and undocumented by academicians. While I am pleased that I have been able to collaborate with Raquel over the years—mentoring her initially and editing her first collection of poetry as well as producing two of her plays—I acknowledge others played key roles in her artistic development and success, too.

How should this end? Well, the way it began. I got lost looking for the HR office at TAMIU, not knowing I was headed this way, but here I am—or more precisely, here we are—in the midst of, to borrow a word from Alurista's lexicon, a genuine *floricanto*. In other words, a festival of flowers and song. *¡Brava, Raquel!* Your spirit and work as a poet, painter, and playwright have brought us together; your courage made this possible! *¡Mil gracias!*

NOTES

1. Raquel was in the original Macondo Writers Workshop that Cisneros started in 1995.
2. Both WTWP and STWP are affiliated with the National Writing Project, whose beginnings date back to 1974, when administrators at the University of California, Berkeley, expressed concern over students' deficient writing skills. In turn, Jim Gray, a teacher educator and former high school teacher, organized the first invitational summer institute at the university, where K–12 teachers from the Bay Area gathered to share, discuss, and develop best practices in the teaching of writing. The site was named the Bay Area Writing Project. With grants from foundations and the federal government, more sites were established throughout the states, and the network became known as the National Writing Project.
3. The Chicano/Latino Literary Prize was established in the Department of Spanish and Portuguese at the University of California, Irvine, in 1974. Among the first national literary contests open to Chicanos and Latinos, it published, from 1974 to 2006, some of the leading lights of Chicano literature, such as Ron Arias, Gary Soto, Carmen Tafolla, María Josefina López, and others. Two of its most renowned directors have been Alejandro Morales and the late Juan Bruce-Novoa.
4. Raquel provided the English translation used in the following discussion.

WORKS CITED

Koch, Randy. "The Politics *y el Placer* of *la Poesía Confesionaria*." Review of *The Ones Santa Anna Sold*, by Raquel Valle-Sentíes. Unpublished manuscript, November 26, 2015.

———. "Raquel Valle-Sentíes: Painter, Poet, Eavesdropper, and Diva." *LareDOS: A Journal of the Borderlands*, March 2003, 42+.

Valle-Sentíes, Raquel. "In Gratitude." Translated by Raquel Valle-Sentíes. 2020.

———. *Latinopia Teatro: "Nothing to Declare."* Produced by Barrio Dog Productions. 2012. Video, 4:55. https://vimeo.com/25953716.

———. *The Ones Santa Anna Sold*. Introduction by Carmen Tafolla. Moorpark, Calif.: Floricanto and Berkeley Presses, 2014.

———. *Soy como soy y qué*. Introduction by Norma Elia Cantú. San Antonio, Tex.: M&A Editions, 1996.

———. "Soy como soy y qué." Translated by Raquel Valle-Sentíes. 2020.

RAQUEL VALLE-SENTÍES

Portraits of Self-Empowerment and Cosmopolitan Collective Consciousness

MARÍA JESÚS CASTRO DOPACIO

C HICANA LITERATURE has gained an international reputation, particularly since the 1990s. A globalized marketplace has appeared as a consequence of the transnational flows currently taking place. Nonetheless, most Chicana visual art has not achieved such a notoriety. Throughout history several factors have perpetuated the invisibility of Chicanas: gender, ethnicity, sexuality, class, and cultural stereotypes, among others. With the aim of overcoming such silencing, feminist epistemologies have claimed a space of their own, trying to construct feminine subjects whose voices and images transcend the borders of their own communities, while reinvigorating their presence within the U.S. artistic scenario. Thus, we see the oftentimes short-sighted vision held by the hegemonic canon widened.

This essay focuses on the pioneering Tejana visual artist Raquel Valle-Sentíes, whose portraiture integrates self-representation with a cosmopolitan collective consciousness as it turns Chicana writers into subjects of art. Valle-Sentíes, a native of Laredo, pays homage to fellow contemporary writers in her ongoing *Chicana Writers* series at the same time that she inscribes her name as an artist in a more inclusive art history that makes room for a Chicana gaze. The final collection, begun in 1998, is made up of twelve oil paintings that constitute a group portrait of renowned women writers. The original series features two portraits of Ana Castillo; two of Gloria Anzaldúa; one portrait each of Carmen Tafolla, Cherríe Moraga, Montserrat Fontes, Norma E. Cantú, Sandra Cisneros, Denise Chávez, Demetria Martínez, Olga Valle-Herr, Angela de Hoyos, and Lorna Dee Cervantes; and Valle-Sentíes's self-portrait. Even though portraiture had been done before in the Chicano/a arts,[1] the originality of this project lies in the assemblage of a group of writers who are meant to be embodiments of female artistry and whose strength is iconic for others in and outside their communities, fusing the local with the global to attain human resonance. By bringing to light a female gaze in art, Valle-Sentíes advances a sense of community as well as visibilizing female agency and representation in the arts.[2]

I adopt a cosmopolitan approach here in order to highlight dialogue and conviviality through the many borders this painter crosses with her art. Her standpoint reveals an attitude of openness and ethical engagement with others, two basic features of cosmopolitanism (Di Paola, 4; Appiah, 85). According to Modesta Di Paola, a "cosmopolitical aesthetics" emerges as artists respond with hospitable and responsible behavior toward the world in its totality. Given the variety of sociopolitical contexts of emergency in the contemporary world, artistic practices are essential to reflect on how certain subjects are considered as "belonging" whereas others are not (Di Paola, 13). Kwame Anthony Appiah also cautions that in the human community habits of coexistence and association need to be developed (xviii). Living together in a cosmopolitan world implies a continuous reassessment of one's identity. After all, the Other, the Stranger, arrives with questions, challenging and endangering the existing order (Fotou, 18). In this light, the *Chicana Writers* series becomes paramount, since it fills a gap in the arts world by establishing a dialectics that moves beyond binaries like presence/absence, colored/white, self/other, male/female, thereby connecting with concerns that affect global communities. In *After Cosmopolitanism* Rosi Braidotti, Patrick Hanafin, and Bolette Blaagard propose the notion of "cosmopolitics" to refer to the embedded and embodied perspectives that consider situated location as starting point, engaging individually and collectively with issues the global world deals with (4).

Following Marsha Meskimmon's theoretical approach to contemporary art from a cosmopolitan hermeneutics, identity politics merges with body politics to pose ethical and social claims:

> What role does art play in conceiving and reconfiguring the political, ethical and social landscape of our time? Embedded within this question is my commitment to articulating works of art beyond the logic of representation where that entails art's operation as a mute mirroring, a mere reflection of the conditions of the world, rather than as an active constituent element within them. I would argue that art is a vital form of articulation, that visualization and materialization are active and forceful modes in the production of the real, and that they can transcend the limits of current understanding by pushing the boundaries of imagination, in the most rigorous sense. (5–6)

The cosmopolitan imagination is crucial in generating transformations in viewers by enunciating bridges on which aesthetics and politics crisscross. In the case that occupies us here, this cosmopolitan awareness is grounded in a very specific location: the Mexican American border, a border between two languages, two nation states, two cultures, two world views. Valle-Sentíes perceives this hybrid third space she inhabits as "neither and both" (Spanos). Consequently, interaction between both is a focal point in her art, laying the foundations of her creative process.

Far from showing feminine passivity while attaching to normative gender roles, with her series the Texan painter defiantly demands visibility for professional Chicanas who have chosen writing as their career path. Valle-Sentíes vindicates this genealogy of contemporary cultural workers as producers of culture, thus promoting an iconographic revolution in the U.S. art scenario. Much in the same way that Gloria Anzaldúa claimed "a theory in the flesh" (Moraga and Anzaldúa, 23), Raquel Valle-Sentíes displays evidence of a relationship of solidarity that affirms women artists by establishing a community of writers instead of depicting isolated individuals. This cosmopolitan collective consciousness challenges the sensation of otherness Chicanas suffer both within their own communities and from hegemonic groups who assume gender, class, race, ethnicity, and sexual orientation as markers of difference. It is against such a disempowered vision that Valle-Sentíes rebels. With this series she is bringing center stage her own positive interpretation of Chicana difference, deconstructing the association of difference with negative connotations. Her unique artistic vision brightly illuminates directions that open up possibilities for women artists. Her images of writers are not just colored faces, but talented intellectual women who are being validated in their own right.

Contrary to a traditional Western art gaze that focused on the exterior physical aspects of women, the painter also has eyes for the interior of the women she portrays, providing viewers with some insight into their personalities. In *Making Face, Making Soul*, Anzaldúa critically comments on the demand to live up to the image the community wants of Chicanas or else face ostracism, alienation, isolation, and shame (xv). The visual artist adopts a praxis of "haciendo caras" in the subversive sense of questioning and challenging traditions in order to express Chicanas' subjectivities on her canvas. From what Anzaldúa calls "the inter-face," or the space between the masks that women have become accustomed to wearing through the imposition of roles that perpetuate an internalized oppression, it is possible to crack those masks (xv) and "make anew both inner and outer faces": "In our self-reflexivity and in our active participation with the issues that confront us, whether it be through writing, front-line activism, or individual self-development, we are also uncovering the inter-faces, the very spaces and places where our multiple-surfaced, colored, racially gendered bodies intersect and interconnect" (xvi).

The alienation brought about by internalized oppressions that position woman as other allows the artist to reaffirm her interconnections on a global scale. Within the pictorial frame, her imagined new selves reflect unaccustomed images of female embodiment other women may identify with. Valle-Sentíes exposes, therefore, the many faces of Chicanas' subjectivities from a cosmopolitan relational standpoint whose openness to living with difference favors the portrayal of their cultural complexity. Affirmative visions, Braidotti claims, are developed through a redefined cosmopolitan relational ethics that creatively generates sustainable futures in practices of interconnection with others ("Becoming World," 23). As an active agent Valle-Sentíes seems to concur with Braidotti in the latter's enunciation that "the motivation for the social construction of hope is grounded in a pro-found sense of responsibility and accountability" (24). By presenting affirmative visions of the present, Valle-Sentíes bequeaths to future generations a legacy that fulfills the painter's ethical obligations and gives testimony of a personal compromise to promote transformations in long-established social values. As she is an artist, such compromise transcends the personal sphere and imbues the aesthetic one as well, thus championing a feminization of the arts that opens up new path-ways for Chicanas. Her visionary power has the capacity to engender hopeful futures.

In an age when digital images, predominantly photographs, are taken at an incredibly fast rate, the idea of producing a series of com-posed portraits to represent women writers in fine art, in this case oil paintings to be exhibited, implies that simply producing a visual correspondence is not the portraitist's primary goal. These artworks allow viewers to see the dignified features of the women writers from a Chicana perspective. In this sense, Valle-Sentíes reveals herself to be a powerful witness and mediator. If we take into account that "see-ing is a learned, revealed, ever-changing and transformative process" (Pérez, 306), the painter's subjective interpretation guides receivers toward a perception that destabilizes accepted knowledge and tradi-tions, transcending fixed positions and establishing a cultural dialogue. Her personal experience accounts for such a transcultural stand. After having lived in Veracruz, Mexico, for twenty-three years, Valle-Sentíes admits a love-hate relationship with both Mexico and the United States (Spanos). As she is a multifaceted artist, her poem "Soy como soy y qué" is eloquent in this regard:

Soy la mestiza
la pocha,
la *Tex-Mex*,
la *Mexican-American*,
la hyphenated,
la que lucha por no tener identidad
propia y lucha por encontrarla . . . (*The Ones Santa Anna Sold*, 78–79)

Her determination to find her "self" is aided by her creative expression. Her in-betweenness as an insider-outsider grants her what Vince P. Marotta calls "a bird's eye-view," a critical positioning that allows her to see "more clearly, or differently from, those who occupy opposing cultural perspectives" (Marotta, 109).

The fact that her own self-portrait is included in the series is profoundly significant. She is introducing her self-perception as an artistic creator who has the capacity to redirect, and even reeducate, the viewer's gaze. "Perception is an interpretive process conditioned by education," as Anzaldúa states (*Making Face*, xxi). Since her self-portrait is aligned with those of Chicana writers, this individual image is perceived in a new light. Valle-Sentíes is sending out the message about how she wants to be seen, clearly, as part of the series, as a writer as well as a serious professional artist. She actively aims to depart from the margins where Chicana artists have traditionally been occluded. She seeks to foreground the right of Chicana artists to claim their own visual space. Ana Castillo refers to this need to learn about oneself as a step prior to accepting one's identity as an individual and as part of a community: "Then we may educate the world, including our own communities, about ourselves. But more importantly, it will show us another way of seeing life and the world we live in now" (6). Valle-Sentíes is clearly portraying an alternative way of seeing and being in the world.

In contrast with stereotyped images mass-produced by hegemonic media focusing on violence, criminalizing marginalized minorities in the United States, and circulating female objectifications, Valle-Sentíes calls for a reconsideration of Chicanas' positive projections that embrace a more holistic and down-to-earth outlook. Recognizing the presence of women in intellectual and aesthetic milieus is one of her major goals, as she declared in an interview with Tony Spanos: "I wanted to do this record of these women who are writing and doing such good work. I admire these women very much. They are strong women and great writers. They were writing and trying to get published at a time when nobody was interested in Chicano literature, much less Chicana writers. They struggled and persevered and paved the way for the rest of us" (8). The women stand out as a paradigmatic example of cooperation and dialogue. Their intersubjective dimension is at the core of many of their writings. Illustrative of this mutual collaboration are the acknowledgments in Norma E. Cantú's novel *Canícula: Snapshots of a Girlhood en la Frontera*, where Cantú thanks Sandra Cisneros and Ana Castillo, among others, for their support and encouragement (ix).

Valle-Sentíes's personal knowledge of the writers she painted undoubtedly gives a boost to the plastic force of these portraits.[3] Her expressive language displays the interior vision of the artist. As prominent Chicana writers, they represent corporeal role models for their communities, mirrors that counteract what Laura E. Pérez calls "the historical, present-day hypervisibility of images of women in positions of subservience and as objects of male power, sexual desire, and violence" (266). They embody stories of personal and professional achievement that really needed to be painted and exhibited to the public. Acknowledging, recording, and visualizing the existence of these Chicana writers is Valle-Sentíes's way of documenting and transmitting redefined community imaginaries that hopefully resonate with present and future generations. Once out of her studio, the portraits continue to inspire and connect viewers by means of a double process of self-perception and self-reflection. This is where their empowering effect oozes out. Some of the portraits have become visible through exhibitions, such as *Chicanas Abriendo Caminos*, organized in Nuevo Laredo in 2001 and in Laredo in 2003, and some have been used as the central motif of conference posters—for example, the portrait of Denise Chávez was chosen in 2002 and that of Sandra Cisneros in 2005 for the Latina Letters Conference on literature and identity organized in San Antonio in a partnership between St. Mary's University and the Guadalupe Cultural Arts Center. After all, Valle-Sentíes has declared she would like her artistic contribution to move Chicano/a literature from the "ugly duckling" position to the "swan it is becoming" (Spanos). The collection was also exhibited from 2014 to 2021 at Texas A&M International University. Some portraits are available to wider audiences online.[4]

As the series brings to light assertive images of Chicanas, the painter exposes both voice and body, ensuring that their female accomplishments do not go unnoticed, eventually getting them public recognition and cooperating to bring about social transformation in world-making praxis. In fact, her portraits depict only closely cropped, full-frontal views; she does not introduce any content in the background, leaving only plain fields of color. In this manner, the portrayed person draws full attention to herself while facing spectators. In itself this represents an unconventional gaze, since Chicana authors are simultaneously subjects of the paintings, given their agency as cultural producers, and objects of the artist's portraiture. Their subjectivities are inscribed in these artworks as bodies that express themselves creatively through writing and now are painted.

The portraits are intimate in nature; they capture on canvas the psychologies of these women. Valle-Sentíes employs strong colors and fierce brushwork in a fauvist style to achieve this purpose. She uses contrasting colors to highlight the portrayed figures. For backdrops she utilizes plain primary colors: Ana Castillo, Denise Chávez, Demetria Martínez, and Olga Valle-Herr's portraits together with the painter's self-portrait contain a reddish color in the background; Cherríe Moraga's, a yellowish; and Norma E. Cantú and Gloria Anzaldúa's, a bluish. Sandra Cisneros's portrait features a purplish background, a complementary of the yellow light on her face. Another technique Valle-Sentíes makes use of is the creation of shadows in a color complementary to that of the sitter's light, a distinguishing feature in both of Ana Castillo's portraits. Carmen Tafolla and Montserrat Fontes's backgrounds are black, a dark contrast to the artist's otherwise vibrant palette.

Most of these writers' busts contain no ornamentation, which again reveals the painter's artfulness at emphasizing the sitters' personalities and their self-possessed assurance. The inclusion of a man's tie in Cherríe Moraga's outfit intensifies her professionalism and pokes at male gender roles. Denise Chávez is wearing a necklace and earrings; her half-length portrait shows her arms crossed in front of her in a casual pose. Sandra Cisneros's posture is also quite playful, as she rests her head down on her crossed wrists in a relaxed, meditative way while she looks sideways to the left of the frame. Olga Valle-Herr is elegantly dressed in black, wearing a necklace and matching earrings together with a ceremonial headpiece. All the different looks remind us of the complexity of Chicanas identities.

Only Cisneros, Moraga, and one portrait of Castillo do not maintain their gaze fixed on the painter or viewer; the rest of the sitters do. Seeing these portraits all together could well remind viewers of a scene where all the writers are maintaining a conversation with the artist at the same time that she is portraying them and herself. The fact that they never posed for her as models draws attention to her emotional connection with the sitters, whom she depicts with psychological depth. She manages to represent "the inner faces, *las caras por dentro*" (Anzaldúa, *Making Face*, xxvii) of her subjects. Indeed, Valle-Sentíes recognizes that the fierce brushstrokes she began using in Cisneros's portrait eventually led to a breakthrough in her painting (Spanos), wherein she achieved a greater sense of freedom. Viewers perceive a positive impression of vital strength and liberation.

Raquel Valle-Sentíes sets up a direct dialogue between painting and writing by choosing to portray Chicana writers in her art. This choice reaffirms the painter as an artist in control of a subject matter that is often displaced from art's spotlight. Ana Castillo has pointed out that Chicanas "exist in the void, en ausencia, and surface rarely, usually in stereotype" (5). Overturning that norm, in this series Valle-Sentíes exhibits the individuality of each writer, inviting spectators to open themselves to exploring their aesthetic and literary singularities. Both art and literature serve as means for Chicanas' self-definition. Art is said to establish a flow of emotional resonance (Marlin-Bennett). In this case, art and literature become part of this continuum as they intersect in these portraits. The painter illustrates how feminist synergies have been created among artists in both aesthetic fields, their collective power thus becoming more intense. The interaction among the sitters occurs not only at a social level but also in their creation of professional networks. Writing in the context where Chicana authors are situated is understood, in Anzaldúa's terms, as "an act of survival against fears—a woman who writes has power" (Moraga and Anzaldúa, 171). That power means she has the capacity to move and transform others. Inés Hernández-Ávila explains the importance of creating and showing to audiences: "every manifestación of creativity is another victory, *one we share with the world,* as we renew and rebuild comunidad, each of us beginning with our closest loved ones, then spiraling outward in ever grander circles of life-giving connection" (Hernández-Ávila and Cantú, 357; emphasis added). The communal context Valle-Sentíes conceives emphasizes this ability to educate others. By questioning social practices, Chicana artists destabilize borders and design their own "locus of enunciation," to draw from Walter Mignolo's concept (158). Norma E. Cantú expresses this idea in her novel *Canícula*, where she reflects on writing as a "revolutionary act" (xxiv); she creates her own "locus of enunciation" by juxtaposing stories and photographs and finding her own voice through "fictional autobioethnography," as she herself has named it (xi).

In her essay "Border arte," Gloria Anzaldúa observes that "border art is an art that supercedes the pictorial. It depicts both the soul of the artist and the soul of the pueblo" (30). In this conception, border art is a community-oriented practice that ultimately aims at transformation. The choice that Valle-Sentíes makes in her series reveals the plurality and fluidity of border subjectivities, as the portrayed writers represent a polyphony of coexisting voices and points of view. Valle-Sentíes adheres to current tendencies in cosmopolitan art whereby a conversation between global issues and local experiences is enacted through aesthetics. Her portraits may convey meaning for anyone who has experienced migration, displacement, racialization, erasure, or other types of oppressions or repression of rights while retaining a local rootedness, since the paintings portray unique border identities with the specificities of the Chicana condition. In fact, the aesthetic experience negotiates boundaries and builds the exchange with otherness. As Rosi Braidotti suggests, the fact that as subjects we are copresent, living in the world together, defines the ethics of our interaction, opening new ways of cosmopolitan belonging ("Becoming World," 19). Valle-Sentíes's own artistic engagement was strengthened by her interconnections with these writers, who encouraged her to continue writing and following in their footsteps (Spanos). Her muses are part of a necessary collective imaginary that her skill portrays. Despite a shared colored skin, the visual artist transcends mere physicality and shows viewers these Chicana writers from an insider's perspective. She proposes an alternative aesthetic reality that runs counter to globalization and its tendency toward homogenized imagery. She assigns meaning to what it is to be a Chicana artist. Far from depicting utopian dreams, her renditions are highly realistic. The existence of this group of writers is rooted in the survival of the contradictions that define border people. Creativity proves to be a cathartic outlet for all those tensions.

When choosing a medium to articulate her creative imagination, Valle-Sentíes has observed, she feels torn between writing plays, writing poetry, and painting (Spanos). The artist feels painting and writing help each other. In fact, she establishes clear correlations between both: "I think my poetry and plays both print 'lined' faces . . . my writing has 'texture' as well" (Spanos). The blurring of genres is one more instance of the relationality and constant renegotiation of differences that characterize border subjects.

Valle-Sentíes's multifaceted artistry is made manifest in her last poetry collection, *The Ones Santa Anna Sold* (2014), a book that reinforces that conversation with her portraits.[5] In fact, the book cover is illustrated with some of her paintings in the form of a collage, a mix of writers' portraits with others of her own family members. The artist comments on the differences: whereas she aims for realistic portraits with her relatives, in the portraits of the writers she experiments with a greater degree of freedom, trying vibrant tones and playing with texture by using aggressive and powerful paint strokes. This greater sense of freedom contrasts with the realistic demand and the use of more mellow and tempered tones in her commissioned family portraits (Spanos).

Externalizing her cosmovision through painting and poetry, Valle-Sentíes explores formally and thematically both mediums of artistic expression. The elaboration of her pictorial and poetic discourse springs from the appreciation of impressions and personal experiences that allow her to build up subjectivities that transgress the frontiers of gender, ethnicity, sexuality, and class. These individual subjectivities acquire an even greater semantic value when exhibited as a group, creating a pictorial sequence that Valle-Sentíes legitimates as a significantly urgent theme for art historical study. As John Berger argues in *Ways of Seeing*, "A people or a class which is cut off from its own past is far less free to choose and to act as a people or a class than one that has been able to situate itself in history" (33). Valle-Sentíes's collection of portraits positions Chicanas in a contextualized artistic horizon that leads to their people's self-empowerment. The dynamics of contemporary transnational flows and cross-cultural exchanges expands the horizons of the series, as it may well serve purposes beyond its local affiliations by building up cosmopolitan collective awareness around the issues it tackles.

Weaving interconnectedness, the painter-poet stresses a nexus with the literary corpus of Chicana artists, reflecting on their images as writers, revealing how her own identity—and, by extension, that of others in her community—is also shaped by the women around her and the imagery being presented. Eventually, she exposes to the world at large what kind of perception needs to be built around female artistry. She manages to put Chicanas' creativity on the map in her struggle against their oblivion, another tool of oppression. Valle-Sentíes negotiates her identity as an artist by shaping viewers' perceptions of her subject matter. Her series acquires deeper layers of meaning by dint of being comprised of portraits of other women with shared experiences, shared (her)stories, shared crafts(wo)manship. In this way, the painter legitimizes vital female options that had not been contemplated before for Chicanas, like writing or painting (Saldívar-Hull, 213). Women artists become fair protagonists of their own creative spaces in the public realm.

The feeling of sorority among Chicana artists achieves ethical and political significance and declares indispensable some reflexivity about the power mechanisms exercised from a translocal perspective. As cultural workers, Chicanas foster a new way of seeing, constructing referents for Chicanos/as and Latinos/as living on a border without many certainties, for other U.S.-based communities with similar existential conditions, and for a wider public, situating Latina artists within the United States' rich, polyvocal art stage. With her *Chicana Writers* series, Raquel Valle-Sentíes challenges mainstream art and forces it to reassess artistic expressions that must be visualized at present to do away with years of systemic racism, sexism, and classism. The creation of a new visual language gives form to a world beyond the way of seeing imposed by cultural hegemony and current tendencies toward homogenization. The Texan artist has understood the role of art as a social and perceptual system that needs to be crafted and seen with new eyes. In the words of Pérez, Chicana artists, such as the one studied here, "have dared to search for alternative models of greater human and social integrity" (6). A cosmopolitan consciousness, as a hermeneutical category, allows this aesthetic experience to start a conversation in the sense that Appiah grants this word, that of an engagement with others (85). As an artivist who relates art to activism,

Valle-Sentíes makes viewers conscious of the act of viewing, undoing the supposed neutrality visual hegemony enforces. Thus, she creates a cosmopolitan dialogue whereby viewers are urged to negotiate the local, national, and global after the art encounter.

NOTES

Research for "Portraits of Self-Empowerment and Cosmopolitan Collective Consciousness" by María Jesús Castro Dopacio was supported by the Spanish National R&D Programme, project RTI2018–097186-B-I00 (Strangers and Cosmopolitans: Alternative Worlds in Contemporary Literatures) financed by MCIU/AEI/FEDER, EU, and by the R&D Programme of the Principado de Asturias, through the Research Group Intersections (grant number GRUPIN IDI/2018/000167).

1. Artists such as Laredoan César A. Martínez depicted Sandra Cisneros in 1980. He chose a fiction writer and internationally recognized intellectual for a portrait that displays "his ability to capture the emotional depth of the subject within the work of art" (Keller, Erickson, and Villeneuve, 119). Angel Rodríguez-Díaz, a Puerto Rico native living in San Antonio, also chose Sandra Cisneros as the sitter for his oil on canvas done in 1993; it is now in the permanent collection of the Smithsonian American Art Museum in Washington, D.C.

2. At the moment that I am writing this essay, the Smithsonian Institution is holding the exhibition *Her Story: A Century of Women Writers* at the National Portrait Gallery in Washington, D.C. It comprises twenty-four portraits of women writers who have come to prominence in American literature. Since a rich diversity of cultural backgrounds are displayed in this exhibition, one of the featured writers is Sandra Cisneros in a photograph taken by Al Rendón (1998).

3. In a personal exchange with me, Raquel Valle-Sentíes revealed that for her portraits she worked from personal knowledge of the writers as well as using photos.

4. The information can be accessed at https://www.weber.edu/weberjournal/ Journal_Archives/Archive_C2/Vol_20_3/RValle-Sent%C3%ADesPoe.html.

5. My article "Poesía y pintura de Raquel Valle-Sentíes" offers more insights about the relationship between her art and her poetry. María Magdalena Guerra de Charur also explores Valle-Sentíes's poetry in "Las ambivalencias identitarias en la obra poética de Raquel Valle-Sentíes."

WORKS CITED

Aldama, Arturo J., and Naomi H. Quiñonez, eds. *Decolonial Voices: Chicana and Chicano Cultural Studies in the 21st Century*. Bloomington: Indiana University Press. 2002.

Anzaldúa, Gloria. "Border arte: Nepantla, el lugar de la frontera." In *Entre Guadalupe y Malinche: Tejanas in Literature and Art*. Edited by Inés Hernández-Ávila and Norma Elia Cantú. Austin: University of Texas Press, 2016.

———. *Borderlands/La Frontera: The New Mestiza*. 2nd ed. San Francisco: Aunt Lute Books, 1999.

———. *Making Face, Making Soul: Creative and Critical Perspectives by Women of Color*. San Francisco: Aunt Lute Books, 1990.

Appiah, Kwame Anthony. *Cosmopolitanism: Ethics in a World of Strangers*. London: Penguin Books, 2007.

Berger, John. *Ways of Seeing*. London: Penguin Books, 1972.

Braidotti, Rosi. "Becoming World." In *After Cosmopolitanism*. Edited by Rosi Braidotti, Patrick Hanafin, and Bolette Blaagard. Abingdon, England: Routledge, 2013, 8–27.

Braidotti, Rosi, Patrick Hanafin, and Bolette Blaagard, eds. *After Cosmopolitanism*. Abingdon, England: Routledge, 2013.

Cantú, Norma Elia. *Canícula: Snapshots of a Girlhood en la Frontera*. Albuquerque: University of New Mexico Press. 1995.

Castillo, Ana. *Massacre of the Dreamers: Essays on Xicanisma*. New York: Plume, 1994.

Castro Dopacio, María Jesús. "Poesía y pintura de Raquel Valle-Sentíes: Filiaciones estéticas comprometidas." In *Tradition and (R)evolution: Reframing Latina/o Identities in Contemporary U.S. Culture*. Edited by Carmen Méndez García. Alcalá de Henares, Spain: Instituto Universitario de Investigación en Estudios Norteamericanos "Benjamín Franklin," Universidad de Alcalá, 2018, 59–68.

Di Paola, Modesta. *Cosmopolitics and Biopolitics: Ethics and Aesthetics in Contemporary Art*. Barcelona: Publicacions i Edicions de la Universitat de Barcelona, 2018.

Fotou, Maria. "Ethics of Hospitality: Envisaging the Stranger in the Contemporary World." Thesis London School of Economics and Political Science, 2016. http://etheses.lse.ac.uk/3403/.

Guerra de Charur, María Magdalena. "Las ambivalencias identitarias en la obra poética de Raquel Valle-Sentíes: *Soy como soy y qué*." In *Geographies of Identity: Mapping, Crossing, and Transgressing Urban and Human Boundaries*. Edited by Esther Álvarez López. Alcalá de Henares, Spain: Instituto Universitario de Investigación en Estudios Norteamericanos "Benjamín Franklin," Universidad de Alcalá, 2016, 37–45.

Hernández-Ávila, Inés, and Norma Elia Cantú. *Entre Guadalupe y Malinche: Tejanas in Literature and Art*. Austin: University of Texas Press, 2016.

Keller, Gary D., Mary Erickson, and Pat Villeneuve. *Chicano Art for Our Millennium: Collected Works from the Arizona State University Community*. Tempe, Ariz.: Bilingual Press, 2004.

Marlin-Bennett, Renée. "Art-Power and Border Art." *Arts and International Affairs*, October 27, 2019. https://theartsjournal.net/2019/10/27/marlin-bennett -2/ Accessed 6 September 2021.

Marotta, Vince. "The Cosmopolitan Stranger." In *Questioning Cosmopolitanism*. Edited by Stan van Hooft and Wim Vanderkerckhove. Studies in Global Justice 6. Dordrecht, Netherlands: Springer, 2011, 105–20.

Meskimmon, Marsha. *Contemporary Art and the Cosmopolitan Imagination*. London: Routledge, 2011.

Mignolo, Walter D. "The Many Faces of Cosmo-polis: Border Thinking and Critical Cosmopolitanism." *Public Culture* 12, no. 3 (Fall 2000): 721–48. https://doi .org/10.1215/08992363-12-3-721.

Moraga, Cherríe, and Gloria Anzaldúa, eds. *This Bridge Called My Back: Writings by Radical Women of Color*. New York: Kitchen Table, 1983.

Pérez, Laura E. *Chicana Art: The Politics of Spiritual and Aesthetic Altarities*. Durham, N.C.: Duke University Press, 2007.

Saldívar-Hull, Sonia. "Feminism on the Border: From Gender Politics to Geopolitics." In *Criticism in the Borderlands: Studies in Chicano Literature, Culture, and Ideology*. Edited by Héctor Calderón and José David Saldívar. Durham, N.C.: Duke University Press, 1994, 203–20.

Spanos, Tony. "Living and Working on the Border: A Conversation with Raquel Valle-Senties." *Weber Journal* 20, no. 3 (Spring/Summer 2003). https://www .weber.edu/weberjournal/Journal_Archives/Archive_C2/Vol_20_3/RValle -Sent%C3%ADesConv.html.

Valle-Sentíes, Raquel. *Chicana Writers* Series. https://www.weber.edu/ weberjournal/Journal_Archives/Archive_C2/Vol_20_3/RValle-Sent%C3 %ADesPoe.html.

———. *The Ones Santa Anna Sold*. Introduction by Carmen Tafolla. Moorpark, Calif.: Floricanto and Berkeley Presses, 2014.

ANGELA DE HOYOS

ANGELA DE HOYOS

A Poet Artivist

MARÍA ESTHER QUINTANA AND
MARÍA MAGDALENA GUERRA DE CHARUR

A NGELA DE HOYOS was an internationally renowned and awarded poet who fought for the Chicanx community and women. Poet Raúl Salinas named de Hoyos "the den mother of the Chicano Movement,"[1] a writer who used her literature to lead true social fighters in fostering awareness of the abuse and discrimination against Mexicans and Mexican Americans and in affirming their cultural pride (Milligan, "Den Mother"). She was also an artist, an editor, a translator, and an activist who left a vast body of work as a legacy not just for Chicanx and Latinx people but for other minorities as well. In the late twentieth century, as Chicanx writers were finding their place in the early Chicano Movement and emphasizing poetry of protest with a focus on the oppression of the working class, one poet in San Antonio—de Hoyos—persisted in celebrating Chicanismo not only by writing poetry that was at once personal and political but also through her artwork and her tireless efforts to empower Chicanxs and women.

What follows is a brief biography of de Hoyos. The rest of the essay will examine her multifaceted work by discussing her different areas of artistic endeavor, with a special emphasis on her poetry. We will be looking at her collections *Arise, Chicano! and Other Poems*

(1975), *Chicano Poems: For the Barrio* (1975), *Selected Poems/Selecciones* (1976), *Woman, Woman* (1985), and three books that were published posthumously by de Hoyos's husband, Moisés Sandoval: *Sweet 16, Shades of Sappho*, and *Gata Poems: El desquite*. The poems from the latter three were included in *Selected Poems of Angela de Hoyos*, published by Arte Público Press in 2014.

FIRST YEARS

Angelina Andrea Sandoval de Hoyos was born in Coahuila, Mexico, a state that borders the United States, on January 23, 1924.[2] At a very young age, she and her family moved to San Antonio, Texas, where an accident with a gas heater would cause her to suffer severe burns on her chest and neck. During her long convalescence, her siblings would lend her crayons to draw, and her mother would read poetry to her from a wide range of authors, such as Sor Juana Inés de la Cruz, Amado Nervo, and Rubén Darío. She also listened to her maternal grandfather, Amado de Hoyos, improvise satirical, witty four-liners. Then, she would spend hours creating rhymes and stories to alleviate the pain and boredom. The poet noted that she would "try to write out words that rhymed—cat, bat, hat. I was desperate to express myself, for there was nothing else I could do in bed. . . . When you must rise to an emergency, something compels you" (Young).

During her sophomore year of high school, the poem "Our San Antonio Book" became her first published poem, along with an illustration she made titled "Mesquite." This made her the only student to contribute poetry and art to the San Antonio Technical and Vocational High School art department project book in 1941. At this time, she signed her poem as Angelina Sandoval. On May 24, 1943, she earned her high school degree. After high school, de Hoyos decided to enroll in classes related to her interests in literature and art in different institutions, such as the University of Texas at San Antonio, San Antonio College, the Art Institute of San Antonio, and the Witte Museum. These studies contributed to her lifelong creative power as a poet, visual artist, composer, translator, and editor.

LYRICIST

A less researched aspect of de Hoyos's talent is her role as a lyricist. Toward the end of the 1950s and the beginning of the 1960s, de Hoyos, still under the name of Angelina Sandoval, wrote the lyrics to several songs, primarily with Daniel Garzés and Emilio Cáceres as composers. The Strachwitz Frontera Collection of Mexican and Mexican American Recordings at the University of California, Los Angeles, houses recordings of songs written by her, such as "Eso no," "Mentiritas," and "Pero que lástima," with music by Cáceres, and "Amor de Dios" and "Cómo has cambiado," with music by Garzés, among other titles.[3]

Most of de Hoyos's songs were recorded by such small record labels as Ideal, Sombrero, Corona, and Falcon, all of them based in Texas. These companies specialized in promoting Tejano music and singers at a time when major labels were not interested in this musical genre. The music composed for her lyrics ranged across different song forms, from bolero and bolero mambo to guaracha and ranchera. The recurring themes in her songs were love, disillusion, humor, reflection, and sorrow. These songs were written and recorded in Spanish. The record companies also took advantage of de Hoyos's artistic talent, using her image of a Mexican charro hat as a logo for the Sombrero and Ideal recording labels.

VISUAL ARTIST

As an artist, de Hoyos created a massive collection of illustrations, oil paintings, and watercolors that have gone unnoticed by most critics. Many of these pieces later served as illustrations for her poetry. She credited her artistic talent to her mother, whom she considered a very talented painter (Baeza Ventura, xii).

In 1948, de Hoyos's oil portraits were displayed in her first art exhibit, a group show called the *San Antonio River Art Show*. She was the only Mexican artist in the exhibit. In the early 1950s, de Hoyos painted a full-body self-portrait filled with contrast between dark and light tones. In this image, the artist uses soft and fine lines to show a serene young de Hoyos wearing a mustard-colored dress that added light to the portrait. Arte Público Press chose the image for the cover of its 2014 book *Selected Poems of Angela de Hoyos*. The anthology contains an appendix with some of her illustrations, such as the one she created for the poem "Campesinos" in support of farmworkers in March 1975. The sketch portrays the drawing of a map of Texas on the sole of a foot. The image is accompanied by the statement of a fifty-eight-year-old woman: "Traigo el mapa de Tejas en la planta de mis pies y los invito a que me ayuden a cargarlo hasta Osten" (I've got the map of Texas on the sole of my foot, and I invite you to help me carry it up to Austin), a reference to Chicano demonstrations at the Texas State Capitol.

Although she produced some commercial designs (such as logos for record companies) and other sketches (like the ones included in the book *Ten Short Poems, 32 Sketches with Witty Words, I Never . . . Sinned Until I Met You*, published posthumously in 2014),[4] her art stemmed mainly from her Chicanx consciousness, her poetry, and her concern for female empowerment.

One of her hallmark illustrations, the political print *Pa' Delante Vamos*, was published on the cover of *Caracol* in January 1978. *Caracol* was a journal founded in 1974 in San Antonio, intended as a forum for raising Chicanx consciousness during Texas's Chicano literary renaissance. *Pa' Delante Vamos* portrays five mestizo women, some of them young girls: one is waving a flag with the map of Texas; another one carrying a pennant with the motto "Arise, Chicano!"; one holding a child on her lap; another one speaking over a microphone; and, in the background, a teacher writing the statement "El que habla dos idiomas vale por dos" (He who speaks two languages is worth twice as much) on a blackboard. At the bottom of the print appears the phrase "Pa' Delante Vamos" (We Are Moving Forward), which represents both a statement of how Chicanx are moving forward in their struggle for political, social, economic, and cultural changes in favor of Chicanx rights in the United States and an exhortation to keep fighting in El Movimiento. The artist underscores another political message, "Arise, Chicano!," by inscribing it on a pennant held by the young girls in the image. Not by coincidence, "Arise, Chicano!" constitutes the title of one of her most iconic political poems as well as of her first collection of poetry. In *Pa' Delante Vamos*, de Hoyos conveys a subtle feminist message by bringing attention to Chicanas' pivotal presence in their communities. However, de Hoyos's message is somewhat timid, as she depicts these Chicanas solely in traditional roles. In her future collections of poetry, such as *Woman, Woman* (1985), de Hoyos will make a stronger critique of women's subordinate status in Chicanx society.

In addition to acknowledging the prominent role Chicanas played in the Chicano Movement, this print also emphasizes the pivotal role of Spanish—a colonized language in the USA—in bilingual and bicultural Chicanx culture and the value of bilingual education for future generations. According to Areli Navarro Magallón, in her introduction to de Hoyos's graphic archives on the Recovering the U.S. Hispanic Literary Heritage Digital Collections site, this illustration "could be considered the epitome of de Hoyos with Chicanx circles."

In addition to illustrating many of her poems (for example, her poem poster in memory of César Chávez), Angela de Hoyos also composed other poems in which she incorporated spacing techniques to create a visual effect connected to the message she intended to convey. In that regard, the visual distribution of the lines in "To a Brown Spider: En el Cielo" (included in *Arise, Chicano!*) reinforces the poet's comparison of her own vulnerability to that of a brown spider clinging precariously to its web. Furthermore, de Hoyos underscores their mutual resilience as well as their courage and creativity in the face of adversity:

> Brave arachnid
> Spinning with star-lit dreams
> Your daring web
> —how precarious is your perch!
> I too h
> a
> n
> g by a thread. (*Selected Poems*, 7)

PUBLISHER AND EDITOR

When El Movimiento emerged during the U.S. civil rights movement, Chicanxs advocated social and political empowerment through Chicanismo, or cultural nationalism, embracing their Mexican heritage and fighting for the recognition of their historical and cultural legacy. Along with the political movement arose a literary movement with Chicanx authors writing in diverse genres. Some voices that stood out during this time were Tomás Rivera, Rolando Hinojosa-Smith, Tino Villanueva, Raúl Salinas, Reyes Cárdenas, and Cecilio García-Camarillo. The movement also gave rise to many female voices, such as Cherríe Moraga, Sandra Cisneros, Gloria Anzaldúa, Ana Castillo, and Denise Chávez. For some authors, de Hoyos served as a promoter by publishing their work in her pioneering press M&A Editions, founded in 1974 by de Hoyos and her husband, Moisés Sandoval, to provide a platform for Chicanx authors like Carmen Tafolla, Inés Hernández-Ávila, Evangelina Vigil-Piñón, and Juan Tejeda.

De Hoyos and Sandoval also published cultural and political magazines aimed at Chicanx audiences, including *Caracol* and *Huehuetitlan*. M&A Editions helped to legitimize and disseminate the work of Chicanx authors when established publishing companies were not interested in narratives of resistance to the multiple oppressions Chicanx and women were subject to.

During the 1990s de Hoyos, along with Bryce Milligan and Mary Guerrero Milligan, were the editors of two all-Latina anthologies: *Daughters of the Fifth Sun: A Collection of Latina Fiction and Poetry* (1995), published by Riverhead Books, and *Floricanto Sí! A Collection of Latina Poetry* (1998), published by Penguin Books.

M&A Editions ceased publishing in 1996, but after de Hoyos's death in 2009, some of her unpublished works were posthumously published by the press.

LITERARY WORK

According to an unpublished autobiography, de Hoyos started writing the poems contained in *Arise, Chicano! and Other Poems* and

Chicano Poems: For the Barrio around 1968. However, the books were not published until 1975. In this autobiography she states that she started writing in a blend of Spanish/English because she wanted to preserve something of her Mexican-Indian-Spanish ancestry. From her first published poems, in 1975, de Hoyos's work was recognized and translated into various languages, including Spanish, Italian, and Portuguese.[5] Her poetic work was published in books and magazines around the world. In addition, she earned international awards and several honors, such as one granted by Rome's Centro Studi e Scambi Internazionali, Accademia Internazionale Leonardo Da Vinci. De Hoyos also distinguished herself in the translation of such books as Mireya Robles's *Tiempo artesano/Time, the Artisan* (1977) and Teresinha Pereira's *While Springtime Sleeps* (1975) and *Help! I'm Drowning!* (1975).

The Chicano Movement impacted de Hoyos profoundly. The literary movement that grew out of it was dominated by poetry that "beyond its antagonistic and political tone demonstrated the imaginative quality of a people embarking in the quest of self-defining their culture through a literary language" (Gaona, 266). She used her poetry and prints to give voice to the varied issues faced by Mexican Americans. As did many other activists, she utilized her artistry to exhort Chicanx to fight against exploitation and discrimination by Anglo-American society. At the same time, and unlike her compañeros in the movement, de Hoyos denounced the subjugation of Chicanas by males within their own culture. Her poetic production reflected her concern not only for the Chicanx community in general but specifically for Chicanas who were oppressed by Anglo-Americans for being women in general *and* women of color and by Chicanos for being female. In an unpublished interview with Norma Elia Cantú, de Hoyos said that to write about women's problems, she was inspired by a line from the poem "El poeta" by Atahualpa Yupanqui: "que lo primero es ser hombre / y lo segundo, poeta" (A man needs to be man first / and then a poet). De Hoyos realized that in her case she had to be a woman first and then a poet. As a poet, she had to feel empathy for the suffering of others, because only by being able to understand other people's pain would she be able to express a full gamut of emotions in a poem. As she explained in 1982, in an unpublished interview by Norma Elia Cantu, that was her way to help improve the situation of women, including Chicanas: "I try to speak for women, I try to contribute."[6]

Although her main influences in poetry were her mother and grandfather—it is because of him that she started writing under the name of Angela de Hoyos[7]—when interviewed by Cantú, de Hoyos said that classical authors in the English and Spanish languages contributed to her formation. She added that what other poets wrote triggered her creations: she responds to César Vallejo in her poem "Brindis por el barrio," for example, and to Octavio Paz in "Respuesta de las palabras I" and "Reply of the Words II," two poems in *Woman, Woman.*

Another influence she mentioned in the same interview came from the Mexican writer Juan Rulfo. De Hoyos said that in Rulfo "there is an urgency to say a lot in a few words," and she would try to do the same with her poems: "'Realidades macabras a la Rulfo' could not have been written if I had not read something about his style." The influence of other writers likewise detonated her creative work.

De Hoyos also dedicated many of her poems to colleagues, writers and artists, local and nationwide civic leaders, and cultural events. Some examples of these poems are "Poema Anaya, tres veces," written for Rudolfo Anaya; "Tonantzin morena," dedicated to her mother; and "Chicano Music Festival." Upon her death, her husband, Moisés Sandoval, published *Dedicatorias: Poemas for People* (2013), a compilation of all the poems she wrote for people or events between 1975 and 1990. In those poems the poet expressed her admiration for individuals who genuinely search for the good and the truth in their lives and in society. She noted, in the interview with Cantú, why she wrote these poems and how she got the inspiration to create them. One example she presented was the poem she wrote for Yolanda Julia Broyles, whom she considered "the epitome of la mujer chicana" as she instilled pride in her Chicano students. She told Cantú: "It is something that is in the subconscious, something or someone that I have known and suddenly a person appears to crystallize what is there and helps me put it into a coherent and meaningful poem, as in 'A tí, maestra.'"

Her first book, *Arise, Chicano! and Other Poems*, published in 1975 with a Spanish translation by the award-winning Cuban American author and literary critic Mireya Robles, comprises nine poems focused almost entirely on the oppression and marginalization of Chicanxs. Some of the poems included in this collection date from the late 1960s, a period when de Hoyos's growing social and political consciousness incited her to produce poetry to debunk the stereotypical literary portrayals of Chicanxs: "We had to stand up and shout: 'here I am! Not as you have stereotyped me, but as I really am!' and from that premise proceed to record our reality; these books are part of that reality; they represent my commitment primarily to myself and to my people who inspired them" (quoted in Aguilar-Henson, 12).

Bryce Milligan positions de Hoyos as one of the first Chicanx poets giving voice to Texas migrant workers and poor Mexican Americans dwelling in the cities ("Ever Radical," 218), while at the same time she represented the social and political concerns of the young Chicano movement in Texas ("Den Mother"). De Hoyos's thematic focus on Chicanx's oppression has been underscored by other critics, but they have also identified an equally relevant thematic plane represented by her more introspective and philosophical poems (Ramos, 10). Luis Arturo Ramos describes the poetry of the first area of focus as "engaged literature," whose roots emanate from the poet's urgent need to become a spokesperson for "los desheredados" (the disinherited). The second thematic focus of her poetry Ramos describes as "antiheroic," as it features an "'unimportant' and ironic poetic 'I', trapped in the social conventions and demands typical of the middle class" (27). Ramos's characterization of Angela de Hoyos's poetry, however, is too reductive since, on the one hand, only a few of her poems center on domestic life and bourgeois values, and on the other, her introspective poems also deal with universal philosophical themes, such as the source of emotions, religious concerns, relationships, life, and death. While these two stylistic and thematic planes have coexisted since the composition of *Arise, Chicano! and Other Poems* (as we will explain later in our analysis of the book), they do not coalesce until her second book, *Chicano Poems: For the Barrio* (1975), where the speaker finds comfort for her grief and sense of hopelessness in her connection with the Chicanx community.

The title poem, "Arise, Chicano!," powerfully illustrates the exploitation of Mexican migrant workers as they toil from daybreak to sunset to earn a meager salary. De Hoyos deconstructs idealized images of houses as safe and comfortable homes or as cozy shelters where, as French philosopher Gaston Bachelard states in *The Poetics of Space*, the dwellers can daydream happily in peace. Unlike Bachelard's depiction of his ideal childhood home, de Hoyos renders migrant farmworkers' houses as cold and unwelcoming, especially for the "unsmiling children" who have to sleep on icy-cold beds while they listen to the same "wry song, / a ragged dirge, / thin as the air." In the next stanza, the speaker refers to the slave-like conditions of migrant workers, plowing under "long suns of brutal sweat" while even their dreams of "sweeter dawns" are "confiscated" by their cruel masters. The hopelessness of the migrant workers is reinforced by the image of a "shroud," a metonymic reminiscent of Christ's burial, as she suggests a comparison between the dreams of migrant workers and Christ's dead body. The conclusion of the poem extends an urgent call to Chicanx to ignite a spiritual and cultural rebellion:

> Arise Chicano!—that divine spark within you
> surely says—Wash your wounds
> and swathe your agonies.
> There is no one to succor you.
> You must be your own messiah. (*Selected Poems*, 2)

Aguilar-Henson concludes that in "Arise, Chicano!" the admirable use of pivotal Christian concepts, primarily the idea of the Messiah as liberator of his people through his resurrection from death, communicates de Hoyos's emancipatory message to Chicanx: do not resign yourselves to your fate, but instead "be your own messiah" (19). Nonetheless, in this poem, as well as in others in the collection, de Hoyos rebels against many Christian values—for example, the acceptance of suffering as a way to submit to God's will.

"Brindis: For the Barrio," the second poem of *Arise, Chicano!*, is another piece in which de Hoyos subverts Christian values as well as communicates her empathy for Chicanx's physical and emotional hunger. In this case, however, rather than focusing on migrant workers, she looks at Mexican Americans living in working-class neighborhoods, or barrios. The imagery in the first stanza evokes once again a biblical image, this example from the Old Testament:

> Brothers, today we drink
> the fresh milk of dawn
> —for once, not tasting
> of sourness (*Selected Poems*, 4)

The idea of feasting on milk seems to be inspired by a quote from the Exodus 3:8 in which God promises the Israelites "a land flowing with milk and honey." However, in contrast to the story in the Bible where the Israelites eventually arrive to the Promised Land and enjoy its sweet fruits, Chicanx live in a country where they are offered only "bitter food." The allusion to sourness suggests the image of Christ on the cross, tasting vinegar as his last willing act in order to fulfill the prophecies about him (John 19:29–30). As opposed to Jesus's acceptance of suffering and sacrifice, the poet proposes that her fellow Chicanx drink milk at a table "with plates full of hope." However, despair also surfaces in the next verses, as she cannot promise Chicanx that they will feel consolation for their losses or satisfy their hunger by "consuming" only the hope of a better future:

> Not that the hollows
> in your sad face of death
> will ever be filled;
> —or the seedy, stale figure
> of the poor
> feel at ease in fine clothes—(*Selected Poems*, 4)

These last three verses can be interpreted as Anglo-American society's negative view of Chicanx as purportedly incapable of fitting into hegemonic culture. In the final verses of this poem, the speaker extends a joyous invitation to her fellow brothers and sisters to enjoy a banquet as a community while they comfort one another for the pain and sense of alienation that, according to the poet, Anglo-American society has inflicted upon Chicanx:

> but today we eat
> to soothe the pain
> —a pain of alien-hungers
> Vallejo never knew. (*Selected Poems*, 4)

"Brindis: For the Barrio" quotes "La cena miserable" by Peruvian poet César Vallejo, a poem in which he describes life as a meager, solitary, and seemingly endless meal. For Vallejo, there is hope only in the afterlife, where people will no longer experience physical or emotional hunger and will feel connected to one another. In the aforementioned interview by Cantú, de Hoyos affirmed that even though Vallejo's suffering did not emerge from a sense of oppression or cultural alienation, she felt compelled to "converse" with the Peruvian poet: "In César Vallejo's poem something in my subconscious became the Chicano movement, I correlated these two things and compared them. There was something to add. I try to be a voice for the people." In other words, as Vallejo does, de Hoyos addresses human suffering; however, she connects it to Chicanx oppression while she tries to alleviate their pain with the hope for a better future.

Equally introspective, "The Feeling Is Mutual" includes one of the main leitmotifs in de Hoyos's poetry: people's antagonism toward their fellow humans in spite of Christ's command to love one another in John 13:34. The speaker ironically reveals that while she is in church her sins are forgiven, but as soon as she is back home her "normal" self "growls at the world / and the world / returns the compliment." Her cynicism underscores, on the one hand, the automatization of religious beliefs and, on the other, the disenchantment with Catholicism. For de Hoyos, Catholicism has failed as a source of a deep spirituality, and hence it provides no inspiration for Chicanx's liberation.

An even darker poem, "The Oasis Exists," conveys a sense of hopelessness as the speaker wanders through the desert without finding a helping hand or an oasis to quench her thirst. The only thing to which she is allowed to aspire is a mirage "in the endless desert / of [her] thirst." The poem also transmits a sense of alienation when the speaker alludes to being forbidden from entering the oasis, a proscription doubly unjust as she has earned the right to enter and therefore it should be her "well-earned prize." This poem can be interpreted in a myriad of ways; however, given the main leitmotif of the book, namely Chicanx's oppression and marginalization, it can be associated with the sense of otherness felt by de Hoyos as a Chicana in a land that once belonged to her ancestors and that she now experiences as foreign, a sentiment that she communicates in her next collection of poetry.

"The Final Laugh," which concludes *Arise, Chicano! and Other Poems*, reiterates the brutal contradiction between Mexican Americans' longing for social acceptance in Anglo-American culture and the discrimination and marginalization against them by mainstream society.[8] The poem contains a peremptory warning to Chicanxs: either they lose their remaining "ethnic pride" by succumbing to the "alien white" "gluttonous omnipotent world," or instead they "burst [their] shackles" and "fling the[ir] final parting laugh" at the oppressive hegemonic society. According to Gabriela Baeza Ventura, "The Final Laugh" renders the author's conviction for a brighter future for Mexican Americans as a direct consequence of the Chicano Movement (xvii).

De Hoyos's second book, *Chicano Poems: For the Barrio* (1975), reiterates her concern for the increasing loss of Mexican heritage by Mexican Americans and their potential disappearance as a distinctive cultural community. *Chicano Poems: For the Barrio* focuses on the subjugation of Chicanx by U.S. hegemonic culture and society while it also questions the single-perspective narratives surrounding the historical relations between Mexico and the United States, especially in the Southwest. Moreover, de Hoyos's poetry in this volume features codeswitching as a literary tool to undermine the diglossia between English and Spanish in the United States, in other words, the higher status of the former over the latter. In this manner, the poet conveys Chicanx's bilingual and code-switching abilities in order to subvert the stereotypical assumption of their lack of mastery of either language. With regards to bilingualism in de Hoyos's poetry, Marcela Aguilar-Henson observes a progressive development in the use of Spanish starting with an almost exclusive use of English in *Arise, Chicano! and Other Poems*, code-switching in *Chicano Poems: For the Barrio*, and Spanish, English, and code-switching in her later collections (11). In a similar vein, Baeza Ventura observes that de Hoyos employs different linguistic registers in both English and Spanish (such as caló, the language of the Chicano neighborhood, Tex-Mex, pochismo, and Spanglish) "to represent and communicate with her readers," sometimes including footnotes to explain certain words or entire sentences (xiv–xv). As Aguilar-Henson precisely states, the barrio constitutes both an interlingual and an intercultural world (42), and, as such, it is a distinctive space in danger of disappearing because of the powerful influence of a hegemonic Anglo-American culture.[9]

One of the objectives of *Chicano Poems: For the Barrio* is to foster cultural pride in Mexican Americans so that they value their historical

and cultural contributions in the USA, a heritage that is often marginalized in American historiography. In order to remedy the imperialistic
versions of U.S.-Mexican history, she offers a critique of key historical events from the point of view of the vanquished. For example,
the poem "Hermano" (Brother) employs irony to debunk the epic
interpretation in Texas history textbooks of the phrase "Remember
the Alamo!" as honoring what is traditionally considered a defeat of
a small group of heroic Texans fighting against the Mexican army. De
Hoyos encourages the reader to ponder the other side of the history
of the War of Texas Independence, namely, the Mexican heritage of
Texas, which has been traditionally absent in most history textbooks
in Texas. In the epigraph to "Hermano," "'Remember the Alamo' . . .
and my ancestors who had the sense to build it," the author articulates a counternarrative by making the reader aware that Mexicans
were legitimately defending a territory established by their forefathers
and foremothers. She describes the Anglo-Americans who conquered
Texas as "hombres rudos que te hurtaron" (barbaric men who stole
you [Texas]) and

> pilgrim[s]
> who arrived here only yesterday
> whose racist tongue says to me: I hate
> Meskins. You're a Meskin. Why don't you go back where you came
>   from? (*Selected Poems*, 13)

Furthermore, she defends her right to live in a land that once belonged
to her ancestors and sarcastically challenges the descendants of the
English pilgrims (traditionally considered the legitimate founders of
the country) to leave the United States: "—and you can scare up your
little "Flor de Mayo"—so that we can all sail back / to where we came
from: the motherland womb." The predominance the poem gives to
the presence of the Spaniards over the British is reinforced by the use
of Spanish. Its importance is announced in the title, "Hermano," and
also emphasized in the translation of Mayflower as "Flor de Mayo." As
we noted before, de Hoyos's use of her native Spanish in the poem
undermines the supposed higher prestige of English. In the final verses
of "Hermano," the author transmits her hope that the cultural clash

between Chicanx and Anglo-Americans will end when the latter learn to treat Mexican Americans with dignity: "I must wait for the conquering barbarian / to learn the Spanish word for love: Hermano." As Aguilar-Henson states, "The missing ingredient in Anglo culture, then, is love, a sense of humanity"—and, we might add, an awareness of kinship, which the word *hermano* suggests (47). Baeza Ventura explains that de Hoyos wrote "Hermano" in response to a newspaper article she read when she was a teenager in which the author asserted that people of Mexican descent must leave the USA and return to "their country of origin" (xviii). Here de Hoyos acts as an educator trying to remedy the ignorance of Mexican American history displayed in the article. By so doing, she hopes that Anglo-Americans will acknowledge their commonalities with Chicanx rather than focusing on their cultural differences.

Just as in other poems in *Chicano Poems: For the Barrio*, de Hoyos laments the status of Chicanx youth in terms of cultural loss. The poem "Small Comfort" conveys the poet's sadness over the increasing loss of language and tradition by the younger generation of Chicanx and the disintegration of the barrio under the pressure of acculturation and the acceptance of American values:

En tierra de gringo
vamos poco a poco
sepultando todo (*Selected Poems*, 17)

(We are little by little
burying in the USA
everything we are)

The final two verses of the poem ("I'm even forgetting / how to say / *mande usted*") address the catastrophic potential loss for the Chicanx not only of their Mexican traditions and culture to which the poem alludes (the siesta, the Mexican pastry shop, popular music) but also of a sense of a linguistic community conveyed in "mande usted," a phrase connoting respect in Mexican culture and lacking a literal translation in contemporary American English. The loss of a sense of community transmitted through language duplicates the idea of cultural loss anticipated in the first verse of the poem: "So much for ethnic ties." The message of the poem is that losing one's ethnic ties and cultural heritage for the sake of gaining social acceptance by the dominant culture is a "small comfort," a powerful point that perhaps mirrors the poet's own sense of loss and her determined position as a poet to resist the assimilation that is implied.

As we stated before, de Hoyos's introspective dimension blends with the social-political one. In poems like "Mujer sin nombre," the speaker expresses her existential anguish by depicting herself as "nobody's daughter," born on a "bed of hungers" and wrapped in "a cloak of thorns." Her desolate description of herself as an orphan hints at her sense of alienation from the Christian family, and her reference to "a cloak of thorns" indirectly alludes to Christ's crown of thorns as a metonymic image of her sorrow. The speaker's sense of loneliness and profound sadness arguably comes from her loss of faith; moreover, since it is also triggered by the awareness of her own mortality, she finds solace in her connection with her fellow brothers of the Chicano Movement:

> Chicano, amigo mío,
> dame tu aliento
> para llevar conmigo
> algo de tí
> cuando me devore el tiempo (*Selected Poems*, 24)

> (Chicano, my friend
> give me your breath of life
> so that I can bring it with me
> when time devours me)

It is unclear how de Hoyos maintained connections to poets and publishers in Mexico, but the fact that her third book, *Selected Poems/ Selecciones* (1976), was published in Mexico by Universidad Veracruzana with Spanish translations by Mireya Robles brings to the forefront her continued link to the country of her birth. Compared to her previous books, de Hoyos's third collection of poetry constitutes a more introspective and pessimistic work, since it contains only a few poems where the speaker either finds relief in human connection for her sense of loneliness and alienation ("For the Road," "To a Novice," "When Your Eyes Speak," "For Mireya") or escapes from a cruel and materialistic world via the arts ("The Artist" and "Recommendation to the Psalmist").

The leitmotif of suffering in *Selected Poems* is summarized in the brief poem "Reply to Sappho," where the speaker defies the Greek poet for what the speaker considers Sappho's presumptuous belief that she has "coined" the word "suffering":

> You speak of suffering
> and tender the word
> as if it had been
> coined for you. (*Selected Poems*, 60)

The conclusion "—have you / ever / looked / into my eyes?" underscores de Hoyos's sense of alienation as a woman of color from Western literary renditions of human experience.

Most poems in the collection explore grief and sorrow as the unescapable destiny for all human beings. Paradigmatically, "The Mortal Trap" portrays life and death as a two-faced creature, a sort of Janus, presiding over people's past and present and laughing at their naïve search for happiness. In this poem life disguises itself as a beguiling female lover luring an "unsuspecting mortal" into her "boudoir," where she eventually transforms herself into a murderous Marcus Brutus. To the poet, despite our desire for joy and pleasure, we are destined to suffer and die; however, even if we are acutely aware of this truth, we inevitably fall into life's traps as it falsely promises us love, peace, and happiness. Moreover, the illusion of its enchantments is better than the reality of the other option, namely, death and, for the poet, nothingness, since the speaker has no hope for the existence of life after death.

In de Hoyos's view, this two-faced reality leads humans to confuse the desire for death with the desire for life, as they are two sides of the same coin, as Antonio Chazarra Montiel argues when he says that *Selected Poems/Selecciones* depicts "the instinctual desires for life and death" (quoted in Milligan, "Ever Radical," 221). In this regard, the epigraph to *Selected Poems/Selecciones,* "Hasta que el cuerpo aguante, señor, uno debe de vivir" (You have to live until you drop dead from exhaustion),[10] announces the speaker's struggle to fight against the death instinct even if she experiences life as a series of painful events that she is expected to endure stoically, as the last poem of *Selecciones* suggests. However, despite the fact that life inflicts insufferable pain and the "warm" "womb of earth" offers her "bleeding heart" an end to her sorrow, she chooses life over death in "Mi dolor hecho canción mi canción hecha dolor . . .":

> but everything
> bind me to you, Life
> —even these illusions: Love
> Peace
> Happiness—and the slings of dawn
> find me, the ever-obedient child
> bravely singing,
> waving
> my worn-out flag of truce (*Selected Poems,* 35)

In spite of her awareness of the illusionary nature of happiness and pleasure, they at least constitute a better option than dwelling on death, since, in the absence of a religious faith, death equals despair and nothingness.

In "In Spite of You," the speaker transforms from the aforementioned defeated hero, incapable of resisting the illusions of life's pleasures, into a defiant one. De Hoyos creates an allegory in which the speaker appears personified as perennial grass after a brutal winter. The grass tells her survival story to Life, also personified in the poem:

> I've come up anew
> for a taste of sun
> and—why not?—for the sparkling
> wine of laughter
> to drink away this dryness of sleep
> (before it becomes a habit)
> in my mouth (*Selected Poems,* 38)

The powerful metaphors employed by the poet put forth her desire for joy and pleasure despite the opposition of her formidable antagonist, who cropped her "careless head" with her "vicious winter-bite." As the speaker demonstrates her resilience vis-à-vis Life's blows, she proposes a truce, and, moreover, she defies Life to prepare for a more ferocious battle should she decline her peace offering:

> Because I'm a seasoned fighter
> —better known as *that old die-hard*
> and if you really want to finish me
> you'll have to do better than that. (*Selected Poems*, 39)

The last poem of the collection, "This Fitting Farewell," concludes the book with de Hoyos's belief in the power of poetry as a catalyst for her sorrow and, furthermore, as the only source of strength for a skeptical and disillusioned poet like herself. Paradoxically, as a source of knowledge, poetry constitutes a poison for de Hoyos, as it constantly reminds her of her own mortality.

After ten years publishing mostly in self-published and independent Chicanx venues, de Hoyos moves toward acceptance by publishers as the renowned Latinx publishing house Arte Público Press, under the auspices of Nicolás Kanellos, accepts her next collection for publication. At the height of her career, de Hoyos demonstrates her consummate skill as a poet in *Woman, Woman* (1985), once again using code switching as a literary tool and writing in Spanish as well as English. The titular poem, "Woman, Woman," sets the feminist tone for the totality of the collection, while it also announces its emancipatory impulse. If "Arise, Chicano!" urges migrant workers to rebel against exploitation, "Woman, Woman" tells women to have the audacity to grab the moon and stop it from telling lies about them—in other words, from repeating patriarchal narratives surrounding femininity:

> climb up
> that ladder
> bring down
> the moon

or she
will tattle
tattle falsehood
to the skies
(and who
can tell the
truth from lies?)
that it
is you
forever Eve
who rules
mere man
without
reprieve. (*Selected Poems*, 71)

The anadiplosis, consisting here in the repetition of the word "tattle" at the end of one verse and at the beginning of the following,
draws attention to stereotypical and misogynist stories surrounding
women, such as the myth of Adam and Eve in the Garden of Eden,
where the former was purportedly created by God to rule over creation. The speaker debunks this belief by stating "that it / is you /
forever Eve / who rules / mere man / without / reprieve," thus inviting women to strive for their autonomy rather than to depend on
males, as in romantic stories and fairy tales. Since the organization
of the last verses is not syntactically clear-cut, this poem could also
be interpreted in the opposite direction: even though the moon has
been preaching that women (matriarchs?) have been ruling over
males, this is a lie.

Woman, Woman demonstrates the author's mastery in her poetic
voice in both English and Spanish. For example, "Two Poems: Inebri-
eties" is a two-part poem: the first one, subtitled "Poem to (What
a) Wine / Poema al (qué) vino," is in English, and the second part,
"Poema al (que) vino," in Spanish. In the first section the speaker,
who must swim to save her life, compares the eyes of her love interest with the ocean into whose waves she has tumbled:

into the passion-seas
of your eyes
quite by mistake
(adventure-vent)
I have fallen. (*Selected Poems*, 83)

In the second section, the poet puns on the double meaning of *vino*: as a noun (*wine*) and a verb (*came*) "Poema al (que) vino" thus can be translated in two different ways: "Ode to Wine" and "Poem to the One Who Came." In this part of the poem the speaker proclaims that she is no longer alone, as a human face has appeared in the bottom of her glass of wine. This sudden vision "invades" her creative process, as well as her desire to be alone, enjoy a glass of wine, and write about it. Consequently, she cannot save the poem, since it cannot convey her original intent: "y yo que esperaba / Salvarle el pellejo" (I hoped in vain to save it). Therefore, while the English section communicates the speaker's longing for romantic love, the section in Spanish connects her desire with the loss of her autonomy. The previous poem in the volume, "Words Inspired by Wayward Husbands, Pontifical Lovers, and Innocuous Deviants," provides a clue about the speaker's inability to save the poem due to the sudden "apparition." In "Wayward Husbands" she states that

the
distance
between
thee
and
me
. . . .
therein
lies
the
poem. (*Selected Poems*, 76)

The quoted verses suggest the speaker's need to keep her distance (her autonomy) from the "thee"—in other words, the "Wayward Husbands, Pontifical Lovers, and Innocuous Deviants" of the title—for her poem to exist. As she sees herself and her poetry as one, the latter can survive only if the former is also free from her lover's control over her.

If, on the one hand, the speaker strives to keep her distance from her romantic partners in order to safeguard her autonomy, on the other, in "Portrait: Non-progress," she despairs at her failed attempt to match her ideal of a romantic partner ("an artist's / dream of a demi-god") with the busy human being who shows no devotion toward her. The speaker explains that she sees her lover through a mythological lens: he is "chasing some labyrinthian / Mad-Corinthian" or getting involved in other, equally grandiose projects that preclude him from being present with her. She expresses dismay at her frustrated desire to paint him: he is "bigger than canvas," and even when she tries, her painting turns into liquid, running away from her while "she has not even a good cup to scoop it up." De Hoyos's well-constructed allegory transmits the futility of the artist trying to capture the identity of her lover, as she well knows that what she wants to possess is a fleeting subjectivity.

In addition to the books mentioned thus far, three other poetry collections were published posthumously by de Hoyos's husband, Moisés Sandoval: *Sweet 16*, *Shades of Sappho*, and *Gata Poems: El desquite*. *Sweet 16* features eighteen of her earliest poems, most of which deal with romantic love and are rhymed and constructed in stanzas, unlike her most mature poems, which are composed mostly in free verse. "The Mantis' Prayer" shows the younger de Hoyos's creativity as she employs an insect narrator to address environmental threats, such as the use of fertilizers and other chemicals like DDT. The conclusion of the poem utilizes humor to underscore the poet's environmental message:

How long before I leave, O Lord,
this man-made world behind?
. . . I want to go before, O Lord,
the atom takes my hide!! (*Selected Poems*, 147)

Although the mention of God by a praying mantis creates a humorous effect, in "The Lord God, Lover of Children," the tone changes into a solemn one as the speaker asks God to instruct parents in the art of raising their children. The author's firm faith depicted in this poem contrasts with her later rebellion against Christian values, prominently underscored in *Arise, Chicano!* In "The Lord God, Lover of Child," de Hoyos transmits a deep conviction in her Catholic faith when she describes the Virgin Mary as "a diosa-Madre / . . . with love infinite for inocentes" and Joseph as "an earthly Padre" who embodies human fatherhood and performs his role in a saintly manner (*Selected Poems*, 146).

Shades of Sappho also features a few of de Hoyos's earliest poems, and, like *Sweet 16*, it delves into romantic relationships from a pessimistic point of view. The poems concentrate on the danger of following prescribed gender roles that generate false expectations of happiness and self-fulfillment. In "The Outlaw," the poet debunks the ideal of romantic love by describing it as a cage trapping naïve women, who eventually learn to fight back. In a similar manner, in "The Ship of Matrimony," she posits marriage as a source of boredom that frustrates people's belief in the possibility of achieving long-lasting marital bliss.

In *Gata Poems: El desquite*, de Hoyos satirizes middle-class Mexican American women for their vanity and their obsession with complying with patriarchal gender role expectations, such as dressing in a modest yet coquettish manner. In "No me gustan los comentarios" (I Don't Like Gossip), de Hoyos exemplifies what Judith Butler calls "gender performativity." This performativity results from the stylization of the body, actions and gestures that become deceivingly "natural" by their constant repetition, but that in reality are "manufactured" by political, scientific, religious, and juridical discourses (xv). In the poem, the speaker decides not to wear a blue dress because, according to her, this color would wrongly imply that she is looking for a romantic partner, and people would judge her negatively, since women are not allowed to show any erotic agency. Furthermore, de Hoyos underscores the performative nature of race when the woman in the poem wants to pass as white by choosing a color of garment that, according to her, blends perfectly with her recently bleached hair. "No me gustan los comentarios" delves into the lack of authenticity women engage in when they blindly follow stereotypical views of femininity—including beauty paradigms—modeled on white middle-class women. In contrast, other poems in this collection foreground women's resilience and survival skills. For example, "Nothing New" compares women's resourcefulness to that of alley cats that are capable of surviving in a hostile environment and "always / land squarely on all fours." According to Ventura Baeza, *Gata Poems* was "intended to empower Chicanas in the United States, to demonstrate that they possess talents and skills that enable them to survive and succeed in the oftentimes inhospitable [Anglo-American] environment [in which] they live" (xxvi).

CONCLUSIONS

The vast visual and literary work of the award-winning poet Angela de Hoyos has not been fully analyzed. It would be impossible to separate her visual craft and her poetry, since they are intertwined. In her paintings she uses cheerful colors and portrays mostly mestiza women. Her illustrations were created specifically for poems and book covers, an outgrowth of her passion for Chicanx culture.

From *Arise, Chicano!* to *Woman, Woman*, Angela de Hoyos's poetry displays a rich gamut of themes, from the more openly sociopolitical (the cultural clash between Chicanx and Anglos, the urgency of Chicanx to rebel against racism and oppression, the advantages to preserving Chicanx's Mexican heritage in order to resist acculturation into white Anglo-American culture) to the more introspective (the struggle between the desire to live and the desire to die, the fragility of human relationships, the antagonistic tendencies of human beings, the sense of alienation) to the feminist themed (women's search for autonomy, the danger for Chicanas of following paradigms of beauty from white, heterosexual, middle-class women, the subversion of myths surrounding romantic relationships). Regarding Angela de Hoyos's poetic devices, we have shown her mastery in employing irony to subvert traditional gender stereotypes and her remarkable use of allegory and metaphor (especially personification), among other poetic devices, to convey a political or philosophical message. Furthermore, in connection with her bilingual abilities, her poetry writing evolves from an almost exclusive use of English to code switching and finally to full use of her bilingualism. As we expect to have demonstrated in the analysis of her poems, Angela de Hoyos was a consummate Chicanx poet who, in her most memorable literary compositions, masterfully fused social and political themes with timeless philosophical questions. In short, Angela de Hoyos has earned an honorable place in the pantheon of poets, and she will always be "one of our giants," as Rudolfo Anaya once put it.

NOTES

The word *artivist* joins *artist* and *activist*. While most often used for muralists and other artists, we are using it here to describe de Hoyos, given that her work as a poet and publisher embodied the qualities of artivists elsewhere in the art world. See Sandoval and Latorre.

1. Raúl R. Salinas (1934–2008) was a Texan poet who became known for his prison poetry and his contribution to Chicano literature.

2. There is widespread disagreement among critics regarding the year of her birth; while some critics cite it as 1924, others say 1940. However, documents such as her high school diploma and her obituary point to 1924 as her year of birth, a fact that was confirmed during a phone interview her husband, Moisés Sandoval, on January 23, 1923.

3. "Eso no," Decca: https://frontera.library.ucla.edu/recordings/eso-no-5; "Mentiritas," Falcon: https://frontera.library.ucla.edu/recordings/mentiritas-2; "Pero que lástima," Falcon: https://frontera.library.ucla.edu/recordings/pero-que-lastima-1 (image of the musical partitur for this song appears in the appendix of *Selected Poems* [2014]); "Amor de Dios," Falcon: https://frontera.library.ucla.edu/es/recordings/amor-de-dios-2; "Cómo has cambiado," Falcon: https://frontera.library.ucla.edu/es/recordings/como-has-cambiado-4.

4. As its title indicates, the book contains ten previously unpublished poems and thirty-two illustrations found archived by her husband, Moisés, after her death.

5. Her first published book, *Arise, Chicano!*, is a bilingual edition, translated into Spanish by Mireya Robles.

6. Unpublished interview by Norma Elia Cantú, 1982.

7. This name change probably happened in the early or mid-1960s, since in the previous decade, she was signing her song lyrics as Angelina Sandoval.

8. *Interlingual* refers to the capacity to think and speak in two languages at the same time (Novoa, 37).

9. Aguilar-Henson explains that the female representation of death is "perfectly normal for Hispanic thinking, for 'life' has a specific gender in the Spanish language" (36).

10. The epigraph constitutes an intertext that shows the connection between de Hoyos and Mexican writers such as Raúl Hernández Viveros, whose short story "La invasión de los chinos" provides the epigraph to *Selected Poems*.

BIBLIOGRAPHY

Aguilar-Henson, Marcela. *Multi-Faceted Poetic World of Angela de Hoyos*. Austin, Tex.: Relampago Books, 1985.

Bachelard, Gaston. *The Poetics of Space*. Translated by Maria Jolas. New York: Penguin Books, 2014.

Baeza Ventura, Gabriela. "Introduction." *Selected Poems of Angela de Hoyos*. Houston: Arte Público Press, 2014, xi–xxvii.

Bruce-Novoa, Juan. *Retrospace: Collected Essays on Chicano Literature, Theory, and History*. Houston: Arte Público Press, 1990.

Butler, Judith. *Gender Trouble: Feminism and the Subversion of Identity*. New York: Routledge, 2006.

De Hoyos, Angela. "Ángela's Biography by Herself." HOYO bio04. Recovering the U.S. Hispanic Literary Heritage Digital Collections (website). http://usldhrecovery.uh.edu/items/show/1847.

———. *Arise, Chicano! and Other Poems*. San Antonio: M&A Editions, 1980.

———. *Dedicatorias: Poems for People*. San Antonio, Tex.: Angela Moisés Press, 2013.

———. *Selected Poems of Angela de Hoyos*. Edited by Gabriela Baeza Ventura. Houston: Arte Público Press, 2014.

———. *Ten Short Poems, 32 Sketches with Witty Words, I Never . . . Sinned Until I Met You*. San Antonio, Tex.: Angela Moisés Press, 2014.

Gaona, María Elena. "En torno a la poesía de Ángela de Hoyos." In *Mujer y literatura mexicana y chicana: Culturas en contacto 2*. Coordinated by Aralia López González, Amelia Malagamba, and Elena Urrutia. Mexico City: Colegio de México, 1990, 265–71.

Gewecke, Frauke. "La literatura chicana entres resistencia, transgresión y asimilación." *Review of Handbook of Hispanic Cultures in the United States: Literature and Art*, edited by Francisco Lomeli. *Notas: Reseñas iberoamericanas; literatura, sociedad, historia* 3, no. 3 (1996): 2–47.

Milligan, Bryce. *Daughters of the Fifth Sun: A Collection of Latina Fiction and Poetry*. San Antonio, Tex.: Wing Press, 1995.

———. "Den Mother." *Texas Observer*, December 29, 2009.

———. "Ever Radical: A Survey of Tejana Writers." In *Texas Women Writers: A Tradition of Their Own*. Edited by Sylvia Ann Grider and Lou Halsell Rodenberger. College Station: Texas A&M University Press, 1997, 207–46.

Navarro Magallón, Areli. "Respecting Beauty: Angela de Hoyos' Visual Art." Recovering the U.S. Hispanic Literary Heritage Digital Collections (website), January 5, 2021. http://usldhrecovery.uh.edu/exhibits/show/visualartadh/adhpoliticalprints.

Ramos, Luis Arturo. *Angela de Hoyos, A Critical Look*. Albuquerque, N.M.: Pajarito Publications, 1980.

Sandoval, Chela, and Guisela Latorre. "Chicana/o Artivism: Judy Baca's Digital Work with Youth of Color." In *Learning Race and Ethnicity: Youth and Digital Media*. Edited by Anna Everett. Cambridge, Mass.: MIT Press, 2007.

Young, Melanie. "The Chicana Poet from Two Worlds." *San Antonio Express-News*, October 2, 1994.

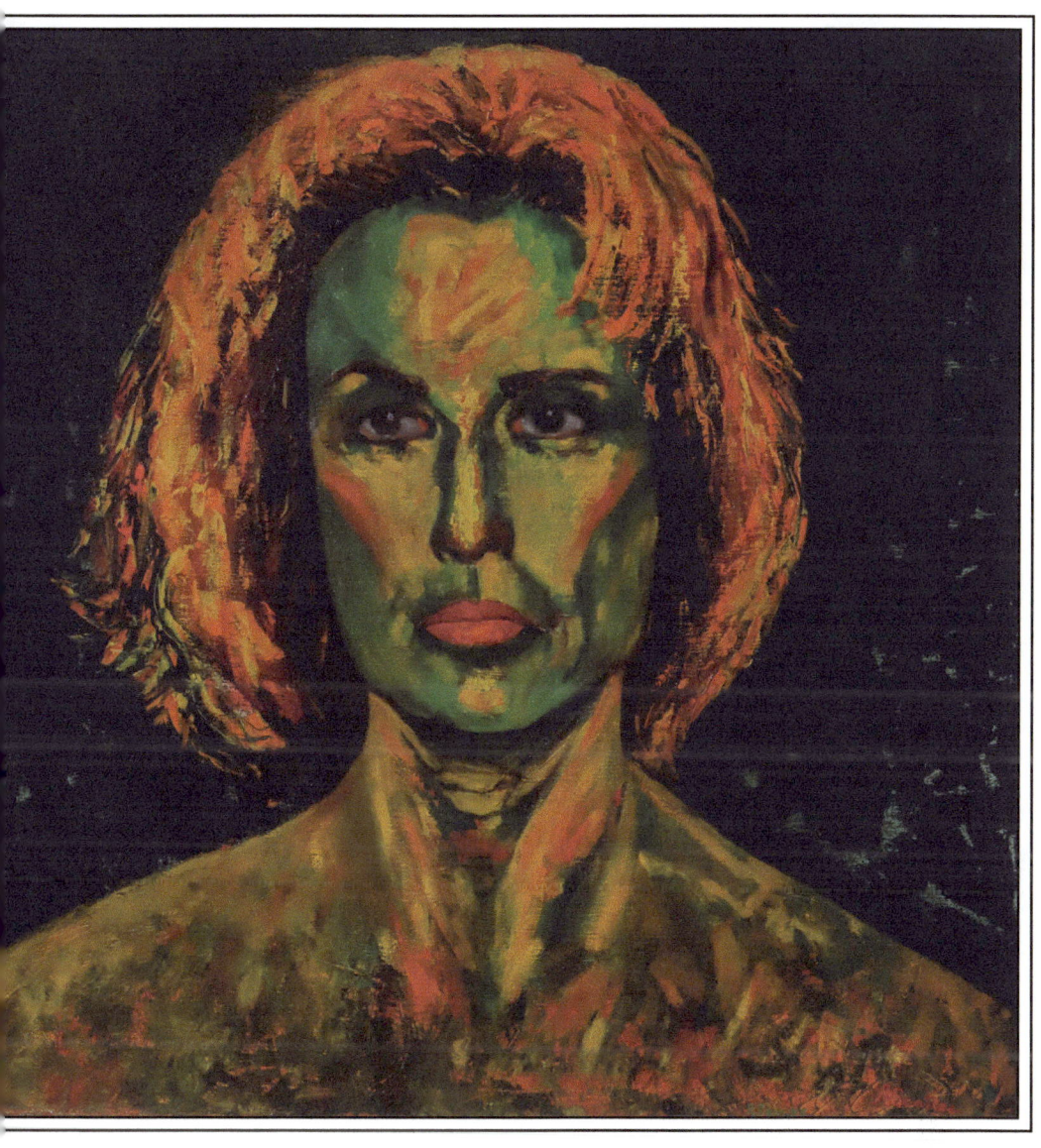

MONTSERRAT FONTES

MONTSERRAT FONTES

Teacher and Writer

MARY PAT BRADY

I T TAKES so many resources to write a book: time, determination, courage, humility, ambition, the support of friends, and smart, critical readers. It takes all of that and a surplus of gumption when you are teaching hundreds of middle school and high school students full-time and so your writing must be confined to the outer edges of already long days. High schools aren't known as ideal environments or as incubators for writers who want to nourish their craft by cultivating a poem or story. When a high school teacher publishes something, it's an exception, worth a celebration. Of course, many influential Chicana/o writers have been school teachers—Lucha Corpi and Tomás Rivera immediately come to mind. Montserrat Fontes is just such another, having achieved, before her retirement, wide acclaim for her fiction as well as her teaching.

Fontes is a legendary teacher. Google her name, and you will find more than one scholar or journalist who thanks her for the inspiration she provided them while they took her high school English and journalism courses, inspiration that spurred their own curiosity about piracy or Russian history, for example. Student activists found her classroom an invigorating space for debate, a space where they could sketch their ideas and strengthen their argumentative prowess. Some, like the radical feminist Susie Bright (also known as Susie Sexpert), found in Fontes a generous mentor as they sought to develop their own radical voices, their own understandings of systems of power and strategies of repression and exploitation.[1] Yet while Fontes taught so generously, worked so prodigiously with students—which she did for decades in various middle and high schools as well as community colleges and universities around Los Angeles until her retirement in 2000—Fontes wrote and sold screenplays, enough to become a member of the Writers Guild of America West, a marker of professional achievement if no guarantee of a lucrative career as a film and TV writer. She also contributed reviews to forums such as the *Philadelphia Inquirer*, and she researched and wrote three novels, two of which were released by one of the most prestigious publishing houses in the world.

And as a dedicated teacher and writer, Fontes also studied. Research for her novels took her across Mexico, and she won many grants to support both this research and her teaching. She also won National Endowment for the Humanities Fellowships to study the icons of the U.S. Southern gothic tradition, William Faulkner and Flannery O'Connor. These were two of the authors Fontes regularly introduced to her students, two of the writers she felt an affinity with as she contemplated her family's own complex, multigenerational, sometimes violent saga. For not only did Fontes study these two writers as profound commentators on U.S. histories of violent racialization, as astute observers of the ways violence seeps into everyday practices and relationships, as mordantly funny and vicious in their observations of hypocrisy and greed, she also studied them as writers, as master technicians of a craft she sought to hone for herself.

Indications that the years of writing through rejection and while teaching must have been tough to sustain surfaces shyly in a short essay Fontes published in the *Flannery O'Connor Bulletin* in 1995. There she describes her research trip to Milledgeville, Georgia—a trip she suggests had a formidable impact on her life. There in Milledgeville, the small Georgia town where O'Connor grew up and lived as an adult writer after her years studying in Iowa, Fontes explored O'Connor's residence. Milledgeville is also home to one of the largest mental health facilities in the country and to O'Connor's papers. Like a good scholar, Fontes spent her evenings exploring the town and her days examining O'Connor's papers, especially the working drafts of her fiction. Fontes remembers her trip with some humor, joking about her struggle to understand the central Georgia accents and to navigate the curious blue laws that prohibited the purchase of alcohol with food in restaurants. Here was a pilgrimage to a beloved writer's world and to its explicitly different culture.

Fontes writes that in 1985, when she made the journey, she only "fancied" herself a novelist. Her self-deprecating comment reveals a vexed sense of her own writerly abilities, especially when we remember that by 1984 she had already completed a draft of *First Confession*, and shortly after this trip she would publish another novel, *High Contrast*. But perhaps during that hot summer when she journeyed to Milledgeville she knew mostly rejection as a writer, a contrast to the success she had garnered as a teacher. Maybe she hoped to unlock a secret to writing success when she sat down to look at the drafts of stories held in the O'Connor archives. Drawn to O'Connor's gamble with the gothic, she wanted to understand the great writer's writing process. And Fontes does suggest she found a key, although perhaps not the key she had initially sought. Paging through the manuscripts, Fontes was struck by the labor on exhibit in these papers: "the countless revisions, the bevy of crossouts, rephrasings, and endless word replacements" that made clear the patient labor behind O'Connor's published fiction. Such a plethora of revisions signaled how O'Connor worked and reworked every aspect of her fiction; how the words themselves could not be taken for granted; how they had to be curated and cultivated to capture the energy of the story O'Connor sought to convey.

Fontes suggests that she felt somewhat humbled by the labor O'Connor poured into her work: "I discovered, sitting before me, raw, naked endurance" (89). Lying before her in the archives was a map toward an elusive perfection, toward a good enough that could not come easily because the good enough revealed itself only in the process, in the revision and dedication and endurance. To sit with failure as a writer and to strike at the text again and again, Fontes learned, meant a different kind of resilience, one that could not be clothed in romantic metaphors. Fontes realized not just how carefully O'Connor layered word upon word to produce the world she conjured into being, but how much that layering was the product of struggle with consonants and vowels, with imagination, and timing and nuance. This discovery, Fontes suggests, was actually a little unwelcome: "I didn't want to know that writing is painful and lonely, that the search for the perfect word was not about polish—as in the word luster. Instead, the search was about scoring the truth" (90). To score the truth entails perhaps discovering it like one might obtain a cache of drugs, or it means to score it as one might a loaf of bread so that it expands as it bakes. However one reads Fontes' musings it's clear that she values writing that makes an impression, that generates a broader, even precious understanding. If Fontes comes to admire O'Connor even more having visited her archives, a sense of contradiction nonetheless hangs over the essay. Fontes implicitly asks, Why is the work of creating, of inventing whole worlds with their own people and places and plants, whole socialities so insanely lonely? That's the hard part; it's the loneliness that must be endured, because without it the work can't get done. This somber insight must have weighed heavily on her over the next several years; or perhaps it gave her courage to sit with the struggle as she began publishing novels—three in a decade, each more substantial than its predecessor, until she gained critical acclaim and national awards.

Given this encounter with Flannery O'Connor, it's not surprising that loneliness, or the "raw, naked endurance" that writing requires, comprises one of the central themes across all three novels—even as each adumbrates loneliness and endurance in its own way and even as each novel, wildly different from the others, commands strikingly varied plotlines. Fontes was not content to repeat a winning plot formula nor recycle a good character. If she was drawn, however, to exploring what loneliness could enable, what could emerge from the distasteful cauldron of isolation, it does not appear as if Fontes was ever lonely. Not only was she a wildly popular teacher, not only was she a contributing critic for prestigious publications like the *Philadelphia Inquirer*, not only was she an active writer with a supportive writing circle, but she was also then, as now, happily partnered to the actress, writer, and dancer Clarice Gillis.

Born in Laredo, Texas, in 1940 to families both prominent in Northern Mexico and with proud ties that extended across Mexico's history to its years as a Spanish colony, Fontes learned early on that history matters. Her parents were educators and the children of Mexican army generals decorated for their exploits while participating in Mexico's revolutionary break from the dictator Porfirio Díaz. Her mother traced her roots to northern Sonora and to what Roberto Cantú describes as "one of the biggest cattle ranch families; of Sephardic ancestry, they converted to Catholicism when the Inquisition reached Mexico" (143). But this family did not remain loyal to Mexico's ruling elite. As Cantú further explains:

> At the outbreak of the Mexican Revolution, Fontes's maternal and paternal grandfathers spearheaded military forces against Porfirio Díaz. One of the grandfathers, Colonel Paulino Fontes, was a railroad promoter and a member of President Venustiano Carranza's elite guard; the maternal grandfather, General Arnulfo R. Gómez, was a presidential candidate in 1927, running against Alvaro Obregón. The execution of General Gómez in Veracruz made international headlines and partly inspired one of Mexico's modern literary masterpieces, *La sombra del caudillo* (1928) by Martín Luis Guzmán. (143)

Not surprisingly, with such a storied (in multiple senses of the word) background, Fontes grew up immersed in Mexico's history. As she told Roberto Cantú, "All of us grew up with the Fontes/Gómez clan talking about the revolution, the exiles, the suicides, the love affairs, the battles, the history, the executions" (143). These would have been romantic stories for young children, and Fontes drew on them when she turned to her own fiction.

At the tender age of nine she left her parents to live in Los Angeles with her maternal grandmother, who had started what became a legendary restaurant, El Carmen. Fontes mostly grew up in Los Angeles, but moved to Mexico City to join her family and complete high school. She subsequently returned to Los Angeles, where she attended Los Angeles City College and California State University, Los Angeles. Graduating with a bachelors of arts in 1966, she then completed a master's in comparative literature, reflecting her passion for the density and drama of Russian literature. She also taught part time at Rio Hondo College for a decade before attending the University of California, Los Angeles, to study creative writing in an extension program. Between teaching and taking classes, she hung out at her family's restaurant. Popular with Hollywood's glitterati, El Carmen was also the locale where, as a young woman, Fontes met and fell in love with Clarice Gillis, who would become her life partner. Or, as Gillis (writing under her stage name, Brandy Wilde) recalls in her own memoir, Fontes first spotted Gillis entering the restaurant and "thought, 'I have found you'" (380–81).

A few years after her trip to Midgeville, Fontes turned the story of Gillis's adventurous life, their friendship, and their love into her first published novel, *High Contrast* (1987). Telling the double tales of a prim, judgmental white art student, Carole, who meets a slightly older white student, Nikki, in a college classroom, *High Contrast* offers glimpses of midcentury queer life and art alongside a look at a demeaned art form, erotic dancing, that rarely receives praise from the dressed-up, institutionalized dance world. As it paints portraits of nightclubs and performers working in Texas, Los Angeles, and Quebec, it also provides a narrative of transformation as the art student, Carole, learns to overcome the bourgeois conventions of her wealthy family and as Nikki shifts away from her demanding schedule as an internationally acclaimed dancer. And while the contrast between the two, one a highly accomplished dancer and the other a budding photojournalism student, provides the conceit of the novel and its titular theme, this contrast also structures the framework for the novel's happy exploration of erotic pleasure as well as its critique of judgmental normative conventions that get in the way of pleasure, connection, and trust.

One could describe *High Contrast*, with its autobiographical resonances and its veiled portrait of Clarice Gillis, as simply a coming-out story, but that would be to mischaracterize the reckoning it demands. Instead, the novel cleverly contrasts the formal education Carole obtains while she pursues an institutionally sanctioned art, photography, against the informal, but nevertheless systematic, training Nikki undergoes to become a professional dancer. It then details the labor, skill, and artistry involved in intimate, boundary-pushing dance. The reader follows this path through alternating narrative voices, which provide distinctive readerly experiences. If *High Contrast* plays on distinctions between Nikki and Carole, underscoring the varying ways respectability infuses discourses of art, it also offers a sweet portrait of connection, romance, show business, and queer life, suggesting a kind of pedagogy of pleasure, of the fun involved in undressing another, of the textures of desire, the somatic possibilities of fluid impulses and newly aware forms of bodying forth into adulthood.

The literary form of the novel, for all its prim history, provides a useful platform to name competing socialities, to evoke connections that slip together with and apart from the logics of social rule and political power. Flannery O'Connor eschewed the hypocrisy of normative social formations, the submerged violence such hypocrisy initiated and sustained. Her fiction tends toward piercing revelations, but rarely does it turn toward the lives of artists or of youth navigating the informal economies produced by hypocrisy. It's easy to imagine that O'Connor would have admired Fontes's novel for its gentle attack on the very norms of respectability and the proper that elevated the novel form to social prestige (even if its subject might have troubled her Catholic commitments), perhaps because *High Contrast*'s world is one that Flannery O'Connor might have eschewed *and* loved.

Yet if the principal lesson O'Connor's archives imparted to Fontes was that writing takes a willingness to endure the tedium of loneliness and a further willingness to hurl oneself into the difficult and painful vulnerabilities of being, she also seemed to glean something else. Fontes seemed to catch the sociality of writing, the fact that writing emerges in collaboration with readers and editors and in the give and take of conversation and dispute, the push to return, to revisit, to do again that friends—astute, stubborn, engaged friends—provide. And Fontes's novels show evidence of this sociality, just as O'Connor's letters and manuscripts do. In every text Fontes thanks members of writing groups with whom she met for years, many of whom also became successfully published authors with vibrant writing careers. They read one another's work, offered editorial advice, and provided the kind of nurturing sensibility that made possible the long hours of writing at the end of days occupied with other full-time jobs. And it was just through such sociality that Fontes met a New York agent who championed her subsequent novels.

Though she published *High Contrast* first, Fontes actually started working on the novel she published second, *First Confession* (1991), when she began taking formal creative writing classes. Drawn from her own experience of childhood in Nuevo Laredo and illustrating the long tentacles of childhood (mis)deeds, *First Confession* should be read as an important intervention into the romantic representations of childhood innocence that characterize both children's literature in general and a number of Chicana and Chicano texts published in the decades before it. Although Rudolfo Anaya, Sandra Cisneros, Tomás Rivera, and Helena María Viramontes, to take only the most prominent examples, published dense accounts of childhood that addressed the perplexities and contradictions that Chicana/o children must navigate, none of their fiction takes as deep a dive into the way children, left to their own devices and inadequately equipped to understand the dynamics structuring their world, can cause profound and lasting damage with their antics. Moreover, these earlier examples of Chicanx fiction trace an arc of childhood fun within the matrices of working-class life, whereas *First Confession* details the complex shroud of support that enable the elite to mostly (or seemingly) hide from the consequences of their deeds.

Taking place in a Mexican border town modeled after Laredo/Nuevo Laredo and told by Andrea, a nine-year-old hellion liberated by an indulgent father from the discipline of summer school despite her failing grades, *First Confession* also tells a story of extreme contrasts. It tracks Andrea and her cousin Victor as they discover sex work, poverty, and death. Their lives have been shaped by their families' refusal to expect much of them, and so they swipe glasses and crush them in parking lots, spy on poor people, and steal money from a storekeeper supplementing her income with sex work. The two children condescendingly decide they should redistribute the cash by buying toys and taking them to the working-poor neighborhoods set along the border river. Their efforts are not especially well received, and as they try to lie their way out of the resulting trouble, they inadvertently initiate a dynamic that will lead to the murder of one of their maids. The ensuing scandal catapults Andrea's father into a weeks-long drinking binge that precipitates a second death and ultimately the partial dissolution of the family: Andrea is packed off to live with her grandmother in Los Angeles, and her parents move to Mexico City.

Like O'Connor, Fontes laces her portrait of indulgence and consequence with humor, alongside portrayals of the antics of people warped by isolation and repression as well as accounts of the children's misguided efforts to break free from that isolation and repression by, for example, standing on the side of busy streets yelling obscenities. *First Confession* is framed around the children's preparation for their first confession, a sacramental ritual of cleansing meant to prepare the young Catholics for their first Holy Communion. As such, the children obsess over lies, witnessing, and divine forgiveness, but the novel itself obsesses over the impossibility of telling the truth. Caught in a chain of lies, the children ultimately turn on each other, so much so that even amid the grief they feel over the catastrophes their antics set in motion, they cannot comfort each other. At the close of the novel Andrea sees a path toward expiation, but out of a confused desire to rebuild a connection with her father, she foregoes that path. This decision, the novel suggests, leaves Victor with a grief so enormous he will finally take his own life.

For the children, the river, as border, is a no-contact zone—they are forbidden to go there unattended. So, of course, they do. But for the reader the river comes to signal both boundaries and rites of passage, the sign of the relations of economic exploitation that leave people unhoused and desperate, as well as the marker of refusal and possibility. The river offers a boundary between the United States and Mexico and as such symbolizes the contrasting cultures that Andrea's parents navigate as well as the entanglements necessary to produce racial formations and vast wealth disparities. The river, for all of its poverty, also symbolizes the multiple debts that go unpaid and unacknowledged within violent systems of exploitation. The children are left without guides to this system—taught to treasure their privilege, hide from its submerged brutality, and imagine the possibilities of redemption without recompense. Their route to the river, however, offers something more, for what *First Confession* insists on is a confrontation with the terrible cost of witnessing brutality.

The young Andrea cannot confess that she has witnessed a rape; to do so would be to admit to other infractions, and this knowledge ferments into an anger with no outlet: "I wanted vengeance against Smelly Hands—to hurt him, hit his face, crush his legs. I yearned to do something terrible to him . . . I let hate run wild throughout my head, my heart. I wished I were ten feet tall so I could stab or stomp Smelly Hands to death" (232). Her vehemence underscores her sense of powerlessness threaded with ignorance. She has lost her connection to Victor; the adults in her life are variously distracted and unwilling to explain the events that affect her; she has borne witness to violence and rendered someone even more vulnerable; and she cannot discuss either what she has witnessed or what she has done. With no road map toward emotional relief, she imagines only the satisfaction of brutality.

To some extent the novel itself is narrator Andrea's adult version of "stomping out" the legacies of a transgression that has burned away at her, leaving ongoing isolation and disconnection. It is the adult narrator's first actual confession. Moreover, just by reading it, by absorbing the story, readers become participant witnesses to the larger crime of racial capitalism and the violence that sustains it. In this way, the novel offers an almost remorseless account of the brutality sustaining Mexican social and economic relations just as it offers an indication of the social habits that naturalize this brutality. Because if the novel examines the ripple effects of nasty, mean-spirited behaviors, of mischief catapulted into malice, it does so by insisting that readers attend to the depredations made possible when one has money and power and hence protection. It asks readers to gaze at vulnerable people scrambling to sustain themselves amid this hierarchy. To witness this gulf, *First Confession* suggests, is to seek an impossible extirpation, an expiation, just as it ultimately gestures toward the clash of cultures, the contrasts between Anglo and elite Mexican cultures that mystify Andrea as a child and that leave her casting about for the solidity of real information amid the diaphanous truths created by layers of lies.

The brooding loss that concludes *First Confession* does not carry over to Fontes's next novel, *Dreams of the Centaur* (1996), which turns the clock back almost a century to a period in Mexico's history too little known in the United States. Published five years after *First Confession*, *Dreams of the Centaur* similarly insists on a hard critique of racial capitalism; it does so, however, through a different set of premises—albeit still portraying young women, of whom not much is expected, growing into fierce and powerful figures. This novel too turns a critical eye on Mexican class relations, on the way racialized narratives are used to shore up exploitation and, ultimately, to prevent sustainable life outside of the hierarchical violence enforced by the state. But if the novel tells a complex story involving a young woman's journey to sensual consciousness, to a new political understanding of her emplacement within a nested hierarchy producing social control, it also tells the story of a young man's efforts to break free from this intractable regime of racialized masculinism and militant corruption. It accomplishes this, furthermore, by insisting that readers learn something of the Yoeme (or Yaqui) people who were repeatedly attacked by these violent systems. Thus, like *High Contrast* and *First Confession*, Fontes's third novel explores the often grotesque contradictions and complicities made evident when one pays attention to contrasting conditions.

Dreams of the Centaur, however, situates itself firmly as a historical novel, as a novel bent on recovering a genocidal crime committed by President Porfirio Díaz's violent reign.[2] During Díaz's dictatorship, the hemp plantation owners in the Yucatán developed a powerful hold over the rope market across the globe, but they also burned through laborers and sought vulnerable people wherever they could to ensnare in labor systems that worked them to death. Eventually the Díaz regime used the spurious argument that the Yaqui people's refusal to acknowledge Mexican sovereignty over them justified their forced removal from their lands; as further punishment, the army forcibly removed them to the Yucatán to engage in brutal labor on the plantations. *Dreams of the Centaur* follows a young woman, Felipa Durcal, married to an entrepreneurial and hard-headed Sonoran rancher, José Durcal. As Felipa adapts to ranch life, giving birth to three sons, she becomes a crucial part of the ranch's success while also learning about sexual pleasure and devastating loss. The novel also follows her son, Alejo, a hard-headed young man who learns the folly of revenge and subsequently champions the Yaqui people's fight for self-determination and sovereignty against the onslaught by the Mexican state and its satellite elite.

Here, as with her prior novels, Fontes is quick to outline the ridiculous bigotry of convention and to illustrate its dampening impact on the imagination as well as its ultimately disciplinary effects. For, as the novel illustrates, social conventions in the service of racial capitalism discipline both the elite and the poor (if not in similar ways or to similar ends). And during the Porfiriato, social conventions were utilized to reinforce the ravenous power of the state by preventing alliances between vulnerable, precarious people. Moreover, *Dreams of the Centaur* shows how enmity, in particular, is useful for the production and maintenance of social stratification. It shines a light on a specific target of enmity for the late-nineteenth-century Mexican state: the Yaquis who refuse to accede to Mexican sovereignty. When the novel opens it shows José, a hardworking ranch owner, defying such conventions. He learns the Yaqui language and appears to respect their culture and sovereignty, but he also exploits them and rapes a young Yaqui servant. When José is killed in part because he is gaining ground against the local elite, his eldest son, Alejo, seeks vengeance and ends up sentenced to prison, where he meets and befriends his Yaqui half brother, Charco. Together they withstand the brutality of prison, ultimately escaping after they learn of the murderous violence of the henequen plantation system. Alejo and Charco rush to Yaqui country, hoping to inform them of the terrible enslavement Díaz, through his system of forced removal, has sanctioned as punishment for their resistance to his army. Alejo and Charco are nearly killed in a fictionalized version of a historic slaughter of Yaquis by the Mexican army. Felipa ultimately helps them escape to Arizona, where they begin a new life while Felipa returns to her ranch. Through this story Fontes exposes the treachery, the duplicity, of the Mexican elite and its casual exploitation of bigotry to maintain its power. Both Felipa and Alejo are transformed as their conscience awakens to their own complicity in the system. The novel also ends where *First Confession* begins, at the border between the United States and Mexico, at a moment when Mexico is on the cusp of a revolution.

The recipient of substantial critical attention as well as of the American Book Award from the Before Columbus Foundation, *Dreams of the Centaur* may well be credited with initiating the current reckoning among Chicana feminists with the settler colonial violence that Spanish, Mexican, and U.S. colonial and imperial legacies enjoin. With this text the long-held romance of Mexican mestizaje undergoes rigorous critique as the novel points to racial anxiety with sly brilliance.

Speaking of one woman's perception of him, the son of José Durcal and an unnamed Yaqui woman, Charco, wryly notes, "She looks at me out of one eye and she sees Yaqui, out of the other she sees a Yori" (346). Charco's choice of terms are especially astute. Yaqui is the name colonists assigned the people who call themselves Yoeme, and Yori is the name the Yoeme assign Mexicans. With this Charco points to the discursive work of racialization, but in his reference to what might be called a Mexicana's cross-eyed vision, he also suggests how racialized conceptions come to be embodied and by being embodied, maintained. In this and across the novel Fontes shows no patience for this legacy of racialization.

Critics have recognized the novel's powerful critique as central to contemporary Chicanx feminist examinations of history. Not only does Felipa model the figure of a strong woman who takes charge of her own life, embracing sexual pleasure and refusing bigotry, she also illustrates what the process of coming into consciousness might look like. Beyond this critique, Nicole Eitzen Delgado, in a rich reading of the novel's engagement with the discourses of liberalism, argues that *Dreams of the Centaur* is "notable for its inversion of Mexican modernity's narrow narrative logic which places agency on the masculinist mestizo subject and takes agency away from the female, indigenous one" (229). Elisabeth Mermann-Jozwiak argues that the novel can be understood, in part, as a travel narrative. This travel narrative, in contrast to the more famous ones offered by figures such as the Beats, advances a "post-colonial critique" that ultimately "counteracts the image of Mexico as ancient, rural landscape; the country is instead part of a global community connected to the world through trade and immigration" (109). This argument picks up on Mexico's long engagement with the global economy of trade, an engagement often lost in romanticized narratives portraying Mexico as apart from history, left behind from a market-driven modernity.

One of the first critics to engage with the novel, Roberto Cantú, reads *Dreams of the Centaur* as offering a "fictional configuration of neocolonial historical forces that would ultimately produce the conditions of possibility for the Mexican Revolution" (152) as well as a historical account of Mexico's racial politics. For Cantú, *Dreams* achieves something deeply significant in allowing "the possibilities to rethink the ideological foundations of Chicano cultural studies" (156). J. Douglas Canfield argues that the novel offers a careful critique of Mexican nationalism at an emerging moment of postnationalism; he sees this as especially important because of Mexico's refusal to acknowledge its own genocidal wars against the Indigenous communities who resisted its national project and thus to understand how necessary such acknowledgment is before solidarity can even be contemplated.

If we consider the arc of Fontes's published novels, we can linger with the arc of a literary vision companionably detailed by many other feminist women of color. This vision does not entirely comport with Flannery O'Connor's sensibilities, but, like her fiction, it does respond to crucial touch points in the twentieth century. Fontes's first novel, *High Contrast*, written in the wake of new sexual freedoms and alongside a new and robust effort to expand the realms of publishing and to transform representational opportunities, provides a picture of how middle-class white women began to expand the possibilities for pleasure and connection as they encountered a working-class world formerly walled off by propriety. *High Contrast*'s breezy portrait of queer Los Angeles in the late 1960s gestures toward the violence that always hovered at the edges of a queer life still ensnared within criminalizing logics; it also gestures toward the defiance with which queer women pursued their desires and found networks of affiliation that sustained them. *First Confession* carries this story backward to illustrate how viciously postwar U.S. and Mexican culture policed women's sexuality, treating desire and sex work as something to be eschewed, unspeakable and forbidden. In showing a young girl's lonely effort to understand this world without articulate guides, Fontes traces the path toward the sexual future liberated from silence and constraint that *High Contrast* celebrated. *Dreams of the Centaur* moves further back in time by telling a story about genocide and a possible path toward the development of a revolutionary consciousness that can repudiate and de-animate white supremacy. Yet, in some ways, this novel also signals the concerns that continue to trouble Chicanx and Latinx activist life in contemporary times. It lays out, without flinching, the settler-colonialist logic that Mexico deployed to propel itself toward a modernity dependent on racial capitalism, on hierarchies of valuation within a dense habit of exploitation. The legacies of these practices continue to trouble efforts to envision a less exploitative world, one that feels free from historical complicities. Monserrat Fontes refuses such easy romanticism. For Fontes, the strains of history continue to speak in the present. No one slips past these histories untouched.

NOTES

1. For a discussion of activism in Los Angeles featuring students from Fontes's classroom, see Ides, "Dare to Free Yourself."
2. For another examination of the Díaz regime and its impact on Chicanx history, see Nava, *The City of Palaces*. It too concludes with a border crossing into Arizona.

BIBLIOGRAPHY

Canfield, J. Douglas. "Crossing Laterally into Solidarity in Montserrat Fontes's *Dreams of the Centaur*." *Studies in 20th Century Literature* 25, no. 1 (2001): 1–15.

Cantú, Roberto. "Hybrid Resolutions: Liberal Democracy and Ethnic Identity in Montserrat Fontes's *Dreams of the Centaur*." *Arizona Journal of Hispanic Cultural Studies* 4 (2000): 141–58.

Córdova, Jeanne. *When We Were Outlaws: A Memoir of Love and Revolution*. Midway, Fla.: Spinsters Ink, 2011.

Delgado, Nicole Eitzen. "Captivity Narratives Unbound: Mexican, Mexican American, and Yaqui Becomings of the Latinx Nineteenth Century." PhD diss., New York University, 2020.

Fontes, Montserrat. *Dreams of the Centaur*. New York: W. W. Norton, 1996.

———. *First Confession*. New York: W. W. Norton, 1991.

———[Jessie Lattimore, pseud.]. *High Contrast*. Naiad Press, 1988.

———. "Sometimes—There's God—So Quickly!" *Flannery O'Connor Bulletin* 24 (1995–96): 88–90.

Ides, Matthew. "'Dare to Free Yourself': The Red Tide, Feminism, and High School Activism in the Early 1970s." *Journal of the History of Childhood and Youth* 7, no. 2 (2014): 295–319.

Mermann-Jozwiak, Elisabeth. "An Interview with Montserrat Fontes." *MELUS* 26, no. 3 (2001): 145–61.

———. "Writing Mexico: Travel and Intercultural Encounter in Contemporary American Literature." *symplokē* 17, nos. 1–2 (2009): 95–114.

Nava, Michael. *The City of Palaces*. Madison, Wis.: Terrace Books, 2014.

Wilde, Brandy [Clarice Gillis]. *Tease*. Los Angeles: Purple Distinctions, 2015.

GLORIA E. ANZALDÚA

GLORIA E. ANZALDÚA

A Critical Biography

CORDELIA E. BARRERA

G LORIA EVANGELINA Anzaldúa was born on September 26, 1942, in Raymondville, Texas, the oldest of four children born to Urbano and Amalia Anzaldúa, Mexicanos who had called the Rio Grande Valley of South Texas home for over six generations. She graduated from Edinburgh High School in 1962 and, after a short stint at Texas Woman's University in Denton, completed coursework for a BA in secondary education at Pan American University in 1968 (renamed the University of Texas—Pan American in 1988). Anzaldúa financed her early college career by working odd jobs—including migrant farmwork—and taking classes at night. Before receiving her MA degree in English and education from the University of Texas at Austin in 1972, she worked as a primary and secondary education teacher in various school districts in Texas. In 1974, she enrolled in the comparative literature program at UT Austin at the PhD level, although she did not complete the requirements for this degree. By 1977, she called the San Francisco Bay Area home and began to devote the bulk of her time to writing. In 1988, she was accepted into the PhD program in literature at the University of California, Santa Cruz. At the time of her death in 2004, she was working toward completion of her dissertation. She was awarded a posthumous PhD from UC Santa Cruz in 2005.[1]

Throughout her adolescence, Anzaldúa's family lived in various houses on small farms and ranches within a thirty-mile radius of the Jesús María Ranch north of Hidalgo County, Texas. When she entered school at the age of seven, she did so alongside Mexican children only, as schools at this time remained segregated and white children were bused to nearby Edinburg for schooling. At this time, the school district did not employ Mexicans; it had only white teachers. This experience mirrors Anzaldúa's early teaching career between 1969 and 1973 at Pharr–San Juan–Alamo Independent School District, which did not allow Chicanos to teach at the high school level until the early 1970s.

As an infant, Anzaldúa struggled with a hormonal imbalance that caused her to begin menstruating when she was a baby of three months. Quick growth spurts led her to begin to develop breasts by the age of six. In grade school, her mother pinned a folded rag onto her panties in case she bled, a secret the young Anzaldúa found shameful and punishing. Skinny and tall for her age, she was *prieta*, "dark like an Indian" (Anzaldúa, "La Prieta" 38). A solitary child who felt that she "was not of this Earth. An alien from another planet" (40), she found solace in reading at an early age. With her first book—a twenty-five-cent pocket western gifted to her by her father—she learned quickly that injustices toward nonwhites were not limited to her community; the racist ideologies against Mexicans and Indians held by whites were everywhere.

An imaginative, precocious child, Anzaldúa did not appreciate the way girls—such as she and her sisters—were rarely encouraged to move or even dream beyond engaging in household chores and other domestic pursuits. Even as a young child she knew "there were other worlds out there" (Anzaldúa, "Turning Points," 29), and so she continually sought to develop her imagination and knowledge base by retreating into books, exploring the landscape around her, and making up stories to occupy her mind. Often these stories were about animals or elements drawn from the dry, dusty landscape; she sometimes cast herself as the hero and used her own nickname, Prietita, for her protagonist. She knew she was different, and from an early age she seemed to understand that there were wider psychic and physical energies that connected her body to the landscape. She had no interest in boys, as other girls her age did, and the painful, very early menstrual cycles that monthly ravaged her body brought high fevers, vomiting, and diarrhea and further confounded her sexual identity.

During her adolescence, Anzaldúa worked the fields after school alongside family members, hoeing, picking cotton or melons, and covering watermelons with paper plates during winter months to keep them from freezing. She recalled how every few years or so the family would move to a new chicken or dairy farm not far from the Jesús María Ranch where she was born and which was on her maternal grandmother's land. Some of the homes her family lived in had no electricity or running water, and she described how her father was sometimes a tenant farmer and at other times a sharecropper, the main difference being that sharecroppers generally contributed their labor with no legal claim to the lands or crops they farmed. Thus, although the Anzaldúas once owned the land they worked, after the Treaty of Guadalupe Hidalgo was signed in 1848 and Mexico ceded Texas and other parts of the Southwest to the United States, Anzaldúa's ancestors, like many other Mexicans, lost their lands to U.S. whites because of the imposition of new taxes and other economic manipulations. Her father died when she was twelve, and Anzaldúa continued to work in the fields on weekends and during summers. Significantly, it was her father who encouraged her to go to college.

Upon earning her BA, Anzaldúa taught at the preschool, primary, and secondary levels. After receiving her MA degree in 1972, she was employed by the state of Indiana to serve as liaison between the public school system and migrant farmworkers' children. Significantly, by 1974, after enrolling in the doctoral program in comparative literature at UT Austin, she became involved in the Chicano Movement and various activist groups, such as the Chicano Youth Organization and the Mexican American Youth Organization. Through coursework in Austin and alongside connections made as a member of activist groups like WomanSpace, she was introduced to feminism, the occult, and queer life. It was at this time that she began to make connections between different forms of knowledge and nonordinary and spiritual realities; by 1977, she determined that her writing would take center stage.

HISTORICAL CONTEXT: ON THE BORDERLANDS

Anzaldúa influenced a generation of students as a lecturer in women's studies (now feminist studies) while at UC Santa Cruz before her untimely death due to complications with diabetes in May 2004. As a cultural theorist, she continues to play a crucial role in shaping contemporary Chicana/o theory, feminist philosophy, and lesbian and queer theory. Additionally, her work has influenced new avenues of scholarly thought in widely disparate areas, such as composition studies, spirituality studies, utopian studies, pedagogy, code switching, and social and environmental justice, among others. Anzaldúa's writings, which broadly and most generally fall under the categories of feminist theory, cultural theory, and queer theory, have become increasingly important for scholars, students, and laypeople alike, partly because her theory of a Borderlands identity is one that so many can readily identify with. For example, in the poem titled "To live in the Borderlands means you," she writes:

In the Borderlands
you are the battleground
where enemies are kin to each other
you are at home, a stranger,
the border disputes have been settled
the volley of shots have shattered the truce
you are wounded, lost in action
dead, fighting back (*Borderlands/La Frontera*, 216)

In this poem, the Borderlands do not refer merely to a geographical space, such as the border between Anzaldúa's home state of Texas and Mexico. Although she locates her writings in this borderland space, the borders she refers to are those related to her identity as a queer woman who is both Mexican and American and who speaks both English and Spanish as well as a mixture of both.[2] Throughout her writings, which include poetry, fiction, children's stories, essays, and experimental histories, or *autohistorias*, she is in a constant battle not only to figure out her identity but to challenge how she is identified within both cultures as well as by the status quo. All sides of her culture—the Indigenous, the Spanish, the American, and the Mexican—often criticize her for being different as well as limit her through the use of labels that make for rigidly defined roles. Earlier in the poem, she writes that she is "caught in the crossfire between camps," which refers to the fact that she does not want to be classified as part of only one race or another. This refusal of unchangeable, inflexible roles extends to her sexuality.

Much of Anzaldúa's work surrounds the idea of moving beyond binary (either/or) constructions of identity. This idea is most clearly visible in one of her best-known concepts, the mestiza consciousness. A mestiza consciousness is a consciousness of the Borderlands that incorporates psychic, spiritual, and sexual Borderlands. These Borderlands "represent intensely painful yet also potentially transformational spaces where opposites converge, conflict, and transform" (Keating, *Reader*, 319). For Anzaldúa, moving beyond binary thinking toward mestizaje is a way to embrace the often-conflicting aspects of our fluid, ever-shifting identities.

Indeed, the idea of identity as always in flux is key to understanding the politics of difference so central to Anzaldúa's theories as well as how she reads, or interprets culture, history, and her own subject position. How do we learn to understand ourselves, one another, and the world through multiple points of view? How do we incorporate perspectives that value difference into the ways we speak, act, and engage with others? How do we link ideas and create bridges between different ways of knowing and being in the world in ways that foster and build alliances between varied groups of people with often very different agendas? These are some of the questions that frame much of Anzaldúan theory.

One of her most quoted concepts of the Borderlands is encapsulated in the following: "The U.S-Mexican border *es una herida abierta* where the Third World grates against the first and bleeds. And before a scab forms, it hemorrhages again, the lifeblood of two worlds merging to form a third country—a border culture. Borders are set up to define the places that are safe and unsafe, to distinguish *us* from *them*" (*Borderlands/La Frontera*, 25). Borders, as described here, are more than lines on a map or geopolitical markers. Although they point to historical, material locations, Anzaldúa also uses borders in the metaphorical sense. There are at least two levels of meaning here: the surface, or exterior, level and an abstract, or less obvious, conceptual level. Thus, in the poem that opens *Borderlands/La Frontera*, "El otro México," she writes:

> 1,950 mile-long open wound
> dividing a *pueblo*, a culture,
> running down the length of my body,
> staking fence rods in my flesh,
> splits me splits me
> *me raja me raja* (24)

The geopolitical border, that line that separates the United States from Mexico, metaphorically announces a physical border that tears through her body, her flesh. In this stanza, we see how Anzaldúa conflates the physical landscape with her own body, in essence suggesting that the creation of an "unnatural boundary" (25) evokes, or perhaps even creates, a substantial emotional and quite visceral effect on her body and thus her identity. This concept speaks to her idea of the new mestiza, which moves us beyond biologically based definitions of mestizaje. Mestizaje at the broadest level refers to racial and/or cultural mixing between different ethnic groups, such as Indigenous peoples and those of Mexican, Spanish, or other European descent. Importantly, mestizaje is an ideological stance that in the twenty-first century conjures positive connotations, as opposed to the term *miscegenation*, which is generally considered pejorative.

FOUNDATIONS: *THIS BRIDGE CALLED MY BACK* AND *BORDERLANDS/LA FRONTERA*

In a 1982 interview with Linda Smuckler (Anzaldúa, "Turning Points"), Anzaldúa discusses how, as an adult, she began to discover and revere elements within her culture that she had not previously been encouraged to understand or even acknowledge. As a child, she learned that her Mexican heritage, just like the food she and her family ate and the Spanish language they spoke, was somehow not equal to that of white culture. She describes the Chicano Movement of the late 1960s as the first turning point in her life, when she began reading Chicano poetry, mythology and religion. Through the writing and activism of leaders like Rodolfo "Corky" Gonzales and Cesar Chavez, men who were bringing ideas central to Mexican and Chicano culture into the public sphere, she further distanced herself from her Catholic upbringing. The second turning point in her life came with her involvement in the consciousness-raising meetings and network of activists she met within the burgeoning feminist movement of the mid-1970s. Significantly, the inadequate attention to women of color in both the Chicano Movement and the mostly white, middle-class second-wave feminist movement left much to be desired. In time, her allegiance to consciousness-raising on various levels would become associated with the more broadly based third wave of feminism. Third wave feminists were instrumental in bringing in individuals and communities—such as queers and women of color—who had been left out of earlier feminist goals. Third wave feminists recognized the intersectional nature of oppression and so focused not only on gender but also on race and on interlocking systems of power that affect those who are most marginalized in society.

Anzaldúa is best known for co-editing, with Cherríe Moraga, *This Bridge Called My Back: Writings by Radical Women of Color* in 1981 and for her 1987 semiautobiographical work *Borderlands/La Frontera: The New Mestiza*. In the twenty-first century, both *This Bridge* and *Borderlands* remain highly influential texts for many reasons. *This Bridge* is notable mostly for the way it challenged mainstream white feminism. Significantly, the collection, which is a mix of poetry, letters, interviews, prose narratives, and essays, reminds readers that feminist thought and action must be defined flexibly and broadly. Although it is not the first published anthology by women of color, it became a catalyst by which women of diverse backgrounds framed later activist-based coalitions, especially as these relate to third wave feminism. In the introduction to *The Gloria Anzaldúa Reader*, Anzaldúa scholar and biographer AnaLouise Keating argues that *This Bridge* is remarkable for the way it "demonstrated the transformative possibilities that arise when we theorize in multiple genres and modes" (9). Because the anthology brought together the writings of Black, Native American, Latina, and Asian American women—many of whom identified as lesbians—it foregrounds issues of identity while also focusing on race, class, ethnicity, and sexuality. *This Bridge* remains a significant achievement for gay and lesbian communities because it offers an intellectual framework for many issues relevant to queer studies.

Anzaldúa was a writer who took risks in many ways, as she put academic scholarship itself—which generally shies away from risk-taking and incorporating aspects of the self—on the line. Although it is well documented that she always meticulously revised her writing before it was to be published, students might sometimes be taken aback by what appears to be a meandering logic and writing style in *Borderlands/La Frontera*. The work is a mixture of prose, poetry, history, memoir, and theory. Additionally, she often shifts from English to Spanish quite abruptly and even uses regional dialects like pochismo, Tex-Mex, and Spanglish throughout. These shifts are made, not to confuse readers, but to mirror the experiences of immigrants, non–native English speakers, and bicultural people as they mitigate the American landscape.

Anzaldúa is not a status quo kind of writer. She freely incorporates intimate personal details of her life alongside historical facts and scholarly theories in *Borderlands/La Frontera*. The personal facts, stories, *dichos*, and shifts in language registers are not digressions. Rather, Anzaldúa's continued juxtaposition of the personal with the scholarly or historical within her writing mirrors her worldview as a queer woman caught between worlds. In other words, her writing reflects her way of thinking: it is hybrid and exists between different, and often contrasting, realities and systems of knowledge. Perhaps most significantly, her inclusion of very personal details builds upon her experiences as a brown-skinned Chicana to, in the words of Keating, "transform herself into a bridge" ("Risking the Personal," 2). In this way, scholars agree, much of her work inspires readers to potentially identify with her and to consider how our differences can actually forge connections, as they are compelled to reflect upon their own experiences and personal, familial, and cultural histories.

In *Borderlands/La Frontera* Anzaldúa further articulates a queer identity as a path to knowledge. She discusses this path as one in which the "Shadow-Beast"—the "Other" that many queer persons are forced to repress or hide—ultimately rebels against the tyranny wrought by culture itself. In order to avoid rejection or being labeled a deviant, queers, people of color, and nonbinary, transgender, or other-gendered categories of people are pressured to conform to the values of the dominant culture, pushing the "unacceptable parts of themselves into the shadows. Which leaves only one fear—that we will be found out and that the Shadow-Beast will break out of its cage" (42). In later sections of the book, where she painstakingly articulates her theory of "la conciencia de la mestiza," or a mestiza consciousness, she relates to the reader how she broke free of dominant culture's "despot duality" that says we must be male or female (41). A mestiza consciousness is a nonbinary way of thinking and acting, a way of balancing, or miti-gating, our many and often incompatible identities.

For example, she writes: "I, like other queer people am two in one body, both male and female. I am the embodiment of the hieros gamos (wounded deer): the coming together of opposite qualities within" (41). A mestiza consciousness is transformational but also painful to achieve, as it requires "healing the split that originates in the very foundation of our lives, our culture, our languages, our thoughts" (102). The mestiza "undergoes a struggle of flesh" (100) to coalesce all those aspects of the self that have been fragmented by the dictates of the dominant culture, the aspects that cultural absolutism dictates must be either/or: male or female, queer or straight, American or Mexican. Moving toward a mestiza consciousness involves a constant progression that takes place within the self and is enacted in the outer world. The goal is to break down the subject-object dualities that hold us prisoner; a new consciousness, a consciousness of the Borderlands, gives us a new story to explain the world as well as new, nonbinary value systems.

In my own writing, I have worked to pierce the barriers of main-stream utopian scholarship that have generally discounted Anzaldúan theories. Anzaldúa's writing, like many of the theories she labored to conceptualize throughout her lifetime, places the act of breaking barriers at the forefront. Her desire to reconceptualize the self by first moving inward and to incite broader behavioral changes among the wider populace is linked to aspects of "social dreaming," a utopian incli-nation theorized by the preeminent scholars Ernst Bloch and Fredric Jameson.[3] As scholars themselves break barriers by conceptualizing innovative approaches to her work, Anzaldúan thought does not simply survive, it thrives. In terms of survival, Anzaldúa discusses altar making, meditational practices, and other ritualized activities as central not just to her writing but to her very survival. Much of what we read in *Borderlands/La Frontera* revolves around the inner struggles she faced as a queer Chicana in the Borderlands; however, inner struggles, when theorized in terms of a mestiza consciousness, signify radical acts of self-excavation that can lead to changes in the outer world. To be sure, what Anzaldúa describes throughout much of *Borderlands/La Frontera* is much like the societal rituals and rites of passage that anthropologists have explained surround complex processes of symbolic transition; yet for her, rites of passage and personal transformations—especially those that radically alter our perceptions of the world—are connected to deeper realities, connective networks between humans and the world itself. They are spiritual frameworks.

Often, Anzaldúa privileges the spiritual in the form of silenced Indigenous knowledge rather than institutionalized religions and white rationality. This approach can alienate some readers and scholars, especially because she prioritizes forms of consciousness and knowing that are not connected to rationality or to obvious, external forms of knowledge. "To me, everything is real," she writes. "The body does not discern between different kinds of stimuli; the body doesn't distinguish between what happens in the imagination and what happens in the material world" ("Creativity and Switching," 108). As such, spirituality, for Anzaldúa, is just one more path to knowledge as well as a source of sustenance. Spirituality is another way she transforms her outer reality.

Anzaldúa's insistence on the spiritual is reaffirmed in almost every interview in the collection *Interviews/Entrevistas*. For her, spirituality is a means to move beyond what she calls the "institutional trappings" of Western thought ("Within the Crossroads," 73) that have effectively severed the realities, our stories. Throughout the pages of *Borderlands/La Frontera*, she discusses different Aztec female icons that point to a female mythology; she writes at length about these to demonstrate one's capacity for reconciling aspects of the self that fragment in the face of patriarchy and religious traditions. She begins by associating the myths surrounding female deities such as Coatlicue,

Coyolxauhqui, and la Virgen de Guadalupe and and legendary figures such as la Llorona and la Malinche with broader female struggles, such as those she and other women of color felt within the mostly white feminist movement of the late 1960s and the predominantly male-led Chicano Movement. For Anzaldúa, these archetypal figures epitomize the Shadow-Beast, which she describes as what "emerges as the part of women that frightens men and causes them to try to control and devalue female culture" (*Borderlands/La Frontera*, 38–41). Patriarchal culture has instilled in us a picture of weak, vulnerable women. But in reality, females are subject to dualities; we are capable of being both strong and weak, invincible and vulnerable. She likens women to serpent goddesses who embody heavenly and underworld powers and mother-warrior characteristics linked to these historical female icons whose stories were revised by patriarchal culture to keep women in subordinate positions.

In recovering these female deities and legends, she reminds readers how the patriarchy, or men in power, drove them underground "by giving them monstrous attributes and substituting male deities in their place, thus splitting the female Self and the female deities" (49). In later sections in which she discusses the Coatlicue state, we begin to understand how recovery of stories, histories, and myths and legends— lost, disregarded, or even silenced—can guide women to confront their worst fears. The process is difficult and is summed up by her theory of *nepantla*, discussed in the following section.

The bulk of Anzaldúan scholarship to date focuses on *Borderlands/La Frontera* because this text encompasses her broadest application of ideas. However, numerous ideas and concepts in *Borderlands/La Frontera* contain the seeds of many of her post-*Borderland* theories and speculations. These include inclusionary community-building theories related to El Mundo Zurdo as well as consciousness-raising concepts bound by her theories of nepantla, *conocimiento*, spiritual activism, autohistoria, Coatlicue, *la facultad*, and the Coyolxauhqui imperative, among others. Many of her speculations further encompass ecological concerns and themes of spirituality bound in her vision of an ancestral, democratic, and egalitarian homeland in the U.S.-Mexico borderlands.

For Anzaldúa, self-reflection is key to the transformative processes of self by which individuals can attain a higher spiritual, social, cultural, or even political consciousness. Through her use of autohistoria (personal life stories that concurrently tell the life stories of others), readers envision history as more serpentine than linear, meaning that she moves beyond official or sanctioned histories to scrutinize and recover discursive fields and spaces that continue to shape our lives, our stories. Thus, through her often-painful bouts of self-reflection, she exposes those spaces where colonialist or patriarchal norms pushed forms of knowledge associated with indigeneity, spirituality, the imagination, the occult, and metaphysics underground. Self-awareness is merely the first stage in coming to consciousness, and, indeed, moving "Towards a New Consciousness" (the title of the culminating prose chapter in *Borderlands/La Frontera*) is a goal in the service of social justice. Coming to consciousness on an individual level can foment broader forms of egalitarianism, as seen in her concept of *autohistoria-teoría*, which blends personal histories or forms of memoir and storytelling with other forms of theorizing to expose the limitations of Western-based paradigms of writing and analysis.

CRITICAL CONCEPTS: NEPANTLA AND THE NEPANTLA STAGE

Nepantla is a Nahuatl word meaning "in-between space." By the late 1990s, Anzaldúa began to theorize a theory of nepantla, which she called a paradigm, "a model I'm constructing to explain a set of events—psychological, sociological, political, spiritual, historical, creative and imagined, external and internal" ("Nepantla: Theories," 1). Nepantla involves a journey into both the interior and exterior self; it culminates in a process of death and rebirth of the psyche. It is "the state or stage between the identity that's in place and the identity in progress but not yet formed" ("Queer Conocimiento," 5). Nepantla represents "a space capable of accommodating mutually exclusive, discontinuous and inconsistent worlds." ("Nepantla: Theories," 1) *Nepantleras* are artists/writers who create "strange new contexts" by which to view the familiar world and see it in new ways. Nepantla, however, also describes "the state or stage between the identity that's in place and the identity in progress but not yet formed" ("Queer

Conocimiento," 5) In a 1995 version of the unpublished essay "Nepantla," located within a folder titled "Nepantla: Theories of Composition" in the University of Texas Benson Latin American Collection, where her writing is stored, and later published in a different form in *The Gloria Anzaldúa Reader*, she reflects on the idea of Chicanas as inner exiles:

> Slowly I begin to see the tear in the weavings of reality
> I slip through the holes
> pass to the other side
> and encounter my other face.

Nepantla demonstrates ideas about liminality and potential change. Yet it is out of necessity, writes Anzaldúa, that Chicana artists connect to "unconscious reservoirs of meaning," to that "nepantla state of transition between time periods" in order to wrest images and metaphors whose meanings have been misappropriated, dislocated, lost, forgotten ("Chicana Artists," 165).

Writing in the North American Congress on Latin America *Report on the Americas*, Anzaldúa wrestles with the ethics of appropriating ancient Aztec images in her writing. For Chicanas, she reasons, exploring and, indeed, appropriating "indigenous Mexican symbols and myths in a historical and contemporary context" is a "mechanism of resistance to oppression and assimilation" ("Chicana Artists," 164). Only if and when we actively look beyond the tangible will we discover connections to the underworld, the spirit world—other realities. This becomes necessary to draw out institutionalized historical and cultural oppression that has, for generations, aimed to subjugate Indians, Mexicanos, and Chicanos.

To gain what has been lost requires a digging up of metaphoric and symbolic roots as well as an overturning of dominant, bifurcating Western practices. Just as the community feeds the border artist's spirit, so too must the border artist nurture the ancient spirits, the originary arbiters of meaning that have been effectively pushed into the unconscious. Because "metaphors *are* gods" (164), we must not only uncover the old metaphors—the old gods—we must nourish them. Anzaldúa's nepantla state is the terrain of "those who challenge the status quo and who struggle for social justice, who want to culti-vate visions of a better, more just world" ("Nepantla: Creative," 1). It is a continually shifting zone of transition that signifies a point of contact between the natural and spirit worlds as well as between humans and the numinous; nepantla embraces the joining of these worlds through ritual transformation. When in nepantla, one feels as though he or she is living on the edge, "an edge that fragments you, unbalances you, makes you vulnerable" (1). In this extreme state of being, one bal-ances the worldview of contemporary society alongside nonordinary worldviews.

CRITICAL CONCEPTS: SPIRITUALITY, AUTOHISTORIA-TEORÍA, AND A POET-SHAMAN AESTHETICS

Notably, because the term *spirituality* is slippery, cannot be quanti-fied, and defies logical explanation, attempts to conceptualize spiritual experience can become reductionist. In scholarly studies, spirituality is often dismissed as apolitical, ahistorical, or escapist; it is generally conflated with religious experience. For Anzaldúa spirituality does not equate to organized religion. In a 1998–99 discussion following from a published 1983 interview with Christine Weiland, Keating engages Anzaldúa regarding spirituality as a tool of the oppressed. Anzaldúa reflects on the often-misused term as well as her inability to formulate a word that encompasses her articulations regarding the word: "I've been trying to think of another term. I keep coming back to Mexican indigenous terms to see if I can appropriate cultural figures or words and apply the twenty-first-century experience, but I haven't come up with anything yet. I know it has something to do with the imagination, the inner life, but the terms I come up with don't work" ("Within the Crossroads," 73). In *Interviews/Entrevistas* Keating broadens the playing field of Anzaldúan studies by incorporating discourse omitted in the past, mostly related to what she calls Anzaldúa's "spiritual-imaginal vision," into previously published interviews ("Risking the Personal," 13) The appended interviews include Anzaldúa's words, thoughts, and musings surrounding "an alternate mode of perception, a holistic way of viewing ourselves and our world that empowers individuals to work for psychic and material change on both the personal and collective levels" ("Queer Conocimiento," 11) to highlight her vision of work that encourages and advocates for social justice. Keating rightly positions Anzaldúa's spiritualized worldview in terms of the pragmatic dimensions related to an ethics of reciprocity, an ethics bound by the idea that "spirituality is oppressed people's only weapon and means of protection. Changes in society only come after the spiritual" (11). Significantly, the augmented interviews further unsettle Anzaldúan studies in terms of content and scope, as they defy neat paradigms that often typify feminist, queer, and Chicana studies.

Anzaldúa's metaphysical philosophies ground what Keating describes as a "poet-shaman aesthetics" ("Speculative Realism," 8). Language—words themselves—for Anzaldúa do not *just* signify and represent concepts and ideas. Rather, and in keeping with certain Indigenous philosophies, words are causal, which suggests they can have a materializing force. This means that certain words and images, "when internalized, can trigger the imagination, which then effects our embodied state—our physical bodies—at the cellular level" (53). In this way, Anzaldúa encourages readers to think of *their own writing* as part of a broader creative process that can add to the connective tissue necessary to foment wider cultural shifts. Just as autohistoria-teoría links the individual to the collective when individual histories become part of that collective, so too can the act of writing be like "carving bone" (*Borderlands/La Frontera*, 95). For Anzaldúa, works of art, like words themselves, are not without life. Rather, they "contain the presences of persons, that is, incarnations of gods or ancestors or natural and cosmic powers" (89).

In many ways *Light in the Dark/Luz en lo oscuro* expands upon theories first explored within the pages of *Borderlands/La Frontera*. Chapter 5, titled "Putting Coyolxauhqui Together: A Creative Process," describes Anzaldúa's own creative process and is presented to readers as a kind of meditation in the second person, a strategy of autohistoria-teoría meant to encourage the creation of narratives of healing, self-growth, and transformation; in fact, Anzaldúa classifies *Borderlands/La Frontera* as autohistoria-teoría. Although she describes the process of writing as a kind of dreaming, images, insists Anzaldúa, are more immediate than words. As such, the act of putting words on the page, and the transference from image to word in the mind of the artist, not only evokes "the bones of inert and abstract ideas" (*Light in the Dark*, 105) but transforms the writer into a nagual (shape-shifter), as the artist's creative process brings the imagination's unconscious process to the page (or canvas): "Words are blades of grass pushing past the obstacles, sprouting on the page, the spirit of the words moving in the body is as concrete as flesh and as palpable; the hunger to create is as substantial as fingers and hand" (*Borderlands/La Frontera*, 93). Similarly, dream worlds and dream states are legitimate realities, as are mythic times and mythic states of being.

CRITICAL CONCEPTS: COATLICUE AND THE COATLICUE STATE

In Aztec mythology, Coatlicue is the earth goddess of life and death and mother of the gods; she gave birth to the moon, stars, and the gods of war and the sun. Anzaldúa describes the Coatlicue state as a "prelude to crossing," a phase of confrontation full of painful, sometimes debilitating encounters that result from the shame and divisions wrought by opposing aspects of the self—in Anzaldúa's case, contrasting aspects within Mexican, Indigenous, and Anglo worldviews. She writes of this state metaphorically, using the symbol of the serpent. For Anzaldúa, snakes are symbols "of awakening consciousness—the potential of knowing within, an awareness and intelligence not grasped by logical thought," which coalesces when we redeem our most painful experiences and shape them into productive actions ("now let us shift," 540). She further uses womb imagery to indicate the darkness and isolation associated with this stage; there are, however, provisions for nourishment. This stage represents an increasing spiritual awareness as well as the resistance to new knowledge and other psychic states triggered by intense inner struggle. Although reaching the Coatlicue state is wrought with pain and challenges, as individuals face their worst fears here, they simultaneously allow themselves to be overcome by them, prompting the realization that the demons we face can generate great inner strength and power. The poem titled

"Letting Go" illustrates the process, which (possibly) culminates with the individual finding the divine within the self:

> You must plunge your fingers
> into your navel, with your two hands
> split open,
> spill out the lizards and horned toads
> the orchids and the sunflowers,
> turn the maze inside out.
> Shake it. (*Borderlands/La Frontera*, 186)

The Coatlicue stage represents a resistance to new knowledge and other psychic states triggered by intense inner struggles. More broadly, this state is analogous to traumatic experiences imposed upon the bodies of Chicanas and other minority figures throughout history. Self-transformation does not occur in this stage but in the later nepantla stage.

CRITICAL CONCEPTS: COYOLXAUHQUI, CONOCIMIENTO, AND "LIVING QUEERLY"

In Aztec history and religion, Coyolxauhqui is the daughter of Coatlicue. According to the legend, Coyolxauhqui, upon learning her mother was pregnant, urged her brothers to kill their mother. The attempted matricide was thwarted by Coyolxauhqui's brother, Huitzilopochtli, who emerged from his mother's womb as a fully dressed warrior and decapitated his brothers and sister. This is a strange, complex story that many Mesoamericans consider to be not about murder but "the personification of the struggle between the sun, moon, and southern stars" or "the annihilation of a female-led clan by the emerging patriarchal order" signified by Huitzilopochtli (Gómez-Cano, 115). Anzaldúa draws from this story to develop a theoretical framework that moves from fragmentation to wholeness; it is most clearly aligned with the process of writing and avenues to healing. In "let us be the healing of the wound," Anzaldúa writes: "Coyolxauhqui is my symbol for the necessary process of dismemberment and fragmentation, of seeing that self or the situations you're embroiled in differently. It is also my symbol for reconstruction and reframing, one that allows for putting the pieces together in a new way. The Coyolxauhqui imperative is an ongoing process of making and unmaking. There is never any resolution, just the process of healing" (*Light in the Dark*, 20). The Coyolxauhqui imperative, which she alternately termed "Coyolxauhqui consciousness" and "Putting Coyolxauhqui Together," is a powerful conception, as it speaks to the need to confront our pain and *desconocimientos* (hidden forms of knowledge or a refusal of new knowledge) and to acknowledge them, not simply to be free of them, but to use the new knowledge to move beyond nonbinary forms of thinking. This, Anzaldúa insists, "is the beginning of a long struggle, but one that could, in our best hopes, bring us to the end of rape, of violence, of war" (*Borderlands/La Frontera*, 102).

Conocimientos signal processes of healing psychic wounds resulting from cultural traumas that have effectively split the self. In other words, as patriarchal systems and those in power effectively silenced Indigenous histories and stories, they pushed ancestral knowledge into the deep recesses of the psyche. Anzaldúa insists that citizens, whether mestiza or not, must perform radical acts of self-excavation if they are to link inner changes to public acts or to activism in the external world. Anzaldúa argues that once conocimiento is reached, one must act in light of the new knowledge. Conocimiento, which translates as "consciousness" or "knowledge" in English, reflects a "connectionist mode of thinking" that unfolds within oppressive contexts and entails a deepening of perception (Keating, *Reader*, 320). Given her ideas surrounding conocimiento—which, at its root, is about how our lives, like the work we produce, is ultimately constructed from the ways we perceive both the outside world and our own inner desires and forms of knowledge—it is not surprising that these burgeoning forms of knowledge can lead to spiritual activism or a "queering" of reality. To "queer" something is to look at that thing or idea through a lens that makes it strange or troubles it in some way. As we have seen, Anzaldúa's work is about writing as a witness from many camps, many sides; it is linked to a Borderlands consciousness. A Borderlands consciousness, a way of being and living that continually and actively refuses dualistic thinking, is a subjectivity of the crossroads: it effectively queers much of what the status quo reveres as "natural." However, when we look closely, *beyond* categories that prioritize only rational thinking, we find that much of what the culture deems natural is really a construction, a creation of culture.

CRITICAL CONCEPTS: COMING TO CONSCIOUSNESS

Anzaldúa's writing is intimate, descriptive, discursive, and reflective of her Borderlands identity. The most reprinted and anthologized component of her work is the culminating prose chapter of *Borderlands/La Frontera*, titled "La conciencia de la mestiza: Towards a New Consciousness." This chapter, like the chapters that precede it and the poetry section that follows, embeds code-switching tactics and a mixture of registers that signal her refusal to be restricted by any one group, belief system, or geographical location. Significantly, this chapter describes the "new mestiza consciousness" as a consciousness of the Borderlands:

> Because I, a mestiza
> continually walk out of one culture
> and into another
> because I am in all cultures at the same time (99)

This poem signals the challenge of living in a liminal space, between different races, cultures, and identities. Although she discusses at length the need to develop a tolerance for contradictions, between the lines of her prose and poetry she poses an important central question: As the mestiza navigates different cultures, languages, and value systems, how does she move between counterstances, how does she heal the splits to create a new cultural space of possibility? Borders are not just physical enclosures, edges, or boundaries; on the contrary, borders also separate people, races, men and women; and we also sometimes create borders around ideas in order to keep certain thoughts, practices, or ways of being out. Thus, the new mestiza must develop a tolerance for contradictions and ambiguity: "She learns to be an Indian in Mexican culture, to be Mexican from an Anglo point of view. She learns to juggle cultures. She has a plural personality, she operates in a pluralistic mode—nothing is thrust out, the good the bad and the ugly, nothing rejected, nothing abandoned . . . she turns the ambivalence into something else" (101).

This stance brings the new mestiza to a crossroads. Using such imagery as a porous rock, an ear of corn that bears an inner seed, and the process of tortilla making, which involves grinding, kneading, molding, and shaping, she describes how flesh, the body itself, transforms, unlearns divisive patterns rooted in patriarchy and binary thinking, and, finally, demands action. This is where the "uniting" of all that separates the self can be synthesized. In synthesis, the self adds that necessary "third element which is greater than the sum of its severed parts" (101–102). This third element *is* the mestiza consciousness, which she insists is, above all else, feminist in nature.

This chapter is so powerful and influential because it represents a culmination of her previous chapters. Additionally, in it she discusses the need for men themselves to challenge divisive systems of masculinity and instead, as many queers have, move beyond the false boundaries of dominant culture. Here, too, she stresses that "we must allow whites to be our allies" by educating them regarding Chicano, Indigenous, and Mexican history (107). We must lean on one another's histories and struggles, learn from them, and support our differences. Such an opening to different forms of awareness and recognition of our shared endeavors can lead to a transformation of one's psyche; it can further inspire collective transformations that lead to more just images of the world, history, and self. These transformations can in turn lead to changes in society.

The mestiza way is a process, an often-agonizing endeavor that does not come easily or swiftly; it may take a lifetime to achieve. But as individuals take inventory of the baggage we have inherited from our ancestors or our culture and move toward making a conscious rupture with oppressive conventions and practices, we are in a position to communicate that rupture and reinterpret individual and shared histories using fresh symbols and myths—aspects of culture that have been lost, silenced, or discredited. The result is a world where Chicanas/os and the "troublesome," the queers, "or those who cross over, pass under, or go through the confines of 'the normal'" (25) may restore their dignity and self-respect. In this space she calls "el retorno" we see clearly, beyond race, racial stereotypes, and disquieting binaries and past the patriarchal values that devastate the complexities of our plural identities.

MAJOR ACHIEVEMENTS AND ENDURING SIGNIFICANCE

Gloria Anzaldúa was a critical theorist, anthology editor, fiction writer, essayist, and poet whose work continues to influence feminist studies, postcolonial theory, Borderlands studies, cultural theory, and American studies, creating and building upon concepts central to Latina feminisms and often moving beyond the parameters of cultural theory. Since her passing in 2004, her papers have been housed in the Benson Latin American Collection at the University of Texas at Austin. The materials comprising her archive range from biographical information and personal papers to financial information, personal correspondence, journal entries, and published and unpublished writings. Researchers will be pleased to find doodles, drawings, and a profusion of spirals scattered throughout her published and unpublished works—"plasmagoric" figures that "pleased Gloria every time she drew [them]" (Montes, 41). A handful of these have been reprinted in *The Gloria Anzaldúa Reader*. Items in the archive are not available for checkout but can be viewed by contacting the Benson library directly.

Today there are various awards and societies in her honor, including the Gloria E. Anzaldúa Distinguished Lecture Award at UC Santa Cruz, the Gloria E. Anzaldúa Poetry Prize, and the Society for the Study of Gloria Anzaldúa.[4] Additionally, *This Bridge Called My Back* was the recipient of the Before Columbus Foundation American Book Award in 1986, and in 1987, *Borderlands/La Frontera* was recognized by the *Library Journal* as one of the year's thirty-eight best books and as one of the one hundred best books of the century by both the *Utne Reader* and the *Hungry Mind Review*. In 1991, Anzaldúa was the recipient of the Lambda Lesbian Small Book Press Award and the Lesbian Rights Award, as well as the National Endowment for the Arts fiction award; in 1992, she was awarded a Sappho Award of

Distinction; and in 2001, she was honored with an American Studies Association Lifetime Achievement Award. In 2012, posthumously, she was named by Equality Forum as one of their thirty-one icons (one for each day) of LGBT History Month.

Time and again throughout her published writing and within the pages of her unpublished materials, we are reminded that Anzaldúa did not hold strict allegiances. Enlightenment-based ways of thinking that underscore rational thinking and binary categories such as male/female, straight/queer, and black/white are cages that reduce her field of vision and action: "Incomplete knowledge is a cage," she cautions in a speech titled "Queers of Color." In what she insists is a political, spiritual, and "immensely conscious way of life," she reminds us of the heteronormative traps that inherently victimize: "Identity is a cage whose bars are tightly defined categories. Gender is a cage, being Chicana, being queer, these are all cages that restrict movement" (2). Queerness for Anzaldúa includes sexual identity but also moves beyond it toward other forms of reparation and justice. As queer studies and efforts to gain LGBTQ rights continue to reshape the myriad ways identity is conceived, and as broader methods of discerning aspects of intersectionality remain at the forefront of efforts for inclusivity and social justice, so too will those aspects surrounding queering reality in Anzaldúa's work continue to materialize.

Anzaldúa delivered the speech "Queers of Color" at the University of California, Santa Cruz, on June 3, 1999. Here, she discusses the "cost of being fully human, of being fully queer, of queering reality." Living queerly, she says, is political, spiritual, an immensely conscious way of life. When we take part in a queer conocimiento we galvanize knowledge in a revolutionary way, "one that contests constricting conceptions of identity, of reality, of reading the world" (2). Where we end and the world begins is not easy to distinguish, she says. However, because queerness is a process and a strategic action, when we move beyond the confines of scientific practices that remain trapped in eighteenth-century Enlightenment principles, we no longer exclude that which cannot be tested and replicated in a lab—the spiritual, the mystical, the mythopoetic, the metaphoric.

These ideas bring to mind El Mundo Zurdo, an early concept that she began theorizing in the late 1970s. El Mundo Zurdo, which translates as the "the left-handed world," is about building alliances and communities based on common goals and desires rather than what might be considered essentialist similarities. Those who feel most at home in El Mundo Zurdo include women of color, the physically challenged, queers, women and minorities in general, and those in low socioeconomic groups. Although to date there has not been much scholarly analysis of this concept that focuses on how marginalized groups can build alliances across differences in efforts to bridge those differences and foment revolutionary change, the Society for the Study of Gloria Anzaldúa has coordinated a sesquiennial international Gloria Anzaldúa conference titled El Mundo Zurdo since 2009. This signifies not only that Anzaldúa's vision and work remain topical and relevant in the twenty-first century, but that practitioners of Anzaldúan studies, other interested scholars and educators, and laypeople will continue to develop output that is both practical and theoretical in scope. Indeed, such conferences have multidimensional benefits, including the potential to encourage revolutionary change regarding the way scholarly output is written and disseminated as well as the shape that such output inevitably takes. Of El Mundo Zurdo as a concept, Anzaldúa writes: "*Together* we form a vision which spans from the self-love of our colored skins, to the respect of our foremothers who kept the embers of revolution burning, to our reverence for the trees—the final reminder of our rightful place on this planet" ("El Mundo Zurdo," 196).

Throughout her life and work, Anzaldúa sought to regain lost or hidden forms of knowledge by diving deep into the metaphors and images that those in power continually pushed underground. For example, she revises Judeo-Christian serpent imagery to illume her idea of "la facultad," which she describes as "the capacity to see in surface phenomena the meaning of deeper realities, to see the deep structure below the surface" of things (*Borderlands/La Frontera*, 60). If we recall, she claims the serpent as a symbol of truths discredited by colonialist practices and patriarchal structures. In this way, she embraces descent as a path to knowledge. Jane Caputi discusses the ways that Anzaldúa "honors . . . downward pathways and shapeshifting" as transformational (186). What is most important here is the idea that we all have a creative life force that is capable of altering mind, body, and spirit when we are confronted with new information, skills, or structures. Our individual realities are flexible, and "shifts" in our human consciousness, as she describes in the piece "now let us shift . . . conocimiento . . . inner work, public acts," can actuate further shifts in our worldviews.

For Anzaldúa, the imaginal is not secondary to the material or phenomenal. Contemporary society, however, rarely nourishes such phenomena. She speculates, however, about a future time, a "great turning point" where humans "leave the rigidity of this concrete reality and expand it" ("Last Words?," 285). In this respect, Caputi argues, Anzaldúa "participates in a lengthy philosophical tradition that recognizes imagination as the faculty allowing us to know and describe the realm that can be variously conceptualized as the world of power, the invisible, mythic, spiritual, energetic world" (187). Refusing to shake off images and feelings that enfold the numinous, the animal or primal, or even unconscious desires, Anzaldúan theories, many of which emanate from her body, her unconscious, and her desires for a more just world, are capable of moving us beyond yearning. They can give us a better understanding of the paths we might walk toward "a new story to explain the world . . . a new value system with images and symbols that connect us to each other and the planet" (*Borderlands/La Frontera*, 103). Anzaldúa, in fact, is all about embracing new ways of being in the world, retaking our bodies and minds in efforts that can make us more whole, more happy, more connected to one another and the planet: "I am an act of kneading, of uniting and joining . . . a creature that questions the definitions of light and dark and gives them new meanings" (103). This process of kneading, of continual reflection, of carving words that are heavy and as material as bones, can drive us insane, "but if the center holds, we've made some kind of evolutionary step forward" (103). Here, then, is that "spiritual-material essence" (Keating, "Risking the Personal," 9) that "enables her to create a new identity category and a theoretical moral framework for social change" (9). Here too is *our* invitation to remember to move forward and leave behind those elements of culture or society that fragment our deepest selves. As we read Anzaldúa's words, as we engage the deepest aspects of her longings and desires, we are asked to balance and confront so much. But she has given us the tools, and so we are poised and ready. There are realities and other truths beyond dominant systems and institutions that privilege the few, but we must be willing to make painful spiritual crossings, often distressing negotiations of body, mind, and spirit, sometimes via often brutal paths of knowledge—conocimientos—to discover them.

NOTES

1. The proposal (titled "Lloronas"), table of contents, and chapter outlines are found in appendix 1 of the posthumously published *Light in the Dark/Luz en lo oscuro*, edited by AnaLouise Keating, 2015. Anzaldúa intended *Light in the Dark/Luz en lo Oscuro* to serve as her dissertation at UC Santa Cruz; it was written during the final years of her life.
2. For Anzaldúa, the use of the lowercase *b* in *borderlands* signifies the region on both sides of the Texas-Mexico border. The use of a capital *B* in *Borderlands* moves beyond this geopolitical space to encompass psychic, sexual, and spiritual Borderlands—spaces of potential transformation.
3. See Ernst Bloch, *The Principle of Hope*, vol. 1 (Cambridge, Mass.: MIT Press, 1995), and Fredric Jameson, *Archaeologies of the Future: The Desire Called Utopia and Other Science Fictions* (Brooklyn, N.Y.: Verso Books, 2007).
4. The Society for the Study of Gloria Anzaldúa (SSGA) puts out a monthly newsletter and holds workshops, performances, and cultural events in line with Anzaldúan thought. In conjunction with Aunt Lute Press, the SSGA publishes *El Mundo Zurdo: Selected Works from the Meetings of the Society for the Study of Gloria Anzaldúa*.

WORKS CITED

Anzaldúa, Gloria. *Borderlands/La Frontera: The New Mestiza*. 4th ed. San Francisco: Aunt Lute Books, 2012.

———. "Chicana Artists: Exploring *Nepantla, el Lugar de la Frontera*." *NACLA Report on the Americas* 27, no. 1 (1993): 163–69.

———. "Creativity and Switching Modes of Consciousness." In *The Gloria Anzaldúa Reader*. Edited by AnaLouise Keating. Durham, N.C.: Duke University Press, 2009, 103–10.

———. *Interviews/Entrevistas: Gloria E. Anzaldúa*. Edited by AnaLouise Keating. New York: Routledge, 2000.

———. "Last Words? Spirit Journeys: An Interview with AnaLouise Keating (1998–1999)." In *Interviews/Entrevistas: Gloria E. Anzaldúa*. Edited by AnaLouise Keating. New York: Routledge, 2000, 281–91.

———. *Light in the Dark/Luz en lo oscuro: Rewriting Identity, Spirituality, Reality.* Edited by AnaLouise Keating. Durham, N.C.: Duke University Press, 2015.

———. "El Mundo Zurdo: The Vision." In *This Bridge Called My Back: Writings by Radical Women of Color.* Edited by Cherríe Moraga and Gloria Anzaldúa. Watertown, Mass.: Persephone Press, 1981, 193–96.

———. "Nepantla: Creative Acts of Vision." Manuscript drafts, 2002. Folder 20, box 112. Gloria Evangelina Anzaldúa Papers. Benson Latin American Collection. University of Texas, Austin.

———. "Nepantla: Theories of Composition." Manuscript drafts, 1995. Folders 20–21, box 61. Gloria Evangelina Anzaldúa Papers. Benson Latin American Collection. University of Texas, Austin.

———. "now let us shift . . . conocimiento . . . inner work, public acts." In *This Bridge We Call Home: Radical Visions for Transformation.* Edited by Gloria E. Anzaldúa and AnaLouise Keating. New York: Routledge, 2002, 540–76.

———. "La Prieta." In *The Gloria Anzaldúa Reader.* Edited by AnaLouise Keating. Durham, N.C.: Duke University Press, 2009, 38–50.

———. "Queer Concocimiento." Manuscript drafts, 2000. Folder 25, box 112. Gloria Evangelina Anzaldúa Papers. Benson Latin American Collection. University of Texas, Austin.

———. "Queers of Color." Manuscript drafts, 1999. Folder 26, box 112. Gloria Evangelina Anzaldúa Papers. Benson Latin American Collection. University of Texas, Austin.

———. "Turning Points: An Interview with Linda Smuckler (1982)." In *Gloria E. Anzaldúa: Interviews/Entrevistas: Gloria E. Anzaldúa.* Edited by AnaLouise Keating. New York: Routledge, 2000, 17–70.

———. "Within the Crossroads: Lesbian/Feminist/Spiritual Development: An Interview with Christine Weiland (1983)." In *Interviews/Entrevistas* Edited by AnaLouise Keating. New York: Routledge, 2000, 71–127.

Caputi, Jane. "Shifting the Shapes of Things to Come: The Presence of the Future in the Philosophy of Gloria Anzaldúa." *Entre Mundos/Among Worlds: New Perspectives on Gloria Anzaldúa.* Edited by AnaLouise Keating. London: Palgrave, 2005, 185–94.

Gómez-Cano, Grisel. *The Return to Coatlicue: Goddesses and Warladies in Mexican Folklore.* Bloomington, Ind.: Xlibris, 2010.

Keating, AnaLouise, ed. *The Gloria Anzaldúa Reader.* Durham, N.C.: Duke University Press, 2009.

———. "Introduction: Reading Gloria Anzaldúa, Reading Ourselves . . . Complex Intimacies, Intricate Connections." In *The Gloria Anzaldúa Reader.* Edited by AnaLouise Keating. Durham, N.C.: Duke University Press, 2009, 1–15.

———. "Risking the Personal: An Introduction." In *Interviews/Entrevistas: Gloria E. Anzaldúa.* Edited by AnaLouise Keating. New York: Routledge, 2000, 1–15.

———. "Speculative Realism, Visionary Pragmatism, and Poet-Shamanic Aesthetics." *Women's Studies Quarterly* 40, nos. 3–4 (2012): 51–69.

Montes, Amelia M. L. "What Gloria Said About La Virgen's Hands." *Güeras y Prietas: Celebrating 20 Years of "Borderlands/La Frontera."* Edited by Norma E. Cantú and Christina L. Gutierrez. San Antonio, Tex.: Adelante Project, 2009, 39–46.

Moraga, Cherríe, and Gloria Anzaldúa, eds. *This Bridge Called My Back: Writings by Radical Women of Color.* Watertown, Mass.: Persephone Press, 1981.

NORMA E. CANTÚ

NORMA E. CANTÚ

Norma-lizing What Is Chicanx, a Life of Beautiful Norms in the Interstice . . .

GABRIELLA GUTIÉRREZ Y MUHS

T IS revolutionary to stand in front of a living icon and declare some of their superhuman skills, characteristics, gifts, ambitions, and accomplishments when the road ahead is still long and potentially prolific in their writing, academic, and personal life. It is not surprising that Raquel Valle-Sentíes chose to paint Norma Elia Cantú for her *Chicana Writers* series. Cantú is a scholar, editor, writer, poet, folklorist, visionary, and groundbreaking icon for Chicana scholars, writers, poets, and also painters and other artists. She is a feminist and a woman responsible for mentoring and supporting many women in academia on her way to becoming the Murchison Professor in the Humanities at Trinity University in San Antonio, having previously worked on the faculties of Texas A&M International University in Laredo, University of Texas at San Antonio, and University of Missouri—Kansas City, as well as several other public and private universities.

Norma Cantú stands in front of us as an evolving literary monument, one who is eager to grow continuously and who produces, teaches, and molds multiple possibilities about being Chicana selflessly into her characters' subjectivities. I met Dr. Cantú in 1997, when I brought her to Stanford University to be the first presenter in my

Chicana fellows series for El Centro Chicano y Latino, the university-funded center in support of Chicanx/Latinx scholars. At the time the only internationally renowned Chicana writer was Sandra Cisneros. The general mainstream readership was unaware that there were many other writers waiting to catch their readership. I was adamant about bringing Chicana writers who had not been given the attention they deserved by mainstream America and the academy, exceptional Chicana authors who had not, unfortunately, been invited earlier to Stanford. Indeed, Cantú had never been to our campus prior to this visit.

It is an honor for me to write this chapter, as I have been following the development of Norma Elia Cantú as a writer, a poet, a scholar, and an intellectual leader nationally and internationally for many years. I have had the joyous experience of staying in her parents' house on San Carlos Street in Laredo, where Norma lived as a child, adolescent, and adult, and to sleep in a room where her parents slept. It is not often that a working-class scholar is hailed and is given what she has earned from a lifetime of arduous work and diligence. Hence, I can say we are before someone exceptional who in her exceptionality understands that there could have been other Norma Cantús, at least at some level, who might have excelled academically and might have had the opportunities to support their communities and serve the underserved communities from which they emerged, but were in fact unable to find or seize the opportunities that she found.

Women were not at their historical height during the Renaissance, so we can't call her a Renaissance woman, but it would be appropriate to call her a Latinx hummingbird feminist writer or a Latinx multi-genre feminist egalitarian. Norma has opened doors for Latinx women and other women of color in places where there were none, always graciously: on boards, in university departments, and interdisciplinarily for students, tenure-track professors, scholars, writers, and leaders.

In 2017 I edited the reader *Word Images: New Perspectives on "Canícula" and Other Works by Norma Elia Cantú*. It includes chapters about Norma's work written by thirteen selected critics, a foreword by María Herrera-Sobek, and an introduction by me, all inspired by this magnificent and unique fronteriza, woman of the border. We reissued and updated one essay by Ellen McCracken, who theorizes about space in Cantú's oeuvre as well as "hybridity": "In the case of geographical borders—that separating the United States from Mexico, for example—porosity and firm separation are in constant interplay. The official efforts of governments to established unassailable borders coexist with the constant flow of people and ideas across the divisional barriers. And like the epistemological borders that postmodernism both denies and indirectly affirms, the geographical interstices between countries are the site of both openness and stricture for those who recreate them in literary texts" (*Word Images*, 30). What McCracken is saying is that if you are part of the border, of this interstice, of the borderlands, there will be many contradictions and many communions:

> Employing Gloria Anzaldúa's motif of the border as an open wound, Cantú suggests that the ostensibly smooth and unified appearance of the two geographical divisions on the map is in fact teeming with contradictions and the unsettling narratives to come.
>
> This essay [in *Word Images*] examines the role of this vibrant border space in Cantú's writing in the context of the other border crossings she undertakes, such as genre hybridity, visual verbal hybridity, and the intersection of competing critical, linguistic, and other cultural codes. While the geographic border described above is the central space of tension and unity of her writing, she frequently probes as well the postmodern intersections that replace the previously clear distinctions between genres, languages and cultures. (31–32)

McCracken underlines that Cantú traverses through many types of borders "that physically intersect, while at the same time probing several of the other tenuous cultural borders that postmodernity has brought into focus" (32).

All the other essays were especially produced for the *Word Images* collection in her honor. In the first part of the book, "Critical Essays," Jesús Rosales writes about the importance of community and exile in *Canícula*, as well as the significance of the family, what we call familism, in Chicanx homes and communities. María Socorro Tabuenca speaks about the many subjectivities that Norma Cantú is representing both to mainstream America and to her community in her essay "From Chicana/*Fronteriza* and Critic to Public Intellectual."

Law Professor Steven W. Bender examines Norma's autobioethno-graphical novel *Canicula: Snapshots of a Girlhood en la Frontera* and talks about the law in Texas during the span of Cantú's collection of vignettes, interestingly highlighting the fact that "addressing U.S. immigration policy, border crossings, segregation in the Southwest, and suppression of Mexican culture under Texas law, the legal snapshots supplied [in the essay] aim to enrich the context of Mexican life and *familia* in the borderlands that Cantú navigated" (79).

However, the contributor who best captures her ally and friend is María Herrera-Sobek, who in her foreword to *Word Images* describes Cantú as an "aesthetic activist." "Norma Elia Cantú, creative writer, folklorist, literary critic, feminist, professor, public intellectual, and persona extraordinaire, has produced a significant body of work that adds greatly to the understanding and appreciation of Chicano/a literary and cultural production," writes Herrera-Sobek, calling *Canicula* "a literary gem" (ix). Vanessa Fonseca parallels Cantú's work with Cleofas Jaramillo's *Romance of a Little Village Girl*, positioning Cantú as one of the great writers of Chicana literature, alongside Jaramillo. María Esther Quintana Millamoto underlines the maternal character in *Canicula* and analyzes the relationship between her and the main character, Azucena, as a daughter, unpacking the uniqueness of this subjectivity in Chicanx literature. Norma Cantú shows us the mille-feuilles this subjectivity of "the daughter" encapsulates for Chicanas.

The second part of *Word Images* consists of teaching methodologies for *Canicula*. It opens with a thorough analysis of bilingualism and language in Aldo Ulisses Reséndiz Ramírez's introduction to this section. Carlos Sibaja García comments on and analyzes Norma's third language, "the Tejana" language and sexuality, noting that "the Tejana/o experience becomes as important as the Mexican and the American."(158) Aurora Chang theorizes about "the hidden curriculum in *Canicula*," and Rose Rodríguez-Rabin enters into the world of nepantla and being a "nepantlera": "It is a Nahuatl word describing a place as an 'in-between situation.' The Aztecs used this word to describe the place between their world/culture and the Spanish colonization. During the 1980s Chicanas appropriated the word to describe their marginalized political situation. Nepantla describes changing borders and colonial expansion within borders. In Cantú's novel, nepantla describes the culture in between Laredo, Texas, and Nuevo Laredo, Tamaulipas, Mexico" (175). Her chapter is invaluable because it explains that what Cantú is illustrating for all of us is an evolving border, through the actions and inactions of its citizens: "Although Cantú shows the reader what may seem like just some teenagers behaving like teenagers, what she is actually demonstrating is the cultural dynamics of a border town" (175).

The collection closes with the clever and stellar work of Juan Velasco, who addresses intersectionality, consciousness, and "multiple selves" (v–vi). Velasco is one of Cantú's most dedicated and innovative critics. He has theorized his work on *Canícula* successfully by referring critically to autobioethnography as "a complex form of consciousness" in his unique and fabulous book *Collective Identity and Cultural Resistance in Contemporary Chicana/o Autobiography*.

NORMA ELIA CANTÚ'S OEUVRE: *CANÍCULA*

Norma Elia Cantú's oeuvre consists of her renowned novel *Canícula* (1995), her recently published novel *Cabañuelas* (2019), and her poetry collection *Meditación Fronteriza: Poems of Love, Life, and Labor* (2019). Norma has contributed chapters to many edited collections, has co-edited as well as co-authored many more books, and is responsible for the publication of more books than anyone can enumerate. She is sought after by an enormous number of academics, prose writers, and poets for her support of their work and her guidance.

Canicula: Snapshots of a Girlhood en la Frontera will remain a classic in Latinx literature and also in world literature, unique in its use of photography and its reflections on memory. Following in the tradition of Tomás Rivera, Nellie Campobello, and Sandra Cisneros, Cantú offers us a multigenre collection of post–World War II vignettes set in Laredo, Texas. The book spans the late 1940s to the mid-1960s, dwelling particularly on the year 1965, although it really ends in the 1990s, the narrator's present. The last vignette, "Martin High," connects the people included in the narration to their "future" in the protagonist Azucena's present. John Beverly clarifies, through his studies of autobiography, how the form is linked to the larger story of social justice. Here I quote Sue Bond on the effects of Beverley's work on autobiography, and in this case on autobioethnography: "Beverley talks of testimonio as particular to Latin American social justice autobiographies, texts that bind the personal and the sociopolitical, and which are a 'way of integrating an individual's story into a larger narrative of social injustice or violence'" (Bond, I-1A).

Canícula is not only the story of a child arriving at the crossroads of her existence and then coming of age but also the story of a woman in her forties telling the story of a child and adolescent up to the age of seventeen. Interspersed in this childhood reality are the comments of the fortysomething woman who talks about her life and the people in it thirty years after her childhood: "Thirty years later, when Pepe died, a distraught Lola came to visit me in Madrid, to forget her pain—cried her eyes out listening to Rocío Durcal sing 'Amor Eterno' at the open air concert" (*Canícula*, 48). And again: "Thirty years later I returned with Tía Nicha on Day of the Dead to clean Buelito's tomb; we visited with her Comadre Adela whose parents were also now buried in the cemetery across the street" (73). The story that is *Canícula* begins in Madrid in 1980, when Azucena is "intently going over photographs kept in an old cigar box" (1), her lover's photographs. It is not her story that readers begin imagining through the photographs of the man she is with. This quality is characteristic of Cantú's ability to travel through gender, class, race, generations, sexualities, and cultures in order to reflect other people's realities through her own.

But the majority of the vignettes transport the adult Azucena back to her childhood through a series of memories and events; the book is narrated largely from the child's point of view in the first person. These are stories every person can delve into, precisely because they come from the perspective of a woman author who represents herself as the once-child and adolescent, sharing the most intimate feelings about her family, community, and friends with us, the reader. The author states that she discarded other vignettes and photographs because they were not true to the voice of the child. As in Antoine de Saint-Exupéry's dedication in *The Little Prince*, "To Léon Werth when he was a little boy," writing from the perspective of a child opens up the audiences much more than writing from the voice of an adult. It provides tender sensibilities that the author astutely wants to rely on for the reading of their books. In *Canícula*, this technique informs the content of the book and is invaluable to the spiritual value of the vignettes in and of themselves. And the ingenuousness of the child's voice allows the reader to believe that the adult is writing from the perspective of a child, even though the child is actually the adult remembering the child. The orality of the work permits Cantú to retell the story of the border in a child's voice, with the enthusiasm of a child who just arrived at a circus or to perform the lead in a theater play.

Canícula was written in a few weeks in which the author, inspired by her memories of childhood photographs, decides to write about them while in Albuquerque, New Mexico, away from her community, her friends, and her pictures: "In 1993 during the dog days of summer, the canícula—I became a 'nun' and cloistered myself at Ana Castillo's home in Albuquerque, and wrote and wrote and wrote on a rented PC in a small room behind the kitchen of her house in Old Town. It was the middle of the hottest days of the year. I'd already decided on the photographs as the objective correlative, as T. S. Eliot would say. So I went from there. The stories emerged, merged, flowed and literally bled on the page" (5).

Cantú testifies to having written about the pictures at random, without any particular order, as if pulling them out of a box, or so she says in the introduction to *Canícula*. But in reality, the novel has an internal progression based on age, from her earliest years through high school. The period between high school and the narrator's present remains unvoiced, except for a tangential reference to her life in Madrid as a student. *Canícula* is not a storybook with a beginning, a middle, and an end. Eighty-five vignettes narrated by Azucena (sometimes called Nena), twenty-two photographs, a prologue, and an introduction make up the novel.

The introduction advises us that *Canícula* is the "second part of a trilogy that goes from the late 1800 to the late 1900s." Also important in the introduction is the warning about many of the events being "completely fictional, although they may be true in a historical context" (xi). She states that the book is a collage of stories "gleaned from photographs, randomly picked" (xii), and haphazardly includes Roland Barthes: "the story emerges from photographs, photographs through which, as Roland Barthes claimed, the dead return . . . with our past and our present juxtaposed" (xxi). This last statement is premonitory: the reader will be traversing various frontiers between memory and creativity. The prologue is a synopsis of a love between the protagonist and her Spanish lover, a love we never see develop in the book. The prologue reiterates the importance of photography and family in the telling of stories as well as in the defining of territorial space: "Her childhood home on San Carlos Street holds the photographs of her life; these are stuffed in shoe boxes tied with old shoelaces, treasured and safe in the land in between what she calls la frontera, the land where her family has lived and died for generations" (2).

Canícula is a "novela de crecimiento," as critic María Esther Quintana Millamoto points out in Word Images—a coming-of age-novel, or bildungsroman. In her chapter she focuses on melancholy and the mother, associating Canícula with the female coming-of-age novel in general and situating it at the center of women's ethnic novels and autobiography. Canícula is also a transnational novel; it must be commented upon in the context of the great bildungsromans by Latin American and Spanish women writers and critics. Francisca López, in Mito y discurso en la novela femenina de posguerra en España, discusses how the bildungsroman has evolved since its appearance in the eighteenth century and the favorable effects this evolution has had in our analyzing the literature of women as bildungsromans. She states that when confronting the feminine "bildungs," we must take into consideration sociological and psychological factors that influence women in a different manner than men: gender makes a difference in the telling of the bildungsroman. According to López, women in traditional societies become educated in the interior spaces of the home to which they have been relegated. Canícula is fundamentally about the realizations and consciousness that lead one to come of age, and the spaces López underlines as important to women's bildungsroman resound in its pages, but she also subverts the idea that in Latin America and in the Latinx world, women who write the bildungsroman stay only in interior spaces in their narratives. For Azucena, open spaces, nature, other people's houses, and schools are also places of growth and challenge. And, unlike some of the novels mentioned by López, Canícula's "heroine" does not reject the society she represents. On the contrary, she tells her story and goes as far as to intercalate pictures in her narrative because she is proud of her existence, of her relatives and the richness of her border culture, interior and exterior. The situation that needs to be remedied is the ambiance that her country presents and in turn gives the protagonist a background for her life. The bildungsroman that her autobioethnography represents is not hers as much as it is her country's, implying a larger objective: the perfecting of a whole society.

In an interesting review, "Scenes from a Family Album," critic Sara Castro-Klarén briefly compares *Canícula* to *Las manos de mamá* (1938) by an author from the north of Mexico, Nellie Campobello, and to *Cuadernos de infancia* (1937) by Argentinean author Norah Lange, but I would not make this comparison because neither of the other two novels contains photographs. I find the Texan writer's novel much more similar to Mexican Jewish author Margo Glantz's *Las genealogías* (1981). Glantz's autobiographical narrative also emphasizes memory and includes photographs; it looks back to the Central European origins of Glantz's Jewish family and their "forced piligrimage," settlement, and flowering in Mexico. A feminist testimonial of the Glantz family, *Las genealogías* differs from *Canícula* in that it includes fewer pictures; the photograph is not a central feature of the book. Furthermore, *Las genealogías* is not set up as a collection of vignettes written in the present tense in which the narrator is looking at a set of pictures and commenting upon them; *Las genealogías* is a historical narrative, a family biography combined with the feelings of the narrator. As a whole, although nostalgia and melancholy permeate some of the vignettes in *Canícula*, the main vehicle of delivery in this narrative is, not feelings, but descriptions of events that occur and are acknowledged and spoken, in the voice of a little girl.

In her unpublished memoir about the novel, "How I Wrote *Canícula*: Musings on Writing, Reading, and Life," Cantú identifies the two most significant influences on her writing:

> I could say that my literary influences for *Canícula* have been all the reading I've done in forty years or so. But there are two particular works whose influence can more clearly be noted in the genre I chose to shape my narrative. I read *Six of One* by Rita Mae Brown while I was in Spain in 1986 and I'd read Maxine Hong Kingston's *Woman*

Warrior: Memoirs of a Girlhood Among Ghosts when it first came out. I can honestly say that these two creative nonfiction works, the former a novel that the author calls creative autobiography and the latter a novel the author was encouraged to categorize as autobiography, started me thinking about a narrative set on the border that used this strategy. I came upon the idea of the photos all on my own. I often think up exercises for my writing classes, and in the early 80s I began using the photo for a guided imagery exercise. The students loved it and so did I. (4–5)

We will see a continuation of this formulation of history and the love story in Spain in *Cabañuelas*.

CABAÑUELAS, NORMA'S SECOND NOVEL

In *Cabañuelas* (2019), Cantú's latest novel, the author normalizes the use of Spanish as part of the American English language. No other author before her has written Spanish as part of the experience of everyday American life in such an organic manner, beginning with *Canícula* and continuing with this novel. She employs no italics in the Spanish dialogue in *Cabañuelas*, as authors commonly used to (and sometimes still do) while writing in English; her Spanish is part of the American language. This sets an important precedent for Latinx and Chicanx authors of fiction, memoir, and "fictional autobioethnography," to use the phrase Cantú coined in *Canícula* as part of the critical terminology of evolving genres.

Cabañuelas is divided into four parts, all titled in Spanish. Part I is "Época de desamor" and consists of eleven chapters, also all titled in Spanish. Part II, "La fuerza del destino," has fourteen chapters, six of which are titled in English ("Spring Fever," "Chinese Test," "Walking Talking, Reading Sewing," "Friday Ritual," "Public Displays"), one of which is in French ("Non, je ne regrette rien," named after an Edith Piaf song), one in Catalán, "Valencia's Falles y Ninots," and the remaining six in Spanish, balancing in this way the English and Spanish chapters.

Part III, "Jugar con fuego," consists of fifteen chapters, five titled in Spanish. In Part IV, "La Cruz de mayo," eleven of the twenty-three chapters are in Spanish. This is a reminder of the translanguaging that Norma Elia Cantú has embarked upon from the start of her literary career by giving her first novel a bilingual title, *Canícula: Snapshots of a Girlhood en la Frontera*, beginning with Spanish.

I cite these numbers to prove a point: Cantú is both exposing and unpacking the bilingual mind here. As a native informant, to use the anthropological term, she is letting us know that for us bicultural, bilingual, bisensitive (to borrow Tino Villanueva's word) individuals, some especially important things, such as titles, often come to us in Spanish first.

Some of the characters in *Cabañuelas* will be familiar to us if we have read *Canícula*, most notably Nena, the protagonist of the previous novel. (The two novels are intended as parts of a trilogy, as Cantú wrote in *Canícula*: "I am often asked about the other two books in the trilogy—*Papeles de mujer* and *Cabañuelas*. The former remains incomplete. Written entirely in Spanish and set in the early part of the twenttieth century in Omaha and in Laredo, it may not ever be finished as I am still researching that period in our history and since it is written in Spanish, I would most likely have to translate it to get it published" [xxiii]). The genre-jumping novel *Canícula* begins with Nena living in Madrid and mentioning her lover as the journey to this trilogy begins. He asks her about her childhood in Laredo and Monterrey, México. *Canícula* is a marker in Chicanx literary history because the author gets away with a title in Spanish in a publishing industry that denied Chicanx people their language for a long time and because, as a groundbreaking novel of memory and dissonance, photography and autobioethnography, it sets a precedent in American letters. *Cabañuelas* follows in the footsteps of *Canícula*, showing us folkways of being Mexican both in the United States and in Spain. (The title word refers to the foretelling of weather, in Mexican folkways.) Nena's ability to respect her own traditions allows her to understand cross-cultural and regional issues when she lives in Spain conducting research on regional traditions there. Like *Canícula*, this Chicanx novel is transnational.

In *Cabañuelas*, Cantú continues with her practice of using photography to show us that this work is, in fact, probably not fiction, whether it be recounting a family event, describing a Mexican or an American holiday, or expanding the geography of the Chicanx nation into Spain, the root land for some Chicanx cultural practices. In the tradition of Margaret Randall's guide to *testimonio*—she identifies photography as one of the "documents" that affirms a witness account—we see photography, again, even in the age of Facebook, providing us with the testimonio we need in order to question whether a Chicanx "fictional autobioethnography" is in fact fictional.

Cabañuelas is a solid and innovative novel of 282 pages that consists of an explanation of the title term; a prologue; sixty-five aforementioned chapters divided into four parts, the last two chapters of which are the epilogue; and forty-six pictures, almost twice as many as in *Canícula*. It also includes a map of Spain, marking the places mentioned in the novel. Notably, it has no maps of the places the protagonist visits during her American encounters with others.

Nena speaks about a love/hate relationship with the language and Spain, and we can see that this relationship is being played out through the love story of Nena and Paco, but *Cabañuelas* is also a love story with the land: the Chicanx land, the Texan land, the northeastern part of México, that fronteriza Cantú delivers historically, folklorically, and linguistically by interweaving traditions into the love story between Paco and Nena. The protagonist also tells us of her love for her culture, traditions, and family, all of which she is unable to leave for a man she falls in love with in Spain. Unlike mainstream stories, in *Cabañuelas* a man does not win the love of a woman from the Americas. In this novel and in *Canícula*, region, space, place, identity, and family win over heteronormative love relations.

MEDITACIÓN FRONTERIZA: POEMS OF LOVE, LIFE, AND LABOR

Always a poet—she had published "loose poems" throughout her career in a varied list of distinguished literary journals—Norma Cantú finally gives us a full collection of her poetry in *Meditación Fronteriza: Poems of Love, Life, and Labor* (2019). *Meditación Fronteriza* consists of sixty-five poems, divided into six sections of irregular lengths. Once again normalizing the use of certain words in Spanish, as occurs in the borderlands, la *frontera*, Cantú mixes Spanish and English titles for the sections: "Song of the Borderlands," "Reading the Body," "In the Country of Art," "Miel de Mesquite," "Going Home," and "Meditación Fronteriza."

Her poems in *Meditación Fronteriza* are lyric and historical:

> We live in dangerous times.
> Times that call for dangerous measures.
> That call for witnessing and protesting.
> Like we did in 1911 when they were lynching us
> in South Texas. Brown bodies hang from trees.
> Like we did in 1972 when they were killing us
> in the rice paddies in Vietnam and
> the highways of Aztlán. ("Living in Dangerous Times," 120)

As a writer and an instructor of creative writing, Cantú delivers the trained and exact words, as well as the historical details, of incidents that happened to the Chicano survivers of the U.S. nation. In "Living in Dangerous Times," with rhyme and wit, she offers a testimonial about Vietnam, where the author's brother perished along with thousands of Chicanos; at a time when the U.S. Latinx population was 4.5 percent, between 5.5 and 6 percent of casualties were Latinos ("Vietnam War").

Her genre-jumping technique, very much alive in both her novels, is present in her poems as well. In "Song of the Borderlands," for example, she requires that it be read by three male voices ("MV") and three female voices ("FV"), turning this three-page poem with six voices into a theater piece.

Another one of Cantú's specialties—in all her work, but especially in her poetry—is the development of new Chicanx identities. In "La Llorona Considers the State of Tortillas," she gives us a particularly humorous take on a legendary character we normally think of as a scary mythic entity in Chicanx literature. Here we have a serving of a new type of Llorona, more humanized, a critic of tortillas:

> I could write poems on the smooth surface
> Or fold them up and eat them
> Tortillas are
> At once food and utensil

I scoop up memories with each bite,
and la Llorona
Weeping woman smiles. (80–81)

Along with the work of other Chicana critics and poets, Cantú expands on what was traditionally made much too simple about the entity of la Llorona—here, she also laughs and smiles.

In conversation with Demetria Martínez, a seasoned Chicanx poet at a Latinx symposium I organized at Seattle University in February 2020, Demetria reiterated that Norma's poetry is "a poetry of witness," referring to Cantú's connection with the land, and alluding to the fact that in *Meditación Fronteriza* Cantú "joins forces with descendants of Aztec scribes who are writing the 'new codex' of the borderlands." In her blurb on the back cover of *Meditación Fronteriza*, scholar Amelia Montes writes, "Norma Cantú offers us a prescient and poignant sweep of la fronteriza," highlighting the importance of Cantú representing the fronteriza, the woman from the border who is a product of the interstice, the nepantla between México and the United States, and part of both cultures wholly.

CONCLUSION: THE FRONTERIZA SENSIBILITY

Norma has always marked the fact that Spanish should be considered a normal part of the language spoken in the United States. Bilingualism, translanguaging, and "linguistic terrorism" (as Anzaldúa called the exclusion of Spanish spoken by Chicanos because it's not considered "authentic") are some of the topics we engage in *Word Images*. In "Cantú's Decolonial Imagination Through the Looking Glass," his chapter in *Word Images*, Aldo Ulisses Reséndiz Ramírez brilliantly recognizes *Canícula* as a book resulting from five hundred years of colonization:

Mostly written during such dog days in 1993, which marked the cusp of a five-hundred-year era of indigenous resistance to European invasion and unrelenting neocolonization, *Canícula* came into existence during a momentous time that witnessed a renewed call for decolonization and the shedding of internalized, self-destructive colonial practices, a battle cry that came from multiple fronts and across many native tribes and nations the world over. *Canícula* should thus be read in such a light, as a reinscription of Chicana feminist narrative—on such a historical occasion, the renowned queer theorist Gloria E. Anzaldúa, a fellow Tejana and contemporary of Cantú, would indeed summon writers to do as much—in an effort to uproot hegemonic discourse of oblivion and contribute to the ever-expansive Chicana decolonial imagination. (37)

In other words, Norma Elia Cantú in her oeuvre is packaging what Anzaldúa requested that we as Chicana critics problematize in order to decolonize. Cantú addresses folklore, women, gender and sexuality studies, English, Spanish, comparative literature, literary criticism, history, Chicanx studies, ethnic studies, political science, and other disciplines by establishing paradigm shifts through her example as a literary and arts critic, editor, professor, leader abroad, poet, reviewer, reference for many Chicana scholars going up for tenure and promotion, conference organizer extraordinaire, and more.

Every year, we can envision new literary presents from Norma Elia Cantú. Countless aspects of her fronteriza life still remain to be documented and expressed. As she lives by example, we will not be surprised about any future projects. Cantú even collaborated with artist Marta Sánchez in a poetry collection about train yards that could be read by children of all ages, since her grandfather worked for a railroad company: *Transcendental Train Yard* (2015). Many of us have already benefited from her generosity of spirit, her prolific and creative productivity, and the bountiful outcomes of her efforts. Two more books on teaching Gloria Anzaldúa were recently released with her moral and institutional support and guiding criticism about Anzaldúa, as well as about the work of multiple poets on the border. Her foundational work with CantoMundo and the Society for the Study of Gloria Anzaldúa cannot be ignored. The annual conference El Mundo Zurdo would not have been established without her, nor the nationally renowned annual workshops CantoMundo organizes for Latinx/Chicanx writers. In fact, some of the most successful authors have recently emerged from this organization. Norma Elia Cantú is a woman not yet fully described, unique as a scholar, unique as a creative writer, unique as an educator and a theorist, unique as an engaged intellectual who also raises funding for her local food bank, unique in her continual participation and promotion in community events, whether organized by working-class folks or by academia.

Another issue that we have not highlighted yet is that Norma Elia Cantú is part of many communities, and one of them is the national community of women of color intellectuals and feminists. She is very conscious that her work is seen as symbolic by multiple communities. Juan Velasco rightfully states: "As in Audré Lorde's biomythography, *Canícula* uses photographs and the text to recreate 'snapshots' of what is and what is not here, that which exists only in memory, and that which was destroyed by history, the colonizing experience of loss. Because of her technique, she simultaneously represents La Frontera as a space with gaps and disruptions and also as a space of identity that often moves from intersectionality to interconnectivity" (*Collective Identity*, 180).

Finally, I recently attended San Antonio literary organization Gemini Ink's celebration and fundraiser in honor of Norma Elia Cantú and realized that this essay could never be long enough to encapsulate the many subjectivities, the loyalties, and the strong work ethic of this gregarious, creative, brilliant, and innovative mujerista fronteriza I write about today. I saw hundreds of people Norma had guided, mentored, inspired, and supported, so I must conclude that Norma Elia Cantú is in fact an institution. Scholars Laura Rendón and Aída Hurtado and I commented on the fact that she had gained the respect and admiration of so many people; we recalled no one else being honored in such a manner, as a writer or a scholar, two areas where competition reigns. We were startled and delighted to be part of a historical moment for a bilingual, bicultural Chicana writer-scholar-feminista-academic.

WORKS CITED

Bond, Sue. Review of *The Fiction of Autobiography: Reading and Writing Identity*, by Micaela Maftei. *Transnational Literature* 7, no. 1 (November 2014), 1-1A.

Campobello, Nellie. *Las manos de mamá.* Mexico City: Editorial Juventudes de Izquierda, 1937.

Cantú, Norma Elia. *Cabañuelas.* Albuquerque: University of New Mexico Press, 2019.

———. *Canícula: Snapshots of a Girlhood en la Frontera.* Albuquerque: University of New Mexico Press, 1995.

———. "How I Wrote *Canícula*: Musings on Writing, Reading, and Life." Unpublished memoir, n.d.

———. *Meditación Fronteriza: Poems of Love, Life, and Labor.* Tucson: University of Arizona Press, 2019.

Cantú, Norma Elia, and Marta Sánchez. *Transcendental Train Yard.* San Antonio, Tex.: Wings Press, 2015.

Glantz, Margo. *Las genealogías.* Mexico City: M. Casillas Editores, 1981.

Gutiérrez y Muhs, Gabriella. "Subjectifying Entities/Emerging Subjectivities in Chicana Literature Through the Literary Production of Demetria Martínez and Norma Elia Cantú: Madres, Comadres, Madrinas, Niñas Madres, Tías, Abuelas y Solteronas." PhD diss., Stanford University, 2000.

———. *Word Images: New Perspectives on "Canicula" and Other Works by Norma Elia Cantú.* Tucson: University of Arizona Press, 2017.

López, Francisca. *Mito y discurso en la novela femenina de posguerra en España.* Madrid: Editorial Pliegos, 1995.

Velasco, Juan. *Collective Identity and Cultural Resistance in Contemporary Chicana/o Autobiography.* New York: Palgrave Macmillan, 2016.

"Vietnam War Casualties by Race, Ethnicity and National Origin." American War Library. https://www.americanwarlibrary.com/vietnam/vwc10.htm.

DENISE ELIA CHÁVEZ

DENISE ELIA CHÁVEZ

Staging Theater, Teatroesque Literature, and
Chicana Activism in New Mexico

MYRRIAH GÓMEZ

DENISE CHÁVEZ has spent her life putting books into people's hands, whether as a writer, a bookstore owner, or a *madrina de libros* for the *viajeros* making their way across the U.S.-México border. Throughout her life, she has refused to be boxed in. Her work has run the gamut of genres and in some instances resists categorization. Through it all, Chávez has remained close to her birthplace of Las Cruces, New Mexico, and her homeland has influenced both the content and the style of her writing. Literary critics have argued about the politics of feminism, sexuality, and, to some degree, Chicanx identity in Chávez's work, but little to no attention has been given to her work as a Mexican-identifying Nuevomexicana writing from southern New Mexico and engaging in activism on the U.S.-México border. The detail with which Chávez crafts each individual character in her fiction results in both uniquely New Mexican characters and simultaneously universal figures that have broadened the genre of Chicanx literature. Her theatrical style of writing escapes the pages of her plays and finds its way into her literature, creating what literary critic Alvina Quintana calls *teatroesque* literature. Through it all, Chávez has become the most prolific woman writer in the history of

New Mexico, and her dedication to telling a complex story of Nuevo-mexicanos[1] brands her oeuvre. Through her teatroesque literature and activism, Chávez's stories have helped a widespread audience better understand the people and Culture[2] of the U.S.-México borderlands in New Mexico.

EARLY LIFE

Denise Chávez was born in Las Cruces, New Mexico, in 1948. Her mother, Delfina Rede Faver Chávez, was a schoolteacher who taught Spanish, and her father, Epifanio E. Chávez, was a prominent attorney. In fact, U.S. Senator Dennis Chávez was her *padrino*. She writes that her father "was indebted to his mentor, New Mexico Senator Dennis Chávez, who encouraged him. It is Senator Chavez who became my padrino, who baptized me, and whose name I carry" (*Taco Testimony*, 21). Chávez had an older sister, Faride, and has a younger sister, Margo; both make regular appearances in her work. In fact, readers can find members of Chávez's family in her nonfiction, of course, but also in her fictionalized account of her childhood and adult life. Significantly, she calls her mother, who "kicked ass," her greatest influence (Aldama, 89).

As part of her organic evolution into becoming a writer, Chávez says she began writing in her diary at about the age of eight. What started out as daily musings transformed into a sort of "philosophy of life" that she would hand out to people for birthdays or Christmas (Dunaway). In her essay "Heat and Rain," she shares one of her earliest diary entries, dated Sunday, June 15, 1958: "Dear Diary, Today I didn't go to Mass, I must tell the priest my sin. I'm not to [*sic*] happy about it" (28). Other childhood diary entries published in "Heat and Rain" include passages about her tenth birthday, not doing her homework, praying for her father to come home, and missing school to stay home with her heartbroken mother. In her child's words, we see the lived experiences that would later emerge as important themes in her professional writing, such as religion, feminism, and coming of age.

In her memoir *A Taco Testimony: Meditations on Family, Food, and Culture*, she focuses on her experiences growing up as a southern New Mexican- and Mexican-identifying girl in a household that, though culturally bifurcated, was full of love. Her mother instilled in her the Mexican identity that she has always associated herself with, whereas her father and his family maintained their claim to Spanish heritage. This experience was arguably one of the most formative experiences for Chávez as a writer, though it is easy to overlook. This cultural bifurcation was a unique situation in which Spanish and Mexican butted heads in a home where "Chicano" did not yet exist. Her mother, born in El Polvo, Texas, moved to New Mexico after her first husband's death, just days after the birth of their daughter. Her father, who was born in Doña Ana, New Mexico, moved back to New Mexico after graduating from Georgetown University with a juris doctor degree. Both of her parents used education as a response to racism, but whereas her mother turned toward her Mexican identity, studying in México and becoming a Spanish language teacher, her father turned away from it. The boy who was punished for speaking Spanish on school grounds earned a law degree to move away from his Mexican roots and assimilate into U.S. culture. In fact, the way that Chávez is able to make sense of this proto-Chicana upbringing is by using food as a metaphor. She writes, "It's always back to the tacos. Tacos are my life and my story. They are my hope. They are my salvation, and I don't say that lightly. They are my history. My culture. They are who I am. They are my roots and my Becoming. My pride and my healing" (*Taco Testimony*, 107). And then, "It's so good to be Mexican" (107). She leans on tacos to ground her to place, family, and identity, and this metaphor becomes a symbol for both her Mexican and her New Mexican identity, a Nuevomexicano cultural bifurcation that becomes a prominent theme throughout her work.

During her early life, Chávez dreamed of leaving New Mexico, and we see periods during which she lived in New York or Texas, but she always made her way back home to the state, where she lives today. She recently wrote: "That young girl who dreamed of leaving home and never did, the child who reveled in a well-told drama of the *antepasados*, her kin who moved north to settle a land of promise, still lives within me" ("Libros para el Viaje"). Whether intentionally or accidentally, the irony of Chávez building her life in southern New Mexico has forged the characters and story lines around which she has built her career as a writer and activist.

BECOMING NEW MEXICO'S PLAYWRIGHT

Chávez was a drama student in high school. After winning the best actress award in a play called *Grey Bread* during her senior year at Madonna High School, Chávez used the $200-per-year scholarship award to attend New Mexico State University and major in drama (*Taco Testimony* 145). She earned a bachelor of arts in drama there in 1971; a master of fine arts in theater from Trinity University in San Antonio in 1974; and, in 1984, a master of arts in creative writing from the University of New Mexico, where she was the first Chicana writer to earn a fellowship for that degree (*Menu Girls*, xi). In an interview she said, "When I was a senior in college, I wrote my first play here at New Mexico State [University], and I won a contest. One of my professors gave me an A++++ and +, but he submitted that play to a contest here at New Mexico State [University] and I won $15 for that" (Dunaway). Chávez went on to write over a dozen plays throughout the span of her career.

Chávez's repertoire fits within a longstanding tradition of theater in New Mexico, which scholars have traced to the earliest period of the Spanish Conquest. Historian Ramón Gutiérrez calls these early performances "conquest theater," which includes both the military dramas and the religious *autos* of colonial New Mexico. The colonial dramas were political in nature, and their primary purpose was to evangelize the Indigenous peoples in New Mexico, then a kingdom of the Spanish Empire. These included traditional religious plays, such as *Moros y Cristianos*, *The Arrival of the Franciscan Apostles*, or the *autos sacramentales*, which all served as important points of comparison for Chávez's work and also helped illuminate the feminist reimagining in her writing. For example, the folk plays of the Christmas cycle, *Las posadas* and *Los pastores*, two of the autos that continue to be performed across New Mexico today, are challenged by Chávez's plays *Nacimiento* (1979) and *Sí, hay posada* (1980).[3]

In her early plays, Chávez began to dramatize her experiences as a southern New Mexican woman writer. She quickly built a reputation as a Chicana playwright by permutating colonial plots that had defined theater in New Mexico since Spanish colonization. Whether or not she would admit to the political implications of her early work, it was obvious what she was doing: she was politicizing the experiences of Mexican and Chicana women by foregrounding their lives through her plays with themes relating to religion, sexuality, and feminism. Although she was making these major interventions during the height of the Chicano Movement, she explains, "I wasn't an activist; I was a drama major" (*Taco Testimony*, 114). However, this period was, in fact, the beginning of her activism.

David Richard Jones rightly historicizes dramatic theater in New Mexico, what Brian Eugenio Herrera calls the "complex religious, political, and cultural syncretism of nuevomexicano theatricality" (66). Herrera says of Nuevomexicano theater history: "Most emphatically, it reveals how theatrical performance in New Mexico has, for more than four hundred years, stood as both a part of, yet also emphatically apart from, global theatre history, ever and always a local elaboration of national and international performance traditions" (67). In the 1970s, one way that New Mexico stood apart from theater on other predominantly Chicano and Latino stages could be seen through the work of la Compañía de Teatro de Alburquerque. When la Compañía's director, José Rodríguez, a Puerto Rican transplant by way of New York, saw what Chávez was doing with New Mexico in her plays, he included her work in his efforts to develop a local repertoire.

Chávez began working with Rodríguez to write plays for la Compañía in the 1970s. Marcos Martínez explains how during the years of the Chicano Movement, la Compañía did not address social problems in the agitprop theater style of other Chicano troupes, which often gave the impression that what it was doing was not "Chicano theater." However, because la Compañía presented a "voice from a community that had next to no input in theater," it should be viewed as a meritorious Chicano troupe (109). This approach maintained the "ethic of liberation" (109) that Martínez says was characteristic in Chicano activism and theater, but when Rodríguez saw a community need to switch the dominant language in which la Compañía produced its work from Spanish to English, it became difficult to find relevant works to be produced. He wanted material that would interest a New Mexican (read: Hispanic) audience, and he found it with several prominent Nuevomexicano writers, E. A. (Tony) Mares, Rudolfo Anaya, and Denise Chávez, whom he commissioned to write one-act plays around the themes of "Leyenda, Realidad y Fantasía." Referred to as the *New Mexican Trilogy*, the December 21–23, 1979, premiere of these works "marked the inception of the modern era of Hispanic drama in New Mexico" (Jones, "Introduction," 14). The *New Mexican Trilogy* served as a major turning point toward predominantly English productions. La Compañía went on to produce another one of Chávez's plays, *Plaza* (see discussion below), in New York City for Joseph Papp's Festival Latino and in Edinburgh for the Scotland Arts Festival (Jones, "Brief Introduction to *Plaza*," 82).

Although she is writing fewer plays in the twenty-first century, one thing is still true of Chávez's theater legacy: she remains *the* Chicana playwright from New Mexico. In 1988 Martha Heard wrote, "Consistently active in the theatre since the early seventies, she has written more plays and had more plays produced than any other Hispanic playwright" (91). Heard continues, "Chávez' ear for the nuances of language is evident in the dialogue which captures the character's individuality, his social status, and his culture. She particularly catches that language of the Chicano community in which Spanish flows freely into the syntactic patterns of English" (87). The linguistic aspect of Chávez's work makes her plays and her characters distinctly New Mexican. The linguistic idiosyncrasies in her characters' dialogue create personas that carry with them Nuevomexicano Culture.

PERFORMANCE WRITING AND *TEATROESQUE* LITERATURE

Although theater, both playwriting and acting, has grounded her career, Chávez is best known for her books. In 1986, Arte Público Press published *The Last of the Menu Girls*, which she wrote while a graduate student[4] at the University of New Mexico, under the mentorship of both Rudolfo Anaya and Tony Hillerman. In her introduction to the book Chávez writes, "Some critics call *The Last of the Menu Girls* a series of interconnected stories, others call it a novel. I think of the book in more theatrical terms and wish someone would come up with some sort of terminology to address this dramatic story structure that has its roots in theater" (xiii). Tightly woven together by the repeated presence of the same main characters yet not quite a novel, *The Last of the Menu Girls* catapulted Chávez onto the scene of Chicana literature, and her dramatic story structure would become the signature style of her writing. After publishing *The Last of the Menu Girls*,[5] she published three novels: *Face of an Angel* (1994),[6] *Loving Pedro Infante* (2001), and *The King and Queen of Comezón* (2014). She also published a children's book, *The Woman Who Knew the Language of Animals* (1992), which is additionally a theatrical piece and which Elizabeth Brown-Guillory describes as "a magical fable for children about getting along in an ethnically, culturally and linguistically diverse world" (30). When her memoir *A Taco Testimony: Meditations on Family, Food, and Culture* was released in 2006, she offered a glimpse into how coming of age in the U.S.-México borderlands shaped her life as a writer. The theatrical nature of *A Taco Testimony* makes it read like a one-woman show and helped elevate Chávez's status as a notable Chicana writer.

As her work gained more critical attention, many scholars began to analyze the unique theatrical style of Chávez's prose As she has discussed in various places, her process involves listening to the voices of the characters. She says:

> So I always feel that my work is very theatrical. And I'd like to think that people read it out loud because I work in a deeply auditory kind of way: I listen to the voices, then play the voices back. If I'm having trouble with a section of a narrative, I'll tape it and play it back to myself. I read it out loud; I'll wander around; I'll meander through this fictional room I've created with mirrors. Some have said that I work in the same manner as Charles Dickens—he also had a lot of mirrors around his studio, and he would prance and dance with his characters. (Aldama, 82)

One scholar did, in fact, coin a term for Chávez's theatrical style of writing. In *Home Girls: Chicana Literary Voices*, Alvina Quintana calls Chávez's work "teatroesque." An important aspect of this teatroesque literature is the characters Chávez creates. Chicana literary critic Cordelia Candelaria describes her as "a keen observer of people and of our idiosyncrasies" and says, "I think she is able to do it so well because she's an actress and has the experience of the theater" (quoted in Dunaway). Her teatroesque writing, the lively voices and personages she creates in her characters, help Chávez convey important messages about society and culture.

The Last of the Menu Girls focuses on the life of Rocío Esquibel. In "The Closet," Rocío and her sister, Mercy, fight over who gets to see the picture of the Shroud of Turin that their mother keeps in her closet along with all her other secrets. In a teatroesque passage, Rocío tells Mercy she is going to remove the baby-sized crown of thorns—real thorns—from the crucifix that hangs above their mother's bed and try them on. She says, "Oh, they hurt, but not too much. I never pushed them down all the way. But I can imagine what they feel like. They have long waxy spikes with sharp tips. I can imagine the rest. I've been stabbed by pencils in both my palms. The one on my right looks like one of the stigmata" (22). It is impossible to read this without hearing the squeal of a young girl exclaiming, "Oh, they hurt" or how she might argue that pencils have left her with the marks of the stigmata, a quick reference to Jesus and a symbol of her own martyrdom. Many readers *do* read passages such as this out loud, becoming more intimate with characters like Rocío. Because of its teatroesque style, it is difficult not to want to read it aloud.

CULTURE WITH A CAPITAL *C*: SPACE, PLACE, AND NUEVOMEXICANA/O IDENTITY

Chávez has helped create space within the genres of American literature and Chicanx literature for writing about New Mexico and Nuevomexicana/o life. She has a knack for creating complex characters with complex intersectional identities. Grounded in their distinctive ethnic identities, they are often mislabeled as merely universal rather than interrogated for being uniquely regional. To do this, Chávez digs deep into the psyche, both her own and that of her characters. Literary scholar Tey Diana Rebolledo includes Chávez as one of the literary clairvoyants. She refers to these women as *clarividentes*: they have the ability to see into the future because they remember the past. Similar to Anzaldúa's concept of la facultad,[7] the clarividente uses a psychoanalytic ability that she demonstrates through an "understanding of history, myth, and human nature" (Rebolledo, 142). Rebolledo says of Chávez, "She is a writer who uses ritual, traditions, and culture to examine more deeply how women are affected and what they can do to empower their lives. Her special way of seeing, her clairvoyance, is deeply connected to the land, to the social and cultural life that has developed there" (149). Much of her work exhibits "her special way of seeing," but one of her plays, *Plaza*, best depicts her interrogation of New Mexico as place, space, and Culture; it is among her most compelling theater works.

Plaza, set in the middle of the plaza in Santa Fe, examines the culture of and issues of assimilation in New Mexico. In the *acto*[8] Chávez manages to interrogate Nuevomexicano identity using only six characters. As with much of her writing, Chávez lovingly critiques the commonly held claim to Spanish identity present across New Mexico. Nuevomexicanos and New Mexican writers are notoriously rebuked for celebrating Spanish identity and seldom critiquing it, but Chávez shows how a person can become lost when assuming a Spanish ethnic identity without complicating that identity. Thus, Nuevomexicano identity appears along a spectrum in *Plaza*, which is a more accurate representation of how Nuevomexicanos actually see themselves.

In *Plaza*, Chávez introduces various aspects of Nuevomexicano identity. For example, Benito *el viejito* claims his father "era parte indio"; Minnie the Chimayosa waitress claims her family "venimos de España"; and Tommy *el político* critiques the woman whom he almost married as having a father who thought he "wasn't good enough for him" because "eran españoles, you know how they are around here. . . . I wonder what the old guy would say now. I own half the plaza! His pinched nose and genealogy charts—" (88). The woman to whom Tommy is referring is Iris, who shortened her name from Irisela after marrying a white man and opening an art gallery in Santa Fe. The final characters are Cris (Crisella) and Wilfred, the two youngest of the group. Cris represents a younger generation who, in the 1980s, was trying to reclaim Chicano Culture. She does this, in part, by learning Spanish. Wilfred, who has an intellectual delay, resists assimilation by correcting Tommy when he refers to him as "Willy." Tommy's name is actually Tomás, though that is never discussed, as denoted by his character's name—T. "Tommy" Tafoya.

These varying Nuevomexicano ethnic identifiers are place specific, signifying how the pendulum swings across New Mexico when it comes to identity. For example, Minnie, perhaps the most Spanish-identifying character, is from Chimayó, a place in northern New Mexico near where the Spanish first occupied and violently colonized Indigenous people and land. In the longest monologue of the play, Minnie laments her family's loss of land. She explains how her nephew sold the land in Chimayó given to him by his father, Minnie's brother, which the family had inherited from a Spanish land grant. She says, "What did the wildflowers mean to him, and the unplowed fields? Nothing but work, work!" (87). The irony is that Minnie spends the entire duration of the play trying to buy the Plaza Café but does not have the money to do so, despite dedicating her life to her work. Her character is complex, as she also has split feelings about the land that the restaurant is on. She has no problem asserting that the café is hers, but she says, "Not the land that this place is on, but the land too, and the things on top of the land" (87). This line might seem confusing, but to a New Mexican audience it would be familiar, as many people know that the land was stolen first from Indigenous people by Spaniards and then from Spanish-speaking Nuevomexicanos by Anglos, and so exists the palimpsest that becomes the Santa Fe Plaza, which is the literal center of the play.

If Minnie represents a Spanish-identifying positionality, then Benito represents a Mexican one. Benito is originally from Las Cruces, near the U.S.-México border, and is a retired school janitor. He represents not so much a Mexican positionality but at least a mestizo one. But the play shows the problematics of identifying as mestizo. We see Benito try to align himself with Indigenous people when Charlie, an artist from Santo Domingo Pueblo, enters the scene to sell his jewelry under the portal at the Palace of the Governors, where Indigenous vendors have traditionally gathered to sell their handcrafted work. Benito greets Charlie in Diné (Navajo), although a local audience knows that Keres is the language spoken at Santo Domingo, which changed its name back to Kewa Pueblo in a 2009. Benito, who is not ethnically Indigenous, claims his grandfather was "parte Indio," thus trying to justify his use of the Indigenous greeting. Benito never actually claims a Mexican or even a Mexican American identity, but he

speaks in fluent Spanglish throughout the play, code-switching com-
fortably between Spanish and English. He even attempts to teach Cris
Spanish and encourages her to learn it. Benito asserts his traditional
cultural knowledge as he speaks in *dichos* and *refranes*, and he laments
the changes that he has witnessed as New Mexico and its people move
away from cultural traditions. Toward the beginning of the play, he
critiques Tommy for assimilating by reminding him who his father
was. Benito tells Tommy, "No, hijo, tenía una cosa muy importante . . .
creía en la tradición, he believed in tradition, carrying on the culture"
(88). In this way, Benito serves as the symbol of a dying, or at least
endangered, Culture, as juxtaposed to Cris, the *chispa* who will spark
the resurgence.

Tommy and Iris have fully assimilated into mainstream U.S. hegemonic white capitalist culture. The dollar sign controls them. They
have to use Anglo monikers rather than their Spanish given names,
Tomás and Irisela. They were never allowed to marry each other
because Tommy was not Spanish (or Spanish enough) for Iris's father,
but Iris ended up marrying a non-"Spanish" man whose last name is Le
May. Perhaps the worst trait of these two characters is how they treat
the other Nuevomexicanos. Tommy thinks he is better than everyone
else because he has money, and Iris thinks she is better because she
associates herself with Anglo culture and wealth, but the cultured
life that Iris leads is built on the commodification of Indigenous and
Nuevomexicano art, just as Tommy's wealth is built on selling Nuevomexicano land to Anglos and tourists. They have completely lost
themselves and their connections to Culture, and they might as well
be white. When Minnie tells Tommy, "Don't talk to me about the
bank, Tommy. You're the bank, you're Santa Fe, you're the collateral"
(101), Chávez pokes at Tommy being the collateral damage. By saying
he *is* Santa Fe, she is lamenting a dying Culture that has been replaced
by the Santa Fe–style mythology introduced by Anglo outsiders.[9] In
another scene, Iris calls this change "progress" because she sees value
in capitalizing off of Culture.

Like Tommy, Iris has also assimilated. She owns a gallery, and we
see her planning an elaborate gallery opening with a menu of fancy
cheeses and champagne, but in another scene, when she is talking
to Cris, she expresses her exhaustion from the tourists. She says, "I

wanted to marry someone my dad never liked. We were very Spanish. Oh, we're still so very Spanish, and he wasn't Spanish and he wasn't rich—" (102). What she means by "so very Spanish" is questionable, since we are not privy to cultural markers that might qualify this remark. Iris compliments Cris on her "tan," which Cris tells her is just her natural skin color. This is but one way that Chávez makes clear that Iris longs to heal her internal child, who experienced racism and thus forcefully assimilated. She is now unhappily married and completely ostracized from her Culture and community.

Wilfred represents innocence, and Cris represents the modern Chicana. Wilfred was orphaned when his parents died in a car accident. He enjoys the bliss of having his *vecinos* look out for him. In this way, he mimics the *gente* who are oblivious to the ways in which identity politics both exist and function in New Mexico. Wilfred, a paperboy, sells yesterday's news. He makes his "quarter a paper" reliving the past and sometimes talking about the present. His innocence keeps him amenable. Cris, who, like Benito, is from Las Cruces, is a hip-hop break-dancer who represents the urban teen Nuevomexicana on a path of identifying as Chicana. She hangs out with the "low riders," whom Benito refers to as "pachucos." This terminology is used as a direct cultural reference to the men from Española and Chimayó, which is close to Santa Cruz Lake, where Cris says that had been hanging out. She finds fast friends in Benito and Wilfred, who feed her soul, and Minnie, who literally feeds her. She tries to befriend Iris, who treats Cris like a lowlife. If Wilfred has been literally orphaned, Cris has been figuratively orphaned by a father who is a politico in state government and shows no concern for his daughter. I refer to Cris as a chispa earlier because she shows the spark of resurgence, of reclaiming Nuevomexicana identity, of becoming a new Chicana. Also, Cris's androgynous name allows the reader to question her gender or at least imagine that she might be a symbol of the youthful generation at large. Today we might read her as gender nonbinary.

One of the ways that Chávez marks identity in the play is through the use of Spanish language. Not only do the characters' varying levels of and/or dedication to the Spanish language denote their place on the identity spectrum, but also the Spanglish and word choice with which Chávez chooses to outfit her characters echoes a Nuevomexicano sentiment. For example, Benito says, "La cosa es que vivimos a lo todo trochemoche . . . no time to stop, to rest, to talk to people. Too busy with things" (86). Rubén Cobos's *Dictionary of New Mexico and Southern Colorado Spanish* defines *trochimochi* as "helter-skelter, pell-mell (in a disorderly way or hurry)" (230). Simply put, Benito's message is that nowadays, Nuevomexicanos live life too haphazardly to appreciate the things that were once deemed important in society, the meticulous ways of life that made them Nuevomexicano. In another passage he critiques the creation of the chimichanga. He says, "A fried burrito! ¡Hijole! Como dice la Cristella, no way! Para mí, no hay mejor comida que los frijoles, tortillas y el chile verde de Las Cruces" (*Plaza*, 86). First, we see Benito refer to both Cris and Wilfred by their full Spanish names, noting his push against assimilation. Second, we see another reference to a passé, simpler way of life where beans, chile, and tortillas were revered as the quintessential New Mexican meal. It is significant that he calls for green chile from Las Cruces, drawing attention to the local argument about who produces better chile: the *norte* or the *sur*. It comes as no surprise that food plays an important role in determining identity in Chávez's play. "Frijoles, tortillas y el chile verde" are juxtaposed against not only chimichangas but also against the wine and cheese of Iris's gallery opening and the crepes and other delicacies that she says leave tourists aghast.

If Benito is the preserver of the Spanish language and Cris, the chispa who reignites the flame, then Tommy is the assimilation-ist who represents a loss of language. Tommy stands for the baby boomer generation who experienced corporal punishment in school for speaking Spanish and switched their linguistic practices almost entirely to English. Aside from changing his name, we see Tommy's complex relationship to the Spanish language in other parts of the play. Tommy prepares for a political speech to be delivered at the League of United Latin American Citizens[10] by using a Velázquez Spanish dictionary, one of the ultimate authorities on Castilian Spanish, to "bone up on the old español" (98). He practices his speech: "I'd like this opportunity, oportunidad, to continue serving, serviendo, la población Mexicana, Chicana, Latina, Hispano, Mexican-American, American-Mexican" (98). Tommy's generation was made to believe that their Spanish was not sufficient, so instead of seeing him speak with a localized Spanish dialect, as Benito and Minnie do, we see him reach instead for a Castilian Spanish dictionary.

Plaza is a one-act play with a deep, complex cultural critique of age, language, identity, and place in New Mexico. Chávez showcases her understanding of the identity politics across New Mexico and among Nuevomexicanos. In an interview with Frederick Luis Aldama, Chávez said, "I think, too, that my characters, in their acts of teaching and learning, are preservers. They're keepers of our tradition and culture, just as my novels educate and preserve tradition. I also think that my novels open the door for others to understand our culture" (90). The same can be said for *Plaza*, which is not a novel but is still a piece of literature that educates and preserves. The irony of this identity spectrum is that the characters are all uniquely Nuevomexicano. The ending of the play shows Cris joke with Benito that she will see him tomorrow "if you wake up" (106). It does one more thing: it calls on Nuevomexicanos to wake up and see the cultural violence that they both experience(d) and perpetuate(d).

Whereas *Plaza* is one work that can be read easily through the lens of ethnic identity, other works by Chávez more exclusively interrogate feminism. Although she coins a fantastic term to apply to Chávez's style of writing, Alvina Quintana also undermines Chávez's efforts to create complicated Chicana characters. She calls Chávez's work an "accurate portrayal of the ideological perspectives that prevail in New Mexico" (110), yet she does not explain what she means by that statement. Instead, she insinuates that Nuevomexicanas are stuck in a conservative cult of *marianismo*. She says that not all Chicanas engage in radical feminism and, without any further explanation, writes that "placing La Virgen de Guadalupe as the central deity of female-structured narratives" (110) centers a traditional Mexican *puta/virgen* ideological dichotomy. Quintana misses the point of Chávez's work, arguing instead that Chávez's teatroesque literary style, marked by her lively characters, a polyphony of female voices, overcompensates for her content.

Chávez's work expands our understanding of how Nuevomexicanas, and Chicanas more broadly, have rearticulated their understanding of and relationship to la Virgen de Guadalupe, the brown goddess of the Americas, who countless other writers and critics have demonstrated is already a subversion of the Blessed Virgin Mary.[11] Chávez herself has said that marianismo "celebrates more of a virgin state whereas Guadalupe is a kick-ass mama. . . . Guadalupe has more of a global goddess awareness" (quoted in Keating and Mehaffy, 140).[12] Not only that, but she ascribes to a "In Guad We Trust" spirituality, in which Guadalupe supplants the hegemonic male version of God. She refers to this as an evolution of sensibility. She says, "I think there can be an evolution of sensibility from the pallid little virgin who's nursing and looking so delicate, to Guadalupe with the rays coming out of her robe, standing in front of the sun and on a serpent. I would hope that that transformation occurs simultaneously with my concept of God and with my women characters' evolution of consciousness: taking responsibility for their lives; being aware of machismo, yet becoming strong women not to be confused with that blind acceptance that Latina women sometimes have" (140). This is how she breaks social mores in her work. Her own evolution of sensibility allows her to create characters who experience an evolution of consciousness, but this also depends on their intersectional identities. What might be radical for one character, given elements such as their age and ethnic identity, would not be radical *enough* for another character (or reader, for that matter).

One of her best known actos and a great example of her inter-sectional characters is *Novena narrativas y ofrendas nuevomexicanas* (1996). In this one-act, one-woman play, the narrator is a writer-artist named María Isabel González. The protagonist, who goes by Isabel, has created eight women characters whose narratives tell a story about what it is to be Nuevomexicana. Together with Isabel's own *narrativa*, the stories make nine, and thus comes the novena of the title. Novenas are popular prayer rituals among Catholics and are typically prayed in the name of a saint or holy person. For nine consecutive days, devotees will offer prayers and sometimes engage in other rituals, like light-ing candles on an altar. In explaining the play, Chávez breaks up her explanation for each half of the title. Chávez writes that "*Novena Nar-rativas* was inspired by cultural traditions of *cuentistas* (storytellers), *santeros* and *ofrendas*. . . . Inspiration came as well from the *altares* and *nichos* one finds in the family homes" (*Novena narrativas*, 150). This is the storytelling, prayer, and offerings aspect of the play. She says the *ofrendas nuevomexicanas* consist of a clay Madonna,[13] her garments, and "other token memorabilia representing parts of the women's lives and culture" (150). Both the women and their offerings are intended to be "familiar to those of us who love New Mexico, its traditions, cultures and daily life—full as it is with significant detail" (150). Although the title of the play has religious underpinnings, Chávez is actually highlighting the cultural traditions of Mexican Catholicism rather than the Christian ideology.

The universal nature of the narrativas is based on the gendered class analysis in which Chávez engages. *Novena narrativas* creates a sort of community of Nuevomexicanas by uncovering their complex relationships to one another. If *Plaza* interrogates ethnic identity along a spectrum, *Novena narrativas* examines class along a similar spectrum, which can be explored only by analyzing the other oppressions experienced by the women in the play, namely, age, occupation, and sexuality. Through their relations—with each other and with other people in their lives—we can uncover the universal spirit that transcends Nuevomexicana identity tied to space and cultural practices.

To begin, none of the women in *Novena narrativas* are upper class. They inhabit one small neighborhood; the community itself appears to be working class or working poor. Several of the women do not work, and one lives off the streets. Isabel describes herself as an artist and says, "Those born rich suffer as much as those born poor" (151), suggesting that she is struggling financially. Jesusita is an old spinster who owns a curiosities shop that has no customers and no business because "people don't need different colors of thread anymore, nobody sews" (152). Minda is an orphaned child who lives "where there's garbage and broken beer bottles all over the place!" (154). Magdalena is waiting on her food stamps and says, "When the kids get bigger I'll get a job" (156). Juana is a factory worker. Pauline is a high school girl who cannot read and wants to be an artist. Finally, Corrine, a self-proclaimed *pinta jotita*, is a houseless woman who stays at the Holy Bible Rescue Mission or the Good Faith Shelter. The only two characters whose class is unclear are Esperanza and Tomasa. Esperanza is rushing to get back to work, suggesting that she is perhaps working class. Tomasa is a *viejita* who has been abandoned by her family in a nursing home. She asks Esperanza to take her to the bank: "How much money do I have? It should be enough to get me out of here" (157). Thus, one of the similarities that unites the women are their narratives of not having money. These characters are all a stark contrast to Iris from *Plaza*.

The class positionalities of the characters are complicated by other aspects of their identity, particularly their sexuality. At least two characters identify as queer, one of them being Corrine, who goes by Cory. She says that after she lost her husband, kids, and house by writing bad checks, she served time "in the pinta in Santa." She met "her Sophia" while in prison. Cory ended up on the streets because nobody wanted "una pinta jotita" who had tattoos all over her body, her hair dyed blonde, and her eyebrows shaved off and painted black. Cory's intersectional identities result in her ultimate poverty, but Chávez still makes Cory an empowered character. Cory subverts her poverty by refusing to accept hand-me-down clothes from a woman she describes as a "Mexican with a little bit of money" (162). In this way, Chávez disentangles a misdrawn conclusion that Cory is *only* poor because she is queer. She did not end up on the streets because no one could love her; she was already poor before she was imprisoned, and the real crime is that she was unable to raise her family because of this economic crisis. She uncovered her sexual identity, but only as a result of a failed system that kept Nuevomexicanas unable to pay the bills.

The women's ritualistic religious practices are overshadowed by the cultural implications of Catholicism, marked by the presence of and reverence to Guadalupe. For example, the teenaged Pauline is coming of age and refers to herself as a freak. We see no Spanish language anywhere in her narrativa; however, her tattoo of Guadalupe suggests a burgeoning Chicana identity. She says, "My girlfriend, Gloria, she says I'm changing. I don't want to go out and get rowdy and drunk all the time now. Ever since this lady came to our school. She made me stand up and talk. She's an artist. Her name is Isabel Martínez. She's Chicana. I never known anybody . . . a lady and a chicana and an artist. . . . It surprised me, you know?" (160). Like Cris in *Plaza*, Pauline is also a chispa who reignites Nuevomexicana Culture, marked by her identifying as Chicana, queer, and ambitious and having her teacher, a self-proclaimed Chicana, as her role model. This is how the women build *comadre*hood throughout the play.

But what is it about this acto that makes the characters uniquely Nuevomexicana? Chávez offers no discussion of place-based cultural practices that might make them obviously Nuevomexicana; instead, their place-based linguistic practices are a main cultural signifier. Jesusita's Spanglish is a smooth back-and-forth engagement between Spanish and English, and she emphasizes her code-switching by exclaiming how different things are: ¡Bárbara! Bárbara is not another woman in the play; rather, it is an eccentric expression for surprise or shock. Words and spellings such as Crismes, Burque, ésa, and chansa are examples of the language of Nuevo México that appear naturally and fluidly throughout the play and within each narrativa. How and where each word is used also helps the reader see the characters' intersectionality. That is why Chávez writes that the characters are "familiar to those of us who love New Mexico, its traditions, cultures and daily life," not because there are many traditions that are represented in this play, but because we can recognize the characters that exist within the Culture and have kept those traditions alive.

"I KNEW THEN THAT I HAD FOUND MY CALL TO SERVICE": LIBROS PARA EL VIAJE

Chávez writes exhaustively about the theme of service, particularly in *Face of an Angel*. She says, "I have always been interested in the theme of service. What does it mean to serve, and to be served? Are we on this earth to serve or be served" (quoted in Brown-Guillory, 39). Not only is service a theme in her written work, but she has investigated this question in her daily life, making it her true ideology. It is a fact that one informs the other, and this is best seen throughout her community activism, particularly in her most recent project, Libros para el Viaje.

In 2013, Chávez, along with her husband, Daniel Zolinsky, opened Casa Camino Real Bookstore in Las Cruces. It sits across the street from a building stuccoed a color that Chávez calls "period red" and around the corner from one of New Mexico's best food spots, Nopalito Restaurant. The little adobe house was built in the 1850s and was owned by former New Mexico Supreme Court justice and cofounder of the Mexican American Legal Defense and Education Fund, Daniel Sosa. They opened the bookstore less than three years before ending the Border Book Festival, which Chávez cofounded in Mesilla, New Mexico, and which became the longest-running book festival in the state. The 2015 decision ended a twenty-five-year run of an annual book event in the Las Cruces area. Bobby Byrd, owner of Cinco Puntos Press in El Paso, said when the festival ended, "It's been the only literary event that celebrated the true *fronterizo* spirit, crossing borders and churning languages with books and works and music" (Renteria). In true service to her community, Chávez's Casa Camino Real maintains that fronterizo spirit by serving as a space for workshops, book readings, and book signings. Lovingly called La Casa, the bookstore has recently offered its latest service by becoming a *santuario* for books that she delivers to viajeros traversing the U.S.-México border. She calls the project Libros para el Viaje.

In her nonfiction writing, Chávez tells candid stories of the frequent trips she took with her mother and sister to Ciudad Juarez and how the people and Culture shaped her life and her work. Upon seeing a need to provide Spanish-language books for refugees and asylum seekers crossing the border, she began searching for books in nearby bookstores that she could donate to the humanitarian nonprofit Border Servant Corps. In early 2019, Chávez contacted the American Booksellers Association about hosting at book drive just before the association held their Winter Institute in Albuquerque. So many thousands of books were collected at the Winter Institute that Fonseca Freight, a local trucking company out of Albuquerque, donated time and resources to move them to Las Cruces, where the Mitsubishi dealership became the de facto warehouse for storage and distribution (Chávez, "Libros").

The book drive formally assumed the name Libros para el Viaje, and Chávez began using her bookstore as its home base. She writes,

> Casa Camino Real began distributing books to local refugee hospitality centers where families would be sent after being released from the ICE facility in El Paso, en route to their sponsors somewhere in the U.S. by either bus or plane. I also began to distribute books on Wednesday mornings at Peace Lutheran Church, in Las Cruces,

following what is, for me, a much anticipated pancake breakfast. My husband and fellow book steward, Daniel Zolinsky, and I spread out a large table of donated books, one side for children, the other for adults. After I introduced myself and the program, families would join us. In time, I began storytelling sessions and language lessons. I knew then that I had found my call to service. ("Libros")

Since the beginning of this project, Chávez fully immersed herself in the literacy work that was being carried out at the U.S.-México border, becoming the madrina de libros. In her "call to service," Chávez opened the pages of a new chapter of her life, one to which she would dedicate thousands of hours. She was raised crossing back and forth over the border with her mother, only now she was carrying books and stories—and there was still food involved.

Perhaps as a coda to her memoir *A Taco Testimony*, Chávez contacted the author of *Dragons Love Tacos* (*Dragones y tacos*), Adam Rubin, about the project, especially the storytelling sessions with the children, and Rubin donated hundreds of copies of his award-winning book. On one particular "pajama party" day during which the children are invited for a monthly storytelling session at the library, Chávez says that they read *Dragones y tacos* "with the delicious smell of tacos being cooked outdoors on a disco, or large metal skillet, wafting through the patio door of the children's room" ("Libros").

In early 2020, Chávez penned an essay for *New Mexico Magazine* on her efforts—really, community efforts—associated with Libros para el Viaje. She set the backdrop by describing her experiences growing up in Las Cruces in the borderlands, sharing stories of the women in her family, and discussing the importance of literacy. The essay called attention to the plight at the border that has, in fact, been an issue for decades. It is no coincidence that Chávez writes, "The word was my life then, as now, and my writing became my answer to how I want to live with *truth*. I have continued this inquiry into the heart of the world with my work in Las Cruces" ("Libros"; my emphasis). The irony here is that Chávez's "truth" contradicts the New Mexico Tourism Department's "New Mexico True" campaign, which the department launched in 2012 with a PR firm based in Austin, Texas, named Vendor Inc. (Pollon). Today, the department continues to outsource its public relations to another Austin firm, Giant Noise.[14]

The "New Mexico True" campaign has received criticism since its launch in 2012, most notably when it made a casting call for "light-skinned Hispanics" in 2014 and most recently with an anti-Indigenous, colonial commercial in which the famous painter Georgia O'Keeffe's words are mixed with other voices to create a voiceover saying, "When I got to New Mexico, that was mine. As soon as I saw it, that was my country" (De Vore). The "New Mexico True" campaign is an "attempt to draw out-of-state tourists" to New Mexico, Spencer R. Herrera writes. "The state's objective, to increase tourism, is indeed served by crafting an appealing narrative about New Mexico. However, community issues and governmental responsibilities throughout the state have become neglected and also need to be addressed and remedied" (117). Like Chávez, others have called attention to the real truths that we experience in New Mexico. Catholic Health Initiatives–St. Joseph's Children, tired of the romanticization of New Mexico in the tourism department's commercials, began their own "New Mexico Truth" commercials to "exploit the shallow messaging" of the tourism department's campaign, as Herrera writes (131). The commercials have received a lot of attention for the facts they present about the health and well-being of New Mexico's children. But whereas the state tourism department cannot stop the "New Mexico Truth" commercials, they intercepted Chávez's article before it was published.

The editors of *New Mexico Magazine* decided they would not run Chávez's story. By telling the "truth" about what is occurring in southern New Mexico, Chávez's article disrupted the idyllic image that *New Mexico Magazine* and the tourism department have worked diligently to create, one that Chávez has always written to break. Phaedra Haywood writes that Chávez felt the New Mexico Tourism Department "objected to [Chávez's] piece because it referenced the plight of refugees along the state's southern border, which wasn't in keeping with the image the department wanted to portray of New Mexico as an enchanted place 'where nothing can go wrong as long as you can have a green chili cheeseburger and we can go skiing'" (Haywood). Chávez is also quoted in the article as saying that the tourism department and its representatives "do not want people to see the other side," which can be interpreted literally, as in the other side of the U.S.-México border, or figuratively, as in the story of migrants and immigrants seeking work and asylum. A person only needs to see one commercial, billboard, or magazine ad with the "New Mexico True" slogan to understand the romanticized image that the New Mexico Tourism Department has created about the state, built upon the same Santa Fe style that Chávez critiqued in the 1980s in *Plaza*. Chávez's truth telling disrupted this message, and the magazine's decision not to publish her essay resulted in a controversy that drew local, national, and international attention, rightfully so.

On February 18, 2020, Chávez published a letter to friends on her Facebook page. She explains the details related to *New Mexico Magazine* pulling her story, as well as the additional fallout. In her letter to her supporters (and maybe the nonsupporters, too), Chávez reveals that the magazine's editor, Alicia Inez Guzmán, resigned from the magazine after the article was pulled. She writes,

> She is the first Chicana Editor EVER at *New Mexico Magazine*, has published over 100 articles and has a Ph.D. She is a native New Mexican who understands and loves our state. It was a great pleasure to work with her as she appreciates the rich history and story of New Mexico with a mature clarity and compassion. She understands exactly what is going on in Southern New Mexico and the U.S./México border. Our article, for it is OURS, reflects a coming together of spirit and mind. I unequivocally ask for the exoneration of this stellar writer and a formal apology. ("Here Is the Story")

In this letter, Chávez calls attention to the pervasive racism and sexism that occurred as a result of her essay, one that similarly highlights the racism and sexism—along with class disparities and human rights violations that occur in the borderlands—that Libros para el Viaje also addresses.

New Mexico Magazine eventually published Chávez's story in the April 2020 issue. In some ways, Libros para el Viaje was able to get more attention because of the brief controversy that the magazine caused, but this was accomplished at a great loss, including the forced resignation of Alicia Inez Guzmán. In the final article, Chávez explains how she has recreated the route of el Camino Real, the Royal Road, where "for centuries, travelers . . . have carried books that retain a power to inspire and to heal" ("Libros"). As she did with her bookstore, la Casa Camino Real, Chávez found another avenue to use storytelling and books to heal the *herida abierta*, the open wound along the U.S.-México border where the first blood was drawn by the Spanish in the sixteenth century and which continues to bleed today.[15] As this brief controversy over the article shows, that wound is still deep, but it has not stopped Chávez from serving the communities impacted by border violence.

THE ENCORE: MUSEO DE LA GENTE

As she continues to work at the behest of the viajeros, Chávez has one final project in the works. Her dream is to create el Museo de la Gente, which she has described as "a cultural resource center that serves to preserve, document and celebrate the story of the Borderlands community in the southwestern United States and northern Mexico" (quoted in Renteria). Surely, there will be a home for Chávez's books, the teatroesque literature, and all her characters. Perhaps each character will have their own room named after them.

Chávez's upbringing in southern New Mexico in a household where her parents identified as either Mexican or Spanish influenced her career as an author. As New Mexico's most prolific playwright and acclaimed Chicana author, Denise Chávez has dedicated her career to writing about the complexity of Nuevomexicano identities in ways that bring characters to life using her teatroesque writing style. Her recent Libros para el Viaje project has channeled her activism into her southern New Mexico borderlands community in a way that represents her true call to service.

NOTES

1.   John Nieto-Phillips refers to New Mexico's Spanish-speaking population as "Nuevomexicanos" (2).

2.   In this essay I choose to follow Chávez's lead and capitalize the word *Culture*, which she says gives it "honor and attention" (*Taco Testimony*, 11). In

A Taco Testimony, Chávez writes about the importance of culture, of which she says, "Culture with a capital C. Culture that doesn't kill, maim, degrade or believe anyone should die that we should live" (12). Conversely, when not used in that way, I lowercase the *c* in the word.

3. Both plays can be found in the Denise Chávez Papers, 1965–1987, at the University of New Mexico Center for Southwest Research and Special Collections in Albuquerque.

4. She has also said in several places that she had pneumonia during the time she wrote some of the stories in *The Last of the Menu Girls*.

5. *The Last of the Menu Girls* was republished by Vintage Books in 2004. Chávez comments briefly about why it took so long to republish the book, saying it was "tied up in litigation for nine years" (*Menu Girls*, xiv). The second printing of the book offers the stories in a new order, which she says is their "true sequencing and moment in time" after, "in their first appearance, they got jumbled up independently of me" (xiv).

6. Chávez won the American Book Award and the Premio Aztlán Literary Prize for *Face of an Angel*. The novel also earned her the Mesilla Valley Writer of the Year Award.

7. See Anzaldúa's *Borderlands/La Frontera*, chapter 3, "Entering into the Serpent." She writes, "*La facultad* is the capacity to see in surface phenomena the meaning of deeper realities, to see the deep structure below the surface. It is an instant 'sensing,' a quick perception arrived at without conscious reading" (60).

8. The term *acto* was coined by Luis Valdez and made famous by el Teatro Campesino. He used the term to refer to short sketches that often portrayed complex issues in a comical light. El Teatro Campesino has notably defined the acto as, basically, a "short skit" performed on "flatbed trucks or union halls" ("Our History"). The acto can be performed with as few as two actors.

9. For more on this, see Chris Wilson's *The Myth of Santa Fe: Creating a Modern Regional Tradition*.

10. For a thorough discussion of the history and significance of the League of United Latin American Citizens, or LULAC, see Cynthia E. Orozco's *No Mexicans, Women, or Dogs Allowed: The Rise of the Mexican American Civil Rights Movement*.

11. See, for example, Norma Alarcón's essay "Traddutora, Traditora: A Paradigmatic Figure of Chicana Feminism."

12. Note the earlier reference where Chávez also called her own mother "kick ass." This is not a coincidence.

13. In the summary of the play, Chávez describes the Madonna who adorns the altar as Nuestra Señora de Leche y Buen Parto; however, the set directions say it is la Virgen de Guadalupe who stands on the chest. Although both representative of the Madonna, there is a notable difference in these two virgins. Nuestra Señora de Leche y Buen Parto is the *virgen* depicted nursing

the infant Christ, whereas Nuestra Señora de Guadalupe is depicted *en cinta*. In other words, the red cord or belt wrapped around her stomach signifies that she is pregnant. Whereas Nuestra Señora de Leche y Buen Parto is commonly used in Florida, where Spanish colonizers established the first shrine to Mary in the Americas, Nuestra Señora de Guadalupe highlights the cultural Catholic practices of women in New Mexico and across the Southwest. It is unclear why the original description says the Madonna is the very "pallid little virgin who's nursing" that Chávez tries to stray away from. Perhaps this is a subconscious representation of her own "evolution of consciousness."

14. Giant Noise took over the New Mexico Tourism Department account in 2020. The firm handles other New Mexico accounts, including Sawmill Market in Albuquerque and Heritage Hotels & Resorts, which alone includes eleven properties and twenty-two bars and restaurants across the state. Additional notable Giant Noise accounts include the H-E-B restaurant chain and Lone Star Brewing Company, among others.

15. My reference to *una herida abierta* comes from Gloria Anzaldúa's *Borderlands/La Frontera: The New Mestiza*, in which she describes the U.S./México border as an open wound, "where the Third World grates up against the first and bleeds" (25).

WORKS CITED

Alarcón, Norma. "Traddutora, Traditora: A Paradigmatic Figure of Chicana Feminism." *The Construction of Gender and Modes of Social Division,* special issue of *Cultural Critique,* no. 13 (Autumn 1989): 57–87.

Aldama, Frederick Luis. *Spilling the Beans in Chicanolandia: Conversations with Writers and Artists.* Austin: University of Texas Press, 2006.

Anzaldúa, Gloria. *Borderlands/La Frontera: The New Mestiza.* 2nd ed. San Francisco: Aunt Lute Books, 1999.

Brown-Guillory, Elizabeth. "Denise Chávez, Chicana Woman Writer Crossing Borders: An Interview." *South Central Review* 16, no. 1 (Spring 1999): 30–43.

Chávez, Denise. "Heat and Rain." In *Breaking Boundaries: Latina Writing and Critical Readings.* Edited by Asunción Horno-Delgado, Eliana Ortega, Nina M. Scott, and Nancy Saporta Sternbach. Amherst: University of Massachussetts Press, 1989, 27–32.

———. "Here Is the Story of the Story. We Must Work Against Censorship No Matter Who We Are and Where We Live." Facebook, February 19, 2020. https://www.facebook.com/permalink.php?story_fbid=2331396797158729&id=100008652936972&__tn__=H-R.

———. *The Last of the Menu Girls.* New York: Vintage Books, 2004.

———. "Libros para el Viaje." *New Mexico Magazine*, April 2020. https://www.newmexico.org/nmmagazine/articles/post/libros-para-el-viaje/.

———. *Novena narrativas y ofrendas nuevomexicanas*. In *Chicana Creativity and Criticism: New Frontiers in American Literature*. Edited by María Herrera-Sobek and Helena María Viramontes. Albuquerque: University of New Mexico Press, 1996, 149–63.

———. Papers, 1965–1987. MSS 361-BC. University of New Mexico Center for Southwest Research and Special Collections, Albuquerque.

———. *Plaza*. In *New Mexico Plays*. Edited by David Richard Jones. Albuquerque: University of New Mexico Press, 1989, 1–17.

———. *A Taco Testimony: Meditations on Family, Food, and Culture*. Tucson: Rio Nuevo Publishers, 2006.

Cobos, Rubén. "Trochimochi." In *A Dictionary of New Mexico and Southern Colorado Spanish*. 2nd ed. Santa Fe: Museum of New Mexico Press, 2003, 230.

De Vore, Alex. "New Mexico True Campaign Refresh Draws Ire." *Santa Fe Reporter*, April 16, 2021. https://www.sfreporter.com/news/2021/04/16/new-mexico-true-campaign-refresh-draws-ire/.

Dunaway, David Richard. "Denise Chávez." *Writing the Southwest*. http://www.unm.edu/~wrtgsw/chavez.html.

Giant Noise (website). https://giantnoise.com/.

Haywood, Phaedra. "Ex-editor of 'New Mexico Magazine' Suing State After She Fought for Article." *Santa Fe New Mexican*, August 6, 2020. https://www.santafenewmexican.com/news/local_news/ex-editor-of-new-mexico-magazine-suing-state-after-she-fought-for-article/article_c7e90f4c-d810–11ea-9f87-c7d2b07ec6a4.html.

Heard, Martha E. "The Theatre of Denise Chávez: Interior Landscapes with *Sabor Nuevomexicano*." *Americas Review* 16, no. 2 (Summer 1988): 83–91.

Herrera, Brian Eugenio. "To Imagine a *Nuevomexicano* Theatre History." In *Theatre and Cartographies of Power: Repositioning the Latina/o Americas*. Edited by Santana Analola and Jimmy A. Noriega Champaign: University of Illinois Press, 2018, 65–73.

Herrera, Spencer R. "New Mexico Triptych: Querencia Etched in Wood, in Media, and in Our Memory." In *Querencia: Reflections on the New Mexico Homeland*. Edited by Vanessa Fonseca-Chávez, Levi Romero, and Spencer R. Herrera. Albuquerque: University of New Mexico Press, 2020, 114–37.

Jones, David Richard. "Brief Introduction to *Plaza* by Denise Chávez." In *New Mexico Plays*. Edited by David Richard Jones. Albuquerque: University of New Mexico Press, 1989, 79–93.

———. Introduction. In *New Mexico Plays*. Edited by David Richard Jones. Albuquerque: University of New Mexico Press, 1989, 1–17.

Keating, AnaLouise, and Marilyn Mehaffy. "Carrying the Message: Denise Chávez on the Politics of Chicana Becoming." *Aztlán: A Journal of Chicano Studies* 26, no. 1 (Spring 2001): 127–56.

Martínez, Marcos. "La Compañía de Teatro de Alburquerque: Community Development Through an Actor-Centered Theater." In *Expressing New Mexico: Nuevomexicano Creativity, Ritual, and Memory*. Edited by Phillip B. Gonzales. Tucson: University of Arizona Press, 2007, 87–114.

Moran, Julio. "My Dream Was to Work at the Dairy Queen." *Los Angeles Times*, November 9, 1994, E1.

Nieto-Phillips, John. *The Language of Blood: The Making of Spanish-American Identity in New Mexico, 1880s-1930s*. Albuquerque: University of New Mexico Press, 2004.

"Our History." El Teatro Campesino (website), 2020. https://elteatrocampesino .com/our-history/.

Pollon, Zelie. "New Mexico Tourism Officials Fight State's Dull Reputation." Reuters, April 16, 2012. https://www.reuters.com/article/usa-tourism-new-mexico -idUSL2E8FGI7K20120417.

Quintana, Alvina. "Orality, Tradition, and Culture: Denise Chavez's *Novena Narrativas* and *The Last of the Menu Girls*." In *Home Girls: Chicana Literary Voices*. Philadelphia: Temple University Press, 1996, 93–111.

Rebolledo, Tey Diana. "*Las Clarividentes*: Chicana Artists and Writers, Creativity, Gender, and Ethnicity." In *Expressing New Mexico: Nuevomexicano Creativity, Ritual, and Memory*. Edited by Phillip B. Gonzales. Tucson: University of Arizona Press, 2007, 141–61.

Rentería, Ramón. "Border Book Festival Ends 20-Year Run, Switches Direction." *El Paso Times*, March 14, 2015.

Unger, Todd. "New Mexico Offers Glimpse of $2 Million Tourism Campaign." KOAT Albuquerque, June 19, 2012. https://www.koat.com/article/new -mexico-offers-glimpse-of-2-million-tourism-campaign-1/5041400#.

Wilson, Chris. *The Myth of Santa Fe: Creating a Modern Regional Tradition*. Albuquerque: University of New Mexico Press, 1997.

CARMEN TAFOLLA

CARMEN TAFOLLA

Evolving the Spirit—Crisis, Oppression, and Survival

JEN YÁÑEZ-ALANIZ

AN INTERESTING rock-art glyph on the exterior surface of Carmen Tafolla's house greets you when you arrive. It was designed by David, a nephew she and her husband, Ernesto Bernal, spiritually adopted as a young boy. Together, David and Tafolla toiled and textured over a boring and predictable pattern of swoops and scallops by carving and chiseling out new details and giving the wall an appearance of an ancient system of petroglyph communication. What was once a common hacienda-style aesthetic would become, in my perspective, an allegory for a language with peculiar depth of energy. This energy in flux, always evolving and always in a state of discovery and invention, seems to spread outwardly from within the surfaces of Tafolla's home. The deeply carved front door, thick with welcome, symbolizes for me a threshold where one's imagination integrates into the world of a story, a poem, a manifesto—the interweaving of a life's experiences fully entangled with an endurance of creation and creativity.

Inside Tafolla's home, one finds a vast representation of art and literature, as well as heirlooms and family artifacts from multiple centuries. These interconnected parts embody a diverse culture and history fortified and enriched throughout many generations. The layered energy alive in these symbols, as Tafolla often reminds her readers and as this critical biographical essay demonstrates through a nonlinear approach,[1] impassions her to create works emanating expressions of strength and reclaiming power beyond adversity. Moreover, as we arrive at Tafolla's most current writing in 2020, three years since she experienced multiple traumas and adaptations to the traumas, her poetry especially will reveal how life's encounters fit into a broader narrative of her experience as she reshapes, reframes, and reassigns empowering language and context to her personal survival.

A painting of a woman draped in a red rebozo in midmotion, a vision of agitation and awakening, hangs prominently in Tafolla's parlor. She exudes a lasting force and illuminates the ghostly presence of *bisabuelas, abuelas, madres, comadres,* and *tías* all scuttling in various directions—stirring, conjuring, and testing the strengths and freedoms not necessarily afforded to them in flesh. This ancestral voice, as Tafolla explains, is a constant echo of inspiration:

> *Escríbalo*, she whispers over my shoulder. . . .
> [She] has been standing there behind me for all these 500 years.
> Her breath is heated, her urgency aging my bones.
> My fingers become . . .
> the soft wind that blows through ceremony. . . .
> I am not alone ("Poetry Around," 10)

This same painting by Catalina Gárate García is published alongside Tafolla's ekphrastic poem "Mujeres del rebozo rojo"[2] (*Rebozos*, 2). In the poem, Tafolla, using poignant expression, creates a vision of revolution through the undulating movement of a woman's body beneath the soft flow of the red rebozo "pulling . . . / pushing . . . /arching . . ." The words "only to be, and / to become" give light to the central theme of awakening in both painting and poem, a theme that will resonate throughout this exploration of transformation and voice empowerment through the collective identities of Tafolla's characters.

In that same vein of rooted existence and ethereal energy, beyond the parlor and across the threshold of the master bedroom endures a discernible memory of Carmen's late husband, Ernesto, a six-foot-tall man with thick, curly hair, muscles pulsing through swarthy skin and a velvet laughter delightful enough to curve the spine in halting pleasure. This love stands watchful. Offering a warmth to comfort through the passion brought in dreams, he wakes her at bewitching hours to scribble of love, sex, and hope, the desires he made her promise to seek and encounter beyond his death. This imagery was inspired by a conversation about the remembrance of Tafolla's husband and the dreams she dreams of him coupled with the poem "hombre de raza cósmica." It was especially impactful as I was privy to several drafts of her searching for the words capable of encapsulating his physical and spiritual memory:

> I gulp down your dreams
> and feel them in the chubasco rapids of my veins
> Wild sorrel mustangs dance their sinew
> across your chest, inside your arms
> inside each breath that sings of sunrise, tierra, libertad
> Mexican centuries dance like liquid mercury
> surfacing across your skin   un desfile de raza cósmica (*Boundless*, 235)

In the space of fifteen months, between May 29, 2016, and September 1, 2017, Tafolla suffered the "Trinity of Deaths"(as she chooses to refer to this period), the loss of her three closest beloveds: soulmate and corevolutionary Ernesto Bernal; mother and coconspirator María Duarte Tafolla; and her brother-in-law, Father Eddie Bernal, whom she always called "Baby Brother." Her children also suffered harsh effects from these deaths. To date, her youngest child struggles with agoraphobia caused by the multiple traumas of bereavement. Her oldest child draws deeper into schizophrenia and lifelong depression. Her middle and only biological child offers support in the often-challenging spaces of Tafolla's now lone parenthood, a place in relationship with his mother where he too is in the process of healing from the chaotic trauma of losing so much. Through it all, Tafolla has offered a steadfast resilience as mother, author, educator, and community activist.

As Tafolla revealed to me, "The death of a soulmate, especially, was a defining and devastating loss" ("Interview"). The relationship had gone beyond a mere partnership in love, family, sexual, and professional terms: it had become a permanent spiritual connection. In her poem "Even the Scars . . . ," the poet's voice allows the reader entry to a mature love by engaging the senses of touch, sight, and movement within spaces of mending and tension. This union is so aligned that even the memory of a dream and the identity of the dreamer lie in question:

> dreams one of us dreamed, the other told
> both forgot which one it was,
> the way the mattress curves into place
> without being asked, the way my hand
> follows your shoulder down the stairs,
> a better banister for balance
> in the avalanche of life (*New and Selected*, 9)

The poem speaks to the mapping of a love in relationship over many years by invoking a sense of malleability, flexibility, and durability: "Everything melted, molded, softened / to the challenge of a new world." The verses parallel the healing scars that arise from some of life's most insurmountable junctures. Carmen emphatically said to me, "This level of depth in a relationship can take anything" ("Interview"), reiterating what she has written in her poetry:

> yes, even the scars
> change, soften, stretch
> and curve to fit
> together. (*New and Selected*, 9)

This foundational declaration of deep love remains with Tafolla beyond the departure of her beloved, but the strain of her husband's passing will have a challenging effect on her sensibilities as she attempts to open herself up to a promise she made to him—"that she would not bury herself with his death, that she would not throw herself onto the pyre" ("Interview").[3] In the following excerpt, Tafolla reminds us of the power and necessity of voice expression within the context of her writing: "How can I possibly survive if I DON'T write? How can ANY of us survive, if these words do not build the houses of reality around us? If they do not help us understand the multiple dimensions behind the tragedies and victories and injustices of life?" ("It Gets Crazy," 3).

In 2012, Tafolla was diagnosed with breast cancer. Though Tafolla has always addressed the themes of suffering, persevering, and surviving within her expansive body of work, many of her writings exploring what she refers to as that "hurricaned" time period of cancer, the mastectomy, her role as a "cancer veteran," and the "Trinity of Deaths" remain in stacks of papers and handwritten journals, polished but percolating patiently along with some of her unfinished works—her scurrying utterances found clutched to the edges of crumpled receipts, scratched onto torn envelopes, and etched into the surfaces of folders, book covers, and small boxes piling up on top of her desk. Though seemingly tiny disconnected scribbles, these words are in fact the sturdy branches of a burgeoning proclamation of poetic verse yet to be fully integrated into a published collection.

DEFINING THAT "HURRICANED" TIME: BEFORE AND DURING

Within the years of 2012–2014 and 2015–2016, Tafolla held two back-to-back positions as San Antonio's inaugural poet laureate and as Texas poet laureate. Tafolla's hope was to increase literacy by providing culturally relevant resources and to inspire an appreciation of culturally diverse voices. In her two-year tenure as San Antonio poet laureate, Tafolla shared and read poetry at over three hundred events, marking her commitment of bringing communities together to celebrate and share through poetry while simultaneously undergoing chemo for breast cancer and teaching classes as a professor of bicultural and bilingual studies at the University of Texas at San Antonio. Becoming the Texas Poet Laureate shortly thereafter, and concerned for the little exposure most students in low-income districts had to literature, she worked to raise funds to allow her to visit, present workshops, and gift poetry books to twenty-two of the most impoverished schools throughout Texas. She accomplished this while navigating the challenges of caring for her ninety-four-year-old mother and her husband, who had begun a rapid decline into Parkinson's disease ("Interview").

LANGUAGE REBELLIONS AND SPIRITUAL FORAYS

In Tafolla's most recent collection of poetry, *Carmen Tafolla: New and Selected Poems*, as well as in *This River Here*, poems began to surface expressing her awareness of the fragility of life, her dealings with cancer, and, later, her grief at the inevitability of losing her spiritual partner. Over the decades, Tafolla has exhibited characteristics in her *obra* exploring the human condition in all of its realities, including death, always allowing her poet's voice to travel profoundly toward, across, in between, beneath, and beyond spaces through transitive imagery, as demonstrated in the poem "Revision—2004":

> I am growing closer to my skeleton
> on more acquainted terms with my death
> I am dipping playful toes in those
> murky waters of a river border
> which I might be tempted to—yes,
> cross, illegally, just for a while. (*New and Selected*, 19)

Tafolla expresses a human experience of the journey toward death with collocations demonstrating intimacy and familiarity, such as "growing closer" and "acquainted terms." Yet she also employs cautionary language: "murky waters" and "cross, illegally." She takes control of her poetic expression by mixing, meshing, connecting, and disconnecting—overtures of a living sensory experience, spiritual forays into the realm of the dead, and a Carmen-esque use of translanguaging, writing beyond monolingual limitations and accessing one's full linguistic repertoire. Tafolla layers language and creates a fluid, boundless, and dynamic experience within the words of her poetry that continue in this excerpt from "Revision—2004":

> *Indocumentada, sin papeles,*
> just un *capricho, un antojito*
> just to visit, *convivir,*
> old family, friends,
> living on the other side. (19)

This characteristic of Tafolla's work, the arrogant claiming of the right to simultaneously inhabit languages, cultures, nations, spiritual spheres, and even time periods, has been evidenced in elaborate analysis. In a chapter titled "Mouthing Off: Polyglossia and Radical Mestizaje" in his book *Movements in Chicano Poetry*, Rafael Pérez-Torres, in relation to Tafolla's work, remarks that the Chicanx voice and body survive by including, not separating, the self from new elements of identity.[4] Employing cross-cultural language adds power and growth (220). The nature of the exploration in and out of the realm of the living through playful language and sound-making mechanisms demonstrates Tafolla's curious yet celebratory approach to death and ongoing connection. She light-heartedly wonders

who will go first . . .
cross over splashing loudly,
clanking femur and humerus together,
clavicle and scapula tinkling thinly. (*New and Selected*, 19)

While seeming to be comfortable connecting with death, in altruistic Tafolla form, she moves into activism by giving voice to the realities persistent and eminent in a wider global context, such as the ongoing crises at the border. The intermingled analogy with death's steel-wall dangers and the unknowns of reaching and interacting with "the other side" are evident in these lines: "I realize the risks / feel the deep currents / receding undertows." And though caution persists in "crossing over" from the onset, the narrator plays with the possibility of death nearly gleefully throughout. However, the language within this final excerpt of "Revision—2004" echoes that no border or steel wall—no limit to where one can go—exists, even "*sin papeles*," legal documentation to travel freely.

I am dipping playful toes in those
murky waters of a river border
which I might be tempted to—yes,
cross, illegally, just for a while. (19)

FIGHTING INJUSTICES AND ANTI-SPANISH-LANGUAGE HYPOCRISIES

Rebellion against restrictions and nonpermeable borders between languages, cultures, and national proprieties are ongoing themes in Tafolla's work dating back to 1975 with her publication in *Caracol*, a San Antonio arts and politics journal, twenty-five cents an issue, published during Texas's Chicano literary Renaissance. Her poems also appear in 1976 in a book she co-authored with Cecilio García-Camarillo and Reyes Cárdenas, *Get Your Tortillas Together*. In both publications, she employs the obstinate crossing of language boundaries in cultural protest in pieces like "Los Corts (5 Voices)" and "Aullido eterno." A maturation of these linguistic rebellions would be visible thirty years later in "Both Sides of the Border," where she summarizes her insistent attitude:

> that deep delicious desire to run on two tracks—at the same time,
>   jump back
> and forth. . . .
>
> wound up with the freeness—sin zapatos
> without límites (*This River*, 40)

This period, as Tafolla recalls, actually starting in 1973, when she assumed the directorship of the Center for Mexican-American Studies at Texas Lutheran University, also marks her involvement with García-Camarillo (founder of *Caracol* and *Magazín*, early Chicano periodicals in San Antonio) and Cárdenas as well as Vangie Vigil, Max Martínez, Tomás Rivera, César Martínez, and Angela de Hoyos in the artist-activist branch of San Antonio's Chicano Movement. Her participation in the second national Festival Flor y Canto in Austin in 1975 would broaden her Chicano Movement literary community to include Inés Hernández-Ávila, Alurista, Lalo Delgado, Rolando Hinojosa, Estela Portillo-Trambley, Juan Felipe Herrera, and many others. Tafolla would go on to say, "What was for Chicanos and their barrios an earth-shaking movimiento redefining their worth and their art, shined an international light on their seething protest against linguistic, cultural, and societal oppression." For Tafolla, the Chicano literary movement touched on her community's centuries-long awareness of prejudice against Mexican Americans.

I submit that Tafolla's devotion to social justice through language, primary and secondary education, and academia is pronounced and clearly evident in her work. According to Tafolla, the artist

> is the prophet of society, in the Old Testament sense of the word prophet, that is—NOT a magic, crystal-ball predictor of future prophecies, but a clear-eyed and sensitive SEE-er of the present, someone who can see what is going on all around us and declare or denounce it openly. . . . This is the natural purpose of art—to express and reflect the human condition. If we even PRETEND to be non-political, to exclude social issues from our work, then we are limiting and insulating our art AWAY from the human condition that surrounds us, and thereby being untrue to our art. . . . This does not mean that every artistic creation has an explicit connection with current social issues, but the totality of our art has to do with every aspect of our human existence, including the political struggle against injustice, and the activism that gives solidity to our stated beliefs. ("Poetry Around Us")

This powerful assertion echoes Tafolla's extensive representation of her art as activism and of herself as a lifelong observer of cultural dynamics within the framework of sociopolitical oppression. She is known for exposing injustice in relation to race, class, and gender through materials, conversations, readings, and more than a thousand dramatic performances since 1990, all capable of engaging the human imagination through language rich in imagery: a true multisensory experience. Tafolla uses an overlapping, intertwining layering to construct power structures for power functions.

EARLY EDUCATION, PUBLICATION, AND LITERARY REVOLUTION

In 1972 Tafolla embarked on what she has described as "the best job I ever had." She tells about her need for a summer job to pay for textbooks for graduate classes. With only a three-month window between graduating with her BA in May and returning for graduate study in September 1983, the not yet twenty-one-year-old Tafolla followed up on every job opening she could find. She received a call that would lead her to Father Edmundo Rodríguez at San Antonio's Our Lady of Guadalupe Church, a former Jesuit provincial who in 1969 had cofounded PADRES (Padres Asociados para Derechos Religiosos, Educativos y Sociales), the national activist Chicano priests' organization.[5] Father Rodríguez hired her to collect the oral histories of the people living in the Westside barrios of San Antonio. The folklore she collected would not only be published by Father Rodríguez in a small monograph entitled *Herencia de oro*, but perhaps more significantly, it became the basis for many of the characters in Tafolla's works. Her interviews resulted in over fifty recorded tapes and inspired a common theme often included in her work, the portrayal of female figures succeeding, despite challenging conditions, by reclaiming voice and self-empowerment. These female characters of Westside San Antonio, through humor, humility, pain, and utterance, became champions of hope blasting through pages of books and performances.

"WHEN I DREAM DREAMS . . ."

Tafolla was witness to and directly experienced language discrimination as a young girl growing up on the Westside of San Antonio, where she was born on July 29, 1951. The speaking of foreign languages on school grounds was outlawed by the state of Texas from 1917 until 1969, the year Tafolla graduated from high school. Tafolla explained that language "was re-focused socially and in school institutions to punish Mexican-American children for speaking any Spanish words, or even for the correct Spanish pronunciation of their own names." This practice created a defective learning environment where energy was wasted on paddling and humiliating children and the logical result became a high dropout/pushout rate (*Sonnets to Human Beings*, 240–42).

For Tafolla, this experience began in first grade and reached its most comical climax in the scolding she received in the hallway from a principal who overheard her Tex-Mex conversation with two friends and bellowed over her shoulder, "You'll never get to high school speaking

Spanish!" Later in the office, as Tafolla recounts, he reminded her that she had potential "to make it all the way to high school." Tafolla recalls his biting implication that she might only "make it" to high school but not reach graduation. In the same breath, she says that even in the best of circumstances, children are aware they are not in charge, no matter what is said to them, no matter to what extent they may be part of a ruling class. And this reality of children's disempowerment becomes even more emphatic when the community to which they belong is disenfranchised economically, linguistically, socially, and culturally. resulting in complex psychological and social impacts ("Interview").

Tafolla's poem "And When I Dream Dreams . . ." speaks to the "injustices and anti-Spanish-language hypocrisies" of the education system in rich and defiant form, exposing the challenges she and her classmates faced:

> when I dream dreams,
> *I dream of YOU,*
> *Rhodes Jr. School*
> and the lockers of our minds
> that were always jammed stuck
> or that always hung open
> and would never close (*Curandera*, 34)

Tafolla's use of the words "jammed," "stuck," and "hung open" reveal the disempowerment experienced in the throes of a racist and discriminatory environment. Moreover, the next three lines lay open the objectification of children by further dehumanizing them as traffic markers: Tafolla's intention was to underline the institutionalized demeaning of the entire student body:

> Hall guards from among us,
> human traffic markers, bumps on the road
> between the lanes. (34)

An antihomage to those words said to Tafolla by the principal of Rhodes Junior High School so long ago forever resonates in the following stanza:

You'll never get to high school
speakin' Spanish, I was told
nice of them, they thought, to not report me,
breakin' state law, school law, speakin' dirty
(speakin' Spanish) (34)

Other works published in *Curandera*[6] fearlessly mix and fuse English with Spanish into a code-switched "super-language"[7] and create new forms of poetry, which Tafolla calls "voice poetry" and describes as dramatic monologues by barrio characters in a spoken word context. "Los Corts 3 (la pachuquita)" is an important piece narrated by a pachuca and voice performed and published during a time when the pachuco culture[8] was represented only by male figures. A key scene in the poem echoes the irony Tafolla often exposes in her work: that of institutions placing more value on school property than on humans, as conveyed in the words strung together by la pachuca as she readies herself for a fight:

Ajá, y a ver a quien más juntamos, porque La Silvia
se junta con todas esas gordonas feotas
que tan pero perras para pelear.
Sí, en las showers, pa que no vea la Miss Hensley,
porque no le gusta que peleamos
en el gym floor. (10)

Beyond and between the words are powerful proclamations stated by characters taking agency over systems of despair. The impact of these words was not lost on Mexican American students nation-wide. Tafolla recalls a comment from then-librarian Oralia Garza de Cortés ("Interview") regarding the San Antonio Public Library having to keep its copies of *Curandera* in the reserved section because so many young Mexican American students had "clutched" it to their chests, taken it home, and never returned it. A favorite in classrooms throughout the Southwest, thirty years later *Curandera* was out-lawed by the Arizona State Board of Education, after the state passed a law in 2010 effectively banning the teaching of ethnic studies and the Tucson Unified School District (TUSD) used it to shut down its high school Mexican American Studies program (MAS) in 2012. To date, the nonprofit Librotraficante maintains a list of books removed from TUSD curriculum because of the MAS program ban (Simón, 2017). That very year, 2012, as Tafolla describes it, was when "I was simultaneously being laureled by the city of San Antonio, banned by the state of Arizona, and buoyed 'up' by the support of a San Antonio community enthused to have its first city poet laureate" ("Banned, Buoyed").

Many of Tafolla's poems are spoken in the voice of the student and document the injustices and other reasons Mexican American students led protests, walkouts, and joined the Chicano Movement. In her essay "Semillas," published in the anthology *Cantos al sexto sol*, Tafolla reflected on the spirit of the Chicano Movement as a time of emboldened strength in the face of racism and discrimination. It was a time for reclamation and for building up a new identity in a fight for social and political empowerment: "Our language and our culture were considered cheap, embarrassing, a dirty joke, or more often, non-existent; that our people's lives and health and education and rights were 'not important'—dawning in the midst of all this sufrimiento was a small cluster of bright miracle rays of possibility" (García-Camarillo, Rodríguez, and Gonzales, xix). El Movimiento Chicano was a time for voice expression and tongue revolution to emerge, heal, expand, and explore beyond constraints, a time to step beyond the subjugation of oppression. It was a time to imagine the upward and outward movement of the Chicanx into all industries, to create representation of cultural identity within all spaces. Tafolla went on to defiantly use Spanish and English in a translanguaging justice-oriented way to recreate skillful, courageous language blasts of hybrid poetry, prose, screenplays,[9] and spoken word works to represent the Chicanx cultural experience around her through daring portraiture and narration.

Tafolla's personal stance against the entire system was to charge on despite the harsh and humiliating censure she experienced. She not only "attended" high school, but as the poet's voice in "And When I Dream Dreams . . ." goes on to claim, "I graduated / from you." And the final two lines, "—how I wish my dreams / had graduated too," are a remembrance of silenced tongues and a defective education system that acted against many.

As the poem proclaims, after graduating high school, Carmen did go on to earn her BA, as well as her MA from Austin College and a PhD from the University of Texas at Austin. And as she continued to forge forward in her roles as author and activist, she received myriad awards and accolades over the years, as documented on Tafolla's official website. Her awards include a 1987 Chicano Literary Award from the University of California, Irvine, for *Sonnets to Human Beings and Other Selected Works*, the Américas Award for best children's book writing, five International Latino Books Awards, two Tomás Rivera book awards, and a Charlotte Zolotow Award. She received the Art of Peace Award from St. Mary's University in 1999 for promoting human understanding, peace, and justice. Her 2008 book, *That's Not Fair! Emma Tenayuca's Struggle for Justice*, was listed as a best children's book in *Críticas Magazine* (Medrano and Rodrigues, 89).

Additionally, Tafolla said that a pivotal moment for her was receiving the affirmation of bestselling author Alex Haley, author of the groundbreaking historical novel *Roots*, who in 1984 called her "a world class writer." In this same interview, she tells me that Rigoberto González, in a review published on June 29, 2008, in the *El Paso Times*, described her as "the Zora Neale Hurston of the Chicano-Mexicano Community" ("Interview").

JUDGE, JURY, CHURCH, AND BLESSING: THE LIBERATION OF GENDER IDENTITY

Resistance and empowerment in Tafolla's work has always been evident in her speaking against the heavily weighted realities of feminine truths. Using these means, Tafolla helped expose the oppressive, male-dominant Chicano power structures that were alive within broader national racial intolerances. She created the living female characters of her mind because of a need to liberate the subconscious from behaviors and expectations imposed (and that continue to be imposed) on women and girls. Tafolla took on a societal history of silence that she herself experienced or witnessed from her childhood home to far-reaching global spaces—silence on the violations of war, rape, neglect, fist, and the muzzle of oppression. She spun narratives and provided voice by proxy through characters who, establishing authority unto themselves, served as a valuable tool of resistance and power, as emphasized by Teresa Córdova: "The act of deconstructing and reconstructing Chicana images is a subversive move against years of ideological mistreatment. What Chicanas speak is a function of their experiences. To speak about those experiences is to find themselves in opposition with those that would define them otherwise. The result, as evident in the writings of Chicana feminists, is an identity of opposition" (382).

In 1985, Tafolla, already a mother and an associate professor at California State University, Fresno, experienced firsthand the injustices of a system biased against women, people of color, and most especially women of color. She was inspired to pen a "mythical no- nonsense super-shero" named Porfiria ("Interview"). The poem "Porfiria," published in *"Sonnets to Human Beings" and Other Selected Works* (18–20), is loaded with explosive, uncensored, and seemingly superfluous language:

Porfiria doesn't exist
but if she did
she'd say "¡Que se chingue Reagan!"
    "¡Rómpenles el borlote!"
    y "Tráigame una cerveza, Carlos." (18)

It is arresting that Porfiria is introduced within a space of nonexistence but contextualized within a capacity for creation and expansion. Porfiria's unveiling immediately decimates a culture of voice silence enforced by a history of the defeminized. Her tone is demanding, loud, foul, considered crude and unladylike. The next few lines describe an army of both men and women under her command as Porfiria now exists as an actual historical figure, Mexican revolutionary Colonel Carmen Robles.[10] Tafolla assigns her words force and ferocity through stealthy grit, her teeth locked down on a "cigar" as she seethes, "Ya ha comenza'o / la revolución" (19). Tafolla, through Porfiria, with one foot on the neck of patriarchy ("mythical no-nonsense super-shero"), brings down the mandates against feminine ability through Porfiria's war-cry: The revolution has begun!

Porfiria, in the full poem, represents a collective voice, an intersectionality of culture, class, gender, and sexuality, depicted by many personas. She pushes back against sociopolitical traditions dominated by the masculine, and Tafolla draws her readers to rally behind Porfiria. But, in fact, "Porfiria doesn't exist," though we are reminded—implored—to

> take a picture
> invent a number
> sign a declaration
> for her
> even if it has to be
> with our very own
> names.[11] (20)

Tafolla's tone in the next poem in *Sonnets to Human Beings* remains crucial to the ongoing theme of voice empowerment and again indicates a structuring centered around recovery of self. "La Malinche"[12] is a poetic reconstructed history of rape as an attempted annihilation against a people and the powerful assertion by an Indigenous female figure of her desired context and envisioned position within this conquest. In reality, well-researched evidence indicates that complicated power situations led to the Spanish conquest of Mexico, including but not limited to a revolt by regional Indigenous minorities against an overbearing Aztec empire and Malinche's linguistic and diplomatic skills in her role as Hernán Cortés's interpreter. In male-dominated history, she would later be defined as a traitor. Other major factors in the Spanish conquest of the Aztec empire included rampant disease, genocidal practices, and subsequent enslavement (Candelaria, 3).

In Tafolla's poem, the character of Malinche assigns herself agency. She rejects the identity of traitor and abhors the image of victim. She increases her knowledge of languages from two to at least four, employing what little power an enslaved Indigenous woman would have been given. She becomes a mighty force:

> And yes—I helped you—
> (against Emperor Moctezuma Xocoyotzín himself!)
> They could not imagine me dealing on a level with you—(69)

Instead of history assigning Malinche intelligence, capability, and keenness, she has been presented as the victim of rape, dispensable. However, Tafolla's Malinche speculates beyond Cortés and the Europeans:

> You cried broken tears the night you saw your destruction.
> My homeland ached within me
> (*but I saw another!*) (69)

Through Tafolla's inventive stroke, la Malinche proclaims, "I was immortalized! Chingada!" As analyzed by Cordelia Candelaria, "Malinche's cry issues from gut level to replace the violated, passive flesh of the old Malinche with the visionary and prophetic greatness of the new" (3):

> I saw a dream
> and I reached it.
> *Another world* . . .
> La raza.
> la raaaaaaa-zaaaaa . . . (70)

The word *raza*, commonly used to designate the mestizo people of the Americas, becomes the chosen meaning for Malinche's existence, as she gains skill in her ability to fuse two cultures into one.

Much like Malinche, Tafolla's protagonist in "19 años" (also in *Sonnets to Human Beings*) seeks to claim power despite her circumstance. A high school dropout at fourteen is subsequently raped and experiences a miscarriage; she becomes a heart-shielded prostitute by the age of nineteen. Tafolla presents the nineteen-year-old as displaying a necessary "self-ascribed" virtue in her womanhood, as expressed in her indignant tone when she speaks of the more "acceptable" societal forms of prostitution:

> Prostitutas elegantes, prostitutas respetadas,
> prostitutas de prestigio, prostitutas de dinero—
> presidentas de prostitutas, reinas de prostitutas
> y toda la alta Sociedad (105)

The protagonist insists that those "prostitutas respetadas," those "respectable married women," sell their lives for a price, with marriage represented as a transfer of property from father to husband. She regards them as flesh commodity. She, however, claims the ability to maintain ultimate control of herself:

yo tengo el control final.
Por tanto que me chingan de afuera,
no me pueden chingar el corazón (105)

In her hardness, she proclaims that despite her body getting fucked from the outside, her heart is protected. The protagonist restructures herself beyond rage and vulnerability in response to the extreme trauma of rape and wound inflicted on her. Her language demonstrates the human capacity to create a spirit that moves toward endurance and further speaks to the undercurrent of Tafolla's own battle cry within her work, as reiterated in our interview and as I have heard her say on countless occasions: "CLAIM your Power!" In her quest, Tafolla, through the voice of the nineteen-year-old, dismantles, reconstructs, and repatriates blame to where it belongs.

Tafolla's high standards for social justice themes in her work are reflected throughout her personal life. She married Ernesto Bernal, a respected scholar and education expert, in 1979, at the peak of her involvement developing awareness training workshops for sexism and racism. She and Ernesto made a commitment that theirs would be as nonsexist a marriage as possible. In her writing, as well as in her performances and speeches, Tafolla's Chicana feminism continued to disseminate new models steeped in Chicanx cultural context. Perhaps nowhere is this more evident than in the short story collection *The Holy Tortilla and a Pot of Beans*,[13] where, in numerous ways and instances, she declares, "I'm the judge. I'm the jury. I'm the church. And I'm giving ME a full blessing,"(80) a quote from "How I Got into Big Trouble and the Mistakes I Made, in Increasing Order of Importance." Tafolla also brings her Chicanx feminist sensibility to bear as she depicts the Chicano leaders' reactions to her attending the all-male *tardeada* portrayed in the story "You Don't Know Marta," which she wrote in reflection to this actual event. Tafolla and her husband, newcomers to Austin, Texas, at the time, mistakenly showed up to the tardeada, which scandalized those present. She explained to me that the publication of the story was perhaps more scandalizing ("Interview").

EMPOWERING EVOLUTION

In further exploration of how Tafolla's use of voice consoles and empowers through invention and evolution, let us look at "October 21st, 9 p.m." (*Sonnets*, 2), where the poet leads us into a transition of tone from bold, brusque, and commanding to witty, intimate, and impassioned. She does this through the attitude of the "ripe autumn night" personified as a woman:

No way she's gonna dress up soft, light, sophisticated
                      and polite
when she's really sharply naked, lustily growin'
at the middle, and with every single
freckle of a star
showin' clear through

. . . so intimate and revealing is that "freckle of a star" that the narrator flaunts with confidence, "showin' clear through." And yet, still the fall continues to grow larger in her sexuality and freedom, and she further spreads and exudes sensuality:

. . . breathin' October-like—
                    shivery and ripe,
late harvest of a lady,
        no springtime gentle flower

Seasons in general symbolize the cycles of life through renewals and transformations. Fall in particular has lived a full breadth of effort, and this "late harvest of a lady" has relinquished the inexperienced "springtime gentle lady" she was. Perhaps the then-thirty-two-year-old Tafolla foreshadowed the power and sensuality of her older self, and that she would continue to be a desiring sexual human throughout the decades of her marriage to her beloved Ernesto. Perhaps she further speculated about a capable and energetic sexuality even beyond Ernesto's death. However, she never anticipated the perils of grieving a severed breast, separation by death from her husband, and encountering digital courtship in a pandemic world.

In 2012, upon being diagnosed with breast cancer, Tafolla began to face the possibility of a mastectomy. She attempted to avoid chemotherapy and surgery in favor of alternative health treatments for five months, but as the tumor grew to huge proportions, she began chemotherapy, and five months into the chemotherapy, as a mastectomy became more probable, she began to envision her right breast as an eternal, glowing, etheric presence on the right side of her chest. The poem "How Will We Say Goodbye?" (*Critical Latina*, 5–6) takes the reader through a resistance of all the cultural history placing value solely on the female flesh. The speaker reclaims the body by issuing transformative language to the reconstructing of body image beyond the physical world:

> Will I enshrine you, redefined by scars, transformed
> to blessed icon of warrior shield, survival's mark on me?
> A shriveled dove wing shyly curled into the heart,
> broken from the beautymold of standards and
> conventions, of healthy twin, of matching anything? (5)

The speaker assigns a duality of physical imagery to the space of the chest with the phrases "warrior shield" and "shriveled dove wing." The lines "broken from the beautymold of standards and / conventions, of healthy twin, of matching anything?" suggest a breaking away from assigned masculine and feminine physical attributes and norms. In the following lines, the narrator uses pre-Columbian mythology to create images of strength in nonstereotypic and nongendered transcension:

> a brave duality emerging from your presence,
> as I rise like Aztec warrior rising with the sun
> symbol of life-death, soft-strong, mother-father
> Ometecuhtli and Omecihuatl, One. (5–6)

Ometeotl is the name of the dual male-female god Ometecutli/Ome-cihuatl in Aztec mythology. A primary characteristic of Ometeotl is the combination of genders and the continuity of sexual and gender unity. Identification with the concept of Ometeotl, according to Susana Matallana-Peláez, is the "privileging of balanced movement and transformation over the fixation of states of being as a way of achieving viable and long-lasting cosmic and social equilibrium [and] underpinned sexual and gender architecture in the Americas" (386).

This spiritual reconstructing of her physical body for Tafolla would extend far beyond reclaiming power in the face of losing the right breast. As Ernesto's condition with Parkinson's simultaneously deteriorated, Tafolla found more and more she would have to continue without him. She was in effect evolving and building a new narrative of self.

Because of a shared ideology contrary to patriarchal tradition, she and her husband were able to move toward a marriage in opposition to the world around them, where friends and families were being limited or destroyed by traditional sex roles and expectations. Tafolla's was a marriage of communication, of vigilance of balance, a simultaneous commitment to cultural, gender, and linguistic equalities, mutual respect, romance, and passion.

Perhaps this very deep intimacy is why Tafolla remained spiritually in tune with her husband as he began to lose his executive functions, voice, and ability to talk. The imagery in her poem "Losing You" (*New and Selected*, 17) is centralized around the speaker losing a connection to a great love: "the lilt of a song disappears / a word lost here, a memory there." The poet's tone is one of sadness and awareness of a parting, as evidenced by the use of the words "lilt" and "lost." However, the narrator demonstrates a recognition of love within the despair by juxtaposing clarity with darkness:

your love
still clear as crystal
sparkles through the grey black clouds.

In the last stanza, despite the speaker's own anguish, she compares the barrier to connection, to a red balloon losing helium from one tiny "pinprick" and floating up into the sky, slowly releasing a new destiny, a great adventure for the ailing loved one,

> to which I
> no longer
> have access.

This poignantly purposed reclaiming of a new narrative for the loved one represents an act of selflessness in the face of turmoil.

After Ernesto's death on September 1, 2017, she faced the devastating reality of a separation from her husband's physical being forever. In her process of mourning, she wrote poems that expressed this overwhelming grief. In the poem "For You I'll Fly," (*Healing*, 89) the narrator uses imagery of a home and structures within a home in the process of breaking or in disrepair to illustrate the deterioration experienced over time by physical bodies.

> The motors burn out
> first the fan and then the garbage disposal. . . .
> . . . .
> The only two burners still lighting weakly
> on the stovetop flicker at me.

The narrator goes on to describe the toll taken on them and amplifies the situation through word repetition:

> Things fall apart
> . . . .
> as crisis after crisis beats us down.
> Deaths and Close-to-deaths
> Loss and Deeper loss.

The next lines describe the loved one's physical state as death becomes imminent:

> You can no longer swallow,
> You reach a hand of bones . . .
> [to] carry the message as softly as you can . . .

Tafolla's hard work served as a transcending space for change and survival despite the coinciding separation by death from her three closest companions, especially Ernesto, coupled with an avalanche of tremors and aftereffects experienced in the family. She continued teaching until her 2019 retirement from the Department of Bicultural-Bilingual Studies at the University of Texas at San Antonio and was subsequently appointed professor emeritus. She remained committed to her writing and other projects; among the works she has drafted but not yet submitted for publication are a biography of the civil rights activist Emma Tenayuca, *The Comadres of Cancer, Dancing with Death, The Prince of Chocolate*, and a memoir written in the late 1980s through early 1990s. Three books have recently been published—*Arte del Pueblo: The Outdoor Public Art of San Antonio, The Last Butterfly/La última mariposa* (cowritten with Regina Moya), and *I'll Always Come Back to You*—and a fourth, *Warrior Girl*, a middle-grade novel in verse written during the COVID-19 shutdown of April 2020 and acquired by Penguin Books in a worldwide pre-empt soon after, is scheduled for publication in 2023.

After nearly three years and involvement in countless projects across San Antonio, including her role as president of the Texas Institute of Letters and the coorganizer of a poetry and conversation event titled "Loving, Grieving, and Surviving: Chicanas Read the Poetry of Healing," Tafolla began to explore the possibility of mature dating in an age of digital courtship. This reawakened traumas interwoven within her body, sexuality, and history, but it also ignited Tafolla's ability to create a new world of resistance within this new individual experience of feminist struggle marked by a personal history against a culture of sexism, racism, and oppression. Her poem "Spit It on the Wind" (*Critical Latina*, 15–16) draws on Tafolla's grandmother's rape and her great-grandmother's rape, memories whispered from a long family tradition of story keeping, where identity and power attested to the strength built from struggles that were conquered before her.

The subtitle of the poem, "a probing conversation between the 67-year-old widow and the 70-year-old plumber" (15), contextualizes around a disturbing experience between the speaker and a casual acquaintance visiting the house. The narrator takes the reader beyond the white privilege language of the first line, "he says he doesn't mind Mexican maids," and delves deeper into his ideology of race superiority.

The plumber tells how his elderly and ill father fell in love with and married the Mexican maid who took care of him,

> *Even though my two brothers threw a fit*
> *I told'em, Well, do YOU want*
> *to take care of Dad?* (15)

The three lines that follow reveal that the wife later got cancer and the plumber called on her daughters to take her back to Mexico now that she was no longer of use to him. The poem opens powerfully by signifying his complete disregard for the woman's life, her relationship with his father, and her ailing condition, hence disposability. The next stanza makes clearer his racist attitude by juxtaposing his disapproval of a Black athlete choosing to wear cornrows with his pride in an image of his own sons:

> *Never DID like Kawhi. Ugly Cornrows! Why can't he just act Normal?*
> shows me pictures of his two pink-cheeked sons
> close crewcuts, bushy-big Duck-Dynasty beards. (15)

By the use of the word "normal" and her description of his earlier behaviors against the Mexican maid/wife, the narrator further amplifies a distinction between what the plumber considers acceptable and what is not. He continues driving racial and gender superiority throughout the conversation.

The narrator goes on to understand his insinuating that he doesn't mind a Mexican taking care of him. At this point he arrogantly puts his arm around her, coming into the speaker's bodily space without seeking her consent, an action that instantly triggers her memories:

> My mind flashes—corn rows and
> bushy-big beards bossing plantations . . .
> jumps to horrified 14-year-old maid,
> madre de mi Abuelita, as El Dueño rapes her;
> drags in slow motion to a 13-year-old maid,
> my other Gramma crying, kicking, alma dying
> as the youngest brother of the household tears her clothes off (15)

These lines speak to a harsh truth around a persistent culture of normalized gender-based violence within the male-dominant areas of political, economic, and social structures. This framework drives the history of violence against women and is highly common between female low-status domestic workers and men in high-status positions. The narrator, shaking herself out of the memory of the family story, asserts herself:

> I remove the arm, close the door, delete the number,
> spit it on the wind to his two sons
> to take him back to . . . (16)

simultaneously honoring her grandmother, her great-grandmother, and the Mexican maid/wife sent home to die of cancer by, ironically, sending him back to his two sons. The final line in her response to the plumber is a clear rejection and stance against anything to do with him, his racism, his sexism, his arm slipping around her as an easily assumed acquisition: "*No, sir, Not this Mexican.*"

In keeping with Tafolla's lifelong desires to transcend the boundaries of language, culture, nations, and time, she creates a necessary tension in her work with the simultaneous presence of the past in the present. Tackling the area of child abuse and molestation, she delves into her own past and revisits old scars and traumas in "Touring 3535 San Fernando Street, 60 Years Later" (*Critical Latina*, 2). By contrasting the event with the first word of the title—so casual is "Touring" when discussing the emotional permanence of a childhood home—the poet amplifies the severity of the theme. And the details on which the speaker focuses seem so small—"the plums," "the tiny phone stand," "a miniature arched grotto"—until she comes to the terror in the night, "the echo of a man's footsteps growing closer to my room." Again, this terror stands in contrast to the final allusion, to something so very small that fell out, or was lost, perhaps an innocence, so many years ago:

> And I have lost all my baby teeth
> both the smooth ones, of the body
> and, those more difficult to extract,
> those that were chipped silent
> of the spirit lost.

Small and huge become equivalents in this mestizo'd concept of significance. And one losing their innocence because of childhood molestation is anything but tiny, a theme further attested to by the horrifying
but empowering short story "The Stuff to Scream With," which Tafolla
published in *The Holy Tortilla*. The story describes a child molestation
in a different setting. It is told in amplified stereo, toggling between
the remembered voice of the child and the voice of the grown woman
facing another situation as a bystander who forcefully interrupts a
different instance of sexual violence.

Tafolla takes us on an emotional "tour" through these pieces, as she
reflects on her life and reviews the significance of both the good and
the bad. The fact that it is sixty years later attests to the power of early
experience and the immense impact of violence on the lives of the
silenced and traumatized young. This is a claiming of voice and of all
parts of a life; she is accepting, healing, incorporating all of it into her
own human experience.

Her ultimate proof of survival, though, is the ability, not merely to
continue, but to thrive, to be and to become through that unfurling
evolution, pulling, pushing, arching, sustaining, and reengaging as an
emotional and sensually alive person. An analysis of the poem "Talking
the Fire Out" (*Critical Latina*, 3–4) reveals the speaker reconciling
with life's casualties and blessings, once again demonstrated by a presence of the past in the present. She recounts an accident remembered
by a man to whom she addresses the poem. As a child, he had seen a
classmate fall against a burning cast-iron woodstove. The teacher sends
for the magic of "the Root Lady," the only medical help available to
them in an impoverished schoolroom in the South. Through mystical
healing, the Root Lady uses her voice to "lean in close, talk the fire out
of his leg," ridding the body of extreme damage,

> out of the blooming, now-oozing blisters
> out of the charred dying flesh
> suck the heat of it out with guided whispers. (3)

With intense, visually descriptive words, Tafolla creates an overwhelming sense of pain, flesh "blooming," "oozing," "charred," and "dying," and
paralyzing life-and-death fear for the classmates watching.

The poem flash-forwards to the present time, the young boy now a man, his witness and memory at his side, that very magic that remains with him throughout his life now talking the fire of pain and injury out of the speaker, as he leans into her emotionally and perhaps spiritually and whispers the pain

> out of my scorched lungs, my loss-weary gut
> out of the screaming hot blisters of my heart,
> . . . the hot white ash of the dry well in my eyes. (3–4)

The power pushes forward through mystic energy growing stronger:

> with guided whispers love root salve
> until life   returned
>
> the healing going deep
> into the heart of the bone
> beyond where words
> can whisper (4)

This iteration of wound reparation is perhaps a new mapping over old scars once mended, molded, and softened throughout the decades of a spiritual union. Perhaps one implicitly understands that to get to the root of ache, a deeper penetration into the heart of the bone is necessary—. And as survival, love, and ever-evolving growth inspire Tafolla, she continues to use the words that she writes to "build the houses of reality around us" to help us understand the multiple dimensions behind the tragedies, the bonds, and the victories we claim in life—not unlike the rock glyph writers[14] from thousands of years ago who marked and mapped important locations and chiseled out stories of survival for generations to come . . .

NOTES

1. This nonlinear critical biographical essay parallels Tafolla's personal memories of events and my observations and personal interactions with her from

March 2019 to the present, as well as incorporating interviews and research leading to her most current writing.

2. See Robert Bonazzi, *Outside the Margins*, 208–209, to read interesting commentary on *Rebozos*.

3. In my interview, Tafolla told me that this was a promise Ernesto asked her to make decades earlier. Because of their age difference, he was convinced that he would die sooner than her.

4. See Rafael Pérez-Torres, *Movements in Chicano Poetry*, 226–33, for an in-depth analysis of polyglossia and radical mestizaje in relation to Tafolla's work.

5. See Richard Edward Martinez, *PADRES: The National Chicano Priest Movement*, for more information on Father Edmundo Rodríguez.

6. Although *Curandera* was first published in 1983, it had been ready for publication since 1978 (*Curandera*, xi).

7. Again, see Pérez-Torres, *Movements*, 226–33, for an analysis of polyglossia and radical mestizaje, especially in the "Los Corts" poems.

8. See Gilberto Perez, "Pachuco."

9. In my interview, Tafolla told me about *El artista*, written for the Southwest Educational Development Laboratory in 1977; her *Sonrisas* series of screenplays from 1978; and a feature-length comedy script coauthored with Sylvia Morales in 1995, *REAL MEN . . . (and Other Miracles)*.

10. See Chicano Communications Center, *450 Años*, 64, for more information on *la valiente jefe revolucionaria* Carmen Robles.

11. In my interview, Tafolla told me that *Our Very Own Names* was the inspired title of a one-woman dramatic show that she first performed in Las Vegas, Nevada, in 1990 for the Hispanic Education Association. It has evolved over the years as she has added new dramatic characters, based primarily on personages in her poems and short stories.

12. See Cordelia Candelaria, "La Malinche, Feminist Prototype," for an in-depth analysis of la Malinche with references to Tafolla's la Malinche.

13. See *The Holy Tortilla and a Pot of Beans: A Feast of Short Fiction* for further exploration of these titles.

14. See Katarzyna Mikulksa and Jerome A. Offner, *Indigenous Graphic Communication Systems*, for insights into the meaning of the rich and varied content of indigenous American graphic expression and culture as well as into the societies and cultures that produce them.

WORKS CITED

Bonazzi, Robert. *Outside The Margins: Literary Commentaries*. San Antonio, Tex.: Wings Press, 2015.

Candelaria, Cordelia. "La Malinche, Feminist Prototype." *Frontiers: A Journal of Women Studies* 5, no. 2 (1980): 3. doi:10.2307/3346027.

Chicano Communications Center, ed. *450 Años del Pueblo Chicano/450 Years of Chicano History in Pictures*. Albuquerque, N.M.: Chicano Communications Center, 1976.

Córdova, Teresa. "Anti-Colonial Chicana Feminism." *New Political Science* 20, no. 4 (1998): 379–97. doi:10.1080/07393149808429837.

García-Camarillo, Cecilio Xilo, Roberto Cintli Rodríguez, and Patrisia Gonzales, eds. San Antonio, Tex.: Wings Press, 2002.

Martinez, Richard Edward. *PADRES: the National Chicano Priest Movement*. Austin: University of Texas Press, 2005.

Matallana-Peláez, Susana E. "From Gender to Omeotlization: Toward a Decolonial Ontology." *Hypatia* 35, no. 3 (2020): 373–92. doi:10.1017/hyp.2020.23.

Medrano, Manuel, and Aaron Rodrigues. "Carmen Tafolla: Chicana Writer, from the Whispers of Her People." In *Illuminating How Identities, Stereotypes, and Inequalities Matter Through Gender Studies*. Edited by D. Nicole Farris, Mary Ann Davis, and D'Lane R. Compton. New York: Springer, 2014, 83–89. doi:10.1007/978-94-017-8718-5_7.

Mikulska, Katarzyna, and Jerome A. Offner. "Indigenous Graphic Communication Systems: A Theoretical Approach." In *Indigenous Graphic Communication Systems: A Theoretical Approach*. Edited by Katarzyna Mikulska and Jerome A. Offner. Boulder: University Press of Colorado, 2020, 3–22. doi:10.5876/9781607329350.c000b.

Perez, Gilberto. "Pachuco." Subcultures and Sociology, Grinnell College (website). haenfler.sites.grinnell.edu/subcultures-and-scenes/pachuco/.

Pérez-Torres, Rafael. *Movements in Chicano Poetry: Against Myths, Against Margins*. New York: Cambridge University Press, 1995.

Simón, Yara. "These Are 12 Ethnic Studies Books Arizona Doesn't Want You to Read." Remezcla, June 26, 2017. https://www.remezcla.com/lists/culture/banned-books-arizona/.

Tafolla, Carmen. "Banned, Buoyed, and Laureled: A Poet Laureate Speaks on Latinophobia, Censorship, and the Revitalizing Power of Diversity." *Austin College Magazine*, Summer 2012.

———. *Carmen Tafolla: New and Selected Poems*. San Antonio, Tex.: Texas Christian University, 2019.

———. *Curandera*. 30th anniv. ed. San Antonio, Tex.: Wings Press, 2012.

———. "For You I'll Fly." In *Healing the Divide: Poems of Kindness and Connection*. Edited by James Crews. Brattleboro, Vt.: Green Writers Press, 2019.

———. *The Holy Tortilla and a Pot of Beans: A Feast of Short Fiction*. San Antonio, Tex.: Wings Press, 2015.

———. "hombre de raza cósmica." In *Boundless. The Anthology of the Rio Grande Valley International Poetry Festival*. Edited by Edward Vidaurre, Sarah Joy Thomson, and Gabriel González Núñez. McAllen, Tex.: FlowerSong Press, 2021, 235.

———. "How Will We Say Goodbye?" *Journal of Latina Critical Feminism* 5, no. 1 (2022): 5–6.

———. Interview by Jen Yáñez-Alaniz, February 18, 2021.

———. "It Gets Crazy in the World." *Langdon Review of the Arts in Texas* 12 (2015–16): 1–3.

———. "Poetry Around Us." *Fifth Wednesday Journal*, Fall 2018, 10.

———. *"Sonnets to Human Beings" and Other Selected Works*. Edited by Ernesto Padilla. San Antonio, Tex.: Wings Press, 1992.

———. "Spit It on the Wind." *Journal of Latina Critical Feminism* 3, no.1 (2020): 15.

———. "Talking the Fire Out." *Journal of Latina Critical Feminism* 5, no. 1 (2022): 3–4.

———. *This River Here: Poems of San Antonio*. San Antonio, TX: Wings Press, 2014.

———. "Touring 3535 San Fernando Street, 60 Years Later." *Journal of Latina Critical Feminism* 5, no. 1 (2022): 2.

Tafolla, Carmen, and García Catalina Gárate. *Rebozos*. San Antonio, Tex.: Wings Press, 2012.

CHERRÍE MORAGA

CHERRÍE MORAGA

Builder of Movements

LOURDES TORRES

C HERRÍE MORAGA has often said that one of the most gratifying aspects of being a writer is the many people who approach her and say, "Your work saved my life." I count myself among this group. I first encountered Cherríe's writing in the early 1980s as a young, closeted Puerto Rican dyke during my days as a graduate student in Illinois. At that time, I contemplated coming out now that I was far from my home in New York, but it was still a fraught process, given the homophobia of my new midwestern Latino/a community. Reading *This Bridge Called My Back* changed all that. For the first time I heard from a community of lesbians of color, and specifically Latina lesbians, who did not apologize for who they were but rather proclaimed it assertively along with all their other intersecting identities and positionalities. These authors gave me permission to be an out Latina dyke.

The first time I met Cherríe was in April 1983. I was on the organizing committee of the Third World Women and the Politics of Feminism conference at the University of Illinois Urbana-Champaign. This conference, initiated and organized by Chandra Talpade Mohanty and Ann Russo when we were all graduate students, brought together over 150 speakers from around the world and provided a space for significant exchanges among women of color. I worked to bring to campus the Latina feminists who had deeply impacted my emerging feminism. These speakers included Cherríe Moraga, Gloria Anzaldúa, and Juanita Ramos. I remember the pushback I got from my own Latina community when they saw the roster of speakers. Why so many lesbians? This response made me nervous and apprehensive.

The conference drew a massive audience of over two thousand people from around the country and much international participation. Among the audience was a small community of Latina lesbians who came to hear and connect with our new Latina lesbian superstars, Cherríe Moraga and Gloria Anzaldúa. I still remember the night of Moraga's plenary talk. My newfound community, the gaggle of Latina lesbians who had been bonding throughout the five-day conference, sat in the first rows of the lecture hall anticipating Cherríe's words. Cherríe presented a talk from her new book, *Loving in the War Years: Lo que nunca pasó por sus labios*. Among the many topics she discussed, she articulated the importance of creating a Third World feminism that would "feed people in all their hungers," including reckoning with women's sexual desire. She argued for building a Third World women's feminism movement that "brings the strands together and addresses the system of interlocking oppression that women of color face including, importantly, the right to passion and sexuality." She talked about longing, the desire for sex and the desire for freedom. While perhaps not a revolutionary articulation of women of color yearnings nowadays, this idea was radically controversial when Moraga introduced it at the conference forty years ago in 1983.

Once the Q and A period started, all hell broke loose. A line of women of color took to the microphone one after another to critique Cherríe. How dare she talk about sex when children were starving? What right did she have to talk about sexual desire when women were dying in Third World countries? Several women angrily expressed their disapproval and stormed out. I still remember with shame that all of us, her fan club, sat quietly in those first few rows, saying nothing, letting our sister take the heat. After the event ended, a few of us walked Cherríe back to her hotel in silence. Cherríe too was silent.

We said good night and walked away, avoiding a discussion of what had just transpired. Years later Cherríe confessed to me that when she returned to her room, alone, she burst into tears. As for me, every time thereafter when I remember my cowardice in that moment I feel a wave of shame.

I begin with this personal vignette because it captures for me the essence of Moraga's writing. She is an author who is not afraid to take risks as she contends with some of the most challenging social, cultural, and political events of our times.

ORIGINS

Cherríe Moraga is a Chicana writer, feminist, poet, essayist, playwright, and activist. Born in 1952, she was raised in Southern California as the child of a Mexican American mother and an Anglo-American father. She earned a bachelor's degree from Immaculate Heart College in Los Angeles in 1974 and a master's degree from San Francisco State University in 1980. She held an artist-in-residence position in theater at Stanford University for twenty years. Then, in 2018, Moraga and her partner, visual artist Celia Herrera Rodríguez, established the Las Maestras Center for Xicana Indigenous Thought, Art, and Social Praxis at the University of California, Santa Barbara, where Moraga is a professor in the Department of English. Moraga is also founder of La RED Xicana Indígena, "a network of Xicanas indígenas based in Arizona, New Mexico and California, who are actively involved in political, educational and cultural work that serves to raise indigenous consciousness among our communities and supports the social justice struggles of people of indigenous American origins North and South."[1] Moraga has been the recipient of numerous awards, including a National Endowment for the Arts Theatre Playwriting Fellowship Award and a United States Artist Rockefeller Fellowship for Literature, the American Studies Association Lifetime Achievement Award, the American Book Award, and the Lambda Foundation's "Pioneer" award, among many other honors. Her work has garnered extensive interest, as is evidenced by the plethora of articles, book chapters, and dissertations inspired by her work. Her papers (the Cherríe Moraga

Papers, 1970–1996) are housed in the Special Collections and University Archives of the Stanford Libraries.

This essay is organized around overarching themes of Cherríe Moraga's work as they surface in her poetry, autobiographies, critical essays, short stories, and plays. I don't aspire to be comprehensive here, but I engage with recurring issues, tensions, and questions in Moraga's work that have sparked debate and generated animated discussions at particular junctures across the decades.

Moraga's work does not conform to conventional writing, and she defies the boundaries of genre. She writes poetry, essays, short fiction, and plays, and she often code switches between English and Spanish as she mixes the genres and creates her own creative blends of literary forms. Certain topics recur across the trajectory of her work, oftentimes in different genres. A line from a poem may become the subject of an essay or a theme in one of her plays. An image that appears in a journal entry might become a major topic of a short story. Through the years, we can see her interrogating different topics with the benefit of new experiences and perspectives.

Her work has always been radical, ahead of its time, taking on complex topics and creating a space for us to have conversations that were not being had in different eras,—for example, around topics such as Chicana/Latina lesbianism in the 1980s, Chicana indigeneities in the 1990s, and transgender identity and homonormativity in the 2000s. Being unafraid to expose her vulnerabilities and work through controversial ideas in her writing occasionally exposes her to criticism while concurrently pushing much needed conversations to new levels on multiple fronts. She has the courage to process contentious issues publicly at the risk of alienating some readers.

Moraga's writing is intimately personal while simultaneously broadly structural. Her poems and essays exploring her experiences and responses to pivotal events are deeply moving and resonate with readers because they tap into a brutally honest vulnerability that sears the soul; her work inspires women of color and other marginalized people. Moraga often returns to what have been her pressing concerns since she started publishing her work forty years ago; an intersectional feminist of color critique of sexism and patriarchy runs through all the decades of her writing, as does an analysis of mixed-raced positionality.

Again and again she centralizes the importance of racial memory and the importance of recovering our past in order to move toward a more fulfilling and just future. She is a foundational thinker around issues of feminism, queer of color theorizing, and Chicana and Indigenous identity. A critique of capitalism, globalization, and the mindless destruction of our environmental landscape is woven through much of her writing, as is a sense of the centrality of erotic power from an embodied stance.

Taken together, the body of Cherríe's work offers an enlightening opportunity to trace political debates in the Latina and feminist of color communities. One can read her work and get a good overview of some of the central questions that have engaged the Latinx community in the last four decades. Wholeheartedly grounded in the idea that the personal is always political, she is convinced that the most effective strategies for social change will emerge when we have examined and are aware of our own positionality within the social, cultural, and political context we inhabit. Moraga's insightful exploration of personal issues around family and religion continues to compel readers rarely exposed to analyses that treat these issues as concurrently intimate and political. Centering her life experiences and family relations, she leads readers to consider systemic issues through the lens of her own emotional and intellectual grappling with topics such as patriarchy, systemic racism, global capitalism, and imperialism. Her work offers a useful compendium of the major social and political upheavals and challenges we have experienced over the recent past.

Any consideration of her work must begin with an appreciation of one of Moraga's fundamental contributions to feminist thinking. With Gloria Anzaldúa, Moraga co-edited *This Bridge Called My Back: Writings by Radical Women of Color*, a groundbreaking anthology that challenged white feminist mainstream thinking and disseminated emerging theories, philosophies, and praxis generated by Black, Latina, Asian American, and Native women writers. This text revolutionized feminist thinking and has been an essential component of women's and gender studies courses since its first publication by Persephone Press, an independent lesbian-feminist press, in 1981. It has been subsequently reissued with new prefaces and forewords four times, and Third Woman Press published a version in Spanish (Moraga and Castillo).[2] In a 2005 oral history interview, Moraga explains that she was twenty-seven in

1979 when Gloria Anzaldúa invited her to work on the project that became *This Bridge* (Moraga, Voices of Feminism, p. 53). While the initial impetus of the book was to respond to the racism experienced in the mainstream white feminist circles, as the project developed, this aspect became just one section of the book, "Racism in the Woman's Movement," and the majority of the text developed an embodied "theory in the flesh" via manifestos, autobiographical poems, and critical essays penned by a diverse group of thinkers. This trailblazing anthology includes contributions by well-known theorists and activists, such as Audre Lorde and Barbara Smith, as well as by authors who were just emerging at the time, such as Rosario Morales, Chrystos, Naomi Littlebear Morena, Nellie Wong, and Merle Woo. Dexterously dissecting "the simultaneity of oppressions" (as the Black feminist Combahee River Collective put it), these contributors rejected single-issue politics and forged instead a generative, intersectional analysis and praxis. The book continues to be relevant because, as Moraga points out in the preface to the fourth edition, "As I age, I watch the divide between generations widen with time and technology. I watch how desperately we need political memory, so that we are not always imagining ourselves the ever-inventors of our revolutions; so that we are humbled by the valiant efforts of our foremothers; and so, with humility and a firm foothold in history, we can enter upon an informed and re-envisioned strategy for social/political change in the decades ahead" (xix).

Unfortunately, the sociopolitical problems and realities addressed in *This Bridge* continue to plague our marginalized communities today; the perspectives, analyses, and strategies invoked by the contributors continue to provoke and inspire new generations. Contemporary social justice warriors turn to *This Bridge* for its enduring lessons. For example, feminist of color leaders like Black Lives Matter founders Alicia Garza, Patrisse Cullors, and Opal Tometi often note how they have been influenced by foundational texts from feminist of color history, including *This Bridge*.

LO QUE NUNCA PASÓ POR SUS LABIOS

The publication of *Loving in the War Years: Lo que nunca pasó por sus labios* was another pivotal moment in women of color publications for

generations of Chicana and Latina lesbians who had rarely seen themselves reflected anywhere in the culture. Prior to the 1980s, Chicana
and Latina lesbians were rendered invisible in both white feminist
movements and Chicana/Latina political mobilizations. Moraga and
Anzaldúa were among the first Chicana/Latina lesbians to articulate
their right to exist and to condemn lesbophobia in the white wom-
en's movement and in Chicano/Latino spaces. Scholars and activists
have subsequently discussed the extreme fear and hatred of lesbians
in Latino/a communities at the time, including in political spaces and
academic circles (Trujillo; Gaspar de Alba).

Expanded and reissued in 2000, firmly staking out a prominent space
for Chicana lesbian subjectivity in all its complexity, *Loving in the War
Years* has become a manifesto for Latina lesbians everywhere. Moraga
details a Chicana lesbian perspective in poems, diary entries, autobiographical fiction, and much-cited essays, such as "La Güera" and "A
Long Line of Vendidas." Moraga situates her lesbianism within a context
of repressive Catholicism, sexual violence, racism, and mixed-race identity. Striking in its bold exploration of Latina lesbianism, for many the
book was the first time we experienced writing that dared to depict sexuality in all its complexity, without hedging or apology, as in this passage:

Sueño: 15 de julio 1982

*During the long difficult night that sent my lover and I to separate beds, I
dreamed of church and cunt. I put it this way because that is how it came
to me. The suffering and the thick musty mysticism of the catholic church
fused with the sensation of entering the vagina—like that of a colored
woman's—dark, rica, full bodied. The heavy sensation of complexity. A
journey I must unravel, work out for myself.*

I long to enter you like a temple. (*Loving*, 90)

Disentangling disparate elements of the female body, religion, passion,
the sacred and profane, and Spanish and English languages, Moraga's
writing offers a bold and daring analysis of intersecting and at times
contradicting dimensions of Latina lesbian sexuality.

Also significant in her exploration of sexuality is the complex
manner in which Moraga associates her coming into her lesbianism

with her profound love for her mother. This intricate relationship is rendered in the essay "La Güera," first published in *This Bridge* and reprinted in *Loving*: "When I finally lifted the lid on my lesbianism, a profound connection with my mother reawakened in me. It wasn't until I acknowledged and confronted my own lesbianism in the flesh, that my heartfelt identification with and empathy for my mother's oppression—due to being poor, uneducated and Chicana—was realized. My lesbianism is the avenue through which I have learned the most about silence and oppression, and it continues to be the most tactile reminder to me that we are not free human beings" (*Loving*, 52). Moraga further explores this relating of maternal love and lesbian sexuality in essays and especially in affecting poems in *Loving* that link her embodying and embracing of her lesbianism with her acknowledgment of and empathy for her Mexican mother's life experiences, disappointments, and unfulfilled yearnings.

> For you mamá, I have unclothed myself before a woman
> have laid wide the space between my thighs
> straining to open the strings held there
> taut and ready to fight.
>
> Stretching my legs and my imagination so open
> to feel my whole body cradled
> by the movement of her mouth, the mouth
> of her thighs rising and falling, her arms
> her kiss, all the parts of her open
> like lips moving, talking me into loving.
>
> I remember the common skin, mamá
> oiled by work and worry.
> Hers is a used body like yours
> one that carries the same scent
> of silence I call it home. (140)

Moraga reveals that she had to temporarily leave her home in order to come into her identity, and it was though looking at the intersections between race and sexuality, particularly the ways in which women are denied their freedom on the basis of both their race and sexuality, that she was able to construct and articulate the dimensions of a specifically Chicana lesbianism.[3]

Moraga's candid critique of the Chicano community from the perspective of a Chicana lesbian unabashedly centers women's relationships with each other at the same time that it poignantly captures the barriers that women face as they attempt to realize these relationships within their community. The dynamic of women "putting the man first" surfaces in much of Moraga's dramatic writing, including her first play, *Giving Up the Ghost*, published in 1986. This revolutionary play captures the difficulty of maintaining a lesbian relationship in a context of homophobia, both externalized and internal. As one of the first complex portrayals of Chicana lesbian desire ever published and produced on the stage, *Giving Up the Ghost* broke new ground. The play visualizes gender sexuality debates, including butch-femme dynamics, sexual desire, sexual abuse and rape, and how they are all interrelated. Moraga powerfully portrays the reality of a Latino patriarchal culture that priorities men despite the damage their violence perpetuates against women. She writes:

> The women I have loved the most
> have always loved the man more than me,
> even in their hatred of them.
> I'm queer I am. Sí soy jota
> because I have never ever been crazy about a man. (15)

This early play reaffirms the challenge even women loving women face as they try to center their own passion when they have been steeped their entire lives in the ethos of patriarchy and *familismo*.

Moraga returns to the sheer terror of coming out publicly in her latest memoir, *Native Country of the Heart*. She writes that she was in Mexico when her first autobiographical work arrived in the mail:

> I prop myself up on that springy hotel bed in a dispassionate Mexico City and read *Loving in the War Years*, word by word, line by line, and page by page, stopping again and again on that paradoxical glyph of words "Chicana Lesbian."

It was 1983 and I had never, in my life, read those two words as the subject of a book.

"Lo que nunca pasó por sus labios." *What have I done?* (97)

Given the centrality of her maternal bond and how women are always placed second to the man in Latino family dynamics, Moraga returns again and again to the challenge of deconstructing sexism and patriarchy.

DISMANTLING SEXISM AND PATRIARCHY

In the much-cited early essay "A Long Line of Vendidas" (published in *Loving in the War Years*), Moraga lays out the interlocking relationship between sexuality, gender, race, and class. In the first section of the essay, titled "My Brother's Sex Was White. Mine, Brown," she details memories from her childhood when she and her sister were required to look after and wait on her brother. She names the heterosexism of her family and her community as intrinsically tied to preserving the culture. She writes, "Because heterosexism—the Chicana's sexual commitment to the Chicano male—is proof of her fidelity to her people, the Chicana feminist attempting to critique the sexism in the Chicano community is certainly between a rock and a hard place" (105). This articulation of the problem of sexism within Chicana culture and well-defined analysis has always resonated with me and my students across the generations, as it is still the case that Chicanas/Latinas are expected to cater to the men in our communities.

Moraga returns to the theme of sexism and heteropatriarchy and their relationship to religion in *Native Country of the Heart*. She goes on to explore her relationship with her brother James, who was introduced in *Loving*, written early in her career. At that time, Moraga illustrated how the Catholic Church and her mother enabled and reinforced the male privilege enacted in the home, where she and her sister were trained from girlhood to cater to their male relatives. Writing decades later, Moraga explores how male privilege extended through the decades and surfaced again even at the end of their mother's life. While present very little throughout her life, her brother as chief patriarch of the family assumes a major role in decision-making around their mother's illness and death. Moraga reminds us, "The amazing efficacy of patriarchy is that it is a covert operation. It is entre nos, just between us—man and woman, sister and brother, father and daughter, queer and not so queer. It takes place behind closed doors, inside la hacienda and back there in the slave quarters. It is so seamlessly woven into the fiber of our lives that to pull at the dangling thread of inequity is to rip open an entire life" (*Native Country*, 223).

And rip at this dangling thread is exactly what Moraga does in her eulogy to her mother from the pulpit of the Catholic Church. Moraga finds the courage to speak eloquently and candidly of Elvira's lifelong "unrequited desire" before family and friends, enraging her brother, who speaking the previous day at the rosary vigil sought to represent a more conventional—and false—narrative of Elvira's life. In contradiction to his romanticized version of her mother's life and the relationship between her parents, Moraga dares to eulogize her mother as a fiercely passionate woman who, despite her deep intelligence and longing, was mostly unfulfilled in life and love. Moraga's public honesty drives a heartbreaking and intractable wedge between brother and sister at the time of their mother's death. Catholic Church and patriarchy once again collude to deny the truth of women's existence.

GENDER AND ITS DISCONTENTS

As a self-identified butch lesbian, Moraga has grappled with issues of the intricacies of gender throughout her work. In *Loving* she articulates her struggles against the gender expectations of church and culture. In her memoir of motherhood *Waiting in the Wings*, Moraga thinks through the contradictions of inhabiting her body as a child-bearing butch dyke. She confesses: "Buried deep inside me, regardless of the empirical evidence to the contrary, I had maintained the rigid conviction that lesbians (that is, those of us on the more masculine side of the spectrum) weren't really women. We were women-lovers, a kind of third sex, and most definitely not men. Having babies was something 'real' women did—not butches, not girls who knew they were queer since grade school" (20). This autobiography captures her coming to terms with her new role as a pregnant woman and then a dyke mother, the latter instilling in her a desire to bolster her butch identity. While appreciating how her body has changed in ways that make her more feminine (i.e., rounded breasts and softer hips and thighs), she states, "I like it and yet in bed feel a strong urge to assert my butchness, my self as a love-maker" (45).

In later works, with the emergence of increased transgender visibility and a transgender rights movement, Moraga returns to thinking through the intricacies of gender politics. While feminism has long rejected simplistic notions about sex and gender, such as the idea that people are forever bound to an innate gender experience because we are assigned male or female sex at birth, feminist debates about transgender identity and politics have been vociferous. Throughout the years, in her writings and speeches, Moraga has shared her thoughts on the relationship between transgender identity and feminism. Controversy ensued concerning Moraga's discussion of transgender identity and lesbian feminist identification in public talks as well as in the essay "Still Loving in the (Still) War Years" (*Xicana Codex*, 175–92). Here, Moraga makes a call for "keeping queer queer." The essay offers a critique of neoliberal mainstream gay and lesbian politics as well as a painfully honest rendering of Moraga's own emerging attempts to situate transgender realities and politics within her understanding of a queer politics. Moraga speaks openly and honesty about the difficulty she experienced as she sought to unravel the relationship between transgender identity and butch lesbian identification. In the essay Moraga, much to the dismay of some transgender people and their allies, mourns the disappearance of butch lesbians and questions trans men's commitment to feminist and queer politics. She discusses her own butch history and wonders if she would have taken the leap to transition if the context had been different and transitioning had been possible in her life. Discussing the students she teaches, she questions if young Latinx butches who transition really comprehend what they are doing or if perhaps they are fragile youth who have capitulated to peer pressure and/or desire to escape into the comfort of heteropatriarchy rather than residing in an uncomfortable radical-queer space.

Some have challenged these musings as patronizing and uninformed. For example, while appreciating Moraga as one of the few

Latina theorists who actually engages with transgender Latinx politics and concerns at all, transgender theorist Frank Galarte takes issue with Moraga's framing in "Transgender Chican@ Poetics: Contesting, Interrogating, and Transforming Chicana/o Studies." He argues, "Pairing a critique of gay marriage with fears and anxieties around the fashioning of transgender identities by youth of color to reinvigorate discussions about what constitutes queer resistance implicates transgender as an identity category invested in recognition, visibility, and legibility in a normative framework" (129). Galarte offers a nuanced and thoughtful analysis of Moraga's essay as he advocates for an expansion of Chicana feminist theorizing that is inclusive of nonbinary gender and transgender realities, specifically in a context of horrific violence against transgender people.

Moraga's public processing of her fears and concerns about transgender identity have been critiqued by those who take these musings to be transphobic rather than an honest attempt to publicly think through new manifestations and conceptualizations around gender. I remember in the 2000s, after she presented a talk at DePaul University, discussing with Cherríe over dinner my own wrestling around understanding transgender issues. I shared with her that the queer activist organization I belonged to, Amigas Latinas, had recently changed our mission to be inclusive of the transgender community and now advocated for not only lesbian and bisexual women but also for transgender people. While we knew that was the right thing to do, we were still grappling with what transgender identity actually meant and our relationship to it as a predominantly lesbian organization. Would we now advocate for both transgender men and women? How was this connected to our woman-centered origins? How could we have this conversation with our cross-generational membership, especially with some of our older members who were new to these particular debates about gender, appropriate language, and inclusivity and felt confused about the shifting terrain? The questions I raised openly with her probably would also have been read as transphobic in some contexts. As always, I was struck by Cherríe's honesty, her willingness to explore her own evolving understanding and uncertainty, and her efforts to incorporate the complexities of transgender identity given her own butch identification.

Moraga always acknowledges that she comes to these questions about gender politics grounded in her particular history as a butch Chicana lesbian who came to inhabit her lesbian identity in the context of the political and social climate of the 1960s and 1970s. In her writings and talks, Moraga does not shy away from asking questions that push conversations forward that she herself is grappling with. As she is a queer icon, the positions she takes are scrutinized from all sides and make some readers and fans uncomfortable. Moraga is not afraid to express her own opinions and evolving understanding, and she remains committed to intergenerational dialogue about issues that separate women.[4]

CHICANA NATIONALISM, BLOOD TIES, AND MAKING FAMILIA FROM SCRATCH

In her essay "Queer Aztlán: The Reformation of Chicano Tribe," Moraga sketches her hopes for the development of a new radical nationalism within her community, one that rejects the sexism and homophobia typical of mainstream nationalisms. The essay first appeared in her 1993 collection *The Last Generation*, which, as the title suggests, finds Moraga reflecting on the pressures of assimilation to whiteness and the question of the continuity and survival of both her immediate family and the Chicana nation in the United States. *The Last Generation* is especially mournful of lost connections to Mexican heritage. Moraga issues a manifesto that serves as a call to consciousness to the Chicano/a community. While critiquing the negative aspects of past nationalisms, including the Chicano movement of the 1960s, she promotes a new type of organizing community and family grounded in Indigenous womanhood and inclusive of queers. She states, "The nationalism I seek is one that decolonizes the brown and female earth. It is a new nationalism in which the Chicana Indígena stands at the center, and heterosexism and homophobia are no longer the cultural order of the day. I cling to the word 'nation' because without the specific naming of the nation, the nation will be lost (as when feminism is reduced to humanism, the woman is subsumed). Let us retain our radical naming but expand it to meet a broader and wiser nation" (150).

While some scholars have been critical of what they see as a Chicano nationalism that excludes other peoples,[5] there is tension within this essay—and in much of Moraga's work—between articulating the primacy of familia as grounded in blood ties and defining familia as that community we create on the basis of shared affinities and similar goals, rather than biological connections. Moraga consistently argues that activists and writers will be the most effective in their struggle to change the world when their politics are deployed from a place of deep understanding of their specific origins and cultural, political, and spiritual worldview. So it is understandable that she would develop her politics from a profound grappling with her own Chicana origins. And perhaps it is precisely her mixed-raced ancestry and her sense of having to struggle for recognition as a Chicana that shape her fierce insistence on the primacy of blood connections. Nonetheless, this tension permeates much of her writing.

In the conclusion to her first play, *Giving up the Ghost*, Moraga offers the following lines, which can be read as recognizing the centrality of queer family making, particularly the nonbiological familias we craft:

> It's like making familia from scratch
> each time over again . . . with strangers
> if I must.
> If I must, I will. (58)

These same lines serve as the epigraph of *Waiting in the Wings*, her memoir on queer motherhood, in which Moraga shares the story of her pregnancy, butch motherhood, her son Rafael Angel's premature birth, and the first three years of his life. She asserts that her concern with continuing the race led her to have a brown baby and to yearn for a specifically Mexican partner:

> *There is no denying that I had this baby that he might be a Mexican, for him to know and learn of mexicanismo, for him to feel that fuego, that llama, that riqueza I call lo mexicano. And for a moment, I miss that Mexican loving in my life.*

I know this is the "half-breed" in me speaking, she who stands at the generational crossroads of a family. She who bears witness as the Mexican vanishes into the generation that precedes her. She who wants to "not vanish" as a people . . . as a person. (91)

And in her most recent work, *Native Country of the Heart*, Moraga again formulates her fears of the erasure perpetuated by an insidious assimilation at multiple levels: "To disappear into Mexicanism is not enough; to disappear into Latinidad is even less of who we are; to disappear into Anglo-America, our colonization is complete. We were not supposed to remember" (238).

In *Native Country* Moraga comes to terms with the loss of her mother and, through her, her connection to her Mexican and Indigenous past. She again returns to questions about the significance of DNA, blood, and their relevance to making familia. At the time of the writing of *Native Country*, Moraga has been making familia with her Chicana/O'dami partner, Celia, for some twenty years. They share their household with her son, Rafa, as well as some of the Celia's children and grandchildren. Late in the memoir, Moraga tells of an angry exchange between Celia and Celia's adult son, Maceo. After a near accident, Maceo angrily confronts his mother Celia with the accusation that she has not shared anything with him about her end-of-life desires. An unabashed homophobe who does not approve of his mother's lesbian relationship, he poses the matter as if dealing with Celia's death were his responsibility alone, exclusive of Moraga, her partner of twenty years. Moraga is forced to consider that this is exactly how she feels about her mother's impending death, in spite of her brother's assumption of the role of family patriarch. She recognizes the similarity between Maceo's and her impulses and asks, *"What's blood got to do with it?"* (203). Later in the memoir, when Moraga ponders blood relations versus the familias we make, she reconsiders. Contemplating the potential loss of Celia, her life partner, Moraga reaffirms the significance of the familia we make when she declares, "But the truth was that if I closed my eyes, inhaled the smoke of that burning prayer, and saw only with my heart, there was nothing to distinguish the loss of my mother from the prospect of the loss of this familia, forged by this fire and built with my bare hands in the grasp of Celia's" (234).

CHICANA INDIGENEITY, ANCESTRAL MEMORY

Ancestral memory and cultural loss permeate Moraga's work, and these themes are lyrically developed in *Native Country of the Heart*. This memoir explores the complex dynamics of the mother-daughter relationship and serves as a retrospective of both their lives. To understand her own trajectory and place in the world, Moraga discovers that she must also explore her mother's story, as well as the story of her ancestors. This leads her to also research the story of San Gabriel, California, the region where she grew up, digging deep to uncover its specifically Indigenous heritage. As noted previously, Moraga consistently adheres to the importance of the specificity of analysis and throughout her work exemplifies the idea of developing a theory of the flesh based on her own experience, very much grounded in Chicana Indigenous thought. The forging of an Indigenous worldview is woven throughout all of her work and resonates particularly strongly in her plays.

Her dramatic writing offers an important contribution to Chicano/Latino theater, clearly influenced by Chicano activist theater such as Luis Valdez's Teatro Campesino. Like the work of the early Teatro Campesino, in plays such as *Heroes and Saints, Circle in the Dirt: El Pueblo de East Palo Alto,* and *Heart of the Earth: A Popol Vuh Story,* Moraga tells the continuing story of Chicano exploitation and farmworkers' campaigns for fair wages and human dignity. Many of these plays advance a pre-Columbian and Native American worldview. Moraga's dramatic work is experimental and often has a connection to an Indigenous past and future. Offering a biting critique of capitalism and Catholicism and invested in working toward social justice, the vision put forth in her plays is grounded in an alternative Indigenous spirituality. The plays are imbued with striking, indelible images that represent tragic stories of the damage inflicted on the planet and propel readers toward an engaged, resistant future. For example, *Heroes and Saints* depicts the United Farm Workers union historic grape boycott and dramatizes the farmworkers' organizing and protesting pesticide use and environmental degradation in 1988. Cerezita, a central character, is a victim of pesticide poisoning, born without a body. To call attention to the explosion of a cancer cluster in the town, rebellious children put up crucifixes with the bodies of children killed by environmental toxins. The symbolism in the play is unforgettable, and the story blends topics such as disability, sexuality, and embodied resistance in a powerful, innovative manner.[6] The play *The Hungry Woman: Mexican Medea* reimagines two mythical stories: Euripides's tragedy *Medea* and the Mexican tale of la Llorona. Again, Moraga brings a Chicana lesbian sensibility to the stage as she tells the tragic story of a woman who is cast from her Native community because of her love of a woman.

Moraga's focus on Native American roots, specifically how they manifest in Chicana mestiza culture, is a central dynamic of her work. Her interest in indigeneity is prompted by a desire to explore this often-erased part of Chicana culture, not for its own sake, but because Indigenous ways and philosophies can point the way to a healthier, more grounded, and sustainable future. This perspective is detailed and elaborated on in the essays in *The Last Generation*. As the title suggests, in this collection Moraga is very much concerned with the future of Chicanidad. As a mixed-raced person, she fears for the eventual loss of her people and of Native ways of knowing under the pressures to assimilate to Anglo culture, which often goes hand in hand with a leaving behind of Indigenous and Chicana ways of being. In all her work Moraga writes against this push toward cultural amnesia. She fears this loss both in the confines of her specific family, where she sees her siblings' children becoming whiter and whiter, and in the context of Chicanos *agringados* in general. She sees the future of Chicanos intertwined with the survival of Indigenous peoples around the world and indeed with the survival of the planet. She looks to Indigenous elders and Native traditions and philosophies to find ways to approach that future.

Claiming an Indigenous identity is not without controversy. While some Chicanos, as mestizos, profess an Indigenous heritage, others neither identify as Indigenous nor claim Indigenous ancestors. However, for Moraga this disavowal or lack of recognition is due to the erasure of racial memory. She argues that more and more Chicanos are now asserting such an identity and engaging in the difficult recovery work uncovering this lineage entails. Mestizaje has a complex history in Mexico and the United States. For Moraga, mestizos in the United

States are Indigenous people who have forgotten their past and have been "de-Indianized."[7]

Assertions of Chicano indigeneity are complicated by the reality that throughout history Mexicans have participated in the dispossession of Indigenous lands (Guidotti-Hernández). The issue of whether or not Chicanos can be seen as colonial settlers is currently debated in Chicano studies; some understand Mexicans in the United States as an oppressed group dispossessed of their land, while others argue that in certain historical moments Mexicans perpetuated violence against Indigenous peoples and appropriated Native lands in the Southwest (Guidotti-Hernández; Pulido; Cotera and Saldaña-Portillo). While some Native Americans accept Chicanos as Indigenous, others do not. Cotera and Saldaña-Portillo argue that Chicanos have a tenuous relationship to claiming Native heritage and identity due to the complex history of indigeneity and colonialism in both the United States and Mexico; they contend that "when Chicanos claim an Indigenous Heritage, they do so from a position of *mestizo* mourning that is not merely an appropriative gesture of Native tribal identity, but rather a psychic restoration of an indigenous past denied them by the exigencies of U.S. colonial history and law" (562–63). In *Native Country of the Heart*, Moraga moves beyond generalizations about Indigenous heritage and gestures to her family's specific, if tenuous, genealogical relations to indigeneity, specifically to the Pueblo Indians in Arizona. At the beginning of the memoir she describes herself as "Mexican, mixed-blood, queer, female, *almost-Indian*" (4; my italics). As she explains, the journey to understand her mother's story leads her on the track of that ancestral racial memory that has been obscured over the centuries. She excavates this past, meticulously tracing fleeting leads of displacement, dispossession, migration, and enforced assimilation. It leads her to a tentative conclusion that remains an open question and thus compels her to describe herself as "almost Indian." She states, "I am a displaced mixed-blood Chicana, whose Native relations on my mother's side may land me somewhere in the deserts of Sonora and perhaps, and quite distantly, in the once paradisal lands of the Tongva. There is something to be found in those sites where memory calls us, in spite of the institutional amnesia force-fed to us for centuries. We return as refugees to that forgotten landscape which we somehow recognize as home" (181). Moraga ends her memoir with a commitment to continue to fight against the erasure of her ancestral memory.

THIRD WORLD WOMEN'S MOVEMENT AND COALITION BUILDING

While Moraga's work is unapologetically grounded in an Indigenous Chicana aesthetic, she is concurrently invested in fomenting coalitions among people of color. Her earliest writing is very much engaged in the work of building a U.S. Third World women's movement. Especially important in this regard is the frequently anthologized essay "A Long Line of Vendidas," which first appeared in *Loving in the War Years*. This essay details the elements of a Third World women's movement—inspired by the work of Black feminists, specifically, the 1977 Combahee River Collective Statement—that speaks to the needs, passions, challenges, and strengths of women of color. Over the years her writing has captured the waxing and waning of periods of hopeful activism and other moments of becoming disillusioned with the prospects of advancing the promise of the movement. Moraga also does not shy away from exploring the obstacles, both internal and external, that impede the development of this powerful movement and make coalition building such hard work. For example, the short story "Pesadilla," which begins with the line *"There came the day when Cecilia began to think about color"* (*Loving*, 36), delves into the difficulty of forging intimate connections between Chicanas and Black women. In spite of the obstacles, Moraga's work evidences a yearning to understand and align with other Third World women and marginalized communities' struggle for social justice. For example, poems and essays included in the early 1990s collection *The Last Generation* express solidarity and common cause with the victims and survivors of U.S. imperialism in Central America. In the essay "Art in América con Acento," Moraga also envisions hemispheric unity for people of color across the Americas: "We must learn to see ourselves less as U.S. citizens and more as members of a larger world community composed of many nations of people and no longer give credence to the geopolitical borders that have divided us, Chicano from Mexicano, Filipino-American from Pacific Islander, African American from

Haitian. Call it racial memory. Call it shared economic discrimination. Chicanos call it 'Raza'—be it Quichua, Cubano, or Colombiano—an identity that dissolves borders. As a Chicana writer that's the context in which I want to create" (*Last Generation* 62).

Later still, her vision expands to engage with worldwide transnational struggles. Moraga's introduction to the fourth edition of *This Bridge Called My Back*, published in 2015, thirty-five years after the first edition, begins with a poem paying homage to the 2010 Egyptian uprising and holding it up as an inspiration for U.S. Chicanos. Watching the revolution unfold in the media, Moraga identifies with the women struggling for regime change in Egypt: "And I hear a woman's voice, 'I have worked for this my whole life.' She is crying and I am crying because her victory is mine. To view the world today through a feminist of color lens shatters all barriers of state-imposed nationality. The Egyptian revolution is my revolution" (*This Bridge*, xvi).

She realizes this transnational vision through an engagement with global challenges, such as climate change and environmental devastation across the planet. These concerns are intimately connected to Moraga's consistent insistence on the centrality of an Indigenous perspective and analysis based on reestablishing a healthy relationship with the land, premised on respecting and working with nature rather than owning or controlling it.

Early plays such *Circle in the Dirt: El Pueblo de East Palo Alto* and *The Hungry Woman* gesture to an Indigenous spirituality as they express the necessity for forming alliances among multicultural marginalized communities at the same time that they capture the complications for realizing such coalitions. For example, *Circle in the Dirt*, commissioned by the Committee on Black Performing Arts at Stanford, engages with the efforts of a multicultural coalition to fight gentrification in East Palo Alto in the 1990s. *The Hungry Woman* takes up the idea of coalition building through the depiction of the mobilization of Indigenous peoples banded with other marginalized groups of the U.S. Southwest and their efforts to reclaim stolen territory. Unfortunately, this fantasy does not end well, as the tenets of homophobia and heteropatriarchy internalized by people of color impede the realization of unity. These dramas demonstrate the difficulty of as well as the rewards and costs of resistance.

CONCLUSION

While I have not attempted to provide an overview of all of Moraga's work, I hope that this introduction serves to inspire new readers to engage with Cherríe Moraga's rich oeuvre. Perhaps it is fitting to conclude with Moraga's insistence on the ongoing work of movement building within a national and transnational context and her effort to inspire a collective project to work toward a more equitable future for all people of color. Moraga has much to contribute to intergenerational feminist struggles and the dream of imagining and then fostering a feminism without borders. Moraga offers us a Chicana feminist perspective that speaks to Chicana/o readers at the same time that her expansive worldview addresses all Latinos/as and people of color across transnational communities. In her preface to the fourth edition of *This Bridge Called My Back*, Moraga writes that "*Bridge's* original political conception of 'U.S. women of color' as primarily including Chinese, Japanese, and Filipina American, Chicana/Latina, Native and African American, has now evolved into a transnational and increasingly complex movement of women today, whose origins reside in Asia, throughout the global south and in Indigenous North America" (xvi).

Moraga discusses the imperative to build solidarity around issues of gender and racial justice across/in-between borders while also articulating the need for a strong Chicana/o Indigenous nation. Are these ideas contradictory? Can they coexist? If the nation-state is a barrier to the urgent need for solidarity, given the common struggles we share around economic injustice, wars and other violence, xenophobia, environmental degradation, and more, what is the role of nationalism in our struggles for freedom? I long to read Moraga's future work, where she will surely unpack this paradox as she helps us develop a theory and praxis toward liberation. One thing I know for sure: Cherríe Moraga will never shy away from asking the difficult questions that will lead us all toward a more just, equitable, sustainable future. My students and I, along with queers and women of color everywhere, will forever turn to her work for her keen observations, astute analyses, and generous sharing of herself, all of which enrich the work of social justice activists and scholars alike. Cherríe Moraga sees us; we are not invisible; she writes for us and addresses the issues that matter to us in a language that is passionate, intense, accessible, and speaks directly to our hearts and minds. Resolutely grounded in a specific Chicana Indigenous perspective, her works grapple with contradictions around the meaning of blood, family, community, nations, and borders. Her crafting of a Chicana Indigenous, queer, feminist theory in the flesh continues to evolve with each new work and will resonate with readers for decades to come.

NOTES

1. See "People, Places, and Política," Cherríe Moraga (website), https://Cherríemoraga.com/index.php/la-comunidad-y-politica/14-la-red for a description of the group and its projects.
2. The second edition was published in 1983 by Kitchen Table: Women of Color Press. The third edition was published by Third Woman Press in 2002; the fourth edition was published by SUNY Press in Albany in 2015. A Spanish-language edition, translated by Ana Castillo and Norma Alarcón, and edited by Moraga and Castillo, was published in 1988. It had photos of some of the contributors and illustrations not included in the English- language version, as well as a few new contributions not found in the English editions.
3. See Lora Romero's essay "When Something Goes Queer" for an enlightening reading of this aspect of Moraga's work. See also the insightful readings of Paula Moya and Sandra Soto.
4. See, for example, the YouTube video of a talk Moraga gave at Stanford University's "Introduction to Identity, Diversity, and Aesthetics" course in 2016: https://www.youtube.com/watch?v=5XeYKZAL9e4. In the Q and A period (1:12:00–1:15:00) Moraga addresses a question about her response to transgender pronouns. She frames her response around the need to have open and honest intergenerational dialogues around gender and sexuality issues. Her comments about the importance of not letting issues of language get in the way of honest discussion was interpreted by some as being dismissive of the right of transgender folks to be addressed as they felt appropriate.
5. See Christina Sharpe for a development of this argument.
6. See Yvonne Yarbro-Bejarano's *The Wounded Heart*, a book that explores how Moraga's writing insists on the body as a site of struggle and reclamation.
7. See Marcos Colón's 2020 interview with Moraga for Moraga's articulation of how mestizos are encouraged to "de-Indianize" and how they can resist this "de-Indianization" through gaining consciencia of their origin story in the United States.

BIBLIOGRAPHY

Colón, Marcos. "'Consciencia' Is Not About 'I' but 'We': Interview with Cherríe Moraga." *Latino Book Review*, March 11, 2020. https://www.latinobookreview .com/consciencia-is-not-about-i-but-we---interview-with-cherriacutee -moraga--latino-book-review.html.

Cotera, María Eugenia, and María Josefina Saldaña-Portillo. "Indigenous but Not Indian? Chicana/os and the Politics of Indigeneity." In *The World of Indigenous North America*. Edited by Robert Warrior. New York: Routledge, 2015, 549–68.

Galarte, Francisco J. "Transgender Chican@ Poetics: Contesting, Interrogating, and Transforming Chicana/o Studies." *Chicana/Latina Studies* 13, no. 2 (2014): 118–39.

Gaspar de Alba, Alicia. "Tortillerismo: Work by Chicana Lesbians." *Signs: Journal of Women in Culture and Society* 18, no. 4. (Summer 1993): 956–63.

Guidotti-Hernández, Nicole M. *Unspeakable Violence: Remapping U.S. and Mexican National Imaginaries*. Durham, N.C.: Duke University Press, 2011.

Moraga, Cherríe. *Circle in the Dirt: El Pueblo de East Palo Alto*. Los Angeles: West End Press, 1995.

———. *Giving Up the Ghost*. Los Angeles: West End Press, 1986.

———. *Heart of the Earth: A Popol Vuh Story*. Los Angeles: West End Press, 2001.

———. *Heroes and Saints*. Los Angeles: West End Press, 1992.

———. *The Hungry Woman*. Los Angeles: West End Press, 2001.

———. Interview by Kelly Anderson, June 6–7, 2005, for Voices of Feminism Oral History Project. Sophia Smith Collection of Women's History. Smith College, Northampton, Mass.

———. *The Last Generation*. Boston: South End Press, 1993.

———. *Loving in the War Years*. Boston: South End Press, 1983.

———. *Native Country of the Heart*. New York: Farrar, Straus and Giroux, 2019.

———. *Waiting in the Wings: Portrait of a Queer Motherhood*. Ithaca, N.Y.: Firebrand Books, 1997.

———. *A Xicana Codex of Changing Consciousness: Writings, 2000–2010*. Durham, N.C.: Duke University Press, 2011.

Moraga, Cherríe, and Gloria Anzaldúa. *This Bridge Called My Back*. 4th ed. Albany: State University of New York Press, 2015.

Moraga, Cherríe, and Ana Castillo. *Esta puente, mi espalda: Voces de mujeres tercermundistas en los Estados Unidos*. San Francisco: Ism Press, 1988.

Moya, Paula. *Learning from Experience: Minority Identities, Multicultural Struggles*. Berkeley: University of California Press, 2002.

Pulido, Laura. "Geographies of Race and Ethnicity III: Settler Colonialism and Nonnative People of Color." *Progress in Human Geography* 42, no. 2 (2018): 309–18.

Romero, Lora. "'When Something Goes Queer': Familiarity, Formalism, and Minority Intellectuals in the 1980s." *Yale Journal of Criticism* 6, no. 1 (1993): 121.

Sharpe, Christina. "Learning to Live Without a Black Family: Cherríe Moraga's Nationalist Articulations." In *Tortilleras: Hispanic and U.S. Latina Lesbian Expression*. Edited by Lourdes Torres and Inmaculada Pertusa. Philadelphia: Temple University Press, 2003.

Soto, Sandra. "Cherríe Moraga's Going Brown: 'Reading Like a Queer.'" *GLQ: A Journal of Lesbian and Gay Studies* 11, no. 2 (2005): 237–63.

Trujillo, Carla. "Chicana Lesbians: Fear and Loathing in the Chicano Community." In *Chicana Lesbians: The Girls Our Mothers Warned Us About*. Edited by Carla Trujillo. Berkeley, Calif.: Third Woman Press, 1991. 186–94.

Yarbro-Bejarano, Yvonne. *The Wounded Heart: Writing on Cherríe Moraga*. Austin: University of Texas Press, 2001.

ANA CASTILLO

ANA CASTILLO

A Multigenre Author

MEAGAN SOLOMON

ANA CASTILLO, award-winning novelist, essayist, playwright, and poet, is widely celebrated as a foundational figure of the Chicana feminist movement. Born on June 15, 1953, in Chicago, Illinois, Castillo was creatively inclined from a young age, initially expressing herself through art before delving into poetry. Following the death of her beloved grandmother in 1963, she began to write as a form of self-expression and healing at the age of ten (Cantú, 60). As she grew up during the civil rights movement, the arts also offered Castillo an outlet to express her budding political consciousness in coalition with other working-class students and activists of color.

After graduating from Jones Commercial High School and completing two years of undergraduate work at City Colleges of Chicago, Castillo graduated with a bachelor's degree in arts education from Northeastern Illinois University in 1975. After college, she made her way to California, where she taught ethnic studies and developed a deeper political consciousness of her Chicana identity against the backdrop of the larger Chicano Movement (Cantú, 60). Returning home to Chicago, Castillo served as writer in residence for the Illinois Arts Council in 1977, not long before completing a master's degree in

Latin American and Caribbean studies at the University of Chicago in 1979. Castillo would go on to complete her PhD in American studies at the University of Bremen in Germany in 1991, later transforming her nontraditional dissertation into the collection of personal and critical essays *Massacre of the Dreamers: Essays on Xicanisma*, in 1994.

Informed by her own experiences as a bisexual Chicana feminist, Castillo's innovative body of work centers on the intersections of race, class, gender, and sexuality in ways that honor Indigenous epistemologies and defy strict genre conventions. Perhaps best known for her imaginative novels, Castillo is also a prominent interdisciplinary scholar and theorist, coining the term "Xicanisma" to signify Chicana feminism in the early 1990s. Deeply personal and political, Castillo's work invokes what Cherríe Moraga and Gloria Anzaldúa call "theory in the flesh" in *This Bridge Called My Back* (23). Her writing foregrounds communal and ancestral memory as a vital source of knowledge at the same time that it grapples with "the pull and tug of having to choose between which parts of our mothers' heritages we want to claim and wear and which parts have served to cloak us from the knowledge of ourselves" (23). Considered a foundational Chicana feminist thinker, Castillo critiques heterosexist expectations of women perpetuated by Chicano nationalists. Speaking back to machista cultural beliefs that demand that motherhood and marriage be at the center of a woman's identity, Castillo crafts narratives that highlight the strength, resilience, and necessity of women's friendship and close bonds. So too does her work engage with the complexities of race, ethnicity, and nation, interrogating the long-lasting effects of colonialism while at the same time elevating Indigenous ways of life. Castillo's expansive body of work has garnered her numerous awards and honors. Her first novel, *The Mixquiahuala Letters* (1986), won the American Book Award from the Before Columbus Foundation in 1987, while *So Far from God* (1993), often considered Castillo's most noteworthy work of fiction, earned her a *New York Times* Notable Book of the Year award, the Carl Sandburg Literary Award, and a Mountains and Plains Independent Booksellers Association award. Castillo's collection of personal essays, *Black Dove: Mamá, Mi'jo, and Me* (2016), received the 2016 International Latino Book Award for best autobiography and the 2017 Lambda Literary Award for best bisexual nonfiction. Her most recent awards include the 2018 PEN Oakland Reginald Lockett Lifetime Achievement Award, the 2018 Site Committee Critical Thought Award from Mujeres Activistas en Letras y Cambio Social, and the 2020 Northeastern Illinois University Distinguished Alumnus Award.

Castillo has also served in many distinguished academic positions throughout her career as a teacher and scholar. In 2012, she was poet in residence at Westminster College in Utah, and she won the American Studies Association Gloria E. Anzaldúa Award for Independent Scholars in 2013. Castillo also held the Lund-Gill Chair of the Rosary College of Arts and Sciences at Dominican University in Illinois in 2014–2015, later serving as faculty for the Bread Loaf School of English summer program at Middlebury College in 2015 and 2016. In addition to receiving fellowships for fiction and poetry from the National Endowment for the Arts, Castillo has also held prestigious academic appointments, including the first Sor Juana Inés de la Cruz Endowed Chair position at DePaul University and the Martin Luther King Jr. Visiting Scholar position at MIT.

As this brief biographical introduction illustrates, Castillo's significance as a Chicana feminist writer and thinker is too great to be properly or fully represented within the parameters of this short chapter. Rather than attempt to detail a complete portrait of Castillo's work, I have chosen to examine central themes within a focused selection of her essays and fiction, including *Massacre of the Dreamers: Essays on Xicanisma*; *The Mixquiahuala Letters*; *Sapogonia* (1990); and *So Far from God*. Readers are encouraged to explore the equally significant works of nonfiction, fiction, poetry, and drama not represented here.

CORE THEMES IN *MASSACRE OF THE DREAMERS: ESSAYS ON XICANISMA*

As referenced earlier, *Massacre of the Dreamers* began as the dissertation project that would earn Castillo her doctorate in American studies from the University of Bremen in 1991. Resisting academia's long-standing belief that knowledge production and scholarship are necessarily objective, Castillo's critical essay collection performs historical and cultural criticism intimately connected to—rather than removed from—her own lived experiences. In line with earlier Chicana feminist theorists Anzaldúa and Moraga, Castillo's essay collection embodies the personal as political, positioning her individual voice as a brown Chicana within a larger political movement and collective. In the introduction, she writes: "Throughout the history of the United States 'I' as a subject and object has been reserved for white authorship and readership. . . . Within the confines of these pages, 'I' and the mestiza/Mexic Amerindian woman's identity become universal. It is to that woman whom I first and foremost address my thoughts" (1). In centralizing brown Chicana perspectives and experiences in *Massacre of the Dreamers*, Castillo consciously speaks back to and subverts their widespread erasure from the white mainstream feminist movement of the late twentieth century and in public scholarship more broadly.

Castillo coins the term "Xicanisma" in *Massacre of the Dreamers* to signify Chicana feminist activism and politics. She deliberately uses the X to honor Nahuatl linguistic practices, emphasizing the Chicana's connection to her Indigenous Mexican ancestry. Rather than rely on a singular term to describe women of Mexican descent, Castillo invokes several throughout her essay collection—"Mexic Amerindian," "Chicana," "mestiza," and "mejicana"—all based on varied historical and political contexts. She writes early on that the complex racial and ethnic histories of women classified as Chicana "cannot be summarized nor neatly categorized" (1). She is therefore careful not to flatten differences or essentialize Chicanas into a singular perspective; instead, she brings their common experiences together to highlight shared struggles against racial, ethnic, class-based, and gendered oppressions.

While she sees language as fluid, contextual, and often incomplete, Castillo is invested in the act of self-naming as "a rejection of colonization" (12). *Massacre of the Dreamers* specifically interrogates and critiques the label "Hispanic" for centralizing European ancestry, seeking instead to connect descendants of Latin America with their Indigenous and African roots. In the essay "A Countryless Woman," Castillo writes:

> Hispanic gives us all one ultimate paternal cultural progenitor: Spain. The diverse cultures already on the American shores when the Euro-

peans arrived, as well as those introduced because of the African slave trade, are completely obliterated by the term. Hispanic is nothing more than a concession made by the U.S. legislature when they saw they couldn't get rid of us. If we won't go away, why not at least Euro-peanize us, make us presentable guests at the dinner table, take away our feathers and rattles and civilize us once and for all. (28)

In this sense, "Hispanic" serves to further the colonial project of Spain every time it is uttered. The catch-all label defines descendants of Latin America by their common colonizer, failing to recognize the diversity of cultures and traditions that preceded and have endured beyond Spanish colonization. Castillo therefore rejects the term, call-ing for readers to recognize and embrace cultural nuances.

Castillo also interrogates gender relations prior to Spanish col-onization and their endurance into the contemporary moment. In "The Ancient Roots of Machismo," she specifically examines how the Mexica peoples structured life around gender roles we still recognize today. Girls and women were responsible for domestic duties and given little schooling, while boys and men served in positions of lead-ership (64). Spanish colonization only perpetuated this imbalance of power as the rise of capitalism necessitated the oppression and com-modification of women. Their domestic labor fueled the production of goods at the same time their bodies were expected to produce future laborers. As Castillo writes, "Conquest women were already living out the blueprint for the following generations of Mexican women" (65). The sociopolitical system of machismo we recognize today, in other words, is directly connected to earlier forms of male dominance and violence.

Castillo specifically addresses the phenomenon in which Mexican men who have been socially and politically marginalized by white elites reestablish a sense of power by dispossessing women in their own communities. Taking advantage of laws and customs that have historically necessitated women's financial dependence on men, Mexi-can men are culturally encouraged to take on the roles of provider and protector of women. In order to maintain this macho mentality, men subjugate women to second-class status and reject their independence. Machismo also requires the policing of women's bodies and sexuality to the extent that girls are expected to maintain a sense of innocence and purity as virgins, only engaging in sex to fulfill their roles as mothers once married.

Women are therefore assumed heterosexual by default; any deviation from heteronormativity would threaten the dependence on men that machismo demands. As Castillo writes in "La Macha: Toward an Erotic Whole Self": "The traditions of our [Mexican] heritage, the rules of the Church, and importantly, economic dependency, still make most women who feel themselves to be lesbian or bisexual opt for a heterosexual lifestyle" (134). Like others who have experienced the pressure of religious indoctrination, particularly that of Catholicism, lesbian Chicanas were—and often still are—expected to repress their sexual identities. Whereas the economic privilege of white lesbians has historically afforded them easier access to financial independence and higher education, lesbian Chicanas have had to overcome multiple oppressive barriers to publicly exist beyond the confines of machismo and heteronormativity.

While Castillo recognizes the long-standing relationship between Mexican communities and Catholicism, she also seeks to revive non-Western spiritual beliefs and practices. She is particularly invested in recovering spiritual connection to the feminine, which she sees as a life-sustaining, nurturing force historically subordinated by white paternalism. In "Brujas and Curanderas: A Lived Spirituality," Castillo examines the significance of *curanderismo* for Chicana feminists seeking reconnection to ancestral spiritual practices. She highlights the importance of reviving such practices with attention to contemporary needs and contexts. Whereas some ancient customs relied on hierarchical gender roles, the modern-day Chicana and *curandera* has the capacity to enact spirituality in ways that empower and honor the feminine. Castillo also subverts negative connotations around brujas, seeking to elevate their spiritual practices as divine gifts. She writes: "In Mexican culture, a brujo is someone to fear and to revere while a bruja is someone to hate to the point of killing if at all possible. However, I claim this term for women who are in tune with their psyches, allow their lives to be informed by them, and offer their intuitive gifts to their communities without fear of being seen as loathsome or mad" (157). With attention to the ways men and patriarchal power have historically governed mainstream religious practices, Castillo revives the figure of the bruja as a vital spiritual practitioner who taps into spiritual realms and healing practices without asserting an imbalance of power between men and women or between humans and nonhumans.

While this section offers only a snapshot of the major ideas taken up in *Massacre of the Dreamers*, my hope is that readers gather the collection's cultural significance for Chicana feminists and all those allied with them. Castillo's articulation of Xicanisma ultimately elevated the long-standing activism, creative work, and spiritual labor of Chicana feminists to new heights. Described as "an ever present consciousness of our [Chicanas'] interdependency specifically rooted in our culture and history," Xicanisma recognizes the intersections of politics, spirituality, sexuality, and activism (*Massacre*, 226). *Massacre of the Dreamers*, considered a foundational Chicana feminist text, heightened Castillo's prominence as a theorist and scholar at the same time that she gained recognition for her poetry and fiction.

FEMINIST FRIENDSHIP AND QUEER POSSIBILITY IN *THE MIXQUIAHUALA LETTERS* AND *SAPOGONIA*

Like her critical essays, Castillo's novels center on Chicana feminist struggles against intersectional oppression. While her fictional narratives offer realistic portraits of machismo and the harm it inflicts on women, they also showcase the subtle and direct ways women resist and seek refuge from patriarchal power in their daily lives. In *The Mixquiahuala Letters* and *Sapogonia*, friendships serve as one such site where women establish solidarity against interpersonal and institutional forms of misogyny. While platonic, these relationships between women embody a level of intimacy unmatched by heterosexual partners in both novels, giving rise to queer interpretation. In crafting such meaningful, life-sustaining bonds between women that blur the line often drawn between friends and lovers, Castillo's novels challenge heteronormativity and imagine futures for women beyond those predicated on life commitments to men.

Castillo's debut novel, *The Mixquiahuala Letters*, centers on the intimate friendship and travels of Teresa, a Chicana writer, and Alicia, a Spanish Romani artist. While the novel details their shared experiences across the United States and Mexico, readers have access only to Teresa's side of their correspondence. Inspired by Argentinian writer Julio Cortázar,[1] Castillo offers multiple plot possibilities by organizing Teresa's letters in separate sequences: "For the Conformist," "For the Cynic," and "For the Quixotic." Each sequence offers different angles from which to view and interpret Teresa and Alicia's friendship. The path "For the Conformist" indicates that Teresa and Alicia eventually retire their adventures across the border so Teresa can establish a family with her husband, while the path "For the Cynic" suggests a betrayal of their friendship when Teresa finds out that one of her ex-boyfriends had been secretly living with and dating Alicia in Puerto Rico. The path "For the Quixotic" speculates the least conventional plot as it portrays the women's friendship outlasting their relationships with men, indicating a conclusion that relies more on the women's life-sustaining connection than their fleeting heterosexual love affairs. While each sequence projects different possibilities surrounding the fate of Teresa and Alicia's friendship, what remains central to the novel is the meaningful role the women embody in each other's lives, particularly to a degree no other relationship fulfills.

Throughout the novel, Teresa recounts personal memories of Alicia with the affinity and fondness of a lover. At some points addressing her as "sister, companion . . . friend" and at other times comparing their relationship "to that of an old wedded couple," Teresa's descriptions of Alicia embody an unparalleled level of trust and understanding (24, 53). While both women maintain sexual and romantic relationships with men throughout the novel, none garner the same level of intimacy readers witness between the two women. In fact, relationships with men are often fleeting, purely sexual, or depicted as mere social obligations to fulfill. In one letter, Teresa reflects on her marriage: "i[2] was never in love with Sergio Samora, although he was attractive and likable. What did love have to do with the order of things? A woman didn't marry for love. . . . She married out of necessity" (68). Unlike her relationship with Sergio, whom she would eventually divorce, Teresa's relationship with Alicia reflects the meaningful and genuine connection one might ascribe to life partners (127). Recalling one of their trips to Mexico, Teresa writes: "It is true we slept together curled up on the double seat of a rickety Mexican bus that wound its way through the nocturnal roads from one strange place to another; a soft shoulder served as a pillow for one another's head. . . . It is true we bathed together in the most casual sense, scrubbed each other's back, combed out one another's wet hair, braided it with more care than grandmothers who invariably catch it on broken tooth combs. . . . For the first half of the decade we were an objective one, a single entity, nondiscriminate of the other's being" (127–128). While Teresa offers an intimate portrait of their relationship, even describing herself and Alicia as "experts at exchanging empathy for heart-rending confusion known only to lovers," she ultimately rejects the label of "lovers" because of its sexualized connotation (127).

Teresa's letters never indicate that her relationship with Alicia is sexual, nor do they suggest a desire for it to be, but the women share an unmatched level of intimacy that many read as queer.[3] Castillo, in fact, displaces sex as the defining feature of queer desire in an interview with Marta A. Navarro. When asked about her characters' potential lesbianism, Castillo says: "I would consider a lesbian relationship to be one in which one makes a very clear lifestyle decision and commitment, whether or not she's having sex with another woman. . . . In this case, with these two women, it's up to the reader to decide whether or not they were in love with each other" (Navarro, 119). Castillo's response coincides with Teresa's sentiments about sex in *The Mixquiahuala Letters*. At several points in the novel, sex with men is described as an urge to be fulfilled rather than an intimate or meaningful form of bonding. In one letter, Teresa deflates both her and Alicia's sexual encounters with men by situating them within the social grip heteronormativity has on their lives, reminding Alicia that "we weren't free of society's tenets to be convinced we could exist indefinitely without the demands and complications one aggregated with the supreme commitment to a man. Even greater than these factors was that of an ever present need, emotional, psychological, physical . . . it provoked us nonetheless to seek approval from [men] through sexual meetings" (*Mixquiahuala*, 45). Here, Teresa embodies Castillo's point that internalized homophobia and the cultural weight of heteronormativity place many women in a state of denial about their queer desire. While she invites readers to speculate about and determine the nature of Teresa and Alicia's relationship on their own terms, she recognizes that the characters themselves are too pressured by compulsory heterosexuality to openly identify with lesbianism.

Castillo's second novel, *Sapogonia*, similarly depicts an intimate friendship between two women that invites queer interpretation. While the novel centers on Max Madrigal as he journeys across Europe and North America in an attempt to make sense of his mestizo identity, it also features a secondary relationship between close friends named Perla and Pastora. Although the women's relationship exists in the background of Max's story, it has garnered attention from readers for challenging the romantic/platonic binary that typically governs Western relationship structures. Both Perla and Pastora engage in heterosexual relationships throughout the novel, but none warrant the same level of intimacy shared between the two friends. Upon first meeting, Perla offers Pastora an immediate sense of familiarity and comfort. Expanding her solo music to include more voices, Pastora is met with an overbearing male vocalist named Saúl, who threatens their professional relationship by coming on to her. Pastora finds relief in Perla's company during rehearsal, "enjoy[ing] Perla's comradery, the empathy of those born of the same sex" (22). This comfort is felt on both ends. Perla opens up to Pastora immediately, sharing her woes of being a single mother who had been rejected from her family for resisting marriage. As Castillo writes, "Pastora hardly said a word, and yet Perla knew that Pastora was with her, understanding the tragedy of her young life" (19). This description of their gendered connection communicates a level of trust between the women that stems from their shared social positionings, which ultimately provides the foundation of their friendship.

The close relationship Perla and Pastora eventually develop threatens men who attempt to pursue them romantically. When Max is initially transfixed by Pastora and asks his friend about the pair, Jacobo responds: "You can't get anywhere with them, believe me, my friend. I've known plenty of men who've tried. I think they're lesbians" (25). This sentiment is echoed multiple times throughout the novel, showcasing their overt intimate relationship. At the same time, Jacobo's response reveals the heterosexist climate ultimately driving the two women close together as they offer each other a distinct sense of empathy and understanding. As women, and Chicanas in particular, Pastora and Perla navigate the world with similar social positionings; they are hypersexualized by men in their community while at the same time read as uptight, "conceited" lesbians for rejecting their advances (25). Pastora and Perla find comfort in each other's company and take pride in their shared resistance to men's unwanted attention.

As their friendship grows, Pastora and Perla merge lives and move in together. Their intimate bond deepens to the point that they resemble "a pair of newlyweds, blissful within the tight cocoon they had woven for themselves" (69). There are subsequent descriptions of intimate gestures Perla performs for Pastora: "Each morning, before Pastora went off to work, Perla prepared for her friend a cup of cafe con leche, dashed with cinnamon. She poured it into an earthenware cup that was painted with gladiolas. She knew this pleased Pastora very much. Perla found dozens of small ways to please her friend, whom she now loved. She might prepare dinner, though out of a can, or save Pastora the trouble [of] warming up her car in the morning by starting out first to confront the cold" (69). This passage amplifies Perla's attention to detail and care in her pursuit of satisfying Pastora, even if it requires discomfort on her part. While the narrator emphasizes the word "friend" here, the partner-like gestures rooted in Perla's love for Pastora exemplify that their friendship, however platonic, is very queer.

Even Perla is aware of the unconventional closeness she experiences with Pastora within their friendship. Not only is she aware of their heightened level of intimacy, but she also chooses to repress her awareness because "it made [her] uneasy . . . that she behaved this way with a woman, while having no patience whatsoever with the wishes of men" (69). Given the deeply heteronormative culture surrounding them, it is no surprise that Perla experiences bouts of internalized homophobia and confusion. Yet the intimacy they share continues to grow to such magnitudes, they routinely ward off male lovers to bask in each other's company instead. Their relationships with men are in fact scarce when they are living together. In their one-bedroom apartment, the women "shared the same bed, the only closet, each other's clothes, make-up, [and] toothbrush" (69). Much like romantic partners or newlyweds, the women's lives become so intimately intertwined, they are nearly inseparable. Men appear only to satisfy fleeting sexual pleasures, and even then, their visits are limited. Instead, Pastora and Perla "celebrated all the possible advantages of sharing life with another woman, while counting the disadvantages one had when sharing it with the opposite sex" (69). Men, at this point, embody temporary and routine roles in the women's lives rather than any substantive connections.

Sex is in fact decentered as the root of intimacy in their lives. The level of trust, empathy, and understanding they share as women and close friends takes precedence over their cursory sexual relations with men. When Pastora's childhood friend Fabiola comes to visit, she is in awe of the home and life the women have built together. On a night out, Pastora and Perla's intimate relationship intrigues Fabiola as she witnesses "what life was like on a given evening with the most delightful couple she had ever known" (70). Fabiola's excitement for the two women absorbs her. She realizes that the only aspect missing from their partner-like relationship is sex. She notes, in fact, that "everything else was obvious; companionship, financial interdependency, as well as individual independence" (70).

Following her visit, Fabiola is inspired by the relationship she witnesses between her old friend and Perla. She begins to reflect on her married life, making note of its shortcomings. The narrator amplifies Fabiola's inner dialogue in a series of questions: "When had Fabiola driven the car with her husband as a passenger when he didn't nearly push her to tears with his constant criticism and commands? . . . When had her husband cooked dinner for her last as she entertained a friend in the living room? . . . When had he said he was confident she was going to succeed in a goal that was outside the home—and was actually prepared to be a shadow in her life as a result of it if necessary to keep her going?" (71). Fabiola envies that Pastora and Perla "lived without the prerequisite of men" (71). After Fabiola and her friend Rosario share a potluck with the pair, they devise a plan to leave their husbands in pursuit of independence. While only one follows through with this pact, the outcome of their visit at Pastora and Perla's signifies the appeal of two women forging their own paths in support of each other without the demands or expectations of male lovers.

When Pastora's sexual relationship with Max heightens, it causes a rift in her relationship with Perla. One night, as the two get ready for bed, they are startled by an unexpected visit from Max. Seemingly jealous, "Perla hadn't understood before then that anything so intimate was going on between Maximo and Pastora" (124). It is only a perceived sense of intimacy, however, as Max's role in Pastora's life serves her only sexually. Even worse, Max's fixation with Pastora fuels his ego rather than his heart. He believes that "Pastora was his sexual counterpart in every sense, that she was as much a manizer, a Jezebel of a thousand lovers, as he was the Cortés of every Vagina he crossed" (124). Smug and insincere, Max treats Pastora as a sexual prop in his life, with no real regard for her as a person. In turn, Pastora turns to Max only for sex, at times with the impression of passionate love. It is clear, however, that their relationship is both toxic and fleeting, with no real intimacy beyond that which they imagine.

Following this incident, Perla is once again confronted with the intensity of her feelings for her friend. She is "disturbed" at the level at which she and Pastora grew attached to one another and at her partner-like devotion to a woman. In "fear that one day Pastora would reject her, might think her too trivial, abandon her," Perla sets out to marry a man who might fulfill her need for Pastora's affections in a more socially acceptable capacity (126). The closeness they once shared eventually dissipates into more heteronormative modes of life. Both eventually marry men, despite their initial resistance, and have children. What this "ending" suggests, more than anything, is the powerful pressure of heteronormative life on women who once resented it. Their marriages come into fruition more as obligations to the status quo than as gestures of love. Yet the strength and intensity of their friendship, however changed, remains an integral part of their lives throughout the novel.

The Mixquiahuala Letters and *Sapogonia* represent only two of the many important contributions Castillo has made to the canon of Chicana feminist literature. In centralizing the experiences of women, particularly Chicanas, Castillo's novels intervene in the long-standing tradition of machista writers who have silenced or flattened women's perspectives in their accounts of Mexican American life. Her characterization of women's friendships, in particular, generates important discussion regarding queer life and its literary resonances beyond explicit identity disclosures or sexual encounters. Castillo's novels also illuminate the cultural weight of compulsory heterosexuality, ultimately offering portraits of women's lives—however incomplete or fleeting—that imagine possibilities for love and relationships outside those determined by men.

SPIRITUALITY, MYSTICISM, AND THE DIVINE FEMININE IN *SO FAR FROM GOD*

So Far from God is another one of Castillo's most notable works. The novel centers on the interconnected lives of Sofi and her daughters, Esperanza, Fe, Caridad, and La Loca, in their small village of Tome, New Mexico. Beginning with La Loca's death and resurrection as a toddler, the novel showcases the town's unexplainable happenings, including miraculous recoveries, clairvoyance, cosmic connections, psychic dreams, and more. At the same time offering criticism of the Catholic Church for institutionally subjugating women, *So Far from God* elevates non-Western epistemologies and spiritual practices— especially those exercised by women. Castillo indeed taps into a new spiritual imagination inspired by a divine feminine energy, one that blends Indigenous cosmologies with popular Catholic traditions that continue to govern many Mexican American spiritual practices.

Each of the daughters in *So Far from God* embodies or experiences what readers might call supernatural occurrences. La Loca, the youngest, is pronounced dead at the age of three . . . until she comes back to life at her funeral, levitates to the rooftop, and tells her community about her travels through heaven, hell, and purgatory. While Father Jerome, the priest overseeing her funeral, questions if La Loca's resurrection is holy or evil, Sofi rejects his authority and embraces her daughter's return as a gift from God. La Loca, too, rejects Father Jerome's paternalism when he tells her that he will pray for her, and she responds: "'No, Padre . . . Remember, it is *I* who am here to pray for *you*'" (24). Each of these instances portrays subtle, yet direct, acts of rebellion against male authority; these figure prominently in the novel. As Theresa Delgadillo writes, "By insisting on the miraculousness of her experience and her communion with other realms, Loca insists on her spiritual power and agency" (895). While community members attempt to take advantage of La Loca's divine energy, she ultimately asserts a firm boundary against social interaction and only exercises her healing powers on her own terms.

Two such instances of La Loca spiritually intervening occur when her sisters Fe and Caridad experience seemingly irreparable emotional and physical wounds. After suffering a sudden, heartbreaking separation from her fiancé, Fe screams uncontrollably for over ten days and nights. Her "bloodcurdling wail became part of the household's routine," an unnatural and unexplainable response to a breakup (*So Far*, 32). At the same time that Fe is unable to stop screaming, Caridad comes home in a near-death state. After living through a horrible assault that left her with no nipples, branded skin, and a stab wound to her throat, Caridad miraculously recovers one day with no physical trace of the assault. Her spontaneous recovery sparks the same in Fe, who, embracing her healed sister, finally stops screaming. Witnessing her sisters' recoveries, La Loca comments, "I prayed real hard," suggesting that she is the one responsible for their sudden improvements (38).

Caridad adopts her own set of mystical powers following her recovery and, in turn, a newfound sense of independence. She undergoes a bout of psychic predictions, including one that reveals her upcoming departure from home. She then moves into a trailer owned by doña Felicia, a landlady over ninety years old. Taking Caridad in as a student, doña Felicia teaches her all she knows about spirituality and healing. As Castillo writes, "Felicia was a non-believer of sorts and remained that way, suspicious of the [institutional] religion that did not help the destitute all around her despite their devotion" (60). It was not until the death of her soldier husband and the task of finding her way home with two infant children that she developed faith "based not on an institution but on the bits and pieces of the souls and knowledge of the wise teachers she met along the way" (60). Eventually reconciling her bruised relationship with religion, doña Felicia develops a hybrid spirituality made of Christian faith and non-Western practices of curanderismo, the knowledge of which she bestows upon Caridad. To treat ailments such as "empacho and bilis, mal de ojo, caída de mollera, and susto," doña Felicia uses herbs, body massages, and "'limpias'—cleansings" (63). Blending prayer with cultural healing practices, doña Felicia represents a spiritual figure whose power depends, not on the paternalistic church, but on the nurturing and intuitive spirit of the divine feminine.

Setting out to connect more intimately with her spiritual teachings, Caridad goes on a pilgrimage to El Santuario de Chimayó, a mystical Catholic site in New Mexico, where she experiences another cosmic force—this time, an explainable force of love and longing. At the sanctuary, Caridad encounters a beautiful woman who completely entrances her. As the narrator explains: "Caridad could do nothing but think of the woman on the wall. . . . She was exhausted and nearly dehydrated and surely she could not have experienced what she felt throughout her entire body just from the sight of a woman!" (76). As her curiosity over the woman grows, so too does her urge to know and love her. Caridad eventually confronts the woman, named Esmeralda, and with only a few exchanged words she finds herself in love. The two women eventually meet the same fate when, on a trip to Acoma Pueblo, they jump to their deaths after seeing a coyote disguised as a tourist. This scene challenges Western depictions of death as the women, despite jumping off a mountain, disappear without a trace—"no morbid remains of splintered bodies tossed to the ground. . . . There weren't even whole bodies lying peaceful. There was nothing" (211). Instead, the Acoma Pueblo spiritual deity Tsichtinako guides Caridad and Esmeralda "down, deep within the soft, moist dark earth where [they] would be safe and live forever" (211). Rather than rise up to a Christian-based heaven, the women descend back into the earth as one.

So Far from God captures a spiritual hybridity that many Chicanxs have come to know intimately. As Delgadillo articulates, many practice a form of Catholicism "shaped by its practitioners into what they need," which oftentimes—as is the case in Castillo's novel—includes "a hybrid practice [that] maintains and recovers the knowledge of a spirituality wherein women partake and heal" (913). Castillo's centralization of women as spiritual beings separate from the church (though often still connected to it in some capacity) serves to elevate the divine feminine against dominant images of paternalism and masculinity. At the same time, Castillo's depiction of non-Western spiritual practices captures the enduring significance of Indigenous ways of life often suppressed or silenced in mainstream religious institutions. An important Chicana feminist text, *So Far from God* will continue to spark necessary discourse surrounding the intersections of race, gender, spirituality, and sexuality.

CONCLUSION

While this chapter has covered only a small sampling of Castillo's work, I have sought to provide a portrait of major themes in both her critical essays and her novels that remain relevant today. Castillo's exploration of women's sexuality, friendship, spirituality, and "Chicana" as a political term and identity remains central to our contemporary understanding of Chicana feminism and its enduring significance. Her formulation of Xicanisma in *Massacre of the Dreamers* serves to elevate Chicana voices and perspectives as connected to, but ultimately distinct from, constructions of Latinidad more broadly. Intertwining personal reflections with cultural criticism, Castillo's essay collection also transcends rigid genre conventions and honors firsthand experience as a vital source of knowledge. Readers can identify a similar approach in her 2016 personal essay collection, *Black Dove: Mamá, Mi'jo, and Me*, which captures her experiences as a bisexual single mother grappling with her son's incarceration and a larger culture of racist policing. A winner of the 2017 Lambda Literary Award for Bisexual Nonfiction, *Black Dove* examines overarching social justice issues through Castillo's personal story.

Her fiction, too, remains widely celebrated for its experimental form and engagement with pressing social and political issues. After she gained status as a protest poet, the publication of her first three works of fiction—*The Mixquiahuala Letters*, *Sapogonia*, and *So Far from God*—heightened Castillo's prominence as a novelist and postmodern writer. Refusing linear plot structures, each of the aforementioned novels recounts the lives of Chicana/o characters through oscillating points of view, flashbacks, and intertextual references. Castillo's first collection of short stories, *Loverboys* (1996), captures memorable stories of love and lust in both queer and heterosexual relationships. Other notable novels include *Peel My Love Like an Onion* (1999), which features a disabled Latina protagonist caught in a love triangle with Romani men and a subsequent clash of cultures, and *Watercolor Women Opaque Men: A Novel in Verse* (2005), which features a bisexual Chicana protagonist coming to terms with her sexual and cultural identities. Castillo's most recent novels include *The Guardians* (2007), which centers on the strength of familial bonds against enduring struggles at the New Mexico border, and *Give It to Me* (2014), winner of a Lambda Literary Award for Best Bisexual Fiction, which features a Chicana protagonist in search of purpose amid sexual adventures and an unusual obsession with her cousin.

Any discussion of Castillo's work and prominence should also recognize her first love: poetry. After publishing three chapbooks—*Otro Canto* (1977), *The Invitation* (1979), and *Women Are Not Roses* (1984)—Castillo would go on to establish her domain as a renowned Chicana poet with the publication of her first major collection, *"My Father Was a Toltec" and Selected Poems, 1973–1988,* in 1995. This collection, versed in both English and Spanish, revisits and extends her earlier poetry, capturing the pains, joys, and lessons of life as a Chicana in the late twentieth century. In 2001, Castillo published her second major collection of poetry, *I Ask the Impossible*, which combines both personal and political musings on love, sensuality, and social justice. Her newest collection of poetry was released in 2021 by High Road Books, an imprint of University of New Mexico Press. Entitled *My Book of the Dead: New Poems*, the collection examines contemporary social and political issues, including the growing environmental crisis and COVID-19 pandemic, enduring racism and xenophobia against Black and brown people, and the horrors and lasting effects of Donald Trump's presidency.

Today, Castillo remains an active writer and activist. She is the editor of *La Tolteca 2.0*, a creative virtual zine centering on the work of marginalized artists and writers, and, as referenced above, she continues to excite readers with forthcoming original work of her own. In a 2019 interview with *Foglifter*, an LGBTQ+ publication based in San Francisco, Castillo reasserted her identity as a political writer whose earlier activism continues into our contemporary moment. Reflecting specifically on her public criticism of Trump's presidency, Castillo responded:

People told me to be careful—in a dictatorship or authoritarian rule, there is no enemy too small. I knew I was on the radar back in the 70's and 80's. Rather than go down with a whimper, let me go down with a bang. Let me just do this, that's what I've been doing all my life. Why am I going to let my sorrow and my fear overtake me? People need to hear, need to be encouraged—as they say—to carry on. So, it's still a struggle, a struggle emotionally and spiritually. In every way that I can, I feel it's important to speak out. (Chan and Galloway)

Castillo's courage to write and speak on pressing issues impacting oppressed communities both locally and abroad has cemented her prominence as a politically engaged artist. Her creative work and activism will continue to inspire readers to imagine a socially just world until it is finally realized.

NOTES

1. *The Mixquiahuala Letters* was inspired by the experimental form of *Hopscotch* (1963) by Julio Cortázar. Castillo dedicates the novel to him for this reason.
2. Throughout the novel the personal pronoun "I" appears in lowercase, which I have maintained in this chapter. In an interview with Bryce Milligan (1999) for *South Central Review*, Ana Castillo comments: "In *The Mixquiahuala Letters*, I used the lowercase 'i' throughout because I feel—I might be wrong about this . . . that I am talking about a lot of people" (26). In this sense, the "i" places Teresa's individual experiences within those of a larger collective of women.
3. See "The Homoerotic Tease and Lesbian Identity in Ana Castillo's Work" (2003) by Ibis Gómez-Vega and "Ana Castillo's *The Mixquiahuala Letters*: A Queer *Don Quijote*" (2007) by Barbara F. Weissberger for scholarly interpretations of lesbianism in Ana Castillo's novels.

WORKS CITED

Cantú, Norma E. "A Conversation with Ana Castillo." *World Literature Today* 82, no. 2 (March 2008): 59–62.

Castillo, Ana. *Black Dove: Mamá, Mi'jo, and Me*. New York: Feminist Press, 2016.

———. *Give It to Me*. New York: Feminist Press, 2014.

———. *The Guardians*. New York: Random House, 2007.

———. *I Ask the Impossible: Poems*. New York: Anchor Books, 2001.

———. *The Invitation*. Self-published, 1979.

———. *Loverboys*. New York: W. W. Norton, 1996.

———. *Massacre of the Dreamers: Essays on Xicanisma*. New York: Plume, 1994.

———. *The Mixquiahuala Letters*. New York: Bilingual Press, 1986.

———. *My Book of the Dead: New Poems*. Albuquerque: High Road Books, an imprint of University of New Mexico Press, 2021.

———. *"My Father Was a Toltec" and Selected Poems, 1973–1988*. New York: W. W. Norton, 1995.

———. *Otro Canto*. Chicago: Alternativa Publications, 1977.

———. *Peel My Love Like an Onion*. New York: Doubleday, 1999.

———. *Sapogonia*. New York: Bilingual Press, 1990.

———. *So Far from God*. New York: W. W. Norton, 1993.

———. *Watercolor Women Opaque Men: A Novel in Verse*. Willimantic, Conn.: Curbstone Press, 2005.

———. *Women Are Not Roses*. Houston: Arte Público Press, 1984.

Chan, Celeste, and Jessie Galloway. "Writers Have to Write Right Now: An Interview with Ana Castillo." *Foglifter*, April 24, 2018. foglifterjournal.com/2018/04/24/writers-have-to-write-right-now-an-interview-with-ana-castillo/.

Delgadillo, Theresa. "Forms of Chicana Feminist Resistance: Hybrid Spirituality in Ana Castillo's *So Far from God*." *Modern Fiction Studies* 44, no. 4 (1998): 888–916.

Gómez-Vega, Ibis. "The Homoerotic Tease and Lesbian Identity in Ana Castillo's Work." *Crítica Hispana* 25, nos. 1–2 (2003): 65–84.

Milligan, Bryce. "An Interview with Ana Castillo." *South Central Review* 16, no. 1 (1999): 19–29.

Moraga, Cherríe, and Gloria Anzaldúa, eds. *This Bridge Called My Back: Writings by Radical Women of Color*. Watertown, Mass.: Persephone Press, 1981, 23.

Navarro, Marta A. "Interview with Ana Castillo." *Chicana Lesbians: The Girls Our Mothers Warned Us About*. Edited by Carla Trujillo. Berkeley: Third Woman Press, 1991, 113–32.

Weissberger, Barbara F. "Ana Castillo's *The Mixquiahuala Letters*: A Queer *Don Quijote*." *Letras Femeninas* 33, no. 2 (2007): 9–23.

LORNA DEE CERVANTES

LORNA DEE CERVANTES

"No Self but in Other Selves"

ELIZA RODRÍGUEZ

AN INTERNATIONALLY acclaimed Chicana poet, Lorna Dee Cervantes is the author of six volumes of poetry: *Emplumada* (1981); *From the Cables of Genocide: Poems of Love and Hunger* (1991); *Drive: The First Quartet; New Poems, 1980–2005* (2006); *Ciento: 100 100-Word Love Poems* (2011); *Sueño* (2013); and *April on Olympia* (2021). Her work has appeared in more than 150 anthologies, including *The Norton Anthology of American Literature* and *The Heath Anthology of American Literature*. She is the winner of the Paterson Prize for Poetry, the Latino Literature Award, and the American Book Award, and she has received two fellowships from the National Endowment for the Arts as well as a Lila Wallace–Reader's Digest Award. Since 1976, Cervantes has presented at more than one thousand poetry readings, lectures, performances, and panel discussions in such places as the Library of Congress, the White House, the Walker Art Center, and major university campuses. Her work has been translated into German, Italian, French, Spanish, and Czechoslovakian. She now lives and works in Seattle, Washington.

Cervantes began her publishing career not only as a writer but also as a literary activist and publisher. She founded Mango Publications in

1976, at a time when Chicana/o/x writing and publication were dominated by men. Her work in the establishment and material production of Latina/o/x literature is, frankly, unparalleled. She published the famous Chicano Chapbook series and *Mango*, a cross-cultural literary and art magazine, nurturing a community of Chicana/o/x writers in print; several luminaries of Latina/o/x literature were first published by her press, including Gary Soto, Sandra Cisneros, Jimmy Santiago Baca, Alberto Ríos, and Ray Gonzalez. Even in the context of the material aspects of literary production and circulation, Cervantes's attention to style is characteristic of her work. Cervantes describes this confluence of form and content, style and living: "I did it out of my kitchen on a little multilith press, which is sort of a pre-offset press. And it came out all smudgy pages and everything. But there was this explosion of this sort of literature being published and it didn't matter, it was anti-slick, it was the anti-aesthetic, you work with what you have, and you make good with what you have, you make it damn good, even though it looks *rasquache*" ("On Allen Ginsberg"). In this and other recollections of her publishing work, she names the specific room in her home where she undertook this labor—the kitchen. This location is both literal and symbolic of the sustaining and caretaking work that creating space for Chicana/o/x and Latina/o/x writers was, and it remains central to the development of this body of work. It is, for Cervantes, heart-driven and hearth-grounded work. Cervantes's celebration of *rasquachismo* in this description, the valorization of making art out of making do, of making something remarkable out of the absolutely ordinary, has long been a hallmark aesthetic central to the aesthetics and politics of working-class Chicana/o/x cultural production.[1]

During the early 1990s Cervantes founded and edited *Red Dirt*, a biannual, cross-cultural poetry journal. She has coordinated writing retreats for women of color, providing space, time, and intensive writing workshops dedicated to developing emerging literary voices. Creating the conditions for the writing, publication, and dissemination of "the poetry of possibility" has remained a driving force across Cervantes's lifetime.[2] Cervantes's evolving poetics are significant in American letters because they form connections across a range of literary traditions and canons, including figures as varied as Pablo Neruda, June

Jordan, Federico García Lorca, and Allen Ginsberg, who explore the linkages between poetry and politics, ethics and aesthetics. I invoke the term *poetics* very deliberately, referencing both the structures of the poems themselves and how they circulate in the world—the being and the doing of poetry. Both of these elements are central to understanding Cervantes's significance for Chicana/o/x literature in particular and the American canon more generally. Cervantes's work demonstrates how to revitalize familiar forms of political and social solidarity and action while offering important models for reading poetry and cultural texts. Cervantes articulates the discursive and historiographic interventions possible in the production and circulation of literature and the transformation of consciousness and politics via poetics. Such transformation depends on engaging *as a reader and as a writer* who undertakes the work of illuminating structures of power that shape human experience and history. In an interview titled "Poetry Saved My Life," Cervantes says, "Reading [the work of] African American women poets politicized me. And it was the fact that poetry politicized me that had to do with [these women poets] saving my life" (Gonzalez and Cervantes, "I Trust Only"). That politicization comes from the aesthetic and embodied experience of the literary—it is why, as Audre Lorde puts it so succinctly, "poetry is not a luxury." In that eponymous essay, Lorde elaborates: "There are no new ideas, there are only new ways of making them felt." This thinking-feeling synthesis drives the urgency of Cervantes's poetics—the back and forth between the form and content, between the beauty and horror that she often writes about and against. That life-saving dynamic is what puts Cervantes in the company of such crucially important feminist of color thinkers and writers of the late twentieth and early twenty-first century such as Lorde and Gloria Anzaldúa, who write from their experiences as working-class, racialized, and/or queer women to articulate foundational theoretical frameworks for feminists of color through the end of the twentieth and its turn to the twenty-first century. Cervantes has always articulated her sexuality as oriented toward men, but joins Anzaldúa and Lorde in their refusal of heteropatriarchal frameworks.

Cervantes was born in the Mission District of San Francisco and grew up in San José, California, in a working-class barrio named Horseshoe, which she references in *BIRD AVE*, the second book in

Drive: The First Quartet. Street violence, gangs, and poverty structured her everyday experiences, at the same time and as surely as working in the garden with her maternal grandmother did. At a poetry reading in 2012, Cervantes described accompanying her mother to clean houses and hotels, and she has written extensively about the poverty and the hunger that characterized that experience. Her writing about being one of a gang of "bad girls" epitomizes how Cervantes articulates the negotiations that such an upbringing—shaped by poverty and everyday violence—necessitates. In interviews, Cervantes describes the contradictions of being raised by a mother who simultaneously valued and nurtured her love of language and literature and at the same time resented and scolded her for it (Gonzalez and Cervantes, "I Trust Only"). Fortunately, her mother's own love for language and writing, which Cervantes references in the dedication to *Drive*, won out:

> In memory of Rose, my mother
> who, upon watching me write five entire poems
> in one day in my fifteenth year, said,
> "You tell 'em, Lorna. And after you tell 'em,
> you tell 'em who told you to tell 'em."

The repetition of "tell 'em" in this modest dedication underlines the importance of telling, which in Cervantes's work functions as an act of critical witnessing and poetic reportage, as Tiffany Ana López argues in her essay, "'Stunned into Being': The Practice of Critical Witnessing in Lorna Dee Cervantes's *Drive*." Such critical witnessing is a central element in the transformative potential of poetry in particular. López locates this witnessing within a discussion of trauma as "critically, politically, and personally generative" (182). I would add that in Cervantes's dedication to *Drive*, she also stresses the need for clear genealogies in the telling. In this dedicatory telling that frames *Drive: The First Quartet*, Cervantes places her mother in the same company as T. S. Eliot, whose lines from *Four Quartets* also open the collection. Cervantes thus intertwines and places working-class Chicana voices alongside Anglo canonical ones.

The voices of *mujeres* are nearly always centered in her work. Indeed, the poems in her first book, *Emplumada*, often focus on the relationships between the women in her family and herself as a writer. In "Under the Shadow of the Freeway," Cervantes describes her childhood home in matriarchal terms:

> We were a woman family:
> Grandma, our innocent Queen;
> Mama, the Swift Knight, Fearless Warrior.
> Mama wanted to be Princess instead.
> . . . .
> Myself: I could never decide.
> So I turned to books, those staunch, upright men.
> I became Scribe: Translator of Foreign Mail,
> Interpreting letters from the government, notices
> Of dissolved marriages and Welfare stipulations.
> I paid the bills, did light man-work, fixed faucets
> Insured everything
> Against all leaks. (11)

As Scribe, Cervantes is the speaker-poet who takes on the "man-work" necessary to maintain the matrilineal household and the innocence of the matriarch. Indeed, both daughters in this scheme assume masculine roles to protect their mothers. Writing, in this familial arrangement, is an extension of the labor (emotional and physical) required in order to maintain a household. And while writing is not necessarily masculine, books themselves are. Contributing to their ranks requires an engagement with action and with protecting the innocence of the Queen and Princess, as her mother before her does. Yet, throughout Cervantes's taking up the mantle of poet, she insists on her embodied experiences as a racialized, working-class woman.

Emplumada was critically celebrated for its articulation of the figure of the Chicana writer navigating a selfhood that is insistently working class, female, and literary, all of which is summed up in the title of this collection, a neologism combining the feminine noun *plumada*, or "pen flourish," and the masculine verb *emplumado*, which means "feathered, in plumage, as in after molting" (*Emplumada*). But any pleasure Cervantes might have enjoyed in the success of this first publication was cut short the following year with the devastating news of her mother's violent murder. The aftermath of this event would color both Cervantes's life and her writing for the rest of her career. Indeed, she would come to refer to her second book, *From the Cables of Genocide: Poems on Love and Hunger*, as her "grief book" (Gonzalez and Cervantes, "I Trust Only"). Indeed, the poems turn inward in a complex lyricism that explores the interiority of grief, love, hunger, and the historical and ongoing context of genocide and colonization. The result is a dense collection of poems in which history and memory, domestic violence, and genocide are so deeply intertwined that they are impossible to separate.

Across her body of work, Cervantes addresses the contemporary forms of that violent history, experienced as racism, class inequality, and misogyny. The scales of this violence range from the most intimate to the historical and material to the mythic. In her first book, *Emplumada*, poems detail sexual violence, domestic abuse, the grinding nature of poverty, and the struggle to lay claim to language. The first section of *Emplumada* is announced by a three-line epigraph:

Consider the power of wrestling
your ally. His will is to kill you.
He has nothing against you. (1)

The impersonal and contradictory nature of this aggression incisively captures the misogyny women face within even progressive social movements; the word "ally" suggests partners in struggle. And while the violence is impersonal, it is also embodied in the most intimate forms of relationship, as sexual violence and as domestic abuse. This poetic observation is made concrete in the statistics available about murdered women in the United States. According to the Centers for Disease Control, less than 16 percent of female homicide victims are killed by strangers, and more than half are killed by intimate partners; the rest are killed by friends and family members.[3] A pair of poems in *Emplumada*, "Lots: I; The Ally" and "Lots: II; Herself" are about a sexual assault in a vacant lot. The final lines of the second poem transform the speaker's injured body into something simultaneously precious and damning of heteronormative violence: "my used skin glistened / my first diamond" (9). Like Anzaldúa, Cervantes incorporates the body's wounding into a consideration of aesthetic production, which results in a transfiguration of the experiences of violence.

In her second book, *From the Cables of Genocide*, genocide is not something that happened five hundred years ago and is over; it is lived every day in the ordinary lives of Indigenous people and Chicanas. In "Pleiades from the Cables of Genocide," Cervantes invokes Chumash and Greek myth, describing the seven star sisters as young women who

> recite strange stories of epiphanies of light,
> Claim canons, cannons, and horses, and the strange
> Men in their boots in patterns of Nazis and Negroes. (44)

Literary, military, and colonial violence spanning from conquest to the twentieth century blur together from the perspective of myth. Historical and mythic time cross over each other in these poems, as do European and Indigenous frames of reference. Cervantes addresses the historical and contemporary violence of capitalism and the state against Indigenous people across the globe, an analysis that continues to shape the work published in *Drive: The First Quartet; Poems, 1980–2005*. Five books in one, each of them differs radically from the others. The volume begins with *"How Far's the War?,"* which includes the poems "Bananas" and "Coffee," detailing the violence of colonization, neocolonial capitalist wars across the Americas, the massacres of Indigenous people and mestizos in these wars, the violence of poverty, and the power of poetry. The second book, *BIRD AVE*, is an autobiographical poetic account of her own adolescence. *Play*, which follows it, is an exercise in ludic formal experimentation. The fourth book, *Letters to David: An Elegiac Mass in the Form of a Train*, addresses the death by overdose of David A. Kennedy, the son of the late U.S. Senator Robert F. Kennedy, set against the destruction of addiction within her own family life. The fifth and final book within the book is *Hard Drive*, which is divided into three parts. The first, "Striking Ash," is about returning to the burned-out house where her mother was violently sexually assaulted before she was murdered and the house torched. The second, "On Line," is comprised of a series of lyric poems about writing. And in the final section of the final book, *"Con una poca de gracia"* ("With just a bit of grace," a line taken from the folk song turned crossover rock hit "La Bamba"), Cervantes presents a poetic bildungsroman.

Like so many other Latina writers, Cervantes refuses to separate historical from contemporary forms of violence, because the structures established by colonization and capitalism that sustain the nation are to this day enforced by the state in ideologies and structures organized by race, class, gender, and sexuality. While identity politics have been roundly critiqued by the left and the right (by white thinkers, primarily), Juana María Rodríguez forcefully argues in her first book, *Queer Latinidad*, that identity remains a critical site of solidarity building, activism, and advocacy for groups that are targeted by structures of power *because* of their identities. Violence and aggression are addressed in Latina literature as structural, historical, material, ideological, and embodied. The genocidal violence of conquest is not located in the past; in this body of work, that violence is also ongoing. The violence that rips open the wound at the border, that brutal encounter between First and Third Worlds, is written on the traumatized and dead bodies of women and children. This is what neocolonialist aggression looks like.

From the Cables of Genocide consists of dense lyrical poems that, rather than speak directly to the issue of genocide, assume it as an underlying fact. The term "genocide" is important because of its historical and political uses. The losses occasioned by genocide shape this poetry in nuanced imagery, linking poems thematically and formally throughout the sections of the volume. The title echoes *Cables to Rage* by the African American poet Audre Lorde, shifting the reader's understanding of where Chicana poetry might locate itself. This affinity with African American feminism, embedded here in the allusion to one of its preeminent figures, is not overtly expressed in the poems, yet it informs Cervantes's poetic sensibility as surely as the history of genocide. In this collection and in her subsequent work, Cervantes extends a Chicana/o/x poetic tradition across cultural lines to connect explicitly with Third World feminist concerns.

Claiming Beat poetry as "Chicanao," Cervantes draws the comparison to Ginsberg's articulation of a poetic sensibility that confronts the end of the world ("On Allen Ginsberg"). She notes: "I have to say, we have to consider the conquest, and this sense of Chicanismo, of being conquered by the sword and the book, had become universalized, globalized, through globalized threat, beginning with the atomic bomb, now with extreme ecological destruction, the destruction of our entire world. And how do you create poetry out of that, how do you write about that? How do you not write about that?" That conquest by book, the Bible, makes the stakes of her specifically literary interventions clear. Not only did the Spanish arrive with the sword and the Book, but they also burned down the libraries they found as part of a concerted military effort to destabilize and undermine bodies of knowledge and, by extension, Indigenous epistemes. They also outlawed amate, the handmade paper used for currency as well as for official religious and government documents. In this historical context, Cervantes's work as publisher, described at the opening of this essay, is perhaps the most direct response to neocolonial erasure: make more books and, specifically, make more Chicana/o/x books. I repeat here her mother's confrontational and encouraging words: "You tell 'em, Lorna. And after you tell 'em, tell 'em who told you to tell 'em." It is through her daughter's writing that the mother is inscribed into history after being erased by the multiple conquests that have shaped Chicana/o/x history.

The influence of the men in her family—her father, the painter Luis Cervantes, and her brother, Stephen Cervantes, a musician—is also remarkable, though perhaps not as central as the influence of her family of women. It is certainly not as legible in her poetry, unless the reader is familiar with her biography. She accompanied her brother on a trip to Mexico City in the early 1970s, for example, where his band was playing at a cultural festival and where she was invited to read her work. That invitation and subsequent performance would be a milestone experience for Cervantes, launching her development as a major figure in contemporary literature. In interviews and in biographical statements, Cervantes reflects on the ways in which she "stole" her education and aesthetic formation as a stunningly perfect *rasquache* Chicana force of nature: "crashing" courses at San José State University, "devouring" books at the library, and claiming for herself the worlds of music and of art that reverberate across her body of work. The text of *Drive: The First Quartet*, for example, is organized alongside paintings that speak to each of the five books in that collection. Moreover, musical forms and influences thread through her writing and shape her editorial choices about her own work as it appears in her books.

In the author's note to *Drive*, Cervantes describes it as being intentionally designed for ease of portability and stresses the everyday nature of poetry: "They are bound together in this edition for affordability and for carrying them with you, perhaps, like me, under some tree. Bound so that you don't have to worry about getting them dirty, books intended to be consumed with wine & cheese, pita & hummus, Soyrizo & tortillas organicas. A book that could serve as a table, a plate, a platform" (309). The linkages here between literary, psychic, and culinary sustenance recall the framework of *From the Cables of Genocide*. (Cervantes's list of foods is also reminiscent of Anzaldúa's declaration that in the Borderlands "you put chile in the borscht / eat whole wheat tortillas" [216].) Cervantes's assertion that the book is also table, plate, and platform invokes the ordinary, the domestic, the structural, and the political elements in her work—all embodied in the kitchen (the plate and table) and the public sphere of politics (the platform). That the book is described as refusing *both* the split between poetry and politics and between the private and the public. This refusal of divisions continues the decolonial epistemology clearly articulated in *From the Cables of Genocide*.

Cervantes completed her BA and graduate studies at UC Santa Cruz in the history of consciousness, focusing on the study of value theory and metaethics, a philosophical education and background that is almost always overlooked in the commentary and evaluation of her body of work and of Latina/o/x letters more broadly. These influences are most clear in *Drive: The First Quartet*, where she takes up T. S. Eliot's articulation of divine time in *Four Quartets*, especially the following lines from "Burnt Norton":

If all time is eternally present
All time is unredeemable.
What might have been is an abstraction
Remaining a perpetual possibility
Only in a world of speculation.
What might have been and what has been
Point to one end, which is always present. (quoted in Mah y Busch, 121)

In an essay that focuses on integrity, ethics, and aesthetics in Cervantes's work, Juan Mah y Busch notes Cervantes's strategic misquoting of Eliot in order to transfigure the possibilities of poetry and history, aesthetic explorations of power, history, and meaning. He reads the lines that she rewrites:

> If all time is eternally present
> All time is *redeemable*.
> *But what* might have been is an abstraction
> Remaining a perpetual possibility
> Only in a world of speculation.
> What might have been and what has been
> Point to one end, which is always present. (*Drive*, 184; my emphasis)

Mah y Busch reads the shift closely to reveal the driving dynamic between ethical and aesthetic forms of value that characterize Cervantes's work. Her aesthetic erudition is formidable, and her exploration of what is at stake in a Chicana feminist poetic engagement with "canons [and] cannons" (*From the Cables*, 44) becomes clear in his close reading of the very slight changes in her quotation of Eliot, a poet most notorious for his conservative stances: he was a man who described himself as "classicist in literature, royalist in politics, and Anglo-Catholic in religion" (quoted in Mah y Busch, 114). Mah y Busch writes: "In the second line, in direct opposition to Eliot, Cervantes makes time redeemable. Since Cervantes writes about forms of time that she believes are redeemable, then we must be as fully present as possible, drawing on the two meanings of "present" found in Eliot's lines. She shifts from metaphysics to history, from God's will to human action; change becomes possible. The next line's conjunction replaces the canonized *and* for a revolutionary *but*, sharpening Cervantes's distinction from Eliot's morality" (122). Indeed, Cervantes's focus on history and its witnessing throughout *"How Far's the War,"* the first book in *Drive*, articulates the revolutionary potential in a series of what she calls "docu-poems," in particular the two long poems, "Bananas" and "Coffee." Both of these focus on the eponymous cash crops and the neocolonial violence and genocide that structure their consumption in the global marketplace, enlacing Acteal, Mexico (the site of a massacre of forty-five Indigenous people by a right-wing paramilitary group in 1997), with Boulder, Colorado (where Cervantes lived and worked for twenty years), and weaving together the brutality of the military massacre with an insistence on truth-telling and imagistic reportage. No wonder, then, that her career has included significant time in academia. As a faculty member at the University of Colorado Boulder, Cervantes directed the creative writing program for twenty years, until her departure from that position in 2007, and she was a University of California Regents' Lecturer at UC Berkeley in 2011–12.

In addition to the influences of Cervantes's mother and grandmother, the young women she grew up with have also shaped her poetic vision and voice. In fact, *Drive*'s second book, *BIRD AVE*, centers them. "Oda a las gatas" is dedicated to "a Bird, Tiny, Mousie, Grumpy, Cat-Eyes, Flaca, Sleepy, Princess, y Betty la Boop."[4] The poem explores their creativity and strength and, most importantly, the negotiations and disidentificatory *movidas* at the heart of their survival. That she does so in an ode, a tightly controlled poetic form that deliberately engages its classical English genealogies from the sixteenth century onward across the modern period, is a way of claiming those genealogies. Traditionally the ode celebrates public occasions, but it has been appropriated throughout the twentieth century into lyric forms that turn inward, rather than outward, focusing, for example, on questions of love or faith. Cervantes's canons, moreover, are not limited to the Anglophone. Pablo Neruda, the consummate poet and public figure (he also worked as a diplomat and Communist leader), wrote three volumes of them: *Odas elementales* (1954), *Nuevas odas elementales* (1956), and *Tercer libro de las odas* (1957). His subjects are sublime and ordinary at once; no wonder, then, that Cervantes repeatedly cites, rewrites, and claims him as forebear. The vaunted and transfigured poetic form of the ode, then, is an exceedingly apt place for her to transmute the derogatory connotations of the caló meaning of *gatas* (cats)—"whore," "slut," and, of course, "pussy"—conferring a nimble feline grace on this group of young women.

Cervantes reflects on the false binary understanding of choice and refusal in the negotiation of structural violence that is the architecture of the young women's existence:

We chose

to stay, tough in the fist of our father's
mercy. No face cards in our deck, we dealt
the devil back his hand. (62)

The doubled meaning generated by the comma between the words "stay" and "tough" anticipates the possibilities within this liminal state. Cervantes refuses to fetishize or romanticize the violence necessary to their own survival, even as it forces them into that state of nepantla, a Nahuatl term for the transitory state between life and death that Anzaldúa and other Chicana feminists have theorized as a necessary transformational state. She writes:

. . . we scorched the virgin
from our breasts, as the sweat of heat upon us

did not free us, but did not bind us either. (63)

The meaning of "scorched . . . virgin" here is also doubled: it recalls the tattoos that characterize masculine cholo adornment, and it suggests both that they burn onto themselves a stolen form of gendered bodily ornamentation and also that they reject the compulsory virginal state imposed on young women by patriarchy.

In the essay "*Emplumada* but Grounded (*por vida?*): The 'Bad' Girls in *BIRD AVE*," Tanya Gonzalez describes the bad girl voice cultivated in this collection. González takes up questions of agency for the Chicana protagonists of the poem and examines the ways in which public space figures in their resistance to interlocking oppressions as young, working-class Chicanas. Their freedom is contingent and particular: they are not liberated forever, nor are their lives made different by being imagined in poetry. In this Gonzalez departs from a familiar trope in Chicana criticism wherein Chicana protagonists are liberated by acts of imagination and their circumstances transformed by writing. She argues that Cervantes "is not interested in a transformation of circumstances, nor are the narrators articulating ironic relationships to the masculinized street. The poems in *BIRD AVE . . .* focus on the ways bad girls strike back on the streets of their circumstance while simultaneously (not contradictorily) finding freedom and loving it" (93).

The significance of *Drive* cannot be underestimated: it represented the return of Cervantes to print after a long absence—nearly twenty-five years since the publication of *From the Cables of Genocide*. In order to call attention to this milestone at the start of the twenty-first century, I edited an anthology of previous and new criticism on Cervantes's poetry. Most significant in *Drive* is the way that Cervantes explores different poetic forms: the docu-poem; the biographical vignette via the ode and the lyric; tight writing-workshop-style poems; as well as an experimental elegy for David Kennedy. The final book in the collection, *Hard Drive*, is made up of unpublished work from the 1980s. *Drive* constitutes a literary biography of Cervantes's career up until its date of release and to my mind remains the most significant publication of her career thus far.

In an essay that addresses the pedagogical function of Cervantes's poetics, Tiffany Ana López reads *Drive* as an act of critical witnessing of violence via poetics in order to stage an understanding of it and to transfigure its meanings. She notes that narratives of

> surviving violence too often get buried within predictable melo-dramatic narratives of evil perpetrators and forsaken victims. While such stories represent very real feelings, these essentializing narratives evade the complexity necessary to produce critical discourse and social change. People come into violence for complicated reasons, and they survive violence in complicated ways. Our ability to navigate an openly hostile and debilitating world depends on being taught active modes of engagement such as those offered through the practice of critical witnessing. And poetry is precisely about sculpting clarity from complexities and contradictions. (182)

López's argument here follows a major thread in Chicana feminist discourse that locates the creative as a site of critical possibility; poetry functions as a site of theory, as a place in which knowledge is generated. Building on this insight, I suggest that Cervantes's deliberate explorations of and experimentations with poetic form compel an understanding of the aesthetic production of knowledge in which thinking/feeling is grounded in the materiality of both the textual and the human (racialized, gendered, and working-class) body. As Cervantes writes at the end of "Bananas," an epistolary poem addressing an Estonian physicist friend:

> But poetry
> is for the soul. I speak of spirit, the yellow seed
> in air as life is the seed in water, and the poetry
> of Improbability, the magic in the Movement
> of quarks and sunlight, the subtle basketry
> of hadrons and neutrinos of color, how what you do
> is what you get—bananas or worry.
> What do you say? Your friend,
>   a Chicana poet. (24)

The "poetry of Improbability" that Cervantes describes here perfectly encapsulates the critical possibilities of poetry, found in "the magic in the Movement." The line break and capitalization amplify the double meaning, referencing the Chicano Movement as well as the actions of subatomic particles. Poetry gives the ineffable mass and color; subatomic particles are woven together in basketry; it makes the connections of language (in poems and in letters) concrete, consumable, and as shareable as the banana bread the poet-speaker shipped to Estonia earlier in the poem. Ultimately, it presents the reader with a choice that is predicated on the agency of humans as thinking and doing subjects in the material world—you get bananas or worry. The "poetry of Improbability" maps the landscapes of hope and beauty, which, while not impossible to reach, in a world shaped by the violence of neocolonial capitalism certainly seem improbable. Ultimately, that sense of possibility is what drives Cervantes's vision, and it is what draws so many readers to her work.

This ability to seemingly leap across binary oppositions with ease is the result of Cervantes's precise manipulation of poetic form. Across her body of work, she carefully develops deferral as a poetic strategy, most explicitly in her manipulation of enjambed lines and doubled meanings. She reveals a prevalent deferral of meaning, desire, and certainty and creates productive tensions and multiplicities of meaning, especially in the long poems in *From the Cables of Genocide* and *Drive*. Consequently, the connections between the personal, mythic, and historical are deeply intertwined. As previously mentioned in this essay, throughout her work Cervantes builds an expanding frame of reference for Chicana poetry. She moves from the pride in the Indigenous roots of Mexican and Chicana/o/x culture that is characteristic of classical[5] Chicano and Chicana literature to a broad engagement with global cultural and political influences. Cervantes's references—which range from the traditional Chicana/o/x tropes of Nahua and other Mesoamerican images to Hispanophone modernist poetry, from Celtic folklore to Greek myth—indicate a shifting of consciousness. Not only is it important, as Cervantes has stressed, to participate in a "cultural break" that disrupts monological versions of history and culture, but it is also important to extend the scope of struggle and the alliances that can be imagined in poetry and formed in the world (Rodríguez y Gibson, 138).

Cervantes's poem "Coffee" remains the culminating expression of her poetics. It is a long poem of six sections. Evoking the military-ordered massacre in Acteal in December 1997, "Coffee" travels across space and time. Beginning with the devastating violence wrought by the United Fruit Company in Guatemala, the poem moves to the Jewish poet Hans Sahl fleeing Nazi persecution in Germany and to events in France and the United States. The poem moves back to Acteal to describe the massacre, then it shifts to a young woman protesting in Denver. It ends in the first-person voice of the poet, whose final words are "*con safos*," a signature of protection and defiance ever present in urban *placas*, or Chicana/o/x graffiti markings. "Coffee" is at once an epic and a personal poem in scope and tone, detailing the horrors of the massacre in the context of global capitalism and neocolonialism as well as the role of poetry in the world.

Questions of aesthetics and history and of literary and cultural tradition are deeply interlinked in Cervantes's work. She does not engage in consolation or in monumentalizing the dead; instead, she identifies with them. Cervantes creates a way of understanding devastating cultural and historic losses, specifically a way of understanding the ways women experience grief. She engages difficult questions about the meanings of historical loss and the possibilities of connection across cultural differences and oppositional worldviews. Throughout her body of work, Cervantes writes poems about Chicanas in gangs, associating them with Chumash and Greek myths while describing the realities of their lives. She writes of poverty, combining dignity with righteous anger. She writes about families and their histories and how she is linked to families on the other side of the globe. The scope of her poetic vision is vast, intimately connective, and deeply democratic. Cervantes is part of a generation of U.S.-based Latina and Latino poets who, along with Martín Espada and Francisco Alarcón, write powerfully about love and beauty and their importance to struggles for social justice.

She published her next two books, *Ciento* and *Sueño*, in very quick succession. *Ciento: 100 100-Word Love Poems* follows a very tight form consistently throughout the collection, demonstrating her control and discipline as a writer, as well as her love of layering meanings. The word *ciento* is both the Spanish prefix for "hundred" and a pun on the word *siento*, or "I feel." In a blurb on the back cover of the collection, Mexican American writer Luis Alberto Urrea offers the following assessment: "The 100 word format unleashes paradoxically vast effects. Full of playfulness, rage, and her traditional fire, *Ciento* is a masterful performance." Given the influence of music on Cervantes's work, the tightly controlled formalist explorations invite comparisons to musical forms that rely on improvisation around structure, like jazz. The same heady mixture of feeling and thinking that Cervantes's formal experimentation and mastery of language create also colors *Sueño*. Jessica Helen Lopez's review in *World Literature Today* characterizes Cervantes's voice in a way that recalls the poet-speaker of *BIRD AVE*: "Cervantes is the original bad-girl poeta. She is a spell-casting code-switcher who asserts her indigeneity in verse. A voice for many, she is both *payasa* (clown) and queen bee. *Sueño*, her fifth major collection of poetry, is a triumphant manifestation of all these gifts, a wonderfully charged volume that makes the reader think and, most importantly, feel" (112).

Cervantes is a major figure in American letters and should be recognized as such. She is a Chicana poet engaged with the world. Concerned with solidarities that emerge from common experiences and epistemes rather than fixed identities, she claims traditions beyond the ethnic canon of American literature and modes that trouble unreconstructed identity politics and cultural nationalism. She reflects on her own position as a writer working within a specifically Chicana/o/x literary tradition: "To be a Chicanao poet is to be dealing with the politics of identity as irony. No self but in other selves. No multiples selves, no individual self, no universal self. It's a very Chicano sensibility, to know that you are in the intersection or are sometimes the target of all of these multiple subjectivizations, which is beyond stereotype" ("On Allen Ginsberg"). Cervantes's work disrupts received notions of Chicana poetry. After a reading that included an erotic poem, "For He Who Wants to Know," she was asked about what made it "a Chicana poem." Her answer, while apparently flippant, is deeply evocative: "Because a Chicana wrote it."[6] Both the question and the answer point to and undermine the expectations about ethnically marked work and the stereotypes that constitute what Rey Chow calls "coercive mimeticism" (the logic that requires minoritarian subjects to inhabit a familiar if stereotypical form in order to be legible as such) (107).

Cervantes's Chicana poetics sidesteps the clichés and stereotypes that limit readers' imaginations, even as she takes up subjects that are represented stereotypically in the mainstream imagination: poverty, urban violence, trauma, and gangs. I return to a brief discussion of printing that opened this essay because it illuminates both the form and content of Cervantes's career in letters. Often used in newspapers, letterpress, and other high-speed printing, a stereotype is made by locking type columns and illustration plates together to make a mold, which is then used to cast the stereotype plate. It is sturdier to work with than columns of type, and it is designed for mass reproduction at speed. Historically, the mass production of print depended on stereotypes, quite literally as well as figuratively, when Cervantes set up her small press at home in the 1970s. She made the means of production her own in order to create work that exceeded the form and the content of *both* meanings of the word *stereotype*. Her body of work demands attention to the material, aesthetic, and historic contexts of Chicana literature. Cervantes illuminates the power and potential of Chicana feminist poetics as a site for transformational possibilities in the aesthetic production of knowledge. In other words, the "poetry of Improbability" illuminates what might be, depending on our actions: "how what you do is what you get / bananas or worry" (*Drive*, 24). Poetry gives us the vision; what we do with it is up to us.

NOTES

1. For two landmark theorizations of rasquachismo, see Tomás Ybarra-Frausto, "Rasquachismo: A Chicano Sensibility," in *Chicano Aesthetics: Rasquachismo* (Phoenix: MARS (Movimiento Artistico del Rio Salado), 1989), 5–8, and Amalia Mesa-Bains, "Domesticana: The Sensibility of Chicana Rasquache," *Aztlán: A Journal of Chicano Studies* 24, no. 2 (Fall 1999): 157–67.
2. The phrase "the poetry of possibility" comes from the poem "Bananas"; it is also quoted in the title to the introductory essay in the scholarly collection *Stunned into Being* because of the ways it encapsulates the generative nature of Cervantes's poetic practices.
3. "Intimate Partner Violence," Centers for Disease Control, https://www.cdc .gov/violenceprevention/intimatepartnerviolence/index.html.
4. Cervantes refers to herself as Bird, and avian tropes such as birds and feathers are distinctive features of her first three books.
5. In *Movements in Chicano Poetry*, Rafael Pérez-Torres uses the term "classical" rather than "authentic" to point to the ways that the poetry of El Movimiento adhered to a characteristic set of neo-Indigenous and urban conventions.
6. The exchange occurred at the "Mosaic Realities: Peaces of Resistance" poetry symposium, Cornell University, Ithaca, New York, March 1998.

WORKS CITED

Anzaldúa, Gloria. *Borderlands/La Frontera: The New Mestiza*. San Francisco: Aunt Lute Books, 1987.

Arteaga, Alfred. *Chicano Poetics: Heterotexts and Hybridities*. New York: Cambridge University Press, 1997.

Cervantes, Lorna Dee. *April on Olympia*. East Rockaway, N.Y.: Marsh Hawk Press, 2021.

———. *Ciento: 100 100-Word Love Poems*. San Antonio, Tex.: Wings Press, 2011.

———. *Drive: The First Quartet; New Poems, 1980–2005*. San Antonio, Tex.: Wings Press, 2006.

———. *Emplumada*. Pittsburgh: University of Pittsburgh Press, 1981.

———. *From the Cables of Genocide: Poems on Love and Hunger*. Houston: Arte Público Press, 1991.

————. "On Allen Ginsberg and the Interplay Between Beat and Chicano Poetry." In *Beats at Naropa*. Edited by Anne Waldman and Laura Wright. Minneapolis: Coffeehouse Press, 2009. Reprinted on Literary Hub, December 21, 2020. https://lithub.com/lorna-dee-cervantes-on-allen-ginsberg-and-the-interplay -between-beat-and-chicano-poetry/.

————. *Sueño*. Foreword by Juan Felipe Herrera. San Antonio, Tex.: Wings Press, 2013.

Chávez Candelaria, Cordelia. "Rethinking the 'Eyes' of Chicano Poetry; or, Reading the Multiple Centers of Chicana Poetics." In *Women Poets of the Americas: Toward a Pan-American Gathering*. Edited by Jacqueline Vaught Brogan and Cordelia Chávez Candelaria. Notre Dame, Ind.: University of Notre Dame Press, 1999.

Chow, Rey. *The Protestant Ethnic and the Spirit of Capitalism*. New York: Columbia University Press, 2002.

Gonzalez, Ray, and Lorna Dee Cervantes. "'I Trust Only What I Have Built with My Own Hands': An Interview with Lorna Dee Cervantes." *Bloomsbury Review* 17, no. 5 (September–October 1997): 3, 8.

González, Sonia V., and Lorna Dee Cervantes. "'Poetry Saved My Life': An Interview with Lorna Dee Cervantes." *MELUS* 32, no. 1 (2007): 163–80. http://www.jstor.org/stable/30029711.

Gonzalez, Tanya. "*Emplumada* but Grounded (*por vida?*): The 'Bad' Girls in '*BIRD AVE.*'" In *Stunned into Being: Essays on the Poetry of Lorna Dee Cervantes*. Edited by Eliza Rodríguez y Gibson. San Antonio, Tex.: Wings Press, 2012, 91–113.

Lopez, Jessica Helen. Review of *Sueño*, by Lorna Dee Cervantes. *World Literature Today* 88, nos. 3–4 (2011): 112–13.

López, Tiffany Ana. "'Stunned into Being': The Practice of Critical Witnessing in Lorna Dee Cervantes's *Drive*." In *Stunned into Being: Essays on the Poetry of Lorna Dee Cervantes*. Edited by Eliza Rodríguez y Gibson. San Antonio, Tex.: Wings Press, 2012, 177–95.

Lorde, Audre. "Poetry Is Not a Luxury." In *Sister Outsider*. Freedom, Calif.: Crossing Press, 1984, 36–40.

Madrigal, Sylvia. Review of *Emplumada*, by Lorna Dee Cervantes. *Imagine* 1, no. 1 (Summer 1984): 137–40.

Mah y Busch, Juan. "The Time for Integrity: On T. S. Eliot and the Ethics That Drive Cervantes's Poetry." In *Stunned into Being: Essays on the Poetry of Lorna Dee Cervantes*. Edited by Eliza Rodríguez y Gibson. San Antonio, Tex.: Wings Press, 2012, 114–35.

Pérez-Torres, Rafael. *Movements in Chicano Poetry: Against Myths, Against Margins*. New York and Cambridge, England: Cambridge University Press, 1995.

Rodríguez, Juana María. *Queer Latinidad: Identity Practices, Discursive Spaces*. New York: New York University Press, 2003.

Rodríguez y Gibson, Eliza, ed. *Stunned into Being: Essays on the Poetry of Lorna Dee Cervantes*. San Antonio, Tex.: Wings Press, 2012.

Saldívar, José David. Review of *Emplumada*, by Lorna Dee Cervantes. *Revista Chicano-Riqueña* 12, no. 2 (Summer 1984): 87–89.

SANDRA CISNEROS

SANDRA CISNEROS

Rebel Mentor for Generations of Hijas de La Mala Vida with a Social Consciousness

GEORGINA GUZMÁN

I CLEARLY REMEMBER the first time I saw Raquel Valle-Sentíes's portrait of Sandra Cisneros. It was in July 2005, when I was a second-year graduate student attending the Latina Letters Conference at St. Mary's University in San Antonio, Texas, to present my paper on Sandra Cisneros herself. Cisneros's portrait was prominently displayed on an easel in an open room where volumes of Chicana/Latina literature and arts and crafts were being sold. Since I already owned all of Cisneros's books except for her children's story *Hairs/Pelitos*, I purchased that volume and held it tightly in my hands as I walked over to admire Valle-Sentíes's portrait of her. Cisneros's chin is resting upon her crossed arms, as if she is contemplating her past and all she has been through, but her arched eyebrow signals a brave plotting of her next revolutionary steps. I loved the painting's colorful composition and the pensive yet powerful look upon Cisneros's countenance. The portrait was a brilliant complement to the conference's main event: Cisneros's keynote address on Astor Piazzolla, the Argentine musician who had greatly influenced her. The keynote showcased her artistic magistery; she made us listeners hinge upon her ode's every heart-wrenching word. Listening to her outpouring of love for Piazzolla,

I thought, "How propitious that she looks up to an artist with such fondness and admiration—that means that when I go introduce myself to her afterward, she will be able to understand just how much she means to me."

I had first read Cisneros's *Woman Hollering Creek* as a nineteen-year old sophomore in Sonia Saldívar-Hull's Chicana/o literature class at UCLA. For me, as a working-class, first-generation student and daughter of Mexican immigrants, reading Cisneros's stories and poems sparked an epiphany, a lightbulb going off in my head the moment I realized that, yes, Chicanas did write books, and we were damn good at it, too. And the relatability—here was a writer interspersing her narrative with bilingual dichos and critiquing Mexican patriarchy at every turn. I recognized the voices and experiences captured in Cisneros's prose as similar to my own, and that representation and validation were invaluable to me. They gave me the strength and inspiration—the informal mentorship—to also pursue a life of letters and become a rebellious "hija de la mala vida" such as herself, defying both Americans' racialized expectations and Mexicans' gendered expectations about the domestic and subservient lives we Chicanas should lead. To this day, Cisneros continues to inspire my life decisions. I watched her in conversation with Erika L. Sanchez on July 14, 2022, on Zoom, and she sagely reminded viewers to "give yourself permission to dream" and that "you don't have to just get what's on the menu." I hurriedly jotted down Cisneros's quotes on my notepad. For over two decades, her wise words have fueled my life goals and given me the strength to manifest them into reality.

Indeed, Sandra Cisneros is perhaps our most illustrious and well-known Chicana writer, the first Chicana writer to be published by a major press and to have been able to reach and touch so many hearts around the world. She is best known for her classic coming-of-age novel, *The House on Mango Street* (1991), which has sold over six million copies, has been translated into more than twenty languages, and is required reading in many elementary schools, high schools, and universities across the nation. She is also the author of the full-length poetry books *My Wicked Wicked Ways* (1987) and *Loose Woman* (1994); a chapbook, *Bad Boys* (1980); a collection of short stories, *"Woman Hollering Creek" and Other Stories* (1991); a children's book,

REBEL MENTOR FOR GENERATIONS | 291

Hairs/Pelitos (1994); the novel *Caramelo* (2002); and the picture book *Have You Seen Marie?* (2012). Most recently she has published a collection of personal essays, *A House of My Own: Stories from My Life* (2015); an illustrated chapbook called *Puro amor* (2018), which reimagines the lives of Frida Kahlo and Diego Rivera and their pet animals; *Martita, I Remember You*, a tale of a young Chicana writer's friendship with immigrant women in Paris, published in a bilingual edition (2021); and her latest poetry book, *Woman Without Shame* (2022). This latest book—which was also published in a Spanish translation as *Mujer sin vergüenza*—demonstrates Cisneros's lifelong dedication to providing lessons as a *maestra* (teacher) in the art of defying patriarchy, racial hierarchies, and upper- and middle-class norms of what is considered "classy."

Cisneros is the recipient of two National Endowment for the Arts Literature Fellowships in poetry and fiction, the Texas Medal of Arts Award, a MacArthur "genius grant," Chicago's Fifth Star Award, the PEN America Literary Award, and the National Medal of Arts (awarded to her by President Barack Obama in 2016), and several honorary doctorates. She received the Ford Foundation's Art of Change Fellowship, was recognized among the Frederick Douglass 200, and was awarded the PEN/Nabokov Award for Achievement in International Literature. From working with major publishers to fostering the careers of many aspiring and emerging writers through two nonprofits she founded—the Macondo Foundation and the Alfredo Cisneros Del Moral Foundation—Cisneros has demonstrated a profound social consciousness and commitment to community, paving the way for many Chicana/o writers after her and creating a home for them (by, for example, helping to organize Los MacArturos, a group of Latino MacArthur fellows who are community activists).

Home has been an important symbolic as well as real site of racial, class, and gender struggles throughout Sandra Cisneros's literary oeuvre and life. Since her childhood, she sought a house of her own—in Chicago, in San Antonio, Texas, in Mexico—a place to belong, to grow in, and from which to build community. Two of her books' titles, *The House on Mango Street* and *A House of My Own: Stories from My Life*, reveal that concern. But in 1997, when she purchased a 1903 Victorian in the mostly white (both racially and aesthetically) King William

Historic District in San Antonio and decided to paint it purple, Cisneros's house made resoundingly clear the battles for Mexican and Chicana/o self-definition in the United States. Her color choice angered the neighborhood's historic review commission, who argued that the color was "not appropriate to history" (*House of My Own*, 174) and that she could choose a house color only from an established bland palette of beiges, browns, and grays. CNN crews descended upon her home to broadcast the battle (Lowry). Cisneros contended that her house stood on lands formerly owned by Mexico, so purple was a perfectly suitable color. Indeed, what the historic review commission "considers history," she wrote, "depends on who is telling the story and what story they consider telling" (*House of My Own*, 173). She refused to whitewash her house. Years later, once her home's purple facade faded under the hot sun, she submitted the faded color to the board, and it was accepted. But by then the purple was too light for her liking, and she repainted the home in *rosa mexicano*, a traditional Mexican color closer to warm fuchsia.

Just as Cisneros defiantly decorated her home in San Antonio in a bold, brilliant, and distinctively Mexican American aesthetic, she has been making metaphorical homes accessible to many of us marginalized Latinas/Chicanas in academia and the literary world. She constructed homes for us in publishing, in creative writing, and in American literature, taking on those who opposed a Chicana presence in the spaces and neighborhoods in which she lived and worked. Above all, that is what Sandra Cisneros represents for many Chicanas like myself: a courageous, trailblazing artist who has helped lift up others and improve the quality of life for the people around her, bringing Mexican Americans dignity, beauty, and self-determination within places where we are (or were) not always so welcomed.

Many of us know a bit about Cisneros because of her public persona as a celebrity and her stature as a writer. But in this essay, I would like to explore some of the more intimate parts of her biography and the formative experiences that helped shape and refine her literary craft. I seek to answer: What fueled Cisneros's passion and her determination to carry out such a diverse and distinctive body of work? How did she do it, and what did she have to overcome? How are her personal battles and accomplishments representative of Chicanas' struggles and achievements in the United States as a whole? In exploring Cisneros's story, we find that for all the accolades and triumphs she's enjoyed, she has also suffered many struggles, injuries, and disappointments. Even though she is a famous writer, what makes her story so compelling is that we can find parts of our own story within hers. In telling her story, this essay will focus on aspects of Cisneros's experiences—particularly with race, gender, and class marginalization—that are important to understanding the underbelly and the narrative arc of her body of work, as well as her defiant politics in the face of those obstacles.

FAMILY HISTORY: EARLY FEMINIST AND CLASS CONSCIOUSNESS

Born in Chicago, Illinois, on December 20, 1954, Sandra Cisneros is the daughter of Alfredo Cisneros Del Moral, a Spanish-speaking Mexican immigrant, and Elvira Cordero Anguiano, an English-speaking Chicana born and raised in the United States. Her father was a middle-class immigrant from Mexico City who came to the United States, not out of necessity, but because he was fleeing his father's wrath after receiving bad grades during his first year at the National Autonomous University of Mexico. Her mother's parents, on the other hand, had migrated to the United States during the 1910s to escape the Mexican Revolution and settled first in Flagstaff, Arizona; her grandfather was a railroad worker and later moved his family north to Chicago (McCracken, 229). Cisneros thus grew up speaking Spanish to her father and English to her mother—linguistic hybridity was part and parcel of her life. Her experiences with two languages, cultures, and classes at home would become the source of many of her stories. The marital tension arising from her parents' different customs, class backgrounds, languages, and first- and second-generation American-ness make their fictional appearances in *Caramelo* as well as the story "Never Marry a Mexican" in *Woman Hollering Creek and Other Stories*, where the narrator tells us her mother cautioned her against marrying a Mexican man:

I guess she did it to spare me . . . the pain she went through. Having married a Mexican man at seventeen. Having had to put up with all the grief a Mexican family can put on a girl because she was from el otro lado, the other side, and my father had married down by marrying her. If she had been a white woman from el otro lado, that would've been different. That would've been marrying up, even if the white girl was poor. But what could be more ridiculous than a Mexican girl who couldn't even speak Spanish, who didn't know enough to set a separate plate for each course at dinner, nor how to fold cloth napkins, or how to set the silverware. (69)

Drawn from her parents' lives, Cisneros's story illustrates the huge class and linguistic diversity and complex racial politics within the Mexican immigrant and Chicana/o community in the United States.

Equally important in Cisneros's upbringing is the fact that she has two older brothers and four younger brothers: "I am the only daughter in a family of six sons. That explains everything" *(House of My Own*, 91). Growing up as the only girl among brothers made her keenly conscious of gender differences and double standards from a young age: "I spent a lot of time by myself because my brothers felt it beneath them to play with a girl in public" (91). We see those autobiographical details fictionalized in *House on Mango Street*: "The boys and girls live in separate worlds. . . . They've got plenty to say to me and Nenny inside the house. But outside they can't be seen talking to girls" (8).

Shame of her home and the humiliation experienced at the hands of nuns and teachers also deeply affected Cisneros. Subsisting on her upholsterer father's single income, her family was not financially well off. Cisneros's father would frequently take his family from Chicago to Mexico to visit his mother and settle in a different house upon return. The constant moving from rundown place to rundown place and the ugly feelings it incurred is captured in Esperanza's character in *Mango Street*. Cisneros attended St. Callistus Catholic school (on scholarship) and also felt ashamed of being equated with her dilapidated home, just as Esperanza, whose teacher/nun from her school looks up at her boarded-up apartment and asks, "you live *there*? The way she said it made me feel like nothing. *There*. I lived *there*" (5). In an interview, Cisneros referred to the nuns at her school as "majestic at making one feel little" (Sagel 1991). The class injuries sustained within educational institutions would continue and follow her all her life.

Cisneros's family's extended trips to Mexico to visit the paternal grandmother also contributed to Cisneros's sense of isolation as a child. In Mexico, she was an outsider because she spoke English and seemed American; in the United States, she was an outsider because she also spoke Spanish and seemed Mexican (Tompkins, 36). Her feelings of displacement influenced most of her later writings, especially *Caramelo*, which centers on a family's cross-border travels to Mexico to visit "the Awful Grandmother." Cisneros's childhood solitude and alienation stemming from gender and cultural differences made her turn to reading and writing as a source of comfort: "that aloneness, that loneliness, allowed me time to think, to imagine, to read and prepare myself for my writer's profession" (*House of My Own*, 91–92).

But because of her mother's unfulfilled life, Cisneros was also aware that the privilege to read and write—as a working-class Chicana woman—was a gift that should be nurtured with care and gratitude. She recounts: "I became a writer thanks to a mother who was unhappy being a mother. She was a prisoner-of-war mother banging on the bars of her cell all her life" (291). It was Cisneros's mother who helped give her daughter the privilege of obtaining the education she never could: "I'm here because my mother let me stay in my room reading and studying, perhaps because she didn't want me to inherit her sadness and her rolling pin" (75). She credits her mother's artistic spirit and her taking her to the library every Saturday (295) for instilling in her a love of reading; it was her mother that gave her the space, the time, and the freedom from domestic drudgery to find her craft as a writer.

Cisneros graduated high school from Josephinum Academy of the Sacred Heart in Chicago, having served as the school's literary magazine editor. She remained living at home when she entered Loyola University Chicago in 1972, graduating with a bachelor's degree in 1976. At Loyola, despite the burgeoning Chicano Movement and the publication of poetry, fiction, and essays of the movement in small presses in the 1970s, Cisneros was the only Chicana English major, and she read mostly white male authors. When she decided to attend the University of Iowa Writers' Workshop—one of the most prestigious graduate writing programs in the United States—she did the unthinkable for a Chicana of her generation, something that not even her brothers did: she left her family home, unwed, to go to another state, live alone, and pursue a career in writing. She earned an MFA from Iowa in 1978.

Since her early writings from graduate school until today, Cisneros's work is characterized by two major themes: a deep desire to live a writer's life alone in her own home and the defiance of a patriarchal culture that this act requires. Cisneros's poetry and stories rail against a patriarchy that would dictate prescribed gender roles to women like her: the role of the good Mexican daughter, one who marries a husband and bears and rears children.

Her traditional immigrant Mexican father and his antiquated patriarchal ideas of marianismo represented the biggest obstacles for her in her twenties. After graduate school, Cisneros recounts, she returned to Chicago but declined her father's wish that she live back at home. Instead, it was arranged that she live in her brother's basement (still under the watchful patriarchal eye), where she became a nanny to her brother's children. This experience was formative because it taught her that she did not want to be a mother. And she did not want to clean up after men. In fact, she did not want to marry at all and never did. She wanted to dedicate her life to writing and spend every waking hour on her craft.

When writing *Mango Street* in 1982, Cisneros left behind her boyfriend to go to Greece and write the book: "I'd chosen my writing over a man. It wouldn't be the last time" (*House of My Own*, 13). She needed solitude and space to create. Like Esperanza, Cisneros dreamed of a house of her own: "Not a flat. Not an apartment in back. Not a man's house. Not a daddy's. A house all my own. With my porch and my pillow, my pretty purple petunias. My books and my stories. My two shoes waiting beside the bed. Nobody to shake a stick at. Nobody's garbage to pick up after. Only a house as quiet as snow, a space for myself to go, clean as paper before the poem" (*Mango Street*, 108). Men came and went. Writing remained.

Homes thus became important in her writing: they represent both class and belonging, as well as female artistic independence. As a girl, Cisneros "dreamt about having a silent home, just to herself, the way other women dreamt about weddings" (*House of My Own*, 271). She would be the first in her family to lead this way of life. She writes, "My mother was a housewife, her mother was a housewife, and her mother, and before her, who remembers?" (133). The continuum of women sitting by the window, wondering what their lives could have been, stopped with her because she had the courage to move out of her family home, get her own place, and write. She confesses: "Sometimes the silence frightened me. / Sometimes the silence blessed me" (*My Wicked*, xi). But facing her fears was the first step in carving out her own path of independence and becoming a rebel mentor for other Chicana writers.

MY WICKED WICKED WAYS AND CISNEROS'S INTERSECTIONAL CHICANA FEMINISM

When Cisneros went off to graduate school at the University of Iowa in 1976, she set out to be free—the first in her family to leave the home without being married. In Iowa, she was trained as a poet and produced a poetry collection as her master's thesis; it would later be published as *My Wicked Wicked Ways*. Reflecting back on those poems, she writes that themes of good and evil and being bad emerged in them, and it's true; during these years she "played at mistress / Tattooed an ass" (xi), drank, and—as the narrative speaker in "Love Poem #1"—treated her old love as "you my religion / and I a wicked nun" (34). She grappled with her many years of Catholic school in these poems. She wrote about her many travels, lovers, and admiring the "ass" of Michaelangelo's *David*, trying on the life of a writer. The worldliness of her travels around the globe marks her as a working-class Chicana moving out into a world of leisure and discovery usually out of reach for most women of our background. She crafted gorgeous, sensual poems that fly in the face of what a "good (Mexican) girl" is supposed to be like and flaunt independence and sexual desire—the poetics of a true *hija de la mala vida*, as Mexican patriarchs would be wont to chide her.

My Wicked Wicked Ways is appropriately framed by an opening poem that reflects on transgressions against patriarchy. In an unpublished essay on the inception of these poems, Cisneros explains that she crafted them at a time when she had obtained all she wanted: to "live away from home and out of her father's eye." And, she adds, "I wanted to control my destiny too" ("Chicana Writer's Struggle," 4). Thus, many of her poems meditate on the Chicana's embracement of self as an "audacious crime / that began by disobeying fathers" (*My Wicked*, 39), since for the Chicana, self-emancipation almost always involves a transgression of patriarchal authority and of controlling religious and familial institutions. Cisneros's independence from her father was a necessary step in her search for self; in order to find her own voice and space, she had to leave the confines of his home.

I focus on this part of Cisneros's story because at the Hispanic-serving (HSI) university where I teach, most Latina students still live at home and commute to school for financial reasons or familial obligations; moving out to go to college is a far-fetched dream for many of them. And those who have moved out and live alone or with roommates are sometimes made to feel like "bad daughters" for leaving their family home. Many struggle with guilt and sometimes question their decision. The pull from home is incredibly strong, and there are few Latina mentors to guide them in their journey. So with them in mind, I recount this part of Cisneros's story because it is one we still need to hear and learn from.

Preoccupation with the father's rule (and its defiance) permeates a lot of Cisneros's early poetic ruminations. "Looking at my life from my father's perspective," she recalls of the poem "His Story," "prompted me to write the following poem" ("Chicana Writer's Struggle," 5):

I was born under a crooked star.
So says my father.
And this perhaps explains his sorrow.

An only daughter
whom no one came for
and no one chased away.

It is an ancient fate.
A family trait we trace back
to a great aunt no one mentions. (*My Wicked*, 38)

Having "six sons / and one female / gone," her father superstitiously blames his daughter's deviant ways on the misalignment of the stars and the inherently dire fate in her bad blood. Adriana Estill writes that Cisneros "casts a certain amount of doubt upon her father's evaluation with the qualifiers 'so' and 'perhaps'" ("In Father's Footsteps," 50). She recounts his unfounded explanations in a rather tongue-in-cheek way, as they are excessively mystical and fatalistic. After providing "his story" for nine stanzas (we can imagine her rolling her eyes all the while), she inserts her own view on the matter:

> You see.
> An unlucky fate is mine
> to be born woman in a family of men. (*My Wicked*, 39)

Cisneros's abrupt interjection in "His Story" subverts her father's voice and interrupts his ranting. By beginning her account with "You see," she underscores her dissenting perspective, as these words mark a correction and rectification of her father's story. She mocks her father by appropriating his fatalistic diction, acknowledging her "unlucky fate." However, she clarifies that, unlike her father claims, her "unlucky fate" was not cosmological but, rather, very grounded in human matters: it was her misfortune to be "born woman" in a patriarchal Mexican "family of men," a repressive home with a father and six fraternal patriarchs in training. Cisneros sets the story straight by demonstrating that the problem is not in the skies, but in her family and culture's machista ways.

Yet, despite establishing an identity by way of confronting her father, when she entered elitist, white-dominant literary and academic spaces, Cisneros's once boldly fashioned subjectivity was marginalized. As a woman of color, Cisneros relates, "I had marched off to college and, with relief, left my father's house, that frying pan, only to leap into the fire of an all-Anglo writers' workshop. The move forced me to have to deal with my 'otherness' for the first time—my race and class difference" ("Chicana Writer's Struggle," 2). Cisneros felt her father's home was inhospitable to her woman-identified self, but it was a "frying pan" in comparison to the combined "fire" of racial, class, and gender alienation she encountered in graduate school. Thus, many of her poems from this period give rise to meditations on her heritage of underprivilege and her determination to access literary production in spite of Chicanas' historical exclusion from it.

In her poems, Cisneros ruminates on her travel experiences "vagabond[ing] the globe / like a rich white girl" (*My Wicked*, xi), but she first grapples with the inheritance of disadvantage that her father has bequeathed her. Unlike upper- and middle-class white women's fathers, Cisneros's father could not provide her with this patrimony of privilege because, as a Mexican immigrant in the United States, he is barred from it himself. And this is where Cisneros's poetry pivots from open defiance to a gentle humanizing of her laborer father's body and their shared class status:

Tell me,
how does a woman who.
A woman like me. Daughter of
a daddy with a hammer and blistered feet
he'd dip into a washtub while he ate his dinner.
A woman with no birthright in the matter.

What does a woman inherit
that tells her how
to go? (x)

"Daddy" cannot provide her the means to become a subject in this society, because he himself does not have them; in U.S. society, he is reduced to merely a pair of hands and blistered feet, a man who works to produce commodities for others' enjoyment at the cost of his own body's deterioration. These poignant lines showcase Cisneros's profound ability to crystallize the relationality of first-generation college-educated Chicanas to their working-class immigrant laborer parents, her exploration of having inherited no guides in this life of letters, this life in academia; ours is a patrimony, as she puts it, of "hammer[s] and blistered feet."

Ultimately, in reflecting on the working-class immigrant heritage she has inherited from her father in her early poems, Cisneros emerges with a working-class consciousness that will permeate her later writings. It is important to trace Cisneros's empathetic examination of working-class immigrant laborer men alongside her growing feminist self because it demonstrates the intersectionality of her politics; she is a feminist who is also attuned to the suffering of working-class immigrant Mexican men like those whom her father represents. In *The House of Mango Street*, she builds a pointed critique of repressive and abusive husbands and fathers (Sally's father and husband, Minerva's husband, Rafaela's husband, Alicia's father), but Esperanza's papa stands out as a hardworking and gentle father: "My papa, his thick hands and thick shoes, who wakes up tired in the dark, who combs his hair with water, drinks his coffee, and is gone before we wake" (57). This is a father who doesn't get enough rest himself, but who works tirelessly to provide his family the home and the peace of mind to be able to sleep. Another classic example is "Geraldo No Last Name," the story of an undocumented young immigrant man who worked hard to send "weekly money orders home"; sadly, he is killed in a hit-and-run accident, and his family in "another country" will never be notified, because the hospital doesn't even know his name and really couldn't care less about "just another brazer who didn't speak English. Just another wetback" (66). Cisneros humanizes all immigrant laborers who deserve their names to be known—and to be recognized and properly memorialized—in the United States.

SHAME AND THE RACE AND CLASS INJURIES OF GRADUATE SCHOOL

In many ways, Cisneros's battles against her father's rule were easier to win than those in graduate school. She was able to escape her home's patriarchy through material action and decisive control of her own destiny, whereas the racial alienation, classism, and masculinist attitudes Cisneros experienced in graduate school caused insidious, systemic battles, oftentimes fought on more internal and psychological fronts. Of the University of Iowa, Cisneros writes: "The move [there] forced me to have to deal with my 'otherness' for the first time—my race and class difference, and to develop, at long last, a feminist consciousness" ("Chicana Writer's Struggle," 3). Tracing her life story, we see how the intersectional forms of marginalization and the alienating learning conditions under which Cisneros studied led her to experience racial and class injuries that would later manifest as a deeply internalized shame.

Indeed, shame is an ongoing, central preoccupation in Cisneros's work—from *The House on Mango Street* to today—because, as Cisneros's experiences show, the very fact of being a first-generation female Chicana student in a U.S. university is often inextricable from this matrix of feeling. At Iowa, Cisneros was the only Chicana in her graduate cohort, and the only other women of color were Joy Harjo and Rita Dove. Most classmates were white and wealthy, and Cisneros felt out of place and insecure, leading her to lose her voice and question "her right to a life of letters." She recounts in her essay "A Woman of No Consequence: Una Mujer Cualquiera":

> I am famous now for being an hocicona (a big mouth), but when I was attending graduate school at the Iowa Writers Workshop I was too afraid to even speak. Partly because I was young, and partly because I was other and didn't know it. What I did know was a terrible source of shame. The language for that shame I carried with me for so many years in the form of things I did not talk about or want known about me; I'm not certain I was aware of it in a conscious way, but it was there nonetheless like a fine shard of glass that had healed under the flesh; poke and it hurt. It did not clarify itself into words until that graduate seminar when we were talking about houses. A house, or lack of one, became my subject. Once I could name that smudge as a shame, as shame of my working-class home, neighborhood, of my doubt about my right to a life of letters, of my fear of not being as good as my classmates, of not being smart enough, I became angry. Fueled with that anger, the poems and stories came in a torrent. (82)

Like a practical theorist explaining how affect theory works on the ground, Cisneros uses clear language to illustrate the acutely self-conscious and embodied nature of the debilitating feelings that can stem from experiencing marginality and alienation. She shows how being shamed or judged as lesser for one's ethnic background can plant self-doubt that breeds and festers within us, leading us to feel inferior and internalize a virulent, ever-flaring case of imposter's syndrome.

She likens that shame to "a fine shard of glass" that painfully remains embedded in the body, is hard to extricate, and continuously hurts inside; yet it remains a hidden injury because of the overwhelming desire to hide the defects that one sees within oneself. For Cisneros, it was the act of identifying, naming, and confronting that shame and self-doubt that enabled her to extricate the glass shard from her flesh and begin to heal. Fired up with indignant anger and a renewed sense of self-worth, in her introduction to the ten-year anniversary edition of *The House on Mango Street*, Cisneros says her political consciousness was catalyzed: "my political consciousness began the moment I could name this shame" (2). And she became determined to give her writing a political purpose.

The oppositional racial, class, and gender politics of Cisneros's writing and the ways that they intersect with the thematics and politics of home thus emerge during her time in the Iowa Writers' Workshop. In her 1987 essay "Ghosts and Voices: Writing from Obsession," Cisneros recounts the subversive genesis of the book when she was a student at Iowa. In a seminar entitled "On Memory and the Imagination," the class was heatedly discussing French philosopher and literary critic Gaston Bachelard's 1958 book *The Poetics of Space* and the metaphor of a house. She writes: "What was this guy talking about when he mentioned the familiar and comforting 'house of memory'? It was obvious he never had to clean one or pay the landlord rent for one like ours" (72). For Gaston Bachelard, the house is "an image of felicitous space . . . it shelters daydreaming, it protects the dreamer, the house allows one to dream in peace. . . . A house constitutes a body of images that give mankind proofs or illusions of stability" (quoted in Olivares, 161). But, as Julian Olivares points out, "a man born in the upper crust family house, probably never having to do 'female' housework and probably never been confined to the house by reason of his sex, Bachelard easily contrives states of reverie and images of a house that a woman might not have, especially an impoverished woman raised in the ghetto" (161). Cisneros's is a different reality, for the notions that Bachelard assumes—such as "the comfort, security, tranquility, and esteem derived from the home"—are incongruous with Cisneros's spatially underprivileged experience (Olivares, 162). Cisneros says that it was at that moment, while discussing Bachelard in class, that she came to a realization: "—a house, a house, it hit me. What did I know except third-floor flats, and fear of rats, and drunk husbands sending rocks through windows, anything as far from the poetic as possible. And this is when I discovered the voice I'd been suppressing all along without realizing it" ("Ghosts and Voices," 72–73). By introducing "flats," "rats," and "drunk husbands" to her own house of fiction in *The House on Mango Street*, Cisneros inverts Bachelard's nostalgic and über-privileged utopia and defies the bourgeois poetics and subject matter that excluded the material realities of women (especially working-class women of color) such as herself. Fully comprehending Bachelard's precepts, Cisneros impolitely discards them. Though her education at Iowa may have provided some of the literary forms and foundations with which to build her house of fiction, it was her own experiences of marginalization that inhabited that house and endowed the otherwise hollow form with substance.

Ultimately, for Cisneros, although the Iowa Writers' Workshop "promised the chance to create . . . it actually worked to foreclose her individual creativity and instead became a barrier to her work" (Hickner-Johnson, 387). Her program stifled her craft and rejected the vignettes that would later lay the groundwork to become *The House on Mango Street* (*House of My Own*, xv). Despite what her professors and classmates thought, Cisneros describes *The House on Mango Street* as a book "that was not part of my graduation requirements, but which served to shelter me during my time there. I needed shelter. Maybe I was never more homeless than during those two years in graduate school" (35). Despite the lack of support, Cisneros was defiant in every way, shape, and form, continuing to write those vignettes even though they didn't satisfy her MFA program's requirements.

LIFE AFTER GRADUATE SCHOOL

Despite overcoming shame and finding her empowered voice and oppositional poetics, Cisneros's self-doubt reemerged—the fine shard of glass was ever hard to extricate. After she graduated from the University of Iowa with her MFA, she says, "I didn't even apply for a job at a university. I was making $12,000 a year working at an alternative high school in Chicago when I came out of Iowa. Why? Because as women, we think we're not good enough. Because as people of color, we have been led to believe, we're colonized to think, we're not smart enough, we're not good enough, we have nothing to share at the university" (quoted in Cahill, 465). Internalizing the feelings of inferiority they had instilled in her there, Cisneros left Iowa forever wary of returning to a university. The injuries she sustained left her regarding universities as otherizing, structurally harmful institutions: "I didn't want to live in New York or teach at a university—the former because I hated big cities (as a poor person), the latter because universities intimidated me (as a poor person)" (*House of My Own*, 12). Lesson learned: if you're poor, brown, and female, university and trauma are often synonymous.

Cisneros explains that post–graduate school, she "wanted to be a writer, but I had no idea how to go about this except to travel" (11). This lack of mentorship and direction sent her into a period of dejection and crisis. Though she did publish a chapbook called *Bad Boys* in 1980, she describes this time in her life as a "period of complete impotency" (29). Being back home with her family didn't help matters much. She held many jobs in Chicago during this time; she taught continuation school for Latino youth who hadn't completed high school, worked as a college recruiter and counselor at Loyola University Chicago, and organized poetry readings and writing classes in the barrio. She had to work to pay her bills and felt frustrated that she didn't have much time to write.

Thankfully, in 1982 she received her first National Endowment for the Arts Fellowship, which allowed her to work full-time on her writing for two years. This cycle of life crises and the fellowships that would rescue Cisneros from financial and emotional ruin happened many a time; the fortuitous awards would arrive just in time to help validate her work and her life's meaning and give her the strength and financial means to carry on writing. With the NEA Fellowship, she was able to live and work in Provincetown, Rhode Island, and on the Greek island of Hydra, where she ended up completing and mailing off the manuscript for *The House on Mango Street* in 1984.

In retrospect, Cisneros realized that it was her community arts organizational experiences, along with her teaching and mentoring of youth of color with hard lives, that had enabled her to find the life stories worth telling; in the process of helping students and building community she discovered the rich subject matter that would populate her books. Cisneros recounts that she incorporated all the voices and stories of the many people she met throughout those difficult years and created a collage of their lives in *Mango Street*.

MANGO STREET: POLITICIZING THE HOUSE OF FICTION WITH LATINA WOMEN'S STORIES

In 1984 Cisneros published *The House on Mango Street* with Arte Público Press. Its second publication was in 1991, by the mainstream publisher Random House. This was a momentous occasion, as Cisneros became the first Chicana to be published by such a major press, ushering in a national interest in multicultural literature. Though she had made it big, Cisneros's writings continued to be marked by politicized subject matter and poetics. Ever longing for a home, in *Mango Street* Cisneros, like many American women writers of the twentieth century, employed the image of the house as a symbol of cultural and female disenfranchisement. The many Latina characters who reside on Mango Street are locked up in apartments by their oppressive husbands, are abused, and long for escape; the neighborhood "is filled with women imprisoned in the domestic space by patriarchal and economic constraints" (Saldívar-Hull, 94). The coming-of-age protagonist Esperanza is a nascent writer who feels for these women, tells their painful stories, and wants to help them get out. She is also in search of a house of her own—a place to write, heal, and share with the underprivileged collective who has never had a home. This story becomes a larger metaphor for Cisneros's body of work, which created homes for those who had never had one in academia or in the publishing industry. Thus, Cisneros also "reinscribed the age-old metaphor of the house in order to explore the themes of sexism and racism and the struggle of the female minority writer to appropriate the word in the Anglo-American 'house of fiction'" (O'Reilly Herrera, 198).

One good thing Cisneros gained from her strict training at Iowa's poetry workshop was her adept use of minimalist aesthetics in her writing. She took this minimalist form—characterized by extremely sparse narrative, an economy with words, repetition, no ornamentation, and gradual variation—and adapted it as an oppositional poetics she used to inscribe working-class women of color's historically marginalized experiences. If Ernest Hemingway had created the theory of literary omission to "strengthen the story and make people feel more than they understood" (75), Cisneros perfected it; by depicting characters who are unable to realize their potential, such as sequestered women, forgotten immigrants, and impoverished students, she examines the lives that were previously omitted in American literature.

A prime example of the latent power of Cisneros's minimalist poetics occurs in "A Smart Cookie" when Esperanza's mother tells her how she dropped out of school because she was ashamed of going there in her poor-looking clothes. She starts the story by saying to Esperanza, "I could've been somebody, you know?" (90). It is a simple statement that encapsulates so much regret and so many lost possibilities in a lifetime. Esperanza then takes over the narrative: "She can speak two languages. She can sing an opera. She knows how to fix a TV. She used to draw when she had time." She recognizes her mother's multifaceted talents despite her lack of formal education and how her gifts have been sidelined by her child-rearing duties. Her mother then warns her, "Esperanza, you go to school. Study hard." All her mother says about her life prior to dropping out is expressed in the latent lamentation, "I was a smart cookie then" (91). That is the last sentence of the story—no follow-up, no details, just a succinct statement resounding with pain and regret. The simplicity of the statement makes us fill in the gaps, pulls at our heartstrings, and causes us to writhe with empathy. Esperanza's mother's lesson is haunting: Esperanza will need to go to school and study hard so that she does not end up like her—an organic intellectual who is full of artistic talent but is reduced to singing operas while stirring a pot of oatmeal for her hungry kids.

"A Smart Cookie" can be read as Cisneros's metanarrative for her and her mother's lives—that's why it's so important to know her biography. By going to college, Cisneros embraced the education that her mother was unable to pursue. Like Esperanza's mother, Cisneros recounts, her own mother "could sing a Puccini opera, cook dinner for nine with only five dollars, draw and tell stories, and probably would've enjoyed a college education but [her] only taste of college was reading the books her children brought back from the university" (*House of My Own*, 75). For Cisneros, education and writing became the means with which to pay tribute to her parents' otherwise forgotten lives. Cisneros and Esperanza's stories provide an allegory of the relationship among first- and second-generation Mexican American women: mothers who have been confined to the home and thrown into anonymity, but whose educated Mexican American daughters have found their way into society and can now help write their mothers into existence.

As we can see from "A Smart Cookie," the short-story cycle of *Mango Street* enables Cisneros to explore both the protagonist Esperanza's personal quest in becoming a writer as well as Esperanza's community's history, but it is *Mango Street*'s deployment of the minimalist form that heightens its politics. Part of the reason Cisneros's text is so poignant in its characterization of the underprivileged is that its concise form swiftly paints people as infinitely interesting, but it also suggests that they are infinitesimal specks liable to be forgotten in the larger scheme of society. Cisneros creates vignettes that can stand on their own or can be read within a sustained narrative of socioeconomic, sexual, or autonomous poverty: as she says, "you can understand each story like a little pearl or look at the whole thing like a necklace" (quoted in Jussawalla and Dasenbrock, 467). Whether read in one form or another, they nonetheless still deploy an aesthetic of marginality; Cisneros's sparse and economical language reflects and underscores precisely the paltry conditions that she is writing about.

As Cisneros shows, for the Chicana writer, omission isn't solely an aesthetic practice—it's a social reality. Excluded from literary discourse, her community risks the danger of social erasure and discursive nonexistence, but it is the domestically confined women around her who face the gravest omittance. Cisneros employs her Chicana daughter-narrator—both of them daughters of socially invisible and historically muted women—to reclaim subaltern female subjects' experiences by writing them into her narrative. Quite literally, Cisneros's text seeks to piece together and validate the mothers' forsaken lives. The story "A Smart Cookie" reveals this project by showing

Esperanza as gathering her mother's, the smart cookie's, crumbs. And in "Hairs," Esperanza envisions her mother with her "warm smell of bread" (6) as the maternal bread of life; though to society she is a void, to her daughter, this Mexican woman is plenitude. Cisneros rescues the testimonies of the mothers, such as homesick Mamacita in "No Speak English," the mother in "There Was an Old Woman She Had So Many Children She Didn't Know What to Do," and Minerva, whose husband abandoned her and their children but periodically comes back to beat her, in "Minerva Writes Poems." By incorporating them into her book, Cisneros's text can be read as a project to recover the histories of a muted culture—and, specifically, its muted women—from non-official oral histories and testimonies (Saldívar-Hull, 53).

Ultimately, Esperanza's character in *Mango Street* mirrors Cisneros: despite the traumas they've witnessed and experienced, these writers are hopeful and determined to collectively uplift and improve their communities themselves. Because after all, as Alicia asks Esperanza, "Who's going to do it? The mayor?" (107). That the rhetorical question makes Esperanza "laugh out loud" indicates that the government has failed these communities. The book ends by articulating a politics of grassroots social responsibility, of helping "the ones who cannot out" (110).

Ever the rebel mentor, Cisneros continues to weave that thread of social consciousness throughout her work, urging us to use our rebel ways on behalf of lesser-privileged women. In "Woman Hollering Creek"—the titular short story in her next book—two Chicanas named Felice and Graciela help an immigrant Mexicana named Cleófilas escape her abusive husband by asking their loud-mouthed, truck-driving friend Felice to drive Cleófilas to the Greyhound bus station while the husband is at work. Graciela rhetorically asks Felice, "If we don't help her, who will?" (54). Continuously championing a solidarity between Chicanas and Mexicanas, Cisneros impels more privileged readers to reflect on our social responsibility to help our immigrant sisters—women, sometimes, much like our own mothers or grandmothers. That this story was based on her own experience of giving a ride to a Mexicana who was leaving her husband shows how Cisneros leads by example.

WOMAN HOLLERING CREEK: LIVING IN SAN ANTONIO, TEXAS, AND EMBRACING THE MEXICAN AESTHETICS OF MAXIMALISM

In 1987, Cisneros received her second NEA grant and used this validation of her work to finally gather the courage to return calls from Susan Bergholz, a New York literary agent who had been trying to represent her for four years. She sent Bergholz "thirty-nine pages of a new volume of stories (*Woman Hollering Creek*) and her new agent was able to sell the not-yet-written book to Random House for a large advance" (McCracken, 231). This was the first time a Chicana author had ever been signed by a major publisher. By 1991, awards, advances, royalties, and speaking fees finally enabled Cisneros not only to support herself with her writing but also to fulfill the dream of buying her own house, that 1903 Victorian in the King William Historic District of San Antonio that I discussed earlier in this essay. The large-press validation, the lucrative contract, and living in her own house in San Antonio, with the San Antonio River flowing right behind her house, empowered Cisneros to tap into boundless creative possibilities in her short story collection *Woman Hollering Creek*, published in 1991.

Cisneros recounts that she felt a lot of pressure to write and represent Chicana/os well. The burden of representation is real, particularly for early Chicana writers such as herself. But in *Woman Hollering Creek*, Cisneros delves deeper into her Mexican culture than ever before. In it, she seems to demonstrate that part of the way she can overcome past racial injuries is by basking in the glory of her utter Mexicanness; she shows that *la cultura cura*—and that she found this curative culture by making her home in San Antonio.

How do we see San Antonio's influence at play in her later work? Well, for one, the voices in the stories in *Woman Hollering Creek* are vastly different from the voices in *The House on Mango Street*. As we saw, minimalist aesthetics characterize Cisneros's first book; though the characters are culturally diverse, she makes very few mentions of specific ethnic cultures, traditions, or places. Esperanza quickly mentions her father's "Mexican records" (10) in the story "My Name," and we learn her friend Marin will go back to Puerto Rico (26), and she has one sentence about Alicia being from Guadalajara (106). But of

most characters' countries of origin or cultural traditions, we are not
given specifics. In "No Speak English," for example, Mamacita longs
for home, and we are told that she "paints her walls of the apartment
pink, but it's not the same, you know?" (77). Similarly, Rafaela "drinks
coconut and papaya juice" and longs for home on "the island" (80), so
we gather that she is from a tropical island in Latin America—perhaps
Puerto Rico, the Dominican Republic, or Cuba. But the stories have
few cultural markers, and we never learn exactly where "home" is.

Perhaps Cisneros's experiences at Iowa made her fearful to have her
writing be "too ethnic" in *Mango Street*; maybe she felt the need to keep
it safe. Many writers who have come out of the Iowa program have said
that cultural difference is derided and expunged there. Recently, for
example, Cathy Park Hong shared in *Minor Feelings: An Asian American
Reckoning* (2020) that her classmates at Iowa shamed her, ridiculed her
race, and made her feel that she needed to erase her Korean Chinese
heritage from her poetry in order to be considered a good poet.

In the stories in *Woman Hollering Creek*, Cisneros *manda Iowa al
carajo* and replaces it with the once-Mexican city of San Antonio,
Texas: racial, geographical, cultural, religious, and linguistic specifics
abound in every story. It's an explosion of all things Mexican—the stories invoke the Alamo, Lucía Méndez and her telenovelas, la Virgen de
Guadalupe, Emiliano Zapata, la Malinche, el Cristo Negro de Esqui-
pulas found in the San Fernando Cathedral in San Antonio, Mayan
kings, Pedro Infante, and Popocatepetl and Ixtacihuatl, among others.
Almost every story draws from the rich racial, cultural, and spiritual
diversity of Mexicans and Chicana/os in or around Texas.

In her memoir, *A House of My Own*, Cisneros shows us how the
experience of living in San Antonio imbued her writing with this Mexican American aesthetic of maximalism. She writes: "across a table
of sopa de conchitas at Torres Taco Haven, this question: 'What is
the Mexican American aesthetic?' A San Antonio architect is asking.
He's trying to translate the private Mexican housescape to the public
building. What is the Mexican American aesthetic? I think and then
respond, 'More is more'" (186). For her, in San Antonio, "more is more"
becomes the guiding force of her aesthetic—a Mexican defiance of
the once-imposed Iowan constrictions of minimalism. That Cisneros
is able to define her politics and aesthetic while sitting, chatting, and

eating a *sopa de conchitas* at this famed San Antonio taqueria high-lights how the location, food, company, and culture she found in that city helped her think through, discover, and embrace the style and subject matter that would propel her art from that point forward.

One can clearly trace how the city of San Antonio and those aes-thetic revelations it inspired make their way into *Woman Hollering Creek* and, later, *Caramelo*. Adriana Estill has wonderfully examined how Cisneros employs the geographies of early and mid-twentieth-century Chicago in *Caramelo* to show how the city "performs a for-mative, dynamic function for the Reyes family [in the novel] and their relationship to Mexico" ("Mexican Chicago," 98). Estill traces how, in *Caramelo*, Chicago "serves a paradigmatic function as a place that enabled Mexicans and Puerto Ricans to understand themselves as 'brown' or 'Mexican' rather than black or white" and how "these understandings affected Mexicanness on the other side of the border" (99). In a similar way, in the stories in *Woman Hollering Creek* we see Cisneros integrally exploring Texas histories, experiences, and places to demonstrate how San Antonio has been shaped by the diverse Mex-icans who have lived there for generations and how the city has in turn shaped their understanding of their own Mexicanness as well.

The book itself and its titular story are named after a real body of water named Woman Hollering Creek found near San Antonio. She takes this creek that no one pays mind to and uses it to tell the story of Cleofilas, an immigrant woman who is drawn to the creek in her moments of darkness (like the woman in the famous cautionary tale of la Llorona) when her husband abuses her. However, Cleofilas escapes that usual narrative, and Cisneros uses the creek to empower her and give her a voice. Cleofilas learns how toxic it is to emulate the ever-suffering telenovela star Lucía Méndez and is instead introduced to new models of strong MeXicanas—like Felice, the hollering, unmar-ried Chicana with a pick-up truck who rescues her and helps her leave her husband. In "Remember the Alamo," Cisneros tells the stories of fierce, glamorous drag queens who perform "every Thursday night at the Travisty. Behind the Alamo, you can't miss it" (63). The usually anti-Mexican, vengeful statement "Remember the Alamo" is used here to instead memorialize the LGBTQ community members who suc-cumbed to AIDS and to show how hard the Latinx LGBTQ commu-nity was hit, though their stories are almost never recounted. "Little

Miracles, Kept Promises" is a long collection of prayers, offerings, and notes of gratitude left by current Mexican American parishioners at the San Fernando Cathedral in San Antonio, built in 1731 when San Antonio was a Spanish colonial settlement. Through those prayers we are able to see the trials and tribulations, the intimate worries and supplications, of the people. All of these stories, full of colorful details and bursting at the seams, tell the stories of Tejanxs rarely told.

At 464 pages in length and with about a hundred footnotes, Cisneros's 2002 novel *Caramelo; or, Puro Cuento* represents a culmination of that maximalism, unable to be contained within the traditional bounds of a novel. *Caramelo* in many ways represents a house antithetical to *The House on Mango Street*. In conceptualizing the stylistic differences between the short story and novel form, in 1994, Cisneros said that "you don't start out by building a house if you haven't learned how to build a room . . . at this point in our career and our craft we're learning how to build the rooms before we can build a house" (quoted in Jussawalla and Dasenbrock, 467). With *The House on Mango Street*'s minimalist assemblage of textual blocks, Cisneros certainly practiced learning how to build her rooms. In *Caramelo*, she takes on transnational settings, plots, endless footnotes, and multiple points of view; she's built nothing short of a mansion. And this is precisely where the form takes on greater political implications. If Cisneros's highly sparse and restricted form in *Mango Street* simulated the impoverished and confining conditions her characters were living in, *Caramelo*'s utter lack of boundaries, margins, or borders reflects the realization of the Chicana subject, no longer confined to forms or norms—or, as Cisneros terms it, "loose."

CHICANA SPIRITUALITY ON HER OWN TERMS

Cisneros also replenished her culture and her spirit through her reconnection to her Mexican Catholic spirituality as well as its syncretism with Buddhist faith, epitomized by the Buddha-Lupe tattoo she got inked on her arm. As Cisneros writes in her essay "Guadalupe the Sex Goddess," it took her a long time to reconnect with and embrace la Virgen de Guadalupe because she had many feelings of anger and resentment toward her: "As far as I could see, La Lupe was nothing but a Goody-Two-Shoes meant to doom me to a life of unhappiness . . .

my culture's role model for brown women like me. La Lupe was damn dangerous, an ideal so lofty and unrealistic it was laughable. Did boys have to aspire to be Jesus?" (*House of My Own*, 164). Cisneros rejected the passive, chaste, and motherly role model that she was supposed to look up to and emulate. Marianismo—the cult of Marian chastity and motherhood—was anathema to her aspirations as a writer, so she defied her for a long time. But her travels to Mexico (Mexico City's Zócalo in 1985, the Basílica de Santa María de Guadalupe near Tepeyac Hill in 1995), her research for her story "Little Miracles," and the work of other Chicana feminists, such as Gloria Anzaldúa, helped Cisneros recover and understand Guadalupe's origins in Coatlicue, an Indigenous deity who had creative and sexual powers before the Catholic Church desexed her. Reconnecting to la Virgen by recovering her womanhood, Cisneros was able to make peace and embrace this previously disempowering symbol in her life. Her reconnection with la Virgen de Guadalupe is emblematic of Cisneros's proclivity for forgiveness, growth, and seeking peace and healing.

Cisneros's spiritual search was equally guided by the teachings of the late Thich Nhat Hanh, the Vietnamese Buddhist monk and peace activist who entreated us to practice mindfulness in our daily lives, to find joy and meaning in the everyday things we do. The search for peace, clarity, and insight often eludes us, but his teachings remind us to practice gratitude. For a writer, these are very important lessons. We can get caught up in the exigencies of the craft and the toll it takes on our bodies and soul. But if we are mindful of our purpose—if we remember, as Cisneros says, that "the writer's duty is to be the Buddha. To serve others with wisdom and compassion" ("Woman of No Consequence," 86)—our writing is infused with a social imperative that brings clarity and purpose to our lives.

MEMORIALIZING HER PARENTS' STRUGGLES

Cisneros's parents' lessons and experiences inspired her to infuse her writings with a sense of feminist and working-class purpose. When they passed—her father in 1997 and her mother in 2007—that clarity and purpose became clearer to her, if temporarily harder to come by because of her overwhelming feelings of grief.

In 2007, just a week before she passed, Cisneros's mother, Elvira, came down from Chicago to San Antonio to see her daughter's newly remodeled house. She was thrilled to see Sandra's library and her big office: "Boy, this place is nice!" (*House of My Own*, 287). At night, right before bedtime, when they would snuggle together in bed, she told Sandra, "'Good lucky you studied.' You mean my office, my life. I say to you, 'Good lucky'" (288). Her mother was so proud of what Sandra had attained for herself all by herself; her daughter's home represented everything that she could have dreamed of. Losing her mother—her greatest champion and advocate—brought Cisneros great pain. But that pain also made her turn more deeply to writing: her writings about her parents became an important way to capture and memorialize their lives in a country that would otherwise never know who they were.

In 2012, Cisneros published *Have You Seen Marie?*, a story ostensibly about a woman's search for her missing cat, but also about her grief in the wake of losing her mother, and a reminder that one's mother's spirit resides everywhere and in everything one does. In 2002, Cisneros had also recounted that she wrote *Caramelo* "out of her desire to honor her father as he approached the end of his life by telling his story." She stated, "I didn't want people to erase him," moreover adding that she had "never [seen] an upholsterer in American literature" (Navarro). In *Caramelo*, Lala's immigrant laborer father, Inocencio, works as an upholsterer, just as Cisneros's father once did. Like Lala's father, Cisneros's father spent a lot of time after work resting his swollen hands and feet so he could start the process all over again the following day. The book is an ode to her hardworking father and the labor that enabled his family to thrive in the United States. Alfredo Cisneros Del Moral may have passed, but his daughter created a foundation in his name and through it has mentored and enabled over a hundred creative writers to continue to write stories that share our rich histories.

LATEST BOOKS: *MARTITA, I REMEMBER YOU* AND *WOMAN WITHOUT SHAME*

One of the social purposes that continues to fuel Cisneros's writing, as we have seen, is her depiction of the life-sustaining and life-changing relationships that can exist between women—the power than emanates from sisterhood. Cisneros returns to this subject in one of her latest books. *Martita: I Remember You* (2021) is a semiautobiographical fiction book of vignettes and letters in which Cisneros also pays tribute to her early struggles as a working-class Chicana writer in Paris—making it on her own, traveling, and seeking the writer's life without money or guides. In the book, the Chicana protagonist, twenty-year old Corina, is running out of money while traveling in Paris as she waits for a letter of acceptance from a French art foundation. She meets and develops intense friendships with other immigrants there—Martita from Argentina and Paola from Italy. The three women bond over their shared poverty and dreams of attaining a better life despite their lack of access to the Parisian upper class. Many years later, back in Chicago, Corina finds her letters from her friends, and she reflects on how those past relationships shaped and sustained her life. In her book, Cisneros posits the importance of women's support networks to surviving in a dangerously patriarchal and classist world that has the potential to kill our dreams and spirits. Only by sharing our stories and our innermost thoughts through our writing can we women thrive, together.

Cisneros's latest poetry book, *Woman Without Shame: Poems* (2022), represents another gorgeous effort in Cisneros's now legendary art of oversharing as a rebellious literary genre. Having set the precedent in her poetry books *My Wicked Ways* (1987) and *Loose Woman* (1995), *Woman Without Shame* takes shame as its central subject. Now in her sixties, Cisneros shares with us why she is not ashamed of her corpulent body, the joy and excitement she's derived from it, and whose other bodies hers has communed with. Her poems are a celebration of the self through the many years of living a rich life on one's own terms. She says, "I am a woman of delightful season. / El Cantarito, little brown jug of La Lotería. / Solid, stout, bottom planted / firmly and without a doubt, / filled to the brim I am. / I said the brim" (*Woman Without Shame*, 11). Bawdy, self-assured, and culturally grounded, Cisneros continues to bring us beautiful poems for every season of our lives. Forever teaching us to stop allowing ourselves to be shamed for our differences, Cisneros shows us how we can instead embrace those differences as the source of our strength, as cultural capital that propels our art, politics, and everyday life.

GOING HOME: A CHICANA IN MEXICO

Ultimately, Cisneros's desire to seek peace and purpose and reconnect with the land of her ancestors is what led her to leave her San Antonio home of twenty-nine years and make the bold move to San Miguel de Allende, Guanajuato, México, in 2013. It was in a way a return home and also a slap in the face to hegemonic ideas about American exceptionalism. Many were shocked that a rich and famous writer would want to leave her Victorian house in the United States for a "Third World" country. But Cisneros has always known better about where happiness resides; intuiting the need to let go of the heaviness of the past, she came to this realization in a dream: "I am not my house. Therefore, I can walk away" (*House of My Own*, 351). Having built her dream home, she realized that the material house was not what was important, but rather the peace of mind, safety, and freedom that could afford her the opportunity to continue to seek her purpose.

Cisneros's purple (and later, fuchsia) San Antonio home was the stuff of Chicana legends, but that kind of legacy's weight can also become an exhausting load to carry after twenty-two years. With her famously colorful house perpetually standing out and easily accessible to any passerby, it became necessary to move to be able to continue to live and write in peace. Cisneros made her mark—she built a home and a literary and political legacy that she could be proud of—and moved on to new geographic and spiritual terrains. Upon putting her San Antonio home on the market, she said: "I leave with no regrets and with certainty that I'll create spiritual refuge elsewhere. . . . La Divina Providencia is mapping the motion of our lives . . . weaving a design larger than our lives, too intricate for the eye to follow, but every thread woven with clarity, purpose, and pattern" (*House of My Own*, 171, 176). That tireless capacity for courageous change and growth is emblematic of Cisneros.

In México, she has continued to build community and build homes for others. On February 26, 2019, she received the prestigious PEN/ Nabokov Award for Achievement in International Literature. Cisneros told ABC News that she planned to donate the $50,000 cash prize from the award to her assistants in Mexico so they could purchase their own homes, stating: "With money and fame comes responsibility, and the amount is exactly what they need . . . I can't describe how happy it makes me to be able to do this for them" (Guzman). When I heard this news about Cisneros's generous offer, I wasn't at all surprised. This is what she has been doing most of her life: single-handedly making metaphorical homes accessible to people of color in the university and in the publishing industry through her art, public lectures, mentorship, and Macondo Writers Workshop. Now her generosity is making a material and transnational impact on the lives of those who need it most.

Cisneros continues to support fellow writers and has become a dear literary madrina to many. In March 2022, I got to spend the day with Reyna Grande when she visited my university for our annual reading celebration, and she told me all about how Cisneros invited her to stay at her house and even got up early in the morning to cook her breakfast (which was a huge act of generosity given that Cisneros is not known to be an early riser!). It was a beautiful anecdote that exemplified Cisneros's legacy and commitment to supporting new generations of writers, and that is a feat to be respected. Cisneros will forever be our first mentor and madrina in the art of speaking our truth and being women *sin vergüenza*.

WORKS CITED

Bachelard, Gaston. *The Poetics of Space*. 1958; repr., New York: Penguin Classics, 2014.

Behar, Ruth. "Talking in Our Pajamas: A Conversation with Sandra Cisneros on Finding Your Voice, Fear of Highways, Tacos, Travel, and the Need for Peace in the World." *Michigan Quarterly Review* 47, no. 3 (Summer 2008): 411–26.

Cahill, Susan. "Sandra Cisneros (1954–)." In *Writing Women's Lives: An Anthology of Autobiographical Narratives by Twentieth-Century American Women Writers*. Edited by Susan Cahill. New York: HarperCollins, 1994, 460–68.

Cisneros, Sandra. *Bad Boys*. San Jose, CA: Mango Publications, 1980.

———. *Caramelo; or, Puro Cuento*. New York: Vintage Books, 2002.

———. "Do You Know Me? I Wrote *The House on Mango Street*." *Americas Review* 15, no. 1 (Spring 1987): 77–79.

———. "Ghosts and Voice: Writing from Obsession; From a Writer's Notebook." *Americas Review* 15, no. 1 (Spring 1987): 72–73.

———. *A House of My Own: Stories from My Life*. New York: Vintage Books, 2015.

———. *The House on Mango Street*. New York: Vintage Books, 1984.

———. *The House on Mango Street*. 10th anniv. ed. New York: Vintage Books, 1994.

———. *Loose Woman*. New York: Vintage Books, 1994.

———. *Martita, I Remember You/Martita, te recuerdo: A Story in English and Spanish*. New York: Vintage Books, 2021.

———. *"My Wicked Wicked Ways*: The Chicana Writer's Struggle with Good and Evil, or Las Hijas de la Mala Vida." Unpublished manuscript, 1985.

———. *My Wicked Wicked Ways*. New York: Turtle Bay Books, 1987.

———. "Ghosts and Voices: Writing from Obsession." *Americas Review* 15, no. 1 (Spring 1987): 69–72.

———. "Notes to a Young(er) Writer." *Americas Review* 15, no. 1 (Spring 1987): 74–76.

———. *"Woman Hollering Creek" and Other Stories*. New York: Vintage Books, 1991.

———. "A Woman of No Consequence: Una Mujer Cualquiera." In *Living Chicana Theory*. Edited by Carla Trujillo. Berkeley, Calif.: Third Woman Press, 1998.

———. *Woman Without Shame: Poems*. New York: Knopf, 2022.

Cruz, Felicia. "On the 'Simplicity' of Sandra Cisneros's *House on Mango Street*." *Modern Fiction Studies* 47, no. 4 (Winter 2001): 911–46.

Estill, Adriana. "In Father's Footsteps: Bad Girls in Ana Castillo's and Sandra Cisneros's Poetry." *Confluencia* 16, no. 2 (2001): 46–60. www.jstor.org/stable/27922794.

———. "Mexican Chicago in Sandra Cisneros's *Caramelo*: Gendered Geographies." *MELUS* 41, no, 2 (Summer 2016): 97–123.

Guzman, Sandra. "At 64, PEN America Winner Sandra Cisneros Is Just Getting Started." *ABC News*, February 12, 2019. https://www.nbcnews.com/news/latino/64-pen-winner-sandra-cisneros-just-getting-started-n970076.

Hemingway, Ernest. *A Moveable Feast*. 1964; repr., New York: Scribner, 1996.

Hickner-Johnson, Corey. "Not with the Program: Sandra Cisneros on Feeling and Being a Latina Writer in the Program Era." *Tulsa Studies in Women's Literature* 37, no. 2 (2018): 377–96. doi:10.1353/tsw.2018.0031.

Hong, Cathy Park. *Minor Feelings: An Asian American Reckoning*. New York: One World, 2020.

Jiménez, Tomás R. *Replenished Ethnicity: Mexican Americans, Immigration, and Identity*. Berkeley: University of California Press, 2009.

Jussawalla, Feroza, and Reed Way Dasenbrock. "Interviews with Writers of the Postcolonial World." In *Writing Women's Lives: An Anthology of Autobiographical Narratives by Twentieth-Century American Women Writers*. Edited by Susan Cahill. New York: HarperCollins, 1994, 286–306.

Kerane, Bridget and Juanita Heredia. *Latina Self-Portraits: Interviews with Contemporary Women Writers*. Albuquerque: University of New Mexico Press, 2000. Pp. 45–57.

Lowry, Kathy. "The Purple Passion of Sandra Cisneros." *Texas Monthly*, October 1997. https://www.texasmonthly.com/style/the-purple-passion-of-sandra-cisneros/

Matchie, Thomas. "Literary Continuity in Sandra Cisneros's *The House on Mango Street*." *Midwest Quarterly* 37, no. 1 (Autumn 1995): 67–79.

McCracken, Ellen. "Sandra Cisneros." In *Latino and Latina Writers*. Edited by Alan West-Duran. New York: Charles Scribners' Sons, 2004, 229–49.

McGurl, Mark. *The Program Era: Postwar Fiction and the Rise of Creative Writing*. Cambridge, Mass.: Harvard University Press, 2009.

Mullen, Harryette. "'A Silence Between Us Like a Language': The Untranslability of Experience in Sandra Cisneros's *Woman Hollering Creek*." *MELUS* 21, no. 2 (Summer 1996): 3–20.

Muñoz, José Esteban. *The Sense of Brown*. Durham, N.C.: Duke University Press, 2020.

Navarro, Mireya. "Telling a Tale of Immigrants Whose Stories Go Untold." *New York Times*, November 12, 2002.

Olivares, Julian. "Sandra Cisneros's *The House on Mango Street* and the Poetics of Space." *Americas Review* 15, no. 1 (Spring 1987): 160–70.

O'Reilly Herrera, Andrea. "'Chambers of Consciousness': Sandra Cisneros and the Development of the Self in the BIG *House on Mango Street*." *Bucknell Review* 39, no. 1 (1995): 191–204.

Sagel, Kim. "Sandra Cisneros." *Publisher's Weekly*, March 29, 1991, 74.

Saldívar-Hull, Sonia. *Feminism on the Border: Chicana Gender Politics and Literature*. Berkeley: University of California Press, 2000.

Tompkins, Cynthia. "Sandra Cisneros." In *American Novelists Since World War II: Fourth Series*. Edited by James Giles and Wanda Giles. Vol. 152 of *Dictionary of Literary Biography*. Farmington Hills, Mich.: Gale Research, 1995, 35–41.

Trujillo, Carla. *Living Chicana Theory*. Berkeley, Calif.: Third Woman Press, 1998.

DEMETRIA MARTÍNEZ

DEMETRIA MARTÍNEZ

A Critical Biography

CRISTINA HERRERA

EMETRIA MARTÍNEZ has established herself as one of the leading Chicana voices of our time.[1] Born in 1960 and raised in
Albuquerque, New Mexico, she writes fiction, poetry, essays,
and journalism that often reference the land of her birth, with all of
its fraught tensions of colonial history and violence. Martínez's distinct
Chicana mestizaje traces its New Mexican family lineage to the founding of Old Town Plaza in Albuquerque and to the Indigenous peoples
who had long lived upon the land that the Spanish claimed, in addition
to ancestry that includes Sephardic Jews who were expelled during
the Spanish Inquisition (Gutiérrez y Muhs, *Communal Feminisms*, 53).
In an interview with Gabriella Gutiérrez y Muhs, Martínez states that
she began writing as a child and teenager, keeping a journal in which
she would document her struggles with body image, rejection, and
depression (54). Martínez earned a degree in public and international
affairs from Princeton University, training that would serve her well in
her advocacy work, journalism, and even creative writing. Upon graduating, she began working as a correspondent for the *National Catholic
Reporter*, after which she served as a religion writer for the *Albuquerque Journal* (Ikas, 113). Both journalist positions proved foundational

for her creative writing, but the topics she frequently addressed in her columns would eventually be unjustly used against her by the United States federal government.

Martínez describes herself as being raised in a family of activists, where she witnessed her parents openly speak against injustices occurring at home or abroad. Her father was the first Chicano elected to the Albuquerque school board, and she credits early memories of sitting at the dinner table with her family watching news coverage of the Vietnam War as the catalyst for her lifelong commitment to anti-imperialism, antiracism, and human rights activism (Gutiérrez y Muhs, *Communal Feminisms*, 58). She admits that she wrote *Mother Tongue*, her most famous text, in a mere nine months, as she was working as a correspondent (Ikas, 117). Learning about the multiple Central American wars and the United States' key role in those conflicts inspired both her activism and her creative writing, acts that she believes are not separate. As she states, her life along the U.S.-Mexico border influenced her growing awareness of state-sponsored violence and her obligation as a Chicana writer to act: "I was too young for Vietnam. When I understood that our government, which had no money for scholarships, managed to spend $1.4 million a day in military aid in El Salvador, I began to wonder what the hell was going on" (119). This early awareness of political hypocrisy would later make its way into her work as a journalist and creative writer.

Martínez is best known for standing trial in 1988 for charges of conspiring against the United States government by transporting undocumented Central American migrants seeking asylum. In March 1986, then-Governor Toney Anaya declared New Mexico a sanctuary state for Central Americans in search of asylum. A Lutheran minister, Rev. Glen Remer-Thamert, invited Martínez to accompany him to Juárez, Mexico, to meet two Salvadoran women; on the basis of this interaction, the federal government accused both Martínez and Remer-Thamert of multiple counts of conspiracy (Holmes). The subsequent trial, which garnered national attention, was the first time that a Chicana writer had her own work brought into court as "evidence" of guilt.

In addition to the public trial with which she has been most associated, Martínez has also used her position as a writer to honestly address her experience living with bipolar disorder. In her 2008 interview with the Latinx literary website *La Bloga*, she says candidly, "It's important to tell the truth about bipolar disorder" (Alvarado). This simple but straightforward statement does not occur in a vacuum; instead, Martínez's words are a powerful reminder of the many taboos and stigmas associated with mental illness. She admits that she began experiencing depression as a teenager, the only balm being the act of writing in a journal, copying down song lyrics and other poems, until she eventually began shaping her own original voice (*Confessions*, 30). Martínez has advocated for a greater understanding of mental illness and the need for universal health care: "Writing is no cure for mental illness, but keeping a journal was a way to step outside the violent whirlwind of my emotions so that I could watch" (30). As a Chicana writer living with mental illness, she finds writing to be a profoundly spiritual, life-affirming practice, a theme that emerges in much of her work.

THE SANCTUARY MOVEMENT AND ACTIVIST HISTORY

Existing scholarship on Martínez's important body of work has rightly referenced her ties to the U.S. sanctuary movement of the 1980s through her journalism and creative writing. Prior to the publication of her fiction, for which she would later become famous, Martínez worked as a freelancer and as a regular columnist for the *National Catholic Reporter* and the *Albuquerque Journal*, as previously mentioned. In this role, she would frequently pen op-eds and feature stories that called into question the limits of U.S. democracy when this nation wielded power over Central American countries through military and financial support. Martínez has used her journalistic pieces to expose uncomfortable truths about the United States' direct involvement in torture, violence, and the suppression of human rights, practices that contradict the values for which this country has purportedly stood.

Martínez's journalistic stories also introduced readers to the U.S. sanctuary movement, which scholar Hilary Cunningham defines as "a religiopolitical coalition that began [in 1982] as a network of churches and synagogues that decided to offer safe haven or "sanctuary" to

Central American fugitives denied political asylum by the U.S. Immigration and Naturalization Service. . . . In response to what they perceived as the immoral deportation of Central American political refugees, and in defiance of the INS, this group of church people developed an underground network that transported and crossed Central Americans into the United States" (xiii). Sanctuary workers and activists refused to abide by U.S. refugee and immigration policies that denied the real atrocities being committed by Central American dictatorships, which were receiving U.S. financing and military support. Given that the Reagan administration denied the majority of asylum requests from El Salvador, volunteers, church leaders, writers, and activists took matters into their own hands. "Admitting that the thousands of Central Americans seeking safe haven in the United States were legitimate refugees," writes Cunningham, "ran counter to the political and economic support the government espoused for regimes that were brutally oppressing their own populations" (xvi). The U.S. backing of repressive authoritarian regimes in Latin America has occurred throughout the twentieth century and continues into the present, the nation long suspecting leftist groups and opposition leaders of Communist activity that threatens U.S. capitalist interests in the region. In this light, Martínez's literary corpus rejects American ideals of exceptionalism and the myth of the United States as the birthplace of democracy. Instead, her writing deftly exposes the United States' contradictory patterns of espousing itself as a bastion of liberty and justice while simultaneously supporting governments that systematically torture, silence, and murder.

As Michael J. McConnell explains, the U.S. sanctuary movement grows out of a long tradition of religious and faith-based organizations offering sanctuary and haven for refugees and enslaved fugitives throughout the nineteenth century. Members of the Southside Presbyterian Church in Tucson, Arizona, considered the birthplace of the U.S. sanctuary movement, declared their church a sanctuary in 1982 for refugees needing haven from Guatemala and El Salvador, two countries receiving military aid from the United States. Because these refugees were routinely denied asylum, Southside Presbyterian, as well as other churches in San Francisco, renounced this policy, effectively breaking U.S. immigration law in favor of theological views that advocated for the protection of persecuted groups. By 1985, prior to Martínez's trial, sixteen sanctuary workers had been indicted on multiple counts ranging from aiding and transporting "illegal aliens" to conspiring against the U.S. government (McConnell). In the present, faith-based humanitarian groups continue to advocate for migrants, providing food, water, and shelter in the Mexican desert, infamous for the treacherous heat that is responsible for killing countless individuals attempting to cross the border each year.

In 1986, Martínez was invited to travel to Juárez, Mexico, to meet and interview two Salvadoran women who were hoping to receive asylum in the United States (Valle). Though she spent time with these women, learning of the circumstances that brought them to Northern Mexico, Martínez never published an article describing this encounter. Nevertheless, in 1988, Martínez was charged with conspiracy against the U.S. government, accused of violating immigration laws and transporting undocumented immigrants. Martínez, along with Rev. Glen Remer-Thamert, stood trial, but she and the minister were acquitted on First Amendment grounds. As Martínez has stated in numerous interviews, though she wrote extensively on the sanctuary movement, she did not participate beyond her capacity as a journalist and poet. Her well-known poem "Nativity: For Two Salvadoran Women, 1986–1987" was used by the prosecuting attorneys as "evidence" of her involvement with the sanctuary movement. The poem's first stanzas are useful to cite in their entirety:

Your eyes, large as Canada, welcome
this stranger.
We meet in a Juárez train station

where you sat for hours,
your offspring blooming in you
like cactus fruit,
dresses stained where breasts leak,
panties in purses tagged
"Hecho en El Salvador,"
your belts, like equators,
mark north from south,

borders I cannot cross,
for I am a North American reporter,
pen and notebook, the tools
of my tribe, distance us
though in any other era I might
press a stethoscope to your wombs,
hear the symphony of the unborn,
finger forth infants to light,
wipe afterbirth, cut cords. (132)

Martínez's speaker laments the "distance" between the women and herself, for she understands that she "cannot cross" the literal borders that cut between north and south. But for this speaker, borders exist beyond actual geographical lines, the "pen and notebook" providing her with the necessary tools of her trade to bear witness to the atrocities her country has had a hand in committing; yet at the same time, the privileged positionality of the speaker as a "North American reporter" means she can only speak of, not experience, the refugee women's trauma.

In her time writing for the *National Catholic Reporter*, Demetria Martínez made her support of the sanctuary movement well known. One 2007 article she penned, "Reviving the Sanctuary Movement," calls for churches and faith leaders to continue the radical work undertaken by sanctuary workers in the 1980s, stating, "It's critical that churches step up to the plate to educate the next generation about our social justice tradition" (20). According to Martínez, churches have an obligation to defend the most vulnerable and marginalized, to use faith as the basis from which to challenge corruption, brutality, and injustice. In her essay "A Moment in History," from her 2005 collection *Confessions of a Berlitz-Tape Chicana*, she refuses to mince words on the crucial role the United States played in the Salvadoran Civil War. In her straightforward, even acerbic tone, she describes El Salvador as a site "where right-wing death squads 'disappeared' those who dared question the status quo; a dictatorship to which the United States was forking over $1 million a day in the name of fighting communism" (*Confessions*, 110). Rather than simply justify the United States' involvement in a brutal regime that targeted its own population, Martínez subsequently defends her right as an artist to document her nation's crimes. Martínez's trial highlighted the ways in which those individuals—be they poets or reporters—who expose a country's deeply unpopular open secrets may potentially pay the price for their actions. Speaking of the trial, in her own words, she says bluntly, "Instead of an article, I ended up writing a poem called 'Nativity.' I read it at Southside [church in Tucson] and explained that the poem had been used against me in the course of my own indictment and trial" (110). As Gabriella Gutiérrez y Muhs says of Martínez, "She is perhaps the only Chicana writer whose poetry has been used against her in court" ("Demetria Martínez"), a fact that underscores the exceptional nature of her activist writing.

Much as literature works by Ana Castillo, Rudolfo Anaya, and Sandra Cisneros were designated as "banned books" in the state of Arizona after the successful elimination of Mexican American studies programs from the Tucson Unified School District in 2011, Martínez's own words were presented as "evidence" of wrongdoing when she was merely speaking of injustices with truth and honesty. Significantly, the very fact of her indictment, despite the eventual acquittal, was in many ways deemed a presumption of guilt before she was proven innocent. As a Chicana, a woman, and a writer, she carries multiple intersecting identities that mark her as already "unpatriotic" and therefore suspect. But Martínez rejects the American expectation to perform a patriotism that aligns love of country with passive acceptance of its wrongdoing. Given that "the U.S.-supported Salvadoran regime regularly targeted civilians, using massacres, torture, political assassination, detention, and 'disappearances' to terrorize the population and to dismantle support for the rebel forces among the population" (Lomas, 365), Martínez sees it as her duty to write, even if her view puts her in danger.

With the 1994 publication of her novel *Mother Tongue*, which would cement Martínez's status as one of the significant Chicana writers of her generation, the author joined an elite group of like-minded Chicana authors who penned texts that were critical of the U.S.-backed dictatorships in Central America. Like Martínez, writers such as Graciela Limón and Helena María Viramontes, for example, published fictional works that uniquely captured a Chicana feminist global critique of U.S. empire, repression, and the racialized, gendered violence of war. In numerous interviews, Martínez has declared that poets and other writers have a duty: "Political engagement on the part of writers is not optional. We simply do not have the luxury of looking the other way" (Johnson, 26). This duty, as she calls it, is further affirmed in her poem "Civics After Grace Paley," in which the narrator states, "It is the citizen's duty to be a pest." Martínez's work affirms the tenet that artists should not merely write of injustice but should embody a resistance politics of liberation for all people.

Martínez's body of work, according to scholar Laura Lomas, "positions the reader as a witness to refugees' testimony about the violence that has marked their bodies" (359). In testimonio, readers are responsible for *hearing* the voice of the disenfranchised, who enact change by using the power of speech to undo the structural silencing they have undergone; Martínez's activist poetics asks this of her readers as well. Moreover, as an artist Martínez sees herself as *responsible*, a sentiment that Cherríe Moraga's groundbreaking essay "Art in América con Acento" conveys. In this essay, the writer poses a crucial question: "*I am Latina, born and raised in the United States. I am a writer. What is my responsibility in this?*" (53). Martínez's vast oeuvre responds to this question. To ask this of herself, to look inward as a means to question her own complicity with U.S. imperial violence, is at the heart of Chicana feminist poetics. Chicana feminist writing asks as much of itself as it does of its readers. Moraga continues: "As a Latina artist I can choose to contribute to the development of a docile generation of would-be Republican 'Hispanics' loyal to the United States, or to the creation of a force of 'disloyal' americanos who subscribe to a multicultural, multilingual, radical re-structuring of América" (56). Like Moraga's, Martínez's art and activism are self-reflective and critical, and they simultaneously refuse to assimilate to the mainstream American myth of democracy, inclusion, and freedom. Martínez's work thus cautions its readers to remain skeptical of willfully problematic mainstream rhetoric to which second, third, and subsequent generations of Latinx people might succumb.

In her poem "Grand Jury Indicts 16 in Sanctuary Movement," Martínez's words capture the calm before the storm, the seemingly arbitrary actions committed by activists of color that are later wielded as a weapon against them:

An embrace, a meal, a bed
harboring, aiding, abetting,
the night we went dancing
will be used against us,
an illicit sacrament we shared
over and over,
we, the priests
of another order
in this invisible country
called the border. (124)

In this country, writing a simple poem constitutes "harboring, aiding, abetting"; the most human activities like "the night we went dancing / will be used against us." Martínez has stated that it "took me a long time to really get over what had happened to me in the trial, you know, that sense of shame, of guilt, of being violated, that sense that I asked for it" (Ikas, 117). Nonetheless, although her words were unfairly used against her in a court of law, this has not lessened Martínez's commitment to justice work and solidarity. The deep emotional impact this trial has had on Martínez's life is all the more significant when we consider that she has continued to flourish as a writer. Rather than retreat, Martínez has remained steadfast in her work as one who speaks out. Warning against complicity, the easy way out, Martínez's work asks, nay, demands action from readers.

MAJOR WORKS: *MOTHER TONGUE* AND *THE BLOCK CAPTAIN'S DAUGHTER*

Without a doubt, Martínez is best known for her 1994 novel *Mother Tongue*, which has been translated into multiple languages and has become what scholars would call a canonical text in Chicanx letters. *Mother Tongue* is part of a larger body of Chicanx literature demonstrating a commitment to anti-imperialist humanitarianism that stands in solidarity with displaced and dispossessed peoples throughout the globe. Alongside the work of major writers, including Luis Alberto Urrea, Ana Castillo, and Reyna Grande, for example, Martínez's fiction, essays, and poetry reflect a deep concern for the plight of undocumented migrants and refugees who are victimized by unjust, punitive U.S. immigration and asylum policies. Further, her fictional works center New Mexican space and landscape, articulating a moral position that advocates for all living beings, human and nonhuman, and for the environment.

The need to care for the land and humanity forms a central premise in Martínez's 2012 novel *The Block Captain's Daughter*, for example, when the protagonist, Guadalupe/Lupe Anaya, in an artistic and entrepreneurial endeavor, stamps images of saints onto leftover birth control pill packets to comment on the interconnectedness of spirituality, reproductive freedom, and environmental waste. This enterprise is later celebrated by a local art gallery, much to the dismay of local Catholic leaders, who deem her artwork a shameful assault on the church's staunchly prolife stance. In this work, as in her essays and poetry, Martínez insists on humanizing and elevating those human beings who live with dignity but who are also erased, marginalized, and dehumanized within the borders of a nation that profits off their labor and sweat. At times humorous, playful, and serious, *The Block Captain's Daughter* utilizes multiple points of view to provide an eclectic but interconnected ensemble of characters living in Albuquerque who all eventually come together to celebrate the birth of Lupe's daughter, Destiny.

In Martínez's first work of fiction, *Mother Tongue*, she deftly explores the nineteen-year-old Chicana protagonist Mary/María's relationship with a Salvadoran refugee, José Luis, who stays in the home of Soledad, María's godmother, after fleeing El Salvador to escape persecution during the country's civil war. Soledad, a sanctuary movement worker, teaches María the strategies necessary not only to hide José Luis but to cover up their actions, which defy U.S. immigration and asylum laws. One of the varied narrative devices used in the novel, a letter from Soledad to María instructs her to *"speak to him in English. Tell him all about how 'the relatives' are doing. When you're safely out of earshot of anyone remind him that if anyone asks, he should say he's from Juárez"* (6). In writing this text, Martínez pays homage to sanctuary workers and volunteers, critically unpacking the fraught history of trauma, violence, and war that impacts Latinxs and Latin Americans along multiple borders, unified by the shared experience of U.S. colonialism. Combining rich narrative strategies, including first- and second-person voices, epistolary texts, flashbacks, monologues, newspaper clippings, and poetry, *Mother Tongue* also explores time and liminality, moving from the early days of the Salvadoran Civil War to two decades after, coinciding with the voice of María's and José Luis's son near the end of the novel. Throughout her relationship with José Luis, María articulates complex feelings of shame and unbelonging arising from her Spanish-speaking skills, identity, and communication, feelings that are at times literally and metaphorically untranslatable. As a young woman still reeling from her mother's death and her ensuing confusion and loss, she at first looks to men as "mirrors that allowed me to see myself at different angles" (19). As Debra A. Castillo and María-Socorro Tabuenca Córdoba posit, María "finds a belated wholeness in her own fragmentary life tale, a completeness that comes full circle as her son takes up the challenge of beginning to learn Spanish, the language of his father, the language partially lost to his mother" (173). Time, space, and motherhood intersect to provide María a road map by which to contextualize her past and present. Twenty years after her relationship with José Luis ends, the older María possesses the language and depth through which to unravel the intricacies of this relationship that occurred during a period of youth, mourning, political turmoil, and trauma.

Much scholarship on *Mother Tongue* has pointed to María's growth throughout the text, beginning with her initial naïve connection with José Luis and moving toward an understanding of nation, power, and identity. Ariana Vigil argues that "María's early perspective concerning her connections to José Luis, while failing to adequately account for difference, serves to point out the very fallible ways in which ideas of community may be constructed, even as her character speaks to the real importance of such connections. The narrative paints a sympathetic portrayal of María's quest for community support and paints such a community—specifically a transnational Latina/o community—as integral to her growth throughout the novel" (59). In a similar vein, Theresa Delgadillo describes *Mother Tongue* as a "fictional testimonio" that recounts María's process of consciousness making (67). Within the first few pages of the text, for example, María recalls the moments after encountering José Luis: "I needed a mystery—someone outside of ordinary time who could rescue me from an ordinary life, from my name, Mary, a blessing name that had become my curse. At age nineteen, I was looking for a man to tear apart the dry rind of that name so I could see what fruit fermented inside" (*Mother Tongue*, 16). Mary's evocative imagery, which conjures both life ("fruit") and decay ("dry rind," "fermented"), is visually stunning yet jarring, as she describes herself as alive yet dead, a zombie, in essence. Yet the violence of the imagery, visualized in Mary's hope to find "a man to tear apart" her name, is also unsettling, as it signals a passive state of being that idealizes the possibility of a relationship with another to unburden her from a life of stasis. Martínez frames the body of the narrative with Mary's/María's evolution: she goes from being a romantic young woman who believes herself "one of those women whose fate is to take a war out of a man, or at least imagine she is doing so" (4) to becoming an older adult who at last confronts and remembers her own traumatic experiences of sexual abuse as a child and of serving as the target of José Luis's flashback-induced rage the night they conceive their son.

María's recollection of this night, in which both romantic passion and horror occur within a matter of minutes, takes the form of a letter she writes to her son. The moon-filled evening on which their son is conceived is quickly shattered when "José Luis's hands turned into fists, one for each friend whose life had been torn like a page out of history. . . . And in his eyes I could see people running and dropping, flames and plumes of smoke, processions of women holding photographs of their children, telephone poles falling, bridges flying to pieces" (160–61). José Luis's traumatic experiences of state-sanctioned violence transfer onto María's body, and she becomes an unwitting victim of displaced horror. Early in their relationship María is unable to comprehend the depths of José Luis's trauma; it is not until she herself becomes the target of his rage that she can imagine the terror that has taken place in her lover's home country. Significantly, it is in this moment of trauma-induced rage that we also witness María's flashback to a moment when her neighbor molested her years in the past, leaving her with "no words for what has happened, no words for evil" (167). The novel's complex use of narrative, seen in the combination of epistolary and flashback passages to document trauma, unearths those voices that are systematically silenced and disempowered by brutal regimes within a nation's borders and by sexual abuse within the boundaries of a home. While both María and José Luis's bodies and minds are victimized through structural abuses of power, they never speak aloud to each other of their shared experiences of horrific violence; instead, readers learn of them in quick succession. In these climactic moments in the novel, Martínez captures the jarring effects of trauma in vivid, stunning fashion.

Published eighteen years after *Mother Tongue*, *Block Captain* utilizes narrative techniques similar to those invoked in the first novel, including flashback, stream of consciousness, epistolary text, and first- and third-person narrative voice. Like *Mother Tongue*, *Block Captain* concerns itself with neocolonial themes, including NAFTA, the exploitation of undocumented immigrant labor, activism, and community building. At the heart of the novel is Guadalupe Anaya, pregnant with her first child, whom she names Destiny. Working as a waitress at La Tropical restaurant in Albuquerque, Lupe has recently been named block captain of her neighborhood watch committee, having run on a campaign motto of "God helps those who help themselves." The text weaves in the narrative voices of Lupe's husband-to-be and father of Destiny, Marcos, along with those of their friends and chosen family, Cory, Peter, Flor, and Maritza. Throughout the novel, readers are also introduced to Lupe's periodic letters to her unborn daughter, which she writes during work breaks from the restaurant. The novel concludes eighteen years in the future, culminating in Destiny's letter to her mother. Crucially, "Lupe's status as an undocumented Mexican woman provides her with a more critical, first-hand perspective on border crossing, NAFTA, and the capitalist exploitation of undocumented labor—critiques that she frequently reveals in letters to her daughter written during lunch breaks or in her second-person narrative voice" (Herrera, 154). As in *Mother Tongue*, Martínez pays homage to the long history of Latinx activists, seen in the figures of Flor and Maritza, who routinely hold prayer vigils and protests against George W. Bush's campaign of retribution and violence in Iraq. This political critique, woven throughout the narrative, structurally and thematically connects with Lupe's own traumatic experience of undocumented border crossing and her subsequent near-death experience due to starvation and dehydration. In weaving antiwar critiques with the NAFTA politics that lead to Lupe's treacherous quest to the United States to avoid destitution, *Block Captain* privileges the voices of activists, undocumented immigrants, and allies to rally against U.S. hemispheric and global abuses of power that victimize Middle Eastern *and* Latin American communities.

At the heart of the novel is Lupe, who is pregnant with the child who will soon be the first of the U.S.-born generation in her family. Lupe's chosen name for her daughter, Destiny, symbolically asserts her daughter's right to chart her own path on U.S. soil, the land that births her but the same one that demarcates bodies like her mother's "illegal." In this vein, *"The Block Captain's Daughter* crystallizes the national struggle of Chicana feminist politics. By showing the national and transnational dilemmas that are historical and contemporary along border zones, the character who bears the name of the title of the book is also a metonym that advances the transnational and interdisciplinary feminist struggles that structure Martínez's visions of the world: the block captain's daughter, or Destiny" (Avilés, 8). In one letter Lupe writes to Destiny, she reflects on her long-held desire to create art, but the racialized, gendered immigration system and economy that exploits undocumented labor negate her work as "menial": "To think your mama had dreams of being a writer so long ago, but it was not to be. Maybe you will pick up on that dream where I left off" (*Block Captain,* 72). While Lupe recognizes that white supremacy defines her as "just another Mexican" (73), supposedly a "lesser" human being, her integrity, work ethic, and entrepreneurial spirit elevate her to the position of artist *and* proudly Mexican: "Through public interest, Lupe challenges stereotypes of migrants as job snatchers, as lazy people, as a strain to the welfare system, and as bodies unable to contribute to society in meaningful ways. She also challenges stereotypes on pregnancy and of reproductive rights" (Avilés, 8). Destiny, bearing the name bestowed upon her by her courageous mother, writes her own letter that closes the novel, embodying the feminist spirit that willed her into being: "Just remember Mama, you too pushed a pen: You pushed and pushed, writing letters to your Destiny, words that shimmer now in this pool of candlelight far from home" (*Block*

Captain, 94). Activism and artistry are thus passed down from mother to daughter, time and space proving inconsequential to a bond rooted in a decolonial Chicana feminist love.

SPIRITUALITY AND RELIGION

Matters of the spirit, faith, and the limits of institutionalized religiosity are mainstays in Chicana literature, and Martínez's work is no exception. As Chicana scholar Theresa Delgadillo examines in her foundational text *Spiritual Mestizaje*, the significance of these themes in Chicana writing owes much to the emergence of an evolving feminist positionality that centers the experiences of women of color as living, breathing bodies: "While its Chicana feminist spirituality is rooted in the specific imaginative, theoretical, and spiritual work of Chicana feminists, it shares in a general trend among the U.S. populace in the latter half of the twentieth century away from a traditional religiosity centered in a local branch of a religious denomination and toward more open-ended spiritual forms and practices" (67). As a writer wholly invested in exploring the depth of human spiritual practices, Martínez insists that scholars should undertake these significant themes: "I am hoping that this is something that people will take a look at because sometimes people have read my book as purely just a feminist reading, or have looked at it at particular levels that have downplayed the parts that are concerned about spirituality" (Gutiérrez y Muhs, *Communal Feminisms*, 55). Unlike religion, with its ties to dogma and institutions of power, matters of the spirit and spirituality, as seen in Martínez's work, invoke a concern for humanity and faith as guiding principles. As Chicana scholars Elisa Facio and Irene Lara assert, spirituality must be understood as a "conscious, self-reflective way of life" that directly "goes hand in hand with a deep sense of respect for and accountability to [the practitioners'] communities, including a specific land base or specific traditions" (4). Martínez has used her New Mexican Catholic upbringing to assert a prochoice stance, in contrast to the church's longstanding position on reproductive freedom. In addition, in both *Mother Tongue* and *The Block Captain's Daughter*, characters who do the necessary work of healing and caretaking are celebrated as spirit workers.

In her essay "Spirit Matters," Martínez proclaims that "the novelist is condemned to earth. We are called to be faithful not to abstract doctrine, so vaunted by organized religion, but to what our five senses tell us about the world around us" (*Confessions*, 54). Christina Garcia Lopez reads Martínez's statement as an assertion that "the storyteller's obligation to be faithful to the senses and to remain loyal to the pulse of the story can translate into a resistance to the boundaries of institutional religion" (7). In *Block Captain*, Martínez addresses the taboo subject of abortion through the character of Maritza, who visits a curandera, Maria, after experiencing recurring, troubling dreams about an abortion she had as a young woman. Rather than chastise Maritza, who is tormented by her supposed "sin," Maria gently encourages the suffering woman before her to turn to the ancestors, not religion, for peace of mind: "Do we know if there was a soul in that fetus? No, we don't. But if there was one, the gods of all our ancestors surely told it to fly away for the time being" (44–45). Maria invokes a spiritual ethos that does not conflate the sacred with institutionalized religion. Her words adhere to a spiritual balance that honors the flesh-and-blood human who is worthy of forgiveness and compassion.

Gabriella Gutiérrez y Muhs's fascinating metaphor of a "literary capirotada" to describe Martínez's use of spirituality in her work is particularly illuminating: "It is made up of various metaphorical breads: traditional Catholic beliefs that are analyzed, interpreted, stretched, and expanded by the authors" ("Capirotada," 140). For Gutiérrez y Muhs, the mixture of spices, yeast, and flour that make up this rich yet common bread item for Mexican and Latinx communities symbolizes the complexity of Chicana spiritual literary practices that cannot be so easily captured in words but can, rather, be conveyed through *una receta*, a recipe. She adds: "Capirotada, as opposed to mestizaje, truly encapsulates the essence of an ever-evolving Chicana spirituality that will continually collide with established tradition, while it ingrains itself upon the basic life values that it represents, as the menu continuously grows with representatives of both Mexican and American popular cultures, including the Sanctuary Movement" (154). As in the example above from *Block Captain*, the gentle exchange between Maria and Maritza, which occurs in Maria's warm kitchen, is the site of communion, as Maria tells the younger woman: "You've been on a long, long journey. It's time for you to eat" (*Block Captain*, 45). The simple act of eating breakfast together, enjoyed after Maritza's confession to an abortion she underwent as a young woman, is elevated to the rank of the sacred. Importantly, the site for this sacrosanct meal is not within the four walls of a church but in the warm home of a Chicana curandera, who instructs Maritza on the need for self-forgiveness and love. Likewise, in her discussion of *Mother Tongue*, Delgadillo describes the novel as a "narrative of spiritual becoming and social and political awakening" (67). Delgadillo's assertion of María's simultaneous spiritual and political awareness underscores Martínez's belief that faith can (and should) guide our most basic human principles of compassion and empathy. Rather than extricate the spiritual from the political, Martínez's writing demands more of our faith-based institutions, echoing sentiments made by sanctuary movement religious leaders and those espoused by liberation theology.

IDENTITY, LANGUAGE, AND LATINX SOLIDARITY

Martínez's oeuvre is marked by a concern for the limits of humanity, solidarity, and compassion; she uses literature in particular as a mode through which to speak of the human impetus to cause pain and suffering. In her novels, *Mother Tongue* and *The Block Captain's Daughter* especially, she explores human connection, kinship, and the desire to establish pan-Latinx solidarity in the Americas to call attention to the destructive consequences of colonialism, violence, war, xenophobia, and capitalism. Writing about *Mother Tongue*, scholar Georgina Guzmán posits that the text "articulates a transnational understanding of ethnicity exemplified by the concept of *latinidad*, providing us new ways of rethinking and remapping the nationalistic contours by which we have traditionally conceived of Chicana/o political struggle in the USA" (74). Rather than invoke Latinidad as "a facile umbrella-term that reduces people of Latin American origin into having an all-inclusive, Spanish-speaking, but decidedly *apolitical* identification," as Guzmán argues, "it is a politicized Latino-Chicana/o-global solidarity that [*Mother Tongue*] is in search of" (77). It comes as no surprise that in the United States, "Latinos/as (especially Chicanos) began increasingly to support antiwar efforts and to participate in underground networks assisting Central American refugees and immigrants" (Rodríguez, 130). As Ana Patricia Rodríguez notes, this alliance with Central American refugees was based on a vision of shared struggle against colonial domination (130). Martínez's works are thus part of a rich landscape of Chicanx political and creative resistance to United States hemispheric control that results in the brutal subjugation of Latin American and Indigenous subjects.

For Martínez, language theft and loss are a direct result of U.S. imperialism, violence, and terror. These themes span the arc of her work, particularly in the case of her first work of fiction, *Mother Tongue*. As Lomas argues, "Martínez's work teaches that the first step in opposing these state-sponsored practices should be reading the signs of the unheard and mistranslated, whose bodies have been scarred by imperial violence" (358). Much as María at first struggles to understand José Luis's trauma, Martínez constructs a speaker in "Prologue: Salvadoran Woman's Lament" who admits, "Nothing I do will take the war / out of my man" (117). For both María and the nameless Salvadoran woman speaker, the traumas of silence and war are gendered, as women are unable to "take the war" out of men scarred by the brutalities of violence and imperialism. Further, both the novel and poem speak from a space of silence, in which women are both silent and silenced.

In her essay "By Any Other Name," Martínez continues to address the simultaneous fluidity and fracturedness of identity, speech, and language: "Nothing is fixed. In the name game, improvisation is the magic word. I'm a Latina to promote pan-American unity. A Nuevo Mejicana to specify place and ancient ties to the land. I'm a Chicana as a result of the great 'naming ceremony' of which Rudolfo Anaya writes" (*Confessions*, 48). While Martínez argues for a sort of borderlessness ("pan-American unity") in relation to identity, her playful wording ("improvisation") is both ironic and lighthearted. Chicanas, as bicultural beings who daily navigate both literal and metaphorical borders, possess the gift of a quickness of tongue, language skills that defy margins, limits, and walls. But, as in *Mother Tongue*, where María becomes Mary in a process that entails trauma, violence, and theft of language, Martínez's work also documents the other side of lighthearted language play, which translates into loss, shame, and fear.

Take, for example, a decidedly different tone the speaker in her poem "Fragments" assumes. While referring to the English language as "My mask, my / sword" (23), she details her relationship with this language as being one in which she is both victim and perpetrator:

> Sometimes frightened,
> I run back to the familiar
> streets of English. . . .
> In moments of grace,
> poetry or prayer,
> English uses *me*.
> But most of the time, I use it.
> I do not always like what I
> have become in this tongue. (*Breathing*, 25)

No doubt influenced by the late Chicana philosopher Gloria Anzaldúa, who powerfully takes to task the policing of language within our communities, Martínez directly addresses the harm caused when our speech is silenced, mocked, shamed, or rigidly held to unfair standards. Anzaldúa asserts in *Borderlands/La Frontera: The New Mestiza*, "Until I can accept as legitimate Chicano Texas Spanish, Tex-Mex and all the other languages I speak, I cannot take pride in myself" (81). Chicanas must shift between environments, and in the lines above, the speaker in "Fragments" alludes to the boundaries of identities, the pieces (or fragments) that make up who she is. She does "not always like what I / have become in this tongue," a tragic consequence of arbitrary borders and rules that determine belonging and community. However, although the speaker suggests she is fragmented, Martínez equally imagines language as a potential salve, a bridge of connection and alliance. For example, in *Block Captain*, Destiny's closing letter to Lupe imagines language as powerful enough to break barriers, as she describes her experience at her university far from home: "At the Latino Center I am making friends with people from all over the Spanish-speaking world, *palabra por palabra cruzando fronteras*, erecting bridges, bull-dozing walls" (93). Language can transcend borders, according to Martínez, but it must be used in a way to unite, rather than disconnect. In the case of Destiny, it is Spanish that functions as a balm for the wound of loss, the uprootedness she experiences as a result of being one of the few Latinas at her college so far from home. Collecting the fragments of language loss through poetry and art is key to achieving wholeness.

Currently, Demetria Martínez resides in the city of her birth, Albuquerque, where she continues to write fiction and poetry. Her writing is crucial to our work as scholars, teachers, artists, and activists who demand a more just and humane world. As a poet whose own words have been turned against her by the very government that purports to represent her as a citizen of this country, she continues to use her public platform to expose injustice in the country of her birth and beyond its borders. She has stated that her writing "is the gift I give to people who have committed their lives to the cause of social justice, who have charged my own life with meaning" (quoted in Johnson, 26). Indeed, when I met Martínez for the first time in February 2020, a mere month before the catastrophic COVID-19 global pandemic hit the United States, I was struck by her generosity and graciousness of spirit. I spoke at a symposium Gabriella Gutiérrez y Muhs organized at Seattle University, discussing the impact Chicana feminist theory has had on theorizing my own experiences with disability. Demetria Martínez quietly approached me afterward to thank me for my words and for my bravery in sharing my experiences when so often the personal daily battles with disability are rendered taboo. While she thanked me, it was I who felt that I had been gifted the beauty of her words. I was humbled and deeply touched by her words and the trust she showed by sharing her experience of living with bipolar disorder. The most human of humans, Demetria Martínez is the rare combination of creator, artist, and advocate for the persecuted and vulnerable. We readers of her work are indeed privileged to bear witness to her creative force that inspires, heals, and calls us to action.

NOTES

1.   The forthcoming volume *The Demetria Martínez Reader*, edited by Gabriella Gutiérrez y Muhs and Cristina Herrera, expands upon the significance of Martínez's work to the larger body of Chicana literature.

WORKS CITED

Alvarado, Lisa. "Demetria Martínez: Walking the Walk." *La Bloga*, May 29, 2008. https://labloga.blogspot.com/2008/05/demetria-martnez-walking-wlak.html.

Anzaldúa, Gloria. *Borderlands/La Frontera: The New Mestiza*. 2nd ed. San Francisco: Aunt Lute Books, 1987, 1999.

Avilés, Elena. "The Trials of Displacement: Transnationalism and Interdisciplinary Feminisms in Demetria Martínez's *The Block Captain's Daughter*." *Label Me Latina/o* 7 (2017): 1–14.

Castillo, Debra A., and María-Socorro Tabuenca Córdoba. *Border Women: Writing from la Frontera*. Minneapolis: University of Minnesota Press, 2002.

Cunningham, Hilary. *God and Caesar at the Rio Grande: Sanctuary and the Politics of Religion*. Minneapolis: University of Minnesota Press, 1995.

Delgadillo, Theresa. *Spiritual Mestizaje: Religion, Gender, Race, and Nation in Contemporary Chicana Narrative*. Durham, N.C.: Duke University Press, 2011.

Facio, Elisa, and Irene Lara, eds. *Fleshing the Spirit: Spirituality and Activism in Chicana, Latina, and Indigenous Women's Lives*. Tucson: University of Arizona Press, 2014.

Garcia Lopez, Christina. *Calling the Soul Back: Embodied Spirituality in Chicanx Narrative*. Tucson: University of Arizona Press, 2019.

Gutiérrez y Muhs, Gabriella. "Capirotada: A Renewed Chicana Spirituality Through a Chicana Literary Lens." In *(Re)mapping the Latina/o Literary Landscape: New Works and New Directions*. Edited by Cristina Herrera and Larissa M. Mercado-López. New York: Palgrave Macmillan, 2016, 139–58.

———. *Communal Feminisms: Chicanas, Chilenas, and Cultural Exile: Theorizing the Space of Exile, Class, and Identity*. Lanham, Md.: Lexington Books, 2007.

———. "Demetria Martínez." In *The Oxford Encyclopedia of Latinos and Latinas in the United States*. Edited by Suzanne Oboler and Deena J. González. New York: Oxford University Press, 2005.

Guzmán, Georgina. "The Twenty-First Century Politics of *Latinidad*: Decolonizing Consciousness, Transnational Solidarity, and Global Activism in Demetria Martínez's *Mother Tongue*." In *(Re)mapping the Latina/o Literary Landscape: New Works and New Directions*. Edited by Cristina Herrera and Larissa M. Mercado-López. New York: Palgrave Macmillan, 2016, 73–92.

Herrera, Cristina. "More Than 'Just a Waitress': The Waitress as Artist and Activist in Contemporary Chicana Literature." In *Latin@s' Presence in the Food Industry: Changing How We Think About Food*. Edited by Meredith E. Abarca and Consuelo Carr Salas. Fayetteville: University of Arkansas Press, 2016, 143–63.

Holmes, Sue Major. "Minister, Journalist Acquitted." AP News, August 2, 1988. https://apnews.com/article/0733534b648d54f461b71c1f31ab152d.

Ikas, Karin Rosa. *Chicana Ways: Conversations with Ten Chicana Writers*. Reno: University of Nevada Press, 2002.

Johnson, Michelle. "The Poet as Political Activist: A Conversation with Demetria Martínez." *World Literature Today* 83, no. 5 (2009): 25–27.

Lomas, Laura. "'The War Cut Out My Tongue': Domestic Violence, Foreign Wars, and Translation in Demetria Martínez." *American Literature* 78, no. 2 (2006): 357–87.

Martínez, Demetria. *The Block Captain's Daughter*. Norman: University of Oklahoma Press, 2012.

———. *Breathing Between the Lines: Poems*. Tucson: University of Arizona Press, 1997.

———. "Civics After Grace Paley." *World Literature Today* 83, no. 5 (2009): 27.

———. *Confessions of a Berlitz-Tape Chicana*. Norman: University of Oklahoma Press, 2005.

———. "Grand Jury Indicts 16 in Sanctuary Movement." In *Three Times a Woman: Chicana Poetry*. Edited by Alicia Gaspar de Alba. Tempe, Ariz.: Bilingual Press, 1989, 124.

———. *Mother Tongue*. New York: Ballantine, 1994.

———. "Nativity: For Two Salvadoran Women, 1986–1987." In *Three Times a Woman: Chicana Poetry*. Edited by Alicia Gaspar de Alba. Tempe, Ariz.: Bilingual Press, 1989, 132–33.

———. "Prologue: Salvadoran Woman's Lament." In *Three Times a Woman: Chicana Poetry*. Edited by Alicia Gaspar de Alba. Tempe, Ariz.: Bilingual Press, 1989, 117.

———. "Reviving the Sanctuary Movement." *National Catholic Reporter* 43, no. 31 (2007): 20.

McConnell, Michael J. "Sanctuary Movement." *The Oxford Encyclopedia of Latinos and Latinas in the United States*. Edited by Suzanne Oboler and Deena J. González. New York: Oxford University Press, 2005.

Moraga, Cherríe. "Art in América con Acento." In *The Last Generation: Prose and Poetry*. Boston: South End Press, 1993, 53–63.

Rodríguez, Ana Patricia. *Dividing the Isthmus: Central American Transnational Histories, Literatures, and Cultures*. Austin: University of Texas Press, 2009.

Valle, Victor. "Poet or Smuggler? Demetria Martinez Says She Was Writing an Article; U.S. Attorney Says She Aided Illegals." *Los Angeles Times,* May 26, 1988. https://www.latimes.com/archives/la-xpm-1988-05-26-vw-5332-story.html.

Vigil, Ariana. "Transnational Community in Demetria Martínez's *Mother Tongue*." *Meridiens* 10, no. 1 (2009): 54–76.

CONTRIBUTORS

Cordelia E. Barrera is associate professor of English at Texas Tech University. She is a scholar of Southwest literature and published *The Haunted Southwest: Towards an Ethics of Place in Borderlands Literature* in 2022. Barrera specializes in Latinx literatures, the American Southwest, U.S. border theory, and multiethnic speculative fictions. She is codirector of the Literature, Social Justice, and the Environment Initiative at TTU. Her research highlights the need to disrupt mythologies of the American West by incorporating border voices and concentrates on the literature of social justice and the environment.

Mary Pat Brady is associate professor of English at Cornell University. Brady is the author of *Extinct Lands, Temporal Geographies: Chicana Literature and the Urgency of Space* (2002), which was awarded the Modern Language Association's prize for the best work of Latina/o and Chicana/o literary and cultural criticism. She is also an associate editor of the sixth edition of *The Heath Anthology of American Literature* (2008–2009). An earlier essay, "The Contrapuntal Geographies of *'Woman Hollering Creek' and Other Stories*," won the Norman Foerster Prize for the best essay published in *American Literature* in 1999. She has also served as the director of Cornell's Latina/o Studies Program.

She is currently working on a project that examines the relationship between neoliberalism and Latina/o literatures and cultures.

Norma E. Cantú is the Norine R. and T. Frank Murchison Distinguished Professor of the Humanities at Trinity University in San Antonio, Texas. She is the founder and director of the Society for the Study of Gloria Anzaldúa and organized El Mundo Zurdo, a gathering of Anzalduístas, from 2007 to 2019. Her most recent publications include three anthologies, *Teaching Gloria E. Anzaldúa: Pedagogies and Practices for Our Classrooms and Our Communities* (2020), *MeXicana Fashions: Politics, Self-Adornment, and Identity Construction* (2020), and *Entre Guadalupe y Malinche: Tejanas in Literature and Art* (2016), as well as *Cabañuelas: A Novel* (2019) and *Meditación Fronteriza: Poems of Love, Life, and Labor* (2019). She serves on the Esperanza Peace and Justice Center Conjunto de Nepantleras and the boards of the Macondo Writers Workshop and the American Folklore Society (as past president). An activist scholar, poet, writer, and folklorist, she has published widely in the field of Chicane studies and border studies. She has co-edited or edited over ten anthologies.

María Jesús Castro Dopacio has published articles on Chicana literature and art. She is the author of *Emperatriz de las Américas: La Virgen de Guadalupe en la literatura chicana* (2010) and the article "Poesía y pintura de Raquel Valle-Sentíes: Filiaciones estéticas comprometidas" in *Tradition and (R)evolution: Reframing Latina/o Identities in Contemporary U.S. Culture* (2018). As affiliated faculty with the Departamento de Filología Inglesa, Francesa, y Alemana at the Universidad de Oviedo, she teaches and belongs to the research group on cosmopolitan studies.

Carlos Nicolás Flores is a retired professor of English from Laredo College in Laredo, Texas. Flores is the author of two novels: *Our House on Hueco* (2006) and *Sex as a Political Condition* (2020). He lives in Laredo.

Myrriah Gómez is an assistant professor in the Honors College at the University of New Mexico. She earned her PhD in English with an emphasis in Latina/o literature from the University of Texas at

San Antonio in 2014. Gómez is a 2011 Ford Foundation Predoctoral Fellow. She writes about Chicanx literature, critical New Mexico regionalism, and environmental justice. Her first book, *Nuclear Nuevo México: Colonialism and the Effects of the Nuclear Industrial Complex on Nuevomexicanos*, was published by University of Arizona Press in 2022. She is a proud Nuevomexicana.

María Magdalena Guerra de Charur is a PhD student and an adjunct professor in the department of modern languages at Texas A&M International University.

Gabriella Gutiérrez y Muhs is currently a professor in modern languages and women, gender, and sexuality studies at Seattle University, where she was the Theiline Pigott McCone Chair in the Humanities from 2018 to 2020 and also served as director of the Center for the Study of Justice in Society. A polylingual poet, critic, and cultural worker, she is the author or editor of eight books of poetry, criticism, and culture and of multiple articles, encyclopedia entries, and opinion pieces. She is co-editor of *Presumed Incompetent: The Intersections of Race and Class for Women in Academia* (2012) and *Presumed Incompetent II: Race, Class, Power, and Resistance of Women in Academia* (2020) and single editor of other books on Chicana criticism, including *Word Images: New Perspectives on "Canícula" and Other Works by Norma Elia Cantú* (2017). Her poetry collections include *The Runaway Poems* (2017) and *A Most Improbable Life* (2002).

Georgina Guzmán is associate professor of English at California State University, Channel Islands. As a teacher-scholar, she has written on the transformative and reciprocal service-learning experiences that her Chicana/o literature students shared with farmworker families in Oxnard and Camarillo, California, while discussing Sandra Cisneros's *The House on Mango Street* in bilingual reading circles (in *Reflections: A Journal of Community-Based Writing and Rhetoric*). She is also the co-editor of *Campus Service Workers Supporting First-Generation Students: Cultural Relevancy and Informal Mentorship in Student Success and Retention* (with La'Tonya Rease Miles and Stephanie Youngblood,

Routledge, 2021) and *Making a Killing: Femicide, Free Trade, and La Frontera* (with Alicia Gaspar de Alba, University of Texas Press, 2010).

Cristina Herrera was born and raised in Oxnard, California. She earned her PhD in English from Claremont Graduate University, specializing in contemporary Chicana/Latina literature. In 2014, she published her first book, *Contemporary Chicana Literature: (Re)Writing the Maternal Script*. She published the first book on Chicana young adult literature in 2020, *ChicaNerds in Chicana Young Adult Literature: Brown and Nerdy*. Her research interests include Chicana/Latina young adult literature, Chicana feminism, and Chicana memoirs and life writing. In her spare time, she enjoys long phone calls with her identical twin sister, reading, and spending time with her family at dog parks and beaches.

María Esther Quintana holds a PhD in Hispanic literatures from the University of California, Berkeley. She is the author of *Los pícaros, bufones y cronistas de "Maluco: La novela de los descubridores"* (2008) and *Madres e hijas melancólicas en seis novelas étnicas de crecimiento de autoras latinas* (2014). She has also published critical essays in refereed journals in Mexico, Cuba, Spain, and the United States. She is an associate professor at Texas A&M University, where her teaching fields are Hispanic and U.S. Latin literatures, women's studies, Latin American culture, and the Spanish language.

Eliza Rodríguez is professor of Chicana/o and Latina/o studies at Loyola Marymount University and co-author of *Funny Looking: Humor and Latina/o Camp in Ugly Betty* (2015). She is the editor of *Stunned Into Being: Essays on the Poetry of Lorna Dee Cervantes* (2012) and co-editor of *The Un/making of Latina/o Citizenship: Culture, Politics, and Aesthetics* (2014). She is currently at work on a book examining how Chicana/o/x cultural production works to articulate a critical, solidarity-driven Latinidad. Her latest essay, "'I Love You Like Chicanos Love Morrissey': Affect, World-making, and Latinidad," was published in the *ASAP/Journal*.

Meagan Solomon is an assistant professor of feminist studies at Southwestern University. A queer Tejana of mixed Mexicana and Jewish descent, her work centers on representations of queer and decolonial intimacies in Chicana feminist literature. Her work is published in *Chicana/Latina Studies: The Journal of Mujeres Activas en Letras y Cambio Social*, *Latino Literature: Encyclopedia for Students*, and *The Handbook of Texas Women*. She is also the co-creator of *Sister Outsider Zine* and a founding member of the Public Scholarship in Action Collective.

Lourdes Torres is the Vincent de Paul Professor of Latin American and Latino Studies at DePaul University. Her research and teaching interests include sociolinguistics, Spanish in the United States, and queer Latinx literature. She is the author of *Puerto Rican Discourse: A Sociolinguistic Study of a New York Suburb* (1998) and co-editor of *Third World Women and the Politics of Feminism* (1991) and *Tortilleras: Hispanic and U.S. Latina Lesbian Expression* (2003). Torres's book on Spanish language use in Chicago (with Kim Potowski) is forthcoming from Oxford University Press, and she is currently working on a history of LLEGO, a national Latinx LGBTQ organization.

Raquel Valle-Sentíes, an artist, poet, and playwright, was born and raised in Laredo, Texas. Her poetry has been published in anthologies, textbooks for Spanish students, and various venues in the United States, Mexico, and India. Her first poetry collection, *Soy como soy y qué*, won the Premio Nacional de Literatura José Fuentes Mares en Letras Chicanas, the first granted to a woman. Valle-Sentíes has authored four full-length plays, *Alcanzando un sueño* (third place in the 1989–90 Chicano/Latino Literary Prize contest), *La mala onda de Johnny Rivera*, *Path of Marigolds*, and the yet-to-be-produced *Two Chicanas in Paris*, as well as three one-act plays. Since the 1990s, she has led workshops and read her writings at various venues across the country. As an artist, Raquel has won numerous awards for her oil paintings in state and international competitions. Her portraits of Denise Chávez and Sandra Cisneros were featured on posters for the Latina Letters Conference in 2002 and 2005.

Jen Yáñez-Alaniz is a Texas-based poet activist. She is the cocreator of the presentation Loving, Grieving, and Surviving: Chicanas Read the Poetry of Healing and cofounder of Welcome: A Poetry Declaration for World Refugee Day, San Antonio's citywide event. Her piece "Matrilineal Poetics: Toward an Understanding of Corporeality and Identity" was featured in the annual event Latinas in Hollywood: Herstories. Her writings are included in the *Journal of Latina Critical Feminism, Rogue Agent Journal*, the *Mom Egg Review*, the *Cutthroat* journal anthology *Puro Chicanx Writers of the 21st Century, I Sing: The Body, Boundless 2021: The Anthology of the Rio Grande Valley International Poetry Festival*, and more. She was a finalist for Kallisto Gaia Press's Julia Darling Memorial Poetry Prize and was nominated for a 2021 Pushcart Prize.

INDEX

Society for the Study of Gloria Anz-
aldúa, 13, 125, 127, 129n4, 149
Soto, Gary, 50n3, 268
South Texas Writing Project, 10, 21, 23,
37
Stanford University, 135
St. Mary's University, 22, 44, 198, 289

Tafolla, Carmen, 14, 23, 33, 35–36, 39,
50n3, 62, 185–211; San Antonio Poet
Laureate: 189; Texas Poet Laure-
ate, 2015–16: 189; *Rebozos*, 186;
Boundless, 187; *Carmen Tafolla: New
and Selected Poems*, 188, 190–91,
205–6; *This River Here*, 190; *Get Your
Tortillas Together*, 192; *Curandera*,
195–96; *Sonnets to Human Beings*,
192–94, 198–203; *That's Not Fair!
Emma Tenayuca's Struggle for Justice*,
198; *The Holy Tortilla and a Pot of
Beans*, 202, 210, 212n13; *Critical
Latina*, 204, 207, 209; *Healing*, 206;
*Arte del Pueblo: The Outdoor Public
Art of San Antonio*, 207; *The Last
Butterfly/la última mariposa*, 207;
I'll Always Come Back to You, 207;
Warrior Girl, 207
Teatro Campesino, 178n8, 233
Teatro Chicano de Laredo, 20, 23–24,
37
Texas A&M International University, 3,
19, 44, 135
Treviño, Jesús, 25

University of California, Berkeley, 50n2,
278

University of California, Irvine, 50n3,
198
University of California, Los Angeles,
59, 92
University of California, Santa Barbara,
219
University of California, Santa Cruz,
105, 106, 108, 125–26, 129n1, 276
University of Chicago, 246
University of Iowa, 295, 297, 301, 304
University of Missouri, Kansas City, 135
University of Texas at Austin, 105, 117,
125, 198
University of Texas at Dallas, 21
University of Texas, El Paso, 21
University of Texas, Río Grande Valley,
13
University of Texas at San Antonio, 58,
135, 185, 207
Urrea, Luis Alberto, 283, 331

Valdez, Luis, 24, 178n8, 233
Valle-Herr, Olga, 39, 45
Valle-Senties, Raquel, 3–4, 6–12, 15n1,
19–50; *Nothing to Declare*, 25; *Fash-
ionably Late*, 25; *Path of Marigolds*,
25; *Soy como soy y qué*, 26–32; *The
Ones Santa Anna Sold*, 33–36, 48–49
Vallejo, César, 64, 67–68
Villanueva, Tino, 62, 145
Villaseñor, Víctor, 23
Viramontes, Helena María, 23, 94, 329
Virgen de Guadalupe, 115, 168–69, 171,
311, 313–14

West Texas Writing Project, 21